Soft Computing for Smart Environments

This book applies both industrial engineering and computational intelligence to demonstrate intelligent machines that solve real-world problems in various smart environments. It presents fundamental concepts and the latest advances in multi-criteria decision-making (MCDM) techniques and their application to smart environments. Though managers and engineers often use multi-criteria analysis in making complex decisions, many core problems are too difficult to model mathematically or have simply not yet been modeled.

In response, as well as discussing AI-based approaches, *Soft Computing for Smart Environments* covers various optimization techniques, decision analytics, and data science in applying soft computing techniques to a defined set of smart environments, including smart and sustainable cities, disaster response systems, and smart campuses.

This state-of-the-art book will be essential reading for both undergraduate and graduate students, researchers, practitioners, and decision-makers interested in advanced MCDM techniques for management and engineering in relation to smart environments.

Soft Computing for Smart Environments
Techniques and Applications

Mohamed Abdel-Basset
Ripon K. Chakrabortty
Abduallah Gamal

CRC Press
Taylor & Francis Group
Boca Raton London New York

CRC Press is an imprint of the
Taylor & Francis Group, an **informa** business
A CHAPMAN & HALL BOOK

First Edition published 2023
by CRC Press
6000 Broken Sound Parkway NW, Suite 300, Boca Raton, FL 33487-2742

and by CRC Press
4 Park Square, Milton Park, Abingdon, Oxon, OX14 4RN

CRC Press is an imprint of Taylor & Francis Group, LLC

© 2023 Mohamed Abdel-Basset, Ripon K. Chakrabortty and Abduallah Gamal

ISBN: 978-1-032-41353-2 (hbk)
ISBN: 978-1-032-41354-9 (pbk)
ISBN: 978-1-003-35768-1 (ebk)

DOI: 10.1201/9781003357681

Typeset in Palatino
by codeMantra

Our families, who had the patience to allow us to work, even at midnights.

Contents

Preface

Introduction

Tiny sensors and processors may now be found in common things because of significant advancements and ongoing shrinking in computer technology. The dream of a smart environment is becoming a reality thanks to incredible advancements in fields such as portable appliances and devices, pervasive computing, wireless sensor networking, wireless mobile communications, machine learning–based decision-making, IPv6 support, human-computer interfaces, and agent technologies. A **smart environment** is a networked miniature world where sensor-enabled linked objects cooperate to improve the comfort of people's lives. The terms smart and environment both relate to the capacity for independently acquiring and putting knowledge to use. As a result, a smart environment is one that has the ability to learn and use that information to adapt to the demands of its residents and enhance their experience in that environment. Integrating the Internet of Things (IoT) with smart surroundings has been the subject of several research projects. By enabling the user to monitor the environment from remote locations, the integration of IoT with a smart environment expands the possibilities of smart devices. Depending on the needs of the application, IoT may be integrated with various smart environments. Smart cities, smart homes, smart grids, smart buildings, smart transportation, smart health, and smart industries are the main categories into which the work on IoT-based smart environments may be divided.

Despite the advancements in enabling IoTs while ensuring real-time monitoring, the application of decision analytics to find the sustained or most optimal option has not been explored in the relevant literature. For example, evaluating and then prioritizing a smart and sustainable city among many alternatives has not been a research focus in the smart environment–related literature. Governments and public organizations prioritize smart management practices in policies and programs for sustainable development, economic growth, and improved quality of life. As a result, selecting a smart and sustainable city should incorporate sustainable economic, social, and environmental goals, which is clearly a multi-criteria decision-making (MCDM) problem. Considering all those limitations in the existing knowledge area, this book has complied with different

MCDM techniques to assess, prioritize, and select the best possible smart environment among many of its competitors.

The competitiveness of our proposed book lies in multiple facets. For example, our book is not only limited to a specific smart environment topic. It also has contents from waste management and disaster response systems to traditional supply chain management. In addition to conventional artificial intelligence–based approaches, this proposed book highlights the contributions of different optimization techniques, decision analytics (predictive and descriptive), and data science. This book will be the first in the literature to bridge the industrial engineering perspectives and computational intelligence for different digitalized (aka, smart) environments.

Contents

This book is for undergraduate students, graduate students, researchers, and practitioners interested in the theory of multi-criteria analysis and its applications in management and engineering. This book develops intelligent machines to provide solutions to real-world problems that are not modeled or too difficult to model mathematically in smart applications. This book would be a reference for students seeking to attain a thorough knowledge in this field. Fresh researchers can take this book as a beginning point. In recent years, multi-criteria analysis has been widely used for decision-making purposes by institutions and enterprises.

This book consists of eight chapters. A brief description of those chapters is as follows.

Chapter 1: An Innovative Framework to Evaluate Smart and Sustainable Cities Using Fuzzy MCDM Method

This chapter aims to define the priorities of the dimensions of smart and sustainable cities and provide an idea of the areas in which smart and sustainable city planning should be invested and expanded. Furthermore, city or nation managers must draw comparisons among themselves using smart city characteristics' priorities (weights), allowing them to identify benchmark possibilities. Furthermore, by using the city comparison data, officials in these cities should be able to identify areas that need development. This chapter proposes a multi-stage approach to assessing smart and sustainable city criteria. The proposed approach is based on applying the Analytical Network Process method and the Technique for Order of Preference by Similarity to Ideal Solution method (ANP-TOPSIS). In general, this chapter provides some recommendations for cities to understand their position concerning other cities and to know what areas policymakers need to strengthen.

Chapter 2: A Conceptual Design and Evaluation Framework for Assessing Smart Health Technologies

Through improved health applications, the adoption and implementation of developing smart health technology may improve living circumstances. The most important accomplishment in smart health solutions is the balanced application of technology and engagement in human-based systems. Poor healthcare technology has the potential to kill people. As a result, the region in which smart health technology will be implemented should be thoroughly analyzed before the most appropriate technology is chosen. Because these assessments are based on people's desires and expectations, they might sometimes be hazy and imprecise. This chapter presents a paradigm for the healthcare industry regarding smart health technology selection and assessment. As a result, smart health technology assessment is treated as a multi-criteria decision-making (MCDM) issue. The MCDM area comprises ideas and methods for achieving the "best suitable" answer for a decision scenario that fulfills several competing criteria. It is both a strategy and a set of procedures or approaches for assisting individuals in making acceptable choices to their value judgments. A hybrid MCDM approach to evaluating smart health technologies has been presented. For this task, we find fuzzy AHP and fuzzy VIKOR methods to be the best approach to solve this problem, prioritize criteria, and rank selected alternatives.

Chapter 3: An Intelligent Approach for Assessing Smart Disaster Response Systems

Disaster management is one of the most significant fields of study since it directly affects the quality of human life. One of the most important foundations of disaster management is responding to catastrophes in a way consistent with protecting residents' lives from their effects. Due to the significance of intelligent disaster response systems, their performance must be assessed using criteria that quantify the usefulness of these systems in various circumstances. As with other decision-making difficulties, evaluating smart disaster response systems is one of the decision-making challenges that provide difficulty under unpredictable settings. To account for any ambiguity in the assessment process, this chapter presents an integrated framework for evaluating the performance of the smart disaster response system in an uncertain environment. Multi-criteria decision-making (MCDM) is used for the issue of performance assessment based on a set of criteria. A hybrid methodology for assessing smart disaster response systems has been presented. For the purpose of this task, we find the integration of the two methods, fuzzy Decision-Making Trial and Evaluation Laboratory (DEMATEL) and fuzzy Evaluation based on Distance from Average Solution (EDAS), which are very well-known approaches to prioritize the main dimensions and their sub-indicators and evaluate specific alternatives for an MCDM problem.

Chapter 4: A Facilitating Paradigm for Analyzing the Adaptation of Internet of Things Obstacles (IoTBs) to Waste Management in Smart Cities

An IoT-enabled smart city is a viable option to meet the demands of urbanization; it has the ability to convert societies into smart communities by improving public services such as transportation, water management, smart buildings, healthcare, and education. This chapter intends to establish a knowledge of and analyze the level or severity of IoT hurdles impacting smart city waste management so that stakeholders may take proactive measures to install IoT-enabled technologies smoothly. This chapter aims to comprehend the IoT adoption situation of smart cities in underdeveloped nations and the different implementation issues that may be experienced. The building of an IoT network, with solid backing from services and technology, needs an integrated waste management control strategy for smart cities. Aside from the technological obstacles, a clear, standardized strategy for implementing IoT and an appropriate direction for smart city activities have not yet been offered. This chapter seeks to identify the key IoT obstacles (IoTBs) and their strengths as they pertain to trash management in smart cities. A multi-criteria decision-making (MCDM) technique was applied to accomplish these goals. The IoTBs are investigated using current literature and validated by specialists. Fuzzy DEMATEL examines the interaction between obstacles to demonstrate the intensity/strength of IoTBs impacting one another and managing waste management methods in smart cities.

Chapter 5: A Fusion Approach for Cloud Service Performance Assessment and Selection from Smart Data

Cloud computing is a new way of allocating computer resources through the Internet. This computing paradigm delivers significant advantages to enterprises by relieving them of low-level activities associated with IT infrastructure setup and allowing them to start with limited resources and scale up as needed, freeing up time for innovation and the production of commercial value. Choosing a cloud service is an example of multi-criteria decision-making (MCDM), a process in which several aspects of QoS play an important part in the decision-making process. As a result, a more effective MCDM strategy could be necessary to cope with client demands and rank cloud services according to their capabilities. In this chapter, we provide a systematic assessment approach for picking an ideal cloud service from a range of multiple comparable options, with the selection being made based on the QoS requirements associated with cloud services. Using this framework, customers can evaluate several cloud service providers according to their preferred choice and several other factors. This chapter proposes a hybrid MCDM approach for evaluating multiple cloud service providers (CSPs). The approach consists of two MCDM approaches: the entropy and the combined compromised solution (CoCoSo). The applied approach was carried out under the q-ROFS environment and using q-rung orthopair fuzzy numbers (q-ROFNs).

Chapter 6: An Evaluation Approach for Prioritizing Performance of Sustainability Indicators for Smart Campuses

Higher education institutions have an urgent need to move toward adopting and establishing a smart framework employing spatial software for campus sustainability. Furthermore, the relevance and significance of building a smart spatial-based framework to analyze the appropriateness and sustainability performance of higher education institution campuses are derived from the worldwide adage "think globally, act locally." A further rationale is a country-specific approach that offers a complete information repository for government and higher education institution managers. This chapter addresses this research vacuum by evaluating the relative relevance of spatial-based indicators that fit with the stakeholders' degree of awareness and the nature of the local context in every given nation. This relative significance will assist the development of a method for smart university campuses to embrace the local environment to achieve a smart city objectively. An MCDM-blended approach is presented to prioritize sustainability indicators' performance and assess the sustainability performance of smart campuses (SCs). The applied approach was carried out under q-rung orthopair fuzzy set (q-ROFS) environment and using q-rung orthopair fuzzy numbers (q-ROFNs). The approach used consists of two methods q-ROFS entropy and the q-ROFS Technique for Order of Preference by Similarity to Ideal Solution (q-ROFS TOPSIS).

Chapter 7: Sustainable Supplier Selection for Smart Supply Chain

The phrase "sustainable supply chain management techniques" refers to a collection of tactical activities that may assist a corporation in achieving more sustainability in the economic, environmental, and social aspects of sustainability. These kinds of activities center on the process of implementing sustainable supply chain management, which significantly impacts the level of sustainability performance a firm achieves. It is generally agreed upon that one of the most important aspects of sustainable supply chain management strategies is identifying sustainable vendors. This is because the activities of suppliers are essential to assisting downstream businesses in achieving a collaborative and sustained competitive advantage. In addition, the selection of a supplier may be thought of as a process of multi-criteria decision-making (MCDM), which is comprised of two stages: the calculation of the weights of the criteria and the ranking of the suppliers. The model used consists of two multi-criteria decision-making (MCDM) methods: the CRiteria Importance through Intercriteria Correlation (CRITIC) method and the Combinative Distance-based ASsessment (CODAS) method. The model used is conducted under the IFS environment and using IFNS. Initially, the CRITIC method prioritizes criteria and determines their weights. Then, the CODAS method ranks and selects the best available alternatives.

Chapter 8: Analyzing and Evaluating Smart Card Systems for Public Transportation

The introduction of an integrated fare system has been met with several challenges. Formal public transportation services might sometimes be unreliable, inconvenient, or even dangerous in certain nations. As a result, many passengers are more inclined to utilize alternative modes of transportation provided by private companies. During the planning phase of the transition project, many elements of smart card systems, including all of their benefits and drawbacks for each kind of transportation, should be considered to ensure that the system is adopted in the most effective manner possible. Because of the nature of this kind of transition, it brings about contradictory goals. Because of this, the current problem area is suitable for applying multi-criteria decision-making (MCDM) methods since a dependable and rational decision support system is required to support authorities through the valuation of differences between the planned system and the existing one. It is essential to have access to a decision model in its own right for decision-makers to clearly understand the enhancements that may be accomplished by switching to a smart system. As a consequence, this chapter's objective is to provide an MCDM framework that is both efficient and accurate in assessing and comparing the performance of various fare systems. The methodology is presented under an intuitionistic fuzzy environment. The methodology used consists of two MCDM methods, namely, the intuitionistic fuzzy CRiteria Importance through Intercriteria Correlation (IF-CRITIC) method and the Intuitionistic Fuzzy Preference Ranking Organization Method for Enrichment Evaluation II (IF-PROMETHEE II) method. The methodology used is performed under an intuitionistic fuzzy environment and using intuitionistic fuzzy numbers (IFNs).

Authors

Mohamed Abdel-Basset is an Associate Professor in the Faculty of Computers and Informatics, Zagazig University, Egypt. His work focuses on the application of multi-objective and robust metaheuristic optimization techniques. His current research interests include optimization, operations research, data mining, computational intelligence, applied statistics, decision support systems, robust optimization, engineering optimization, multi-objective optimization, swarm intelligence, evolutionary algorithms, and artificial neural networks.

Ripon K. Chakrabortty is Program Coordinator for the Master of Decision Analytics and the Masters of Engineering Science Programs, and team leader of the Decision Support and Analytics Group at the School of Engineering and Information Technology, UNSW Canberra. His research interests cover a range of topics in operations research, project management, supply chain management, artificial intelligence, and information system management. Many organizations have funded his research programs.

Abduallah Gamal is a Senior Researcher in the Faculty of Computers and Informatics in the Department of Operations Research at Zagazig University, Egypt. His research interests include computational intelligence, optimization, swarm intelligence, evolutionary algorithms, and neutrosophic sets and logic. He currently works on applying multi-criteria decision-making.

1

An Innovative Framework to Evaluate Smart and Sustainable Cities Using Fuzzy MCDM Method

1.1 Introduction

Because of its scale and complexity, the notion of a sustainable and smart city is one of the most significant problems in today's public policy. Cities were regarded as the major factors that may bring answers to the world's difficulties during the UN-HABITAT-organized Seventh World Urban Forum (WUF7). The relevance of cities in terms of a sustainable future, equality, and quality of life was the emphasis of this organization. A unique section on "the need to integrate critical subjects for sustainable cities and human settlements in the post-2015 Development Agenda" was added to the WUF7 declaration. Since the beginning of the twenty-first century, the popularity of the "smart and sustainable city" idea, which arose in the 1990s, has continuously increased. Even in Asia, Latin America, and Africa, there are numerous megacities with populations exceeding 20 million people when urban growth is considered on a global basis. They are responsible for over 80% of global GDP. They also use 80% of the world's energy and produce at least 70% of carbon emissions.

According to a United Nations Population Fund projection from 2008, 70% of the world's population will be living in cities by 2050. Around 828 million people are believed to be living in substandard housing, and this figure is continuously rising. These issues pose several issues in city planning, growth, and operation. As a result, while developing action plans, city and nation administrators must think of innovative ways to improve their cities' economic activity, energy consumption, environmental conditions, and quality of life. Because they offer services using ICT infrastructure, several cities are classified as smart cities. Furthermore, creating sustainable and smart cities requires providing citizens with the satisfying and flexible job and business possibilities, safe and affordable housing, a more

DOI: 10.1201/9781003357681-1

democratic society, transparent government, and a productive economy. It also entails investing in public transportation, increasing the proportion of green areas, and undertaking urban planning and governance via participatory mechanisms that allow all inhabitants to engage. Information city, sustainable city, talented city, wired city, digital city, and eco-city are all connected to the smart city idea.

The California Institute for Smart Communities was one of the first groups to concentrate on how cities may be constructed to integrate information technology and how communities can be smart. The phrase "smart and sustainable city" is often used in the area of urban planning as a policy instrument. Smart management practices are prioritized by governments and public organizations in policies and programs for sustainable development, economic growth, and improved quality of life. As a result, smart and sustainable city methods should incorporate sustainable economic, social, and environmental goals. It's also challenging to assess the success of smart and sustainable city features and dimensions. Many academics have used indicators-based methodologies to analyze the characteristics of urban smartness and sustainability, especially in recent years. They also attempted to use these strategies to bring these aspects together and assess worldwide cities. These studies attempt to compare a variety of global cities using various weighting techniques and a variety of smart and sustainable city features using a number of indicators ranging from 20 to 80.

This chapter aims to define the priorities of the dimensions of smart and sustainable cities, as well as to provide an idea of the areas in which smart and sustainable city planning should be invested and expanded. Furthermore, city or nation managers are required to draw comparisons among themselves using the priorities (weights) of smart city characteristics, allowing them to identify benchmark possibilities. Furthermore, by using the city comparison data, officials in these cities should be able to identify areas that need development.

1.2 Mathematical Preliminary

This section explains several key properties of fuzzy set theory and fuzzy operations, which are used in the proposed hybrid technique to manipulate information uncertainty.

1.2.1 Fuzzy Set Theory

Zadeh (1975) proposed fuzzy set theory as a mathematical framework to represent the vagueness or imprecision of human cognitive processes. The underlying principle behind the fuzzy set theory is that each element

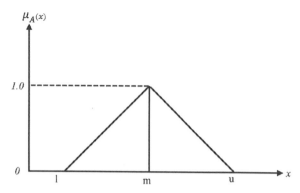

FIGURE 1.1
Implication of a triangular fuzzy number.

in a fuzzy set has a degree of membership. A membership function that transfers items to degrees of membership within a certain interval, commonly [0,1], defines a fuzzy set. In fuzzy logic, several forms of fuzzy membership functions have been utilized. Monotone, triangular, and trapezoidal are the three most prevalent shapes. Because the fuzzy set is a convex function, the trapezoid or trapezoidal function approaches it the best. However, owing to its ease of computation, the triangular fuzzy number (TFN) is more beneficial in fostering representation and information processing in a fuzzy environment. TFN is also the most appropriate feature for expert linguistic assessment, and it is often used in fuzzy multi-criteria decision-making (MCDM) studies (Patil and Kant 2014). A TFN A is presented as a set of three crisp numbers l, m, and u as shown in Figure 1.1, where "*l*," "*m*," and "*u*" describe the lowest, middle, and highest possible values, respectively. The membership function is explained in Eq. (1.1).

$$\mu_{\tilde{A}}(x) = \begin{cases} 0 & x < l \\ \dfrac{x-l}{m-l}, & l \leq x \leq m \\ \dfrac{u-x}{u-m}, & m \leq x \leq u \\ 0 & x > u \end{cases} \tag{1.1}$$

1.2.2 Fuzzy Operation

Suppose there are two TFNs $\tilde{A} = \left(a^l, a^m, a^u\right)$ and $\tilde{B} = \left(b^l, b^m, b^u\right)$, where $a^l, a^m, a^u, b^l, b^m, b^u > 0$. Some fuzzy operations are presented as follows:
Addition:

$$\tilde{A} \oplus \tilde{B} = \left(a^l, a^m, a^u\right) \oplus \left(b^l, b^m, b^u\right) = \left(a^l + b^l, a^m + b^m, a^u + b^u\right) \tag{1.2}$$

Subtraction:

$$\tilde{A} \ominus \tilde{B} = \left(a^l, a^m, a^u\right) \ominus \left(b^l, b^m, b^u\right) = \left(a^l - b^l, a^m - b^m, a^u - b^u\right) \quad (1.3)$$

Multiplication:

$$\tilde{A} \otimes \tilde{B} = \left(a^l, a^m, a^u\right) \otimes \left(b^l, b^m, b^u\right) = \left(a^l \times b^l, a^m \times b^m, a^u \times b^u\right) \quad (1.4)$$

Division:

$$\begin{cases} \tilde{A}^{-1} = \left(a^l, a^m, a^u\right)^{-1} = \left(1/a^l, 1/a^m, 1/a^u\right) \\ \tilde{B}^{-1} = \left(b^l, b^m, b^u\right)^{-1} = \left(1/a^l, 1/a^m, 1/a^u\right) \end{cases} \quad (1.5)$$

Maximum:

$$\mathrm{MAX}\left(\tilde{A}, \tilde{B}\right)\left(\max\left(a^l, b^l\right), \max\left(a^m, b^m\right), \max\left(a^u, b^u\right)\right) \quad (1.6)$$

Minimum:

$$\mathrm{MIN}\left(\tilde{A}, \tilde{B}\right) = \left(\min\left(a^l, b^l\right), \min\left(a^m, b^m\right), \min\left(a^u, b^u\right)\right) \quad (1.7)$$

Sum of product:

$$\sum_{i=1}^{n} \oplus w_i \otimes \tilde{a}_i = \sum_{i=1}^{n} \oplus (w_1, w_2, \ldots, w_n) \otimes \left(\tilde{a}_1, \tilde{a}_2, \ldots, \tilde{a}_n\right) = w_1\tilde{a}_1 \oplus w_2\tilde{a}_2 \oplus \ldots w_n\tilde{a}_n$$

$$(1.8)$$

Multiplication by a scalar:

$$\lambda \otimes \tilde{A} = \begin{cases} \left(\lambda a^l, \lambda a^m, \lambda a^u\right), & \text{if } \lambda \geq 0 \\ \left(\lambda a^u, \lambda a^m, \lambda a^l\right), & \text{if } \lambda < 0 \end{cases} \quad (1.9)$$

Assume that the weight of kth decision-maker is the initial direct-influence average fuzzy matrix that can be gained by gathering the assessment information of experts in Eq. (1.10).

$$x_{ij}^l = \sum_{k=1}^{k} \lambda_k x_{kij}^l, \quad x_{ij}^m = \sum_{k=1}^{k} \lambda_k x_{kij}^m, \quad x_{ij}^u = \sum_{k=1}^{k} \lambda_k x_{kij}^u \quad (1.10)$$

where k denotes the total number of decision-makers, and λ_k satisfies $\sum_{1}^{k} \lambda_k = 1$, where $\lambda = (\lambda_1, \lambda_2, \ldots, \lambda_k)$ and $\lambda_k \geq 0$. x_{ij}^l, x_{ij}^m, and x_{ij}^u denote the lower, middle, and upper limits of the assessment information, respectively.

The distance between two TFNs (i.e., TFN $\tilde{a}$ and TFN $\tilde{b}$) is obtained through the vertex technique as exhibited in Eq. (1.11).

$$\text{dst.}\left(\tilde{a}, \tilde{b}\right) = \sqrt{\frac{1}{3}\left[\left(a^l - b^l\right)^2 + \left(a^m - b^m\right)^2 + \left(a^u - b^u\right)^2\right]} \qquad (1.11)$$

1.3 Solution Methodology

In this part, a proposed multi-stage approach to assessing smart and sustainable city criteria is presented. The proposed approach is based on the application of the Analytical Network Process method and the Technique for Order of Preference by Similarity to Ideal Solution (ANP-TOPSIS) method. In general, this chapter provides some recommendations for cities to understand their position in relation to other cities and to know what areas policymakers need to strengthen. Then, these cities are differentiated by a multi-criteria scenario taking into account several aspects. Thus, the proposed framework consists of several stages, namely, the stage of data collection by volunteers and specialists, the stage of determining the weights of the criteria used in the study, and finally the stage of arranging the specified cities according to their importance from the specified standards. Also, the proposed approach adopts the fuzzy environment as an external framework for conducting the study using TFNs as shown in Figure 1.2.

1.3.1 Connotation of ANP and TOPSIS

The fuzzy ANP approach is used to calculate the final weights of the criteria and to build outer dependencies, i.e., relationships between elements belonging to various groups and criteria. The analytical hierarchy process (AHP) was initially established by Saaty (Saaty 2001) and is now known as the ANP. While the AHP uses a unidirectional hierarchical connection between decision levels, the ANP allows for more generic interrelationships between decision levels and components. The ANP feedback method substitutes hierarchies with networks in which interactions between levels are difficult to characterize as higher or lower, dominant or submissive, and direct or indirect. By including possible interactions, interdependencies, and feedback in the decision-making system, the technique assesses all connections between clusters of the network structure and items inside them. It deals with dependency between components by developing a "supermatrix" to get composite weights. A network structure's node symbolizes a component (or cluster) with elements within it, a

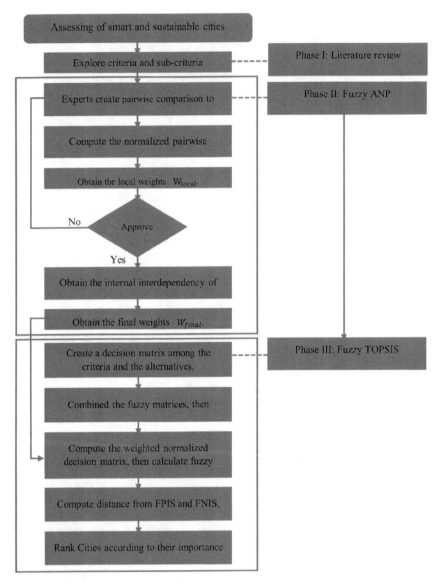

FIGURE 1.2
Steps of the decision framework.

straight line or an arc defines interactions between two components, and a loop denotes the inner dependencies of elements inside a component (Kumar et al. 2021). The ANP technique is appropriate since the parts of the issue in this chapter (factors and criteria) create a network structure owing to interdependencies. The benefits of the ANP approach include the capacity to prioritize groups or clusters of components, as well as the fact that it considers independence in addition to dependency; i.e., it handles independence better than other methods like AHP (Ghosh, Das Chatterjee, and Dinda 2021). The ANP technique assesses the consistency of judgments and simplifies the process of assigning weights by breaking the issue down into smaller components that can be analyzed more thoroughly. On the contrary, ANP has several drawbacks. Because the approach needs a pair of comparisons of items, it is not feasible to examine one element in isolation and find its faults and strengths. The complexity of the issue grows exponentially with the number of components and their interdependencies for the same reason. Figure 1.3 shows the differences between the structure of ANP and AHP methods.

The TOPSIS technique was created by Hwang and Yoon in 1981 (Yoon and Hwang 1985). The goal of this strategy is to find the positive and negative gaps between appropriate and inappropriate solutions. The TOPSIS approach is an important MCDM method that has been utilized by many researchers, policymakers, stakeholders, and academics across a wide range of disciplines. However, since it fails to offer succinct information on the topic and contains ambiguous and undefined difficulties, this strategy has significant limitations in real-world interpretation.

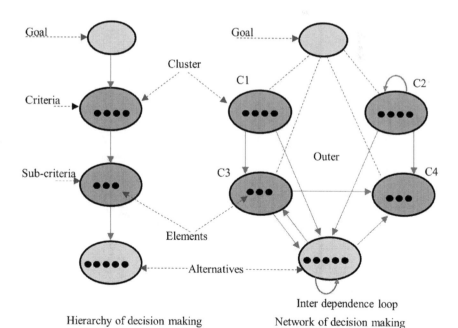

FIGURE 1.3
Details of AHP and ANP methods.

Cardinal information about the qualities to be examined is used by fuzzy TOPSIS. The distance between fuzzy positive ideal solution (FPIS) and fuzzy negative ideal solution (FNIS) to each option is one of the most important steps. Fuzzy TOPSIS is inconsistent and unreliable in some way. It's vital to remember that fuzzy TOPSIS collects and uses only human-generated data. As a result, how much information is "dependable, trustworthy, unfailing, sure, authentic, real, and respectable" affects how close values of interest may be approximated. Despite these drawbacks, fuzzy TOPSIS is a popular MCDM technique (Solangi, Longsheng, and Shah 2021).

1.3.2 The Computational Steps of the Suggested Hybrid MCDM Approach

Step 1: A group of volunteers specialized in the field under study are identified. In this regard, a set of standards have been developed based on which specialists are sought.

Step 2: The aspects of the problem under study are studied by specialists to determine the most important criteria that affect the assessment of smart and sustainable cities.

Step 3: The cities used as alternatives to the problem are selected so that several different cities from all continents of the world are selected.

Step 4: The problem was charted into several different levels. After that, the inner and outer dependencies results of criteria with respect to each criterion have been constructed (Liu et al. 2021).

Step 5: Determine the verbal terms that experts will use while assessing criteria and alternatives based on the criteria that have been chosen. As a result, as indicated in Table 1.1, different verbal measures were established to assess the relative relevance of each criterion. In addition, as indicated

TABLE 1.1

Verbal Vocabularies and Their Corresponding TFNs for Weighting Criteria

Significance	Abbreviations	TFN $\langle l_{ij}, m_{ij}, u_{ij} \rangle$	Reciprocals $\langle 1/u_{ij}, 1/m_{ij}, 1/l_{ij} \rangle$
1	$\langle$EQI$\rangle$	$\langle 1, 1, 1 \rangle$	$\langle 1, 1, 1 \rangle$
2	$\langle$EMI$\rangle$	$\langle 1, 2, 3 \rangle$	$\langle 1/3, 1/2, 1 \rangle$
3	$\langle$MMI$\rangle$	$\langle 2, 3, 4 \rangle$	$\langle 1/4, 1/3, 1/2 \rangle$
4	$\langle$MII$\rangle$	$\langle 3, 4, 5 \rangle$	$\langle 1/5, 1/4, 1/3 \rangle$
5	$\langle$EIM$\rangle$	$\langle 4, 5, 6 \rangle$	$\langle 1/6, 1/5, 1/4 \rangle$
6	$\langle$EVV$\rangle$	$\langle 5, 6, 7 \rangle$	$\langle 1/7, 1/6, 1/5 \rangle$
7	$\langle$VEM$\rangle$	$\langle 6, 7, 8 \rangle$	$\langle 1/8, 1/7, 1/6 \rangle$
8	$\langle$VPM$\rangle$	$\langle 7, 8, 9 \rangle$	$\langle 1/9, 1/8, 1/7 \rangle$
9	$\langle$PMI$\rangle$	$\langle 8, 9, 10 \rangle$	$\langle 1/10, 1/9, 1/8 \rangle$

TABLE 1.2

Verbal Vocabularies and Their Corresponding TFNs for Assessing Alternatives

Verbal Vocabularies	Abbreviations	TFN $\langle l_{ij}, m_{ij}, u_{ij} \rangle$
Extremely low	$\langle$ETL$\rangle$	$\langle 1, 1, 3 \rangle$
Low	$\langle$LLO$\rangle$	$\langle 1, 3, 5 \rangle$
Moderate	$\langle$MOT$\rangle$	$\langle 3, 5, 7 \rangle$
High	$\langle$HIH$\rangle$	$\langle 5, 7, 9 \rangle$
Extremely high	$\langle$EXG$\rangle$	$\langle 7, 9, 11 \rangle$

in Table 1.2, multiple verbal measures were developed to rate the alternatives in terms of relevance. The value of verbal scales is that they allow professionals to express themselves without being limited to numerical scales (Mardani Shahri, Eshraghniaye Jahromi, and Houshmand 2021).

Step 6: Create a pairwise comparison matrix (D) among the criteria and itself by each expert as in Eq. (1.12) by using the verbal vocabularies in Table 1.1 and then by using TFNs as exhibited in Eq. (1.13).

$$
D = \begin{array}{c} \\ C_1 \\ C_2 \\ \vdots \\ C_n \end{array}
\begin{array}{c} C_1 \qquad\quad C_2 \qquad\quad \dots \qquad\quad C_n \end{array}
\left[\begin{array}{cccc}
- & e_{12} & \dots & e_{1i} \\
1/e_{21} & - & \dots & e_{2i} \\
1/e_{31} & 1/e_{32} & - & \dots \\
1/e_{j1} & 1/e_{j2} & 1/e_{j3} & -
\end{array} \right] \qquad (1.12)
$$

where (e_{ij}), $i, j = 1, 2 \dots n$, and e_{ij} is the assessment of the criteria of the ith dimension $C_1, C_2, \dots, C_i$ regarding the jth dimension $C_1, C_2, \dots, C_j$. Also, the key diagonal of the matrix *equals* 1 such that e_{ij} *equals* 1.

$$
D = \begin{array}{c} \\ C_1 \\ C_2 \\ \vdots \\ C_n \end{array}
\begin{array}{c} C_1 \cdot \qquad\qquad C_2 \qquad\qquad \dots \qquad\qquad C_n \end{array}
\left[\begin{array}{cccc}
- & \langle l_{12}, m_{12}, u_{12} \rangle & \dots & \langle l_{1i}, m_{1i}, u_{1i} \rangle \\
1/\langle u_{21}, m_{21}, l_{21} \rangle & - & \dots & \langle l_{2i}, m_{2i}, u_{2i} \rangle \\
1/\langle u_{31}, m_{31}, l_{31} \rangle & 1/\langle u_{32}, m_{32}, l_{32} \rangle & - & \dots \\
1/\langle u_{j1}, m_{j1}, l_{j1} \rangle & 1/\langle u_{j2}, m_{j2}, l_{j2} \rangle & 1/\langle u_{j3}, m_{j3}, l_{j3} \rangle & -
\end{array} \right]
$$

$$(1.13)$$

where l, m, and u characterize the lower, medium, and upper limits, respectively.

Step 7: Calculate the geometric mean of the comparisons for the ith criterion in contradiction to other criteria using Eq. (1.14).

$$ge_i = \left(\prod_{j-1}^{N} e_{ij} \right)^{1/n} \quad i = 1,2,3 \ldots N \tag{1.14}$$

Step 8: Calculate the fuzzy weight of the ith criterion as a TFN by applying Eq. (1.15). Also, the fuzzy weights are standardized by dividing each fuzzy weight by the sum of the fuzzy weights as in Eq. (1.15).

$$w_i = ge_i \times \left(ge_1 + ge_2 + ge_3 + \ldots + ge_N \right)^{-1} \tag{1.15}$$

Step 9: Compute the consistency ratio (CR) for each matrix created by each expert distinctly to confirm the dependability of the comparison matrix as presented in Eq. (1.16), where $CI = \dfrac{\lambda_{max-n}}{n-1}$, λ_{max} is the average of the weighted sum vector divided by the equivalent criterion, and n is the number of criteria. RI is a random index defined by a number of criteria (Saaty 2001).

$$CR = \frac{CI}{RI} \tag{1.16}$$

Step 10: Define the final weights of the criteria by applying the ordered weighted aggregation (OWA) operator of the final weights of all participants.

Step 11: Calculate the sorted vector according to the achieved weights in Eq. (1.15). If the achieved weights above pass the consistency investigation, it will be designed as a matrix; local weight matrix can be achieved as in Eq.(1.17).

$$W_{local} = [w_1, \ w_2, \ldots\ldots\ldots\ldots, w_n]^T \tag{1.17}$$

Step 12: Calculate the internal interdependency of the criterion and other criteria sets as shown in Eq. (1.18), and then get the unweighted supermatrix W_s which is composed of the sorting vectors affected by each criterion.

$$W_s = \begin{bmatrix} w_{11} & w_{12} & \cdots & w_{1n} \\ w_{21} & w_{22} & \cdots & w_{2n} \\ \cdots & \cdots & \cdots & \cdots \\ w_{n1} & w_{n2} & \cdots & w_{nn} \end{bmatrix} \tag{1.18}$$

Step 13: Compute the concluding weights of the criteria by multiplying the local weight in Eq. (1.17) achieved from experts' comparison matrices of criteria by the weight of interdependence of criteria in Eq. (1.18) as exhibited in Eq. (1.19).

$$W_{final} = \begin{bmatrix} w_{11} & w_{12} & \cdots & w_{1n} \\ w_{21} & w_{22} & \cdots & w_{2n} \\ \cdots & \cdots & \cdots & \cdots \\ w_{n1} & w_{n2} & \cdots & w_{nn} \end{bmatrix} \times [w_1, \; w_2, \ldots\ldots\ldots, w_n]^{\mathrm{T}} \quad (1.19)$$

Step 14: Create a decision matrix (X) among the criteria determined and the alternatives selected by the experts as in Eqs. (1.20) and (1.21), using verbal vocabularies and TFNs, respectively, as in Table 1.2.

$$G = [g_{ij}]_{m \times n} = \begin{array}{c} \\ A_1 \\ A_2 \\ \vdots \\ A_m \end{array} \begin{array}{cccc} C_1 & C_2 & \cdots & C_n \\ \begin{bmatrix} g_{11} & g_{12} & \cdots & g_{1n} \\ g_{21} & g_{22} & \cdots & g_{2n} \\ \cdots & \cdots & \cdots & \cdots \\ g_{m1} & g_{m2} & \cdots & g_{mn} \end{bmatrix} \end{array} \quad (1.20)$$

$$G = [g_{ij}]_{m \times n} = \begin{array}{c} \\ A_1 \\ A_2 \\ \vdots \\ A_m \end{array} \begin{array}{cccc} C_1 & C_2 & \cdots & C_n \\ \begin{bmatrix} \langle l_{11}, m_{11}, u_{11} \rangle & \langle l_{12}, m_{12}, u_{12} \rangle & \cdots & \langle l_{1n}, m_{1n}, u_{1n} \rangle \\ \langle l_{21}, m_{21}, u_{21} \rangle & \langle l_{22}, m_{22}, u_{22} \rangle & \cdots & l_{2n}, m_{2n}, u_{2n} \\ \cdots & \cdots & \cdots & \cdots \\ \langle l_{m1}, m_{m1}, u_{m1} \rangle & \langle l_{m2}, m_{m2}, u_{m2} \rangle & \cdots & \langle l_{mn}, m_{mn}, u_{mn} \rangle \end{bmatrix} \end{array}$$
$$(1.21)$$

where n is a number of criteria, m is the number of alternatives, and x_{ij} is the performance evaluation of the ith alternative $A_1, A_2, \ldots, A_n$ regarding the jth criterion $C_1, C_2, \ldots, C_m$.

Step 15: Compute the concluding combined decision matrix among the selected criteria and alternatives by combining the opinions of all experts, by applying Eq. (1.22).

$$l_{ij} = \min_E \{l_{ijE}\}, \; m_{ij} = \frac{1}{E} \sum_{e=1}^{E} \{m_{ijeE}\},$$
$$(1.22)$$
$$u_{ij} = \max_e \{u_{ije}\}, \text{ where } e \text{ is the number of experts}$$

Step 16: Determine the standardized decision matrix as exhibited in Eq. (1.23) for the beneficial criteria by using Eq. (1.24) and for the non-beneficial criteria by applying Eq. (1.25).

$$S = \left[s_{ij} \right]_{m \times n} \tag{1.23}$$

$$\text{Beneficial criteria} : \begin{cases} s_{ij} = \left(\dfrac{l_{ij}}{u_j^+}, \dfrac{m_{ij}}{u_j^+}, \dfrac{u_{ij}}{u_j^+} \right) \\[2ex] u_j^+ = \max_i u_{ij} \end{cases} \tag{1.24}$$

$$\text{Non-beneficial criteria} : \begin{cases} s_{ij} = \left(\dfrac{l_j^-}{l_{ij}}, \dfrac{l_j^-}{m_{ij}}, \dfrac{lo_j^-}{u_{ij}} \right) \\[2ex] l_j^- = \min_i l_{ij} \end{cases} \tag{1.25}$$

Step 17: Calculate the weighted standardized decision matrix (R) by multiplying the weights achieved (w_{final}) with the standardized decision matrix (s_{ij}) as presented in Eqs. (1.26) and (1.27).

$$R = \left[r_{ij} \right]_{m \times n} \tag{1.26}$$

$$r_{ij} = s_{ij} \times w_{\text{final}} \tag{1.27}$$

Step 18: Calculate the FPIS and the FNIS by using Eqs. (1.28) and (1.29), respectively.

$$A^* = \left(r_1^*, r_1^*, \dots, r_n^* \right), \text{ where } r_j^* = \max_i \{r_{ij}\} \tag{1.28}$$

$$A^- = \left(r_1^-, r_1^-, \dots, r_n^- \right), \text{ where } r_j^- = \min_i \{r_{ij}\} \tag{1.29}$$

Step 19: Calculate the distance from each substitute to the FPIS and the FNIS by using Eq. (1.11). Then, define the distance between each alternative and either FPIS or FNIS by using Eqs. (1.30) and (1.31).

$$p_j^* = \sum_{j=1}^{N} p_r \left(r_{ij}, r_j^* \right), \quad i = 1, 2, \dots n, \, j = 1, 2, \dots m. \tag{1.30}$$

$$p_j^- = \sum_{j=1}^{N} p_r \left(r_{ij}, r_j^- \right), \quad i = 1, 2, \dots n, \, j = 1, 2, \dots m. \tag{1.31}$$

Step 20: Compute the closeness coefficient C_j for each substitute by using Eq. (1.20). Lastly, based on the C_j value, the substitutes are rated in ascending order.

$$C_j = \frac{p_j^-}{p_j^- + p_j^*} \tag{1.32}$$

1.4 Application of the Suggested Methodology for the Case Study

This part applies the suggested fuzzy ANP and fuzzy TOPSIS methodology to evaluate smart and sustainable cities. The cities assessed are as follows: Madrid, Paris, Berlin, Moscow, Hong Kong, Tokyo, Sydney, Los Angeles, Dubai, and New York, which are labeled $City_1$, $City_2$, $City_3$, $City_4$, $City_5$, $City_6$, $City_7$, $City_8$, $City_9$, and $City_{10}$, respectively. We will list the steps to implement the suggested approach, beginning with gathering data and determining the criteria to evaluate smart and sustainable cities.

Step 1: A group of participants consisting of three experts in the field of smart sustainability have been identified. Experts collaborated with the authors throughout the research and study period.

Step 2: A set of main and sub-criteria that affect the assessment of smart and sustainable cities have been identified. The main criteria identified are as follows: smart governance (SGC_1), smart economy (SCC_2), smart mobility (SMC_3), smart living (SLC_4), smart people (SPC_5), and smart environment (SEC_6). The sub-criteria determined are as follows: participation in decision-making (PDC_{1_1}), public and social services (SSC_{1_2}), transparent governance (TGC_{1_3}), innovative spirit (ISC_{2_1}), entrepreneurship (ENC_{2_2}), productivity (PRC_{2_3}), economic image and trademarks (ETC_{2_4}), the flexibility of the labor market (FLC_{2_5}), international embeddedness (IEC_{2_6}), local accessibility (LAC_{3_1}), sustainable, innovative, and safe transport systems (SNC_{3_2}), (inter)national accessibility (IAC_{3_3}), availability of ICT infrastructure (AVC_{3_4}), cultural facilities (CFC_{4_1}), health conditions (HCC_{4_2}), individual safety (ISC_{4_3}), housing quality (HQC_{4_4}), education facilities (EFC_{4_5}), touristic attractivity (TAC_{4_6}), social cohesion (SCC_{4_7}), level of qualification (LQC_{5_1}), flexibility (FLC_{5_2}), participation in public life (PPC_{5_3}), affinity to lifelong learning (ALC_{5_4}), cosmopolitanism/open-mindedness (COC_{5_5}), social and ethnic plurality (SPC_{5_6}), creativity (CRC_{5_7}), attractivity of natural conditions (ANC_{6_1}), pollution (POC_{6_2}), environment protection (ENC_{6_3}), and sustainable resource management (SRC_{6_4}).

Step 3: Ten sustainable and smart cities were selected to be used in the evaluation process. These cities were selected from different continents of the world and the Middle East.

Step 4: A network model regarding the goal, and criteria had been constructed as presented in Figure 1.4. The problem was charted into several different levels. After that, the inner and outer dependencies results of criteria with respect to each criterion have been constructed.

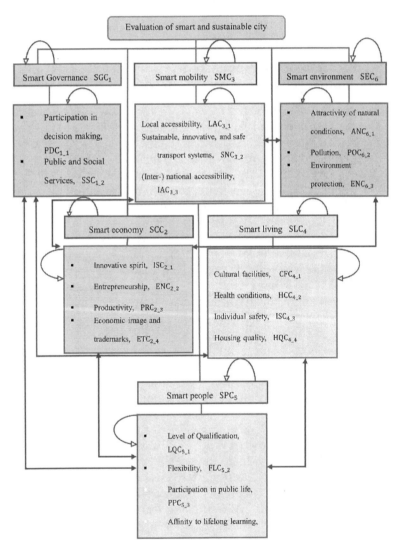

FIGURE 1.4
Structure of the problem's criteria using the ANP method.

Step 5: The verbal vocabularies and their corresponding TFNs that experts use in evaluating criteria and alternatives are identified as shown in Tables 1.1 and 1.2.

Step 6: A decision matrix of the main criteria had been constructed distinctly for each expert to expose the effect of each criterion on the other by applying the verbal vocabularies in Table 1.1 according to Eq. (1.12) as exhibited in Table 1.3. Then, a decision matrix has been constructed for each expert distinctly among the main criteria to expose the effect of each criterion on the other by TFNs in Table 1.1 according to Eq. (1.13), as exhibited in Table 1.4.

Step 7: The geometric mean of the three comparison matrices created by the experts has been computed by using Eq. (1.14) as shown in Table 1.5.

Step 8: The fuzzy weight of the six main criteria determined for each matrix had been calculated distinctly by applying Eq. (1.15) as presented in Table 1.5. Then, the weights of the six main criteria for each matrix are standardized distinctly by dividing each weight by the sum of the weights as presented in Table 1.5.

Step 9: The CR has been computed for each matrix that has been constructed by each expert distinctly to confirm consistency of the pairwise comparisons by applying Eq. (1.16). Then, the consistency level has been ensured to be less than 0.1 for all the matrices in Table 1.5.

Step 10: The concluding weights of the six main criteria had been computed by using the ordered weighted aggregation (OWA) operator of the concluding weights of all experts (i.e., W_{local}) as exhibited in Table 1.6 according to Eq. (1.17).

Step 11: According to the previous steps for computing the local weights (W_{local}) of the six main criteria, pairwise comparison matrices had been created to present the internal correlation of each criterion and its effect on the other set of criteria by all experts as exhibited in Tables 1.7–1.18. Then, the concluding weights of the internal interdependency of the criterion and other criteria are presented in Table 1.19 according to Eq. (1.18).

Step 12: The final weights of the six main criteria were calculated by multiplying the local weight computed from experts' comparison matrices of criteria in Table 1.6 by the weight of interdependence of criteria as presented in Table 1.19, and the final weights had been presented in Table 1.19 and Figure 1.5 according to Eq. (1.19).

Step 13: According to the previous steps in which the weights of the six main criteria were calculated using the ANP method, the sub-criteria weights are calculated for each main criterion. Some results for calculating the weights of the sub-criteria of the smart governance criterion are presented in Tables 1.20–1.29. After that, the global weights of all the sub-criteria were calculated according to the extent to which they were affected by the value of the weight of its main criterion, as shown in Table 1.30 and Figure 1.6.

TABLE 1.3

Evaluation of Main Criteria Using Verbal Vocabularies by All Experts

Expert₁	SGC₁	SCC₂	SMC₃	SLC₄	SPC₅	SEC₆
SGC₁	⟨EQI⟩	⟨EIM⟩	⟨VEM⟩	⟨EIM⟩	⟨VPM⟩	1/⟨EVV⟩
SCC₂	1/⟨EIM⟩	⟨EQI⟩	⟨VPM⟩	⟨PMI⟩	⟨PMI⟩	1/⟨VPM⟩
SMC₃	1/⟨VEM⟩	1/⟨VPM⟩	⟨EQI⟩	1/⟨MMI⟩	⟨VPM⟩	⟨PMI⟩
SLC₄	1/⟨EIM⟩	1/⟨PMI⟩	⟨MMI⟩	⟨EQI⟩	⟨EIM⟩	1/⟨EVV⟩
SPC₅	1/⟨VPM⟩	1/⟨PMI⟩	1/⟨VPM⟩	1/⟨EIM⟩	⟨EQI⟩	⟨VPM⟩
SEC₆	⟨EVV⟩	⟨VPM⟩	1/⟨PMI⟩	⟨EVV⟩	1/⟨VPM⟩	⟨EQI⟩
Expert₂	**SGC₁**	**SCC₂**	**SMC₃**	**SLC₄**	**SPC₅**	**SEC₆**
SGC₁	⟨EQI⟩	⟨EIM⟩	⟨EVV⟩	⟨EIM⟩	⟨VPM⟩	1/⟨EVV⟩
SCC₂	1/⟨EIM⟩	⟨EQI⟩	⟨VPM⟩	⟨PMI⟩	⟨PMI⟩	1/⟨VPM⟩
SMC₃	1/⟨EVV⟩	1/⟨VPM⟩	⟨EQI⟩	⟨MII⟩	⟨VPM⟩	⟨PMI⟩
SLC₄	1/⟨EIM⟩	1/⟨PMI⟩	1/⟨MII⟩	⟨EQI⟩	⟨EIM⟩	1/⟨EVV⟩
SPC₅	1/⟨VPM⟩	1/⟨PMI⟩	1/⟨VPM⟩	1/⟨EIM⟩	⟨EQI⟩	⟨VPM⟩
SEC₆	⟨EVV⟩	⟨VPM⟩	1/⟨PMI⟩	⟨EVV⟩	1/⟨VPM⟩	⟨EQI⟩
Expert₃	**SGC₁**	**SCC₂**	**SMC₃**	**SLC₄**	**SPC₅**	**SEC₆**
SGC₁	⟨EQI⟩	⟨EIM⟩	⟨EVV⟩	⟨EIM⟩	⟨VPM⟩	1/⟨EVV⟩
SCC₂	1/⟨EIM⟩	⟨EQI⟩	⟨VPM⟩	⟨PMI⟩	⟨PMI⟩	1/⟨VPM⟩
SMC₃	1/⟨EVV⟩	1/⟨VPM⟩	⟨EQI⟩	⟨MII⟩	⟨VPM⟩	⟨PMI⟩
SLC₄	1/⟨EIM⟩	1/⟨PMI⟩	1/⟨MII⟩	⟨EQI⟩	⟨EIM⟩	1/⟨VEM⟩
SPC₅	1/⟨VPM⟩	1/⟨PMI⟩	1/⟨VPM⟩	1/⟨EIM⟩	⟨EQI⟩	⟨VPM⟩
SEC₆	⟨EVV⟩	⟨VPM⟩	1/⟨PMI⟩	⟨VEM⟩	1/⟨VPM⟩	⟨EQI⟩

TABLE 1.4

Evaluation of Main Criteria Using TFNs by All Experts

$Expert_s$	SGC_1	SCC_2	SMC_3	SLC_4	SPC_5	SEC_6
SGC_1	$\langle 1,1,1 \rangle$	$\langle 4,5,6 \rangle$	$\langle 6,7,8 \rangle$	$\langle 4,5,6 \rangle$	$\langle 7,8,9 \rangle$	$\langle 1/7,1/6,1/5 \rangle$
SCC_2	$\langle 1/6,1/5,1/4 \rangle$	$\langle 1,1,1 \rangle$	$\langle 7,8,9 \rangle$	$\langle 8,9,10 \rangle$	$\langle 8,9,10 \rangle$	$\langle 1/9,1/8,1/7 \rangle$
SMC_3	$\langle 1/8,1/7,1/6 \rangle$	$\langle 1/9,1/8,1/7 \rangle$	$\langle 1,1,1 \rangle$	$\langle 1/4,1/3,1/2 \rangle$	$\langle 7,8,9 \rangle$	$\langle 8,9,10 \rangle$
SLC_4	$\langle 1/6,1/5,1/4 \rangle$	$\langle 1/10,1/9,1/8 \rangle$	$\langle 2,3,4 \rangle$	$\langle 1,1,1 \rangle$	$\langle 4,5,6 \rangle$	$\langle 1/7,1/6,1/5 \rangle$
SPC_5	$\langle 1/9,1/8,1/7 \rangle$	$\langle 1/10,1/9,1/8 \rangle$	$\langle 1/9,1/8,1/7 \rangle$	$\langle 1/6,1/5,1/4 \rangle$	$\langle 1,1,1 \rangle$	$\langle 7,8,9 \rangle$
SEC_6	$\langle 5,6,7 \rangle$	$\langle 7,8,9 \rangle$	$\langle 1/10,1/9,1/8 \rangle$	$\langle 5,6,7 \rangle$	$\langle 1/9,1/8,1/7 \rangle$	$\langle 1,1,1 \rangle$
$Expert_s$	SGC_1	SCC_2	SMC_3	SLC_4	SPC_5	SEC_6
SGC_1	$\langle 1,1,1 \rangle$	$\langle 4,5,6 \rangle$	$\langle 5,6,7 \rangle$	$\langle 4,5,6 \rangle$	$\langle 7,8,9 \rangle$	$\langle 1/7,1/6,1/5 \rangle$
SCC_2	$\langle 1/6,1/5,1/4 \rangle$	$\langle 1,1,1 \rangle$	$\langle 7,8,9 \rangle$	$\langle 8,9,10 \rangle$	$\langle 8,9,10 \rangle$	$\langle 1/9,1/8,1/7 \rangle$
SMC_3	$\langle 1/7,1/6,1/5 \rangle$	$\langle 1/9,1/8,1/7 \rangle$	$\langle 1,1,1 \rangle$	$\langle 3,4,5 \rangle$	$\langle 7,8,9 \rangle$	$\langle 8,9,10 \rangle$
SLC_4	$\langle 1/6,1/5,1/4 \rangle$	$\langle 1/10,1/9,1/8 \rangle$	$\langle 1/5,1/4,1/3 \rangle$	$\langle 1,1,1 \rangle$	$\langle 4,5,6 \rangle$	$\langle 1/7,1/6,1/5 \rangle$
SPC_5	$\langle 1/9,1/8,1/7 \rangle$	$\langle 1/10,1/9,1/8 \rangle$	$\langle 1/9,1/8,1/7 \rangle$	$\langle 1/6,1/5,1/4 \rangle$	$\langle 1,1,1 \rangle$	$\langle 7,8,9 \rangle$
SEC_6	$\langle 5,6,7 \rangle$	$\langle 7,8,9 \rangle$	$\langle 1/10,1/9,1/8 \rangle$	$\langle 5,6,7 \rangle$	$\langle 1/9,1/8,1/7 \rangle$	$\langle 1,1,1 \rangle$
$Expert_s$	SGC_1	SCC_2	SMC_3	SLC_4	SPC_5	SEC_6
SGC_1	$\langle 1,1,1 \rangle$	$\langle 4,5,6 \rangle$	$\langle 5,6,7 \rangle$	$\langle 4,5,6 \rangle$	$\langle 7,8,9 \rangle$	$\langle 1/7,1/6,1/5 \rangle$
SCC_2	$\langle 1/6,1/5,1/4 \rangle$	$\langle 1,1,1 \rangle$	$\langle 7,8,9 \rangle$	$\langle 8,9,10 \rangle$	$\langle 8,9,10 \rangle$	$\langle 1/9,1/8,1/7 \rangle$
SMC_3	$\langle 1/7,1/6,1/5 \rangle$	$\langle 1/9,1/8,1/7 \rangle$	$\langle 1,1,1 \rangle$	$\langle 3,4,5 \rangle$	$\langle 7,8,9 \rangle$	$\langle 8,9,10 \rangle$
SLC_4	$\langle 1/6,1/5,1/4 \rangle$	$\langle 1/10,1/9,1/8 \rangle$	$\langle 1/5,1/4,1/3 \rangle$	$\langle 1,1,1 \rangle$	$\langle 4,5,6 \rangle$	$\langle 1/8,1/7,1/6 \rangle$
SPC_5	$\langle 1/9,1/8,1/7 \rangle$	$\langle 1/10,1/9,1/8 \rangle$	$\langle 1/9,1/8,1/7 \rangle$	$\langle 1/6,1/5,1/4 \rangle$	$\langle 1,1,1 \rangle$	$\langle 7,8,9 \rangle$
SEC_6	$\langle 5,6,7 \rangle$	$\langle 7,8,9 \rangle$	$\langle 1/10,1/9,1/8 \rangle$	$\langle 6,7,8 \rangle$	$\langle 1/9,1/8,1/7 \rangle$	$\langle 1,1,1 \rangle$

TABLE 1.5

Local Weights of Main Criteria by All Experts

Expert_1	$\left(\prod_{j-1}^{N} e_{ij}\right)^{1/n}$			Fuzzy Weight			Crisp Weight	Normalized Weight	Weight
SGC_1	2.140	2.482	2.834	0.261	0.352	0.450	0.355	0.346	0.331
SCC_2	1.423	1.591	1.783	0.174	0.226	0.283	0.228	0.222	0.217
SMC_3	0.761	0.723	1.012	0.093	0.103	0.161	0.119	0.116	0.160
SLC_4	0.517	0.618	0.729	0.063	0.088	0.116	0.089	0.087	0.067
SPC_5	0.336	0.375	0.423	0.041	0.053	0.067	0.054	0.053	0.052
SEC_6	1.117	1.260	1.411	0.136	0.179	0.224	0.180	0.176	0.173

Expert_2	$\left(\prod_{j-1}^{N} e_{ij}\right)^{1/n}$			Fuzzy Weight			Crisp Weight	Normalized Weight	Weight
SGC_1	2.076	2.419	2.772	0.247	0.327	0.428	0.334	0.326	0.331
SCC_2	1.423	1.591	1.783	0.169	0.215	0.275	0.220	0.215	0.217
SMC_3	1.178	1.348	1.531	0.140	0.182	0.236	0.186	0.182	0.160
SLC_4	0.352	0.408	0.482	0.042	0.055	0.074	0.057	0.056	0.067
SPC_5	0.336	0.375	0.423	0.040	0.051	0.065	0.052	0.051	0.052
SEC_6	1.117	1.260	1.411	0.133	0.170	0.218	0.174	0.170	0.173

Expert_3	$\left(\prod_{j-1}^{N} e_{ij}\right)^{1/n}$			Fuzzy Weight			Crisp Weight	Normalized Weight	Weight
SGC_1	2.076	2.419	2.772	0.247	0.326	0.426	0.333	0.326	0.331
SCC_2	1.423	1.591	1.783	0.169	0.214	0.274	0.219	0.214	0.217
SMC_3	1.178	1.348	1.531	0.140	0.182	0.235	0.186	0.182	0.160
SLC_4	0.344	0.398	0.467	0.041	0.054	0.072	0.055	0.054	0.067
SPC_5	0.336	0.375	0.423	0.040	0.050	0.065	0.052	0.051	0.052
SEC_6	1.151	1.292	1.442	0.137	0.174	0.222	0.177	0.174	0.173

TABLE 1.6

The Local Weights of the Main Criteria

Barriers	Weights by expert_1	Weights by expert_2	Weights by expert_3	W_{local}
SGC_1	0.346	0.326	0.326	0.331
SCC_2	0.222	0.215	0.214	0.217
SMC_3	0.116	0.182	0.182	0.160
SLC_4	0.087	0.056	0.054	0.067
SPC_5	0.053	0.051	0.051	0.052
SEC_6	0.176	0.170	0.174	0.173

TABLE 1.7

Pairwise Comparison Matrix Based on Smart Governance Criterion by All Experts

Smart Governance	SGC$_1$	SCC$_2$	SMC$_3$	SLC$_4$	SPC$_5$	SEC$_6$
SGC$_1$	$\langle$EQI$\rangle$	$\langle$EVV$\rangle$	$\langle$PMI$\rangle$	$\langle$VEM$\rangle$	$\langle$VPM$\rangle$	$1/\langle$MII$\rangle$
SCC$_2$	$1/\langle$EVV$\rangle$	$\langle$EQI$\rangle$	$1/\langle$PMI$\rangle$	$\langle$VEM$\rangle$	$\langle$PMI$\rangle$	$1/\langle$VPM$\rangle$
SMC$_3$	$1/\langle$PMI$\rangle$	$\langle$PMI$\rangle$	$\langle$EQI$\rangle$	$\langle$VEM$\rangle$	$\langle$VPM$\rangle$	$\langle$PMI$\rangle$
SLC$_4$	$1/\langle$VEM$\rangle$	$1/\langle$VEM$\rangle$	$1/\langle$VEM$\rangle$	$\langle$EQI$\rangle$	$\langle$EIM$\rangle$	$1/\langle$MII$\rangle$
SPC$_5$	$1/\langle$VPM$\rangle$	$1/\langle$PMI$\rangle$	$1/\langle$VPM$\rangle$	$1/\langle$EIM$\rangle$	$\langle$EQI$\rangle$	$1/\langle$VEM$\rangle$
SEC$_6$	$\langle$MII$\rangle$	$\langle$VPM$\rangle$	$1/\langle$PMI$\rangle$	$\langle$MII$\rangle$	$\langle$VEM$\rangle$	$\langle$EQI$\rangle$

TABLE 1.8

Interdependency Matrix of the Smart Governance Criterion by All Experts

Smart Governance	$\left(\prod\limits_{j-1}^{N} e_{ij}\right)^{1/n}$			Fuzzy Weight			Crisp Weight	Normalized Weight
SGC$_1$	2.637	3.018	3.447	0.248	0.319	0.414	0.327	0.320
SCC$_2$	0.651	0.726	0.812	0.061	0.077	0.097	0.078	0.077
SMC$_3$	2.540	2.821	3.107	0.239	0.298	0.373	0.303	0.297
SLC$_4$	0.341	0.392	0.459	0.032	0.042	0.055	0.043	0.042
SPC$_5$	0.172	0.192	0.218	0.016	0.020	0.026	0.021	0.020
SEC$_6$	1.995	2.303	2.608	0.187	0.244	0.313	0.248	0.243

TABLE 1.9

Pairwise Comparison Matrix Based on Smart Economy Criterion by All Experts

Smart Economy	SGC$_1$	SCC$_2$	SMC$_3$	SLC$_4$	SPC$_5$	SEC$_6$
SGC$_1$	$\langle$EQI$\rangle$	$\langle$EVV$\rangle$	$\langle$MMI$\rangle$	$1/\langle$EVV$\rangle$	$\langle$VPM$\rangle$	$1/\langle$MII$\rangle$
SCC$_2$	$1/$EVV	$\langle$EQI$\rangle$	$1/\langle$PMI$\rangle$	$\langle$VEM$\rangle$	$\langle$PMI$\rangle$	$1/\langle$VPM$\rangle$
SMC$_3$	$1/\langle$MMI$\rangle$	$\langle$PMI$\rangle$	$\langle$EQI$\rangle$	$\langle$EIM$\rangle$	$1/\langle$VPM$\rangle$	$\langle$PMI$\rangle$
SLC$_4$	$\langle$EVV$\rangle$	$1/\langle$VEM$\rangle$	$1/\langle$EIM$\rangle$	$\langle$EQI$\rangle$	$\langle$EIM$\rangle$	$1/\langle$MII$\rangle$
SPC$_5$	$1/\langle$VPM$\rangle$	$1/\langle$PMI$\rangle$	$\langle$VPM$\rangle$	$1/\langle$EIM$\rangle$	$\langle$EQI$\rangle$	$1/\langle$VEM$\rangle$
SEC$_6$	$\langle$MII$\rangle$	$\langle$VPM$\rangle$	$1/\langle$PMI$\rangle$	$\langle$MII$\rangle$	$\langle$VEM$\rangle$	$\langle$EQI$\rangle$

TABLE 1.10

Interdependency Matrix of the Smart Economy Criterion by All Experts

Smart Economy	$\left(\prod_{j-1}^{N} e_{ij}\right)^{1/n}$			Fuzzy Weight			Crisp Weight	Normalized Weight
SGC$_1$	1.123	1.348	1.600	0.136	0.189	0.260	0.195	0.190
SCC$_2$	0.651	0.726	0.812	0.079	0.102	0.132	0.104	0.101
SMC$_3$	1.386	1.601	1.871	0.168	0.224	0.304	0.232	0.226
SLC$_4$	0.661	0.774	0.914	0.080	0.108	0.148	0.112	0.109
SPC$_5$	0.343	0.383	0.434	0.042	0.054	0.071	0.055	0.054
SEC$_6$	1.995	2.303	2.608	0.242	0.323	0.424	0.329	0.320

TABLE 1.11

Pairwise Comparison Matrix Based on Smart Mobility Criterion by All Experts

Smart Mobility	SGC$_1$	SCC$_2$	SMC$_3$	SLC$_4$	SPC$_5$	SEC$_6$
SGC$_1$	$\langle$EQI$\rangle$	$1/\langle$VEM$\rangle$	$\langle$MMI$\rangle$	$1/\langle$EVV$\rangle$	$\langle$VPM$\rangle$	$1/\langle$MII$\rangle$
SCC$_2$	$\langle$VEM$\rangle$	$\langle$EQI$\rangle$	$1/\langle$PMI$\rangle$	$\langle$EVV$\rangle$	$\langle$PMI$\rangle$	$\langle$VEM$\rangle$
SMC$_3$	$1/\langle$MMI$\rangle$	$\langle$PMI$\rangle$	$\langle$EQI$\rangle$	$\langle$EIM$\rangle$	$1/\langle$VPM$\rangle$	$\langle$PMI$\rangle$
SLC$_4$	$\langle$EVV$\rangle$	$1/\langle$EVV$\rangle$	$1/\langle$EIM$\rangle$	$\langle$EQI$\rangle$	$\langle$EIM$\rangle$	$1/\langle$MII$\rangle$
SPC$_5$	$1/\langle$VPM$\rangle$	$1/\langle$PMI$\rangle$	$\langle$VPM$\rangle$	$1/\langle$EIM$\rangle$	$\langle$EQI$\rangle$	$1/\langle$VEM$\rangle$
SEC$_6$	$\langle$MII$\rangle$	$1/\langle$VEM$\rangle$	$1/\langle$PMI$\rangle$	$\langle$MII$\rangle$	$\langle$VEM$\rangle$	$\langle$EQI$\rangle$

TABLE 1.12

Interdependency Matrix of the Smart Mobility Criterion by All Experts

Smart Mobility	$\left(\prod_{j-1}^{N} e_{ij}\right)^{1/n}$			Fuzzy Weight			Crisp Weight	Normalized Weight
SGC$_1$	0.607	0.723	0.859	0.073	0.100	0.136	0.103	0.101
SCC$_2$	2.289	2.578	2.871	0.276	0.356	0.455	0.363	0.354
SMC$_3$	1.386	1.601	1.871	0.167	0.221	0.297	0.228	0.223
SLC$_4$	0.661	0.774	0.914	0.080	0.107	0.145	0.111	0.108
SPC$_5$	0.343	0.383	0.434	0.041	0.053	0.069	0.054	0.053
SEC$_6$	1.020	1.178	1.342	0.123	0.163	0.213	0.166	0.162

TABLE 1.13

Pairwise Comparison Matrix Based on Smart Living Criterion by All Experts

Smart Living	SGC$_1$	SCC$_2$	SMC$_3$	SLC$_4$	SPC$_5$	SEC$_6$
SGC$_1$	$\langle$EQI$\rangle$	$1/\langle$VEM$\rangle$	$\langle$MMI$\rangle$	$1/\langle$EVV$\rangle$	$\langle$VPM$\rangle$	$\langle$MII$\rangle$
SCC$_2$	$\langle$VEM$\rangle$	$\langle$EQI$\rangle$	$1/\langle$PMI$\rangle$	$\langle$EVV$\rangle$	$\langle$PMI$\rangle$	$\langle$VEM$\rangle$
SMC$_3$	$1/\langle$MMI$\rangle$	$\langle$PMI$\rangle$	$\langle$EQI$\rangle$	$\langle$EIM$\rangle$	$1/\langle$EIM$\rangle$	$\langle$PMI$\rangle$
SLC$_4$	$\langle$EVV$\rangle$	$1/\langle$EVV$\rangle$	$1/\langle$EIM$\rangle$	$\langle$EQI$\rangle$	$\langle$EIM$\rangle$	$1/\langle$MII$\rangle$
SPC$_5$	$1/\langle$VPM$\rangle$	$1/\langle$PMI$\rangle$	$\langle$EIM$\rangle$	$1/\langle$EIM$\rangle$	$\langle$EQI$\rangle$	$1/\langle$VEM$\rangle$
SEC$_6$	$1/\langle$MII$\rangle$	$1/\langle$VEM$\rangle$	$1/\langle$PMI$\rangle$	$\langle$MII$\rangle$	$\langle$VEM$\rangle$	$\langle$EQI$\rangle$

TABLE 1.14

Interdependency Matrix of the Smart Living Criterion by All Experts

Smart Living	$\left(\prod_{j-1}^{N} E_{ij}\right)^{1/n}$.			Fuzzy Weight			Crisp Weight	Normalized Weight
SGC$_1$	0.953	1.148	1.348	0.113	0.157	0.213	0.161	0.157
SCC$_2$	2.289	2.578	2.871	0.271	0.353	0.454	0.359	0.349
SMC$_3$	1.484	1.732	2.054	0.175	0.237	0.325	0.246	0.239
SLC$_4$	0.661	0.774	0.914	0.078	0.106	0.145	0.110	0.107
SPC$_5$	0.312	0.354	0.406	0.037	0.048	0.064	0.050	0.048
SEC$_6$	0.619	0.727	0.865	0.073	0.099	0.137	0.103	0.100

TABLE 1.15

Pairwise Comparison Matrix Based on Smart People Criterion by All Experts

Smart People	SGC$_1$	SCC$_2$	SMC$_3$	SLC$_4$	SPC$_5$	SEC$_6$
SGC$_1$	$\langle$EQI$\rangle$	$1/\langle$VEM$\rangle$	$1/\langle$MII$\rangle$	$1/\langle$EVV$\rangle$	$\langle$VPM$\rangle$	$\langle$MII$\rangle$
SCC$_2$	$\langle$VEM$\rangle$	$\langle$EQI$\rangle$	$1/\langle$EMI$\rangle$	$\langle$EVV$\rangle$	$\langle$PMI$\rangle$	$\langle$VEM$\rangle$
SMC$_3$	$\langle$MMI$\rangle$	$\langle$EMI$\rangle$	$\langle$EQI$\rangle$	$\langle$EIM$\rangle$	$1/\langle$EIM$\rangle$	$\langle$VPM$\rangle$
SLC$_4$	$\langle$EVV$\rangle$	$1/\langle$EVV$\rangle$	$1/\langle$EIM$\rangle$	$\langle$EQI$\rangle$	$\langle$EIM$\rangle$	$1/\langle$MII$\rangle$
SPC$_5$	$1/\langle$VPM$\rangle$	$1/\langle$PMI$\rangle$	$\langle$EIM$\rangle$	$1/\langle$EIM$\rangle$	$\langle$EQI$\rangle$	$1/\langle$VEM$\rangle$
SEC$_6$	$1/\langle$MII$\rangle$	$1/\langle$VEM$\rangle$	$1/\langle$VPM$\rangle$	$\langle$MII$\rangle$	$\langle$VEM$\rangle$	$\langle$EQI$\rangle$

TABLE 1.16

Interdependency Matrix of the Smart People Criterion by All Experts

Smart People	$\left(\prod\limits_{j-1}^{N} e_{ij}\right)^{1/n}$			Fuzzy Weight			Crisp Weight	Normalized Weight
SGC_1	0.650	0.759	0.891	0.068	0.096	0.135	0.099	0.095
SCC_2	2.798	3.313	4.060	0.292	0.417	0.615	0.441	0.422
SMC_3	1.553	2.000	2.423	0.162	0.252	0.367	0.260	0.249
SLC_4	0.661	0.774	0.914	0.069	0.097	0.138	0.102	0.097
SPC_5	0.312	0.354	0.406	0.033	0.045	0.061	0.046	0.044
SEC_6	0.630	0.742	0.884	0.066	0.093	0.134	0.098	0.093

TABLE 1.17

Pairwise Comparison Matrix Based on Smart Environment Criterion by All Experts

Smart Environment	SGC_1	SCC_2	SMC_3	SLC_4	SPC_5	SEC_6
SGC_1	⟨EQI⟩	$1/⟨VEM⟩$	$1/⟨MII⟩$	$1/⟨EVV⟩$	⟨VPM⟩	⟨MII⟩
SCC_2	⟨VEM⟩	⟨EQI⟩	$1/⟨EMI⟩$	⟨VEM⟩	⟨PMI⟩	⟨VEM⟩
SMC_3	⟨MMI⟩	⟨EMI⟩	⟨EQI⟩	⟨EIM⟩	$1/⟨EIM⟩$	$1/⟨EIM⟩$
SLC_4	⟨EVV⟩	$1/⟨VEM⟩$	$1/⟨EIM⟩$	⟨EQI⟩	⟨EIM⟩	$1/⟨MII⟩$
SPC_5	$1/⟨VPM⟩$	$1/⟨PMI⟩$	⟨EIM⟩	$1/⟨EIM⟩$	⟨EQI⟩	$1/⟨VEM⟩$
SEC_6	$1/⟨MII⟩$	$1/⟨VEM⟩$	⟨EIM⟩	⟨MII⟩	⟨VEM⟩	⟨EQI⟩

TABLE 1.18

Interdependency Matrix of the Smart Environment Criterion by All Experts

Smart Environment	$\left(\prod\limits_{j-1}^{N} e_{ij}\right)^{1/n}$			Fuzzy Weight			Crisp Weight	Normalized Weight
SGC_1	0.650	0.759	0.891	0.070	0.098	0.137	0.102	0.097
SCC_2	2.884	3.400	4.152	0.309	0.439	0.640	0.463	0.443
SMC_3	0.833	1.081	1.334	0.089	0.140	0.206	0.145	0.139
SLC_4	0.661	0.774	0.914	0.071	0.100	0.141	0.104	0.099
SPC_5	0.312	0.354	0.406	0.033	0.046	0.063	0.047	0.045
SEC_6	1.145	1.372	1.648	0.123	0.177	0.254	0.185	0.177

TABLE 1.19

Comparative Influence of the Six Main Criteria

Criteria	SGC_1	SCC_2	SMC_3	SLC_4	SPC_5	SEC_6	Local Weight	Final Weight
SGC_1	0.320	0.190	0.101	0.157	0.095	0.097	0.331	0.195
SCC_2	0.077	0.101	0.354	0.349	0.422	0.443	0.217	0.226
SMC_3	0.297	0.226	0.223	0.239	0.249	0.139	0.160	0.236
SLC_4	0.042	0.109	0.108	0.107	0.097	0.099	0.067	0.084
SPC_5	0.020	0.054	0.053	0.048	0.044	0.045	0.052	0.040
SEC_6	0.243	0.320	0.162	0.100	0.093	0.177	0.173	0.219

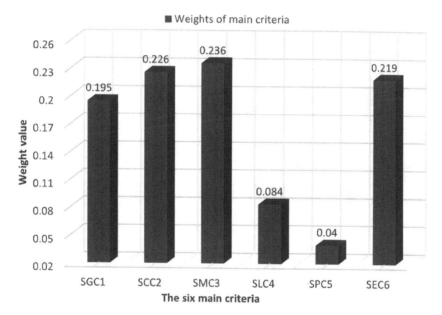

FIGURE 1.5

Final weights of the main criteria are computed by applying the ANP method.

TABLE 1.20

Evaluation of Smart Governance's Criteria Using Verbal Vocabularies by All Experts

Expert$_s$	PDC_{1_1}	SSC_{1_2}	TGC_{1_3}
PDC_{1_1}	$\langle EQI \rangle$	$\langle EIM \rangle$	$\langle VPM \rangle$
SSC_{1_2}	$1/\langle EIM \rangle$	$\langle EQI \rangle$	$\langle EVV \rangle$
TGC_{1_3}	$1/\langle VPM \rangle$	$1/\langle EVV \rangle$	$\langle EQI \rangle$

TABLE 1.21

Evaluation of Smart Governance's Criteria Using TFNs by All Experts

Expert$_s$	PDC$_{1\_1}$	SSC$_{1\_2}$	TGC$_{1\_3}$
PDC$_{1\_1}$	$\langle 1, 1, 1 \rangle$	$\langle 4, 5, 6 \rangle$	$\langle 7, 8, 9 \rangle$
SSC$_{1\_2}$	$\langle 1/6, 1/5, 1/4 \rangle$	$\langle 1, 1, 1 \rangle$	$\langle 5, 6, 7 \rangle$
TGC$_{1\_3}$	$\langle 1/9, 1/8, 1/7 \rangle$	$\langle 1/7, 1/6, 1/5 \rangle$	$\langle 1, 1, 1 \rangle$

TABLE 1.22

The Local Weights of Smart Governance's Criteria by All Experts

Expert$_s$	$\left(\prod\limits_{j-1}^{N} e_{ij} \right)^{1/n}$			Fuzzy Weight			Crisp Weight	Normalized Weight
PDC$_{1\_1}$	1.849	1.944	2.030	0.512	0.562	0.614	0.563	0.561
SSC$_{1\_2}$	0.493	0.514	0.541	0.137	0.149	0.164	0.150	0.150
TGC$_{1\_3}$	0.963	1.000	1.038	0.267	0.289	0.314	0.290	0.289

TABLE 1.23

Pairwise Comparison Matrix of Smart Governance Based on Participation in Decision-Making Criterion by All Experts

Participation in Decision-Making	PDC$_{1\_1}$	SSC$_{1\_2}$	TGC$_{1\_3}$
PDC$_{1\_1}$	$\langle EQI \rangle$	$\langle MII \rangle$	$1/\langle VEM \rangle$
SSC$_{1\_2}$	$1/\langle MII \rangle$	$\langle EQI \rangle$	$\langle MMI \rangle$
TGC$_{1\_3}$	$\langle VEM \rangle$	$1/\langle MMI \rangle$	$\langle EQI \rangle$

TABLE 1.24

Interdependency Matrix of Smart Governance Based on Participation in Decision-Making by All Experts

Participation in Decision-Making	$\left(\prod\limits_{j-1}^{N} e_{ij} \right)^{1/n}$			Fuzzy Weight			Crisp Weight	Normalized Weight
PDC$_{1\_1}$	0.849	0.911	0.970	0.259	0.302	0.349	0.303	0.301
SSC$_{1\_2}$	0.858	0.953	1.049	0.262	0.316	0.378	0.318	0.316
TGC$_{1\_3}$	1.070	1.151	1.260	0.326	0.382	0.454	0.387	0.384

TABLE 1.25

Pairwise Comparison Matrix of Smart Governance Based on Public and Social Services Criterion by All Experts

Public and Social Services	PDC_{1_1}	SSC_{1_2}	TGC_{1_3}
PDC_{1_1}	$\langle EQI \rangle$	$\langle PMI \rangle$	$\langle VPM \rangle$
SSC_{1_2}	$1/\langle PMI \rangle$	$\langle EQI \rangle$	$\langle EIM \rangle$
TGC_{1_3}	$1/\langle VPM \rangle$	$1/\langle EIM \rangle$	$\langle EQI \rangle$

TABLE 1.26

Interdependency Matrix of Smart Governance Based on Public and Social Services Criterion by All Experts

Public and Social Services	$\left(\prod_{j-1}^{N} e_{ij} \right)^{1/n}$			Fuzzy Weight			Crisp Weight	Normalized Weight
PDC_{1_1}	1.956	2.040	2.117	0.537	0.585	0.636	0.586	0.584
SSC_{1_2}	0.858	0.907	0.953	0.236	0.260	0.286	0.261	0.260
TGC_{1_3}	0.514	0.541	0.574	0.141	0.155	0.172	0.156	0.156

TABLE 1.27

Pairwise Comparison Matrix of Smart Governance Based on Transparent Governance Criterion by All Experts

Transparent Governance	PDC_{1_1}	SSC_{1_2}	TGC_{1_3}
PDC_{1_1}	$\langle EQI \rangle$	$1/\langle EIM \rangle$	$\langle MII \rangle$
SSC_{1_2}	$\langle EIM \rangle$	$\langle EQI \rangle$	$\langle VEM \rangle$
TGC_{1_3}	$1/\langle MII \rangle$	$1/\langle VEM \rangle$	$\langle EQI \rangle$

TABLE 1.28

Interdependency Matrix of Smart Governance Based on Transparent Governance Criterion by All Experts

Transparent Governance	$\left(\prod_{j-1}^{N} e_{ij} \right)^{1/n}$			Fuzzy Weight			Crisp Weight	Normalized Weight
PDC_{1_1}	0.891	0.963	1.038	0.250	0.288	0.332	0.290	0.288
SSC_{1_2}	1.698	1.809	1.906	0.477	0.541	0.609	0.542	0.539
TGC_{1_3}	0.541	0.574	0.618	0.152	0.172	0.197	0.174	0.173

TABLE 1.29

Comparative Influence of the Smart Governance's Criteria

Criteria	PDC_{1_1}	SSC_{1_2}	TGC_{1_3}	Local Weight	Final Weight
PDC_{1_1}	0.301	0.584	0.288	0.561	0.339
SSC_{1_2}	0.316	0.260	0.539	0.150	0.372
TGC_{1_3}	0.384	0.156	0.173	0.289	0.289

TABLE 1.30

Final Weights of the Main Criteria and Their Sub-Criteria

Main Criteria	Weights	Sub-Criteria	Local Weights	Global Weights
SGC_1	0.195	PDC_{1_1}	0.339	0.066
		SSC_{1_2}	0.372	0.073
		TGC_{1_3}	0.289	0.056
SCC_2	0.226	ISC_{2_1}	0.096	0.022
		ENC_{2_2}	0.102	0.023
		PRC_{2_3}	0.214	0.048
		ETC_{2_4}	0.139	0.031
		FLC_{2_5}	0.257	0.058
		IEC_{2_6}	0.192	0.043
SMC_3	0.236	LAC_{3_1}	0.212	0.050
		SNC_{3_2}	0.253	0.060
		IAC_{3_3}	0.181	0.042
		AVC_{3_4}	0.354	0.083
SLC_4	0.084	CFC_{4_1}	0.076	0.006
		HCC_{4_2}	0.145	0.012
		ISC_{4_3}	0.185	0.016
		HQC_{4_4}	0.141	0.011
		EFC_{4_5}	0.158	0.013
		TAC_{4_6}	0.119	0.009
		SCC_{4_7}	0.176	0.015
SPC_5	0.040	LQC_{5_1}	0.105	0.004
		FLC_{5_2}	0.137	0.005
		PPC_{5_3}	0.195	0.008
		ALC_{5_4}	0.154	0.006
		COC_{5_5}	0.132	0.005
		SPC_{5_6}	0.129	0.005
		CRC_{5_7}	0.148	0.006
SEC_6	0.219	ANC_{6_1}	0.298	0.065
		POC_{6_2}	0.267	0.058
		ENC_{6_3}	0.243	0.053
		SRC_{6_4}	0.192	0.042

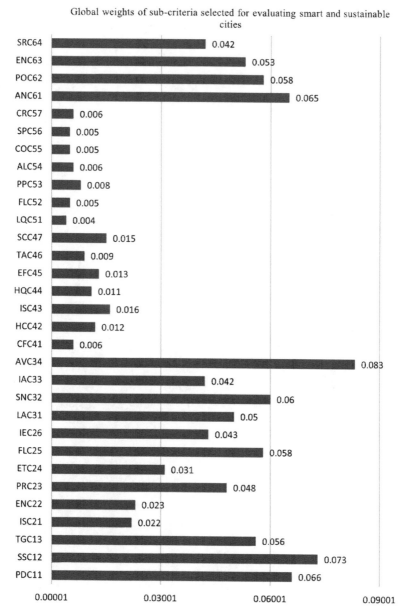

FIGURE 1.6
Final global weights of sub-criteria selected for evaluating smart and sustainable cities.

Step 14: At this phase, the cities identified in the evaluation process are evaluated according to the sub-criteria for each main criterion. First, cities are evaluated according to the smart governance criterion's sub-criteria.

Step 15: The decision matrix was constructed among the smart governance criterion's sub-criteria and the selected cities by the experts using verbal vocabularies according to Eq. (1.20) as presented in Table 1.31 and using TFNs according to Eq. (1.21).

Step 16: The final combined decision matrix between the smart governance criterion's sub-criteria and the selected cities by the experts is presented in Table 1.32 according to Eq. (1.22).

TABLE 1.31

Decision Matrices of Ten Cities According to Smart Governance's Criteria Using Verbal Vocabularies

Expert$_s$	PDC$_{1\_1}$	SSC$_{1\_2}$	TGC$_{1\_3}$
City$_1$	$\langle$MOT$\rangle\langle$MOT$\rangle\langle$MOT$\rangle$	$\langle$LLO$\rangle\langle$LLO$\rangle\langle$LLO$\rangle$	$\langle$LLO$\rangle\langle$LLO$\rangle\langle$LLO$\rangle$
City$_2$	$\langle$MOT$\rangle\langle$HIH$\rangle\langle$EXG$\rangle$	$\langle$LLO$\rangle\langle$LLO$\rangle\langle$LLO$\rangle$	$\langle$LLO$\rangle\langle$LLO$\rangle\langle$LLO$\rangle$
City$_3$	$\langle$MOT$\rangle\langle$MOT$\rangle\langle$MOT$\rangle$	$\langle$HIH$\rangle\langle$HIH$\rangle\langle$HIH$\rangle$	$\langle$EXG$\rangle\langle$EXG$\rangle\langle$EXG$\rangle$
City$_4$	$\langle$ETL$\rangle\langle$ETL$\rangle\langle$ETL$\rangle$	$\langle$LLO$\rangle\langle$LLO$\rangle\langle$LLO$\rangle$	$\langle$LLO$\rangle\langle$LLO$\rangle\langle$LLO$\rangle$
City$_5$	$\langle$LLO$\rangle\langle$LLO$\rangle\langle$LLO$\rangle$	$\langle$LLO$\rangle\langle$ETL$\rangle\langle$MOE$\rangle$	$\langle$ETL$\rangle\langle$ETL$\rangle\langle$ETL$\rangle$
City$_6$	$\langle$HIH$\rangle\langle$HIH$\rangle\langle$HIH$\rangle$	$\langle$HIH$\rangle\langle$HIH$\rangle\langle$HIH$\rangle$	$\langle$MOT$\rangle\langle$MOT$\rangle\langle$MOT$\rangle$
City$_7$	$\langle$ETL$\rangle\langle$ETL$\rangle\langle$ETL$\rangle$	$\langle$LLO$\rangle\langle$LLO$\rangle\langle$LLO$\rangle$	$\langle$LLO$\rangle\langle$LLO$\rangle\langle$LLO$\rangle$
City$_8$	$\langle$ETL$\rangle\langle$ETL$\rangle\langle$ETL$\rangle$	$\langle$LLO$\rangle\langle$LLO$\rangle\langle$LLO$\rangle$	$\langle$LLO$\rangle\langle$LLO$\rangle\langle$LLO$\rangle$
City$_9$	$\langle$EXG$\rangle\langle$EXG$\rangle\langle$EXG$\rangle$	$\langle$EXG$\rangle\langle$EXG$\rangle\langle$EXG$\rangle$	$\langle$EXG$\rangle\langle$EXG$\rangle\langle$EXG$\rangle$
City$_{10}$	$\langle$MOT$\rangle\langle$MOT$\rangle\langle$MOT$\rangle$	$\langle$HIH$\rangle\langle$HIH$\rangle\langle$HIH$\rangle$	$\langle$MOT$\rangle\langle$MOT$\rangle\langle$MOT$\rangle$

TABLE 1.32

Combined Decision Matrix of Ten Cities According to Smart Governance's Criteria Using TFNs

Expert$_s$	PDC$_{1\_1}$	SSC$_{1\_2}$	TGC$_{1\_3}$
City$_1$	$\langle 3, 5, 7 \rangle$	$\langle 1, 3, 5 \rangle$	$\langle 1, 3, 5 \rangle$
City$_2$	$\langle 3, 7, 11 \rangle$	$\langle 1, 3, 5 \rangle$	$\langle 1, 3, 5 \rangle$
City$_3$	$\langle 3, 5, 7 \rangle$	$\langle 5, 7, 9 \rangle$	$\langle 7, 9, 11 \rangle$
City$_4$	$\langle 1, 1, 3 \rangle$	$\langle 1, 3, 5 \rangle$	$\langle 1, 3, 5 \rangle$
City$_5$	$\langle 1, 3, 5 \rangle$	$\langle 1, 3, 7 \rangle$	$\langle 1, 1, 3 \rangle$
City$_6$	$\langle 5, 7, 9 \rangle$	$\langle 5, 7, 9 \rangle$	$\langle 3, 5, 7 \rangle$
City$_7$	$\langle 1, 1, 3 \rangle$	$\langle 1, 3, 5 \rangle$	$\langle 1, 3, 5 \rangle$
City$_8$	$\langle 1, 1, 3 \rangle$	$\langle 1, 3, 5 \rangle$	$\langle 1, 3, 5 \rangle$
City$_9$	$\langle 7, 9, 11 \rangle$	$\langle 7, 9, 11 \rangle$	$\langle 7, 9, 11 \rangle$
City$_{10}$	$\langle 3, 5, 7 \rangle$	$\langle 5, 7, 9 \rangle$	$\langle 3, 5, 7 \rangle$

Step 17: The standardized decision matrix was computed according to Eq. (1.23) for the beneficial criteria by using Eq. (1.24) and for the non-beneficial criteria by applying Eq. (1.25) as exhibited in Table 1.33.

Step 18: The weighted standardized decision matrix is computed as shown in Eq. (1.26) by applying Eq. (1.27), and the results are created in Table 1.34.

Step 19: The FPIS and the FNIS are calculated by applying Eq. (1.28) and (1.29) as presented in Table 1.34.

Step 20: The distance from each city to the FPIS and the FNIS is computed by applying Eq. (1.11) as exhibited in Table 1.35. Also, the distance

TABLE 1.33

Normalized Decision Matrix of Ten Cities According to Smart Governance's Criteria

$Expert_s$	PDC_{1_1}			SSC_{1_2}			TGC_{1_3}		
$City_1$	0.2727	0.4545	0.6364	0.0909	0.2727	0.4545	0.0909	0.2727	0.4545
$City_2$	0.2727	0.6364	1.0000	0.0909	0.2727	0.4545	0.0909	0.2727	0.4545
$City_3$	0.2727	0.4545	0.6364	0.4545	0.6364	0.8182	0.6364	0.8182	1.0000
$City_4$	0.0909	0.0909	0.2727	0.0909	0.2727	0.4545	0.0909	0.2727	0.4545
$City_5$	0.0909	0.2727	0.4545	0.0909	0.2727	0.6364	0.0909	0.0909	0.2727
$City_6$	0.4545	0.6364	0.8182	0.4545	0.6364	0.8182	0.2727	0.4545	0.6364
$City_7$	0.0909	0.0909	0.2727	0.0909	0.2727	0.4545	0.0909	0.2727	0.4545
$City_8$	0.0909	0.0909	0.2727	0.0909	0.2727	0.4545	0.0909	0.2727	0.4545
$City_9$	0.6364	0.8182	1.0000	0.6364	0.8182	1.0000	0.6364	0.8182	1.0000
$City_{10}$	0.2727	0.4545	0.6364	0.4545	0.6364	0.8182	0.2727	0.4545	0.6364

TABLE 1.34

Weighted Normalized Decision Matrix of Ten Cities According to Smart Governance's Criteria

$Expert_s$	PDC_{1_1}			SSC_{1_2}			TGC_{1_3}		
$City_1$	0.0925	0.1541	0.2157	0.0338	0.1015	0.1691	0.0263	0.0788	0.1314
$City_2$	0.0925	0.2157	0.3390	0.0338	0.1015	0.1691	0.0263	0.0788	0.1314
$City_3$	0.0925	0.1541	0.2157	0.1691	0.2367	0.3044	0.1839	0.2365	0.2890
$City_4$	0.0308	0.0308	0.0925	0.0338	0.1015	0.1691	0.0263	0.0788	0.1314
$City_5$	0.0308	0.0925	0.1541	0.0338	0.1015	0.2367	0.0263	0.0263	0.0788
$City_6$	0.1541	0.2157	0.2774	0.1691	0.2367	0.3044	0.0788	0.1314	0.1839
$City_7$	0.0308	0.0308	0.0925	0.0338	0.1015	0.1691	0.0263	0.0788	0.1314
$City_8$	0.0308	0.0308	0.0925	0.0338	0.1015	0.1691	0.0263	0.0788	0.1314
$City_9$	0.2157	0.2774	0.3390	0.2367	0.3044	0.3720	0.1839	0.2365	0.2890
$City_{10}$	0.0925	0.1541	0.2157	0.1691	0.2367	0.3044	0.0788	0.1314	0.1839
A^*	0.2157	0.2774	0.3390	0.2367	0.3044	0.3720	0.1839	0.2365	0.2890
A^-	0.0308	0.0308	0.0925	0.0338	0.1015	0.1691	0.0263	0.0263	0.0788

TABLE 1.35

Distance from Each Alternative to the FPIS and to the FNIS of Smart Governance's Criteria

Experts	p_i^*				p_i^-				C_i	Rank
	$PDC_{1.1}$	$SSC_{1.2}$	$TGC_{1.3}$	$\sum_{j=1}^{n} p\left(\tilde{r}_{ij}, \tilde{r}_j^*\right)$	$PDC_{1.1}$	$SSC_{1.2}$	$TGC_{1.3}$	$\sum_{j=1}^{n} p\left(\tilde{r}_{ij}, \tilde{r}_j^-\right)$		
$City_1$	0.1233	0.2029	0.1576	0.4838	0.1068	0.0000	0.0429	0.1497	0.2363	6
$City_2$	0.0796	0.2029	0.1576	0.4401	0.1815	0.0000	0.0429	0.2244	0.3376	5
$City_3$	0.1233	0.0676	0.0000	0.1909	0.1068	0.1353	0.1943	0.4363	0.6956	2
$City_4$	0.2279	0.2029	0.1576	0.5884	0.0000	0.0000	0.0429	0.0429	0.0680	8
$City_5$	0.1849	0.1832	0.1943	0.5623	0.0503	0.0390	0.0000	0.0894	0.1371	7
$City_6$	0.0616	0.0676	0.1051	0.2344	0.1669	0.1353	0.0910	0.3932	0.6265	3
$City_7$	0.2279	0.2029	0.1576	0.5884	0.0000	0.0000	0.0429	0.0429	0.0680	8
$City_8$	0.2279	0.2029	0.1576	0.5884	0.0000	0.0000	0.0429	0.0429	0.0680	8
$City_9$	0.0000	0.0000	0.0000	0.0000	0.2279	0.2029	0.1943	0.6250	1.0000	1
$City_{10}$	0.1233	0.0676	0.1051	0.2960	0.1068	0.1353	0.0910	0.3330	0.5294	4

between each city and either FPIS or FNIS is computed by using Eqs. (1.30) and (1.31).

Step 21: The closeness coefficient for each city is computed by applying Eq. (1.32) as presented in Table 1.35. Finally, all cities are ranked in ascending order as in Table 1.35 and in Figure 1.7.

Step 22: At this phase, the cities identified in the evaluation process are evaluated according to the sub-criteria for each main criterion. Secondly, cities are evaluated according to the smart economy criterion's sub-criteria.

Step 23: The decision matrix was constructed among the smart economy criterion's sub-criteria and the selected cities by the experts using verbal vocabularies according to Eq. (1.20) as presented in Table 1.36 and using TFNs according to Eq. (1.21).

Step 24: The final combined decision matrix between the smart economy criterion's sub-criteria and the selected cities by the experts is presented in Table 1.37 according to Eq. (1.22).

Step 25: The standardized decision matrix was computed according to Eq. (1.23) for the beneficial criteria by using Eq. (1.24) and for the non-beneficial criteria by applying Eq. (1.25) as exhibited in Table 1.38.

Step 26: The weighted standardized decision matrix is computed as shown in Eq. (1.26) by applying Eq. (1.27), and the results are created in Table 1.39.

Step 27: The FPIS and the FNIS are calculated by applying Eq. (1.28) and Eq. (1.29) as presented in Table 1.39.

Step 28: The distance from each city to the FPIS and the FNIS is computed by applying Eq. (1.11) as exhibited in Table 1.40. Also, the distance

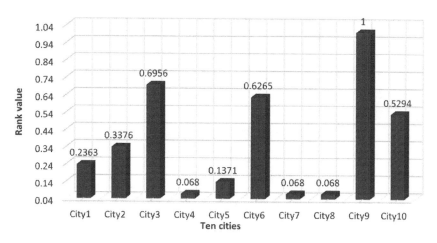

FIGURE 1.7
Final ranking of ten cities according to smart governance's criteria.

TABLE 1.36

Decision Matrices of Ten Cities According to Smart Economy's Criteria Using Verbal Vocabularies

Expert$_s$	ISC$_{2\_1}$	ENC$_{2\_2}$	PRC$_{2\_3}$	ETC$_{2\_4}$	FLC$_{2\_5}$	IEC$_{2\_6}$
City$_1$	⟨MOT⟩⟨MOT⟩⟨MOT⟩	⟨LLO⟩⟨LLO⟩⟨LLO⟩	⟨LLO⟩⟨LLO⟩⟨LLO⟩	⟨ETL⟩⟨ETL⟩⟨ETL⟩	⟨ETL⟩⟨ETL⟩⟨ETL⟩	⟨HIH⟩⟨HIH⟩⟨HIH⟩
City$_2$	⟨MOT⟩⟨HIH⟩⟨EXG⟩	⟨LLO⟩⟨LLO⟩⟨LLO⟩	⟨LLO⟩⟨LLO⟩⟨LLO⟩	⟨ETL⟩⟨MOT⟩⟨MOT⟩	⟨ETL⟩⟨ETL⟩⟨ETL⟩	⟨EXG⟩⟨EXG⟩⟨EXG⟩
City$_3$	⟨MOT⟩⟨MOT⟩⟨MOT⟩	⟨HIH⟩⟨HIH⟩⟨HIH⟩	⟨EXG⟩⟨EXG⟩⟨EXG⟩	⟨MOT⟩⟨MOT⟩⟨MOT⟩	⟨LLO⟩⟨LLO⟩⟨LLO⟩	⟨HIH⟩⟨HIH⟩⟨HIH⟩
City$_4$	⟨ETL⟩⟨ETL⟩⟨ETL⟩	⟨ETL⟩⟨LOW⟩⟨LOW⟩	⟨LLO⟩⟨LLO⟩⟨ETL⟩	⟨ETL⟩⟨ETL⟩⟨ETL⟩	⟨ETL⟩⟨ETL⟩⟨ETL⟩	⟨HIH⟩⟨HIH⟩⟨HIH⟩
City$_5$	⟨LLO⟩⟨LLO⟩⟨LLO⟩	⟨LLO⟩⟨ETL⟩⟨MOT⟩	⟨ETL⟩⟨ETL⟩⟨ETL⟩	⟨ETL⟩⟨ETL⟩⟨ETL⟩	⟨MOT⟩⟨MOT⟩⟨MOT⟩	⟨MOT⟩⟨MOT⟩⟨MOT⟩
City$_6$	⟨HIH⟩⟨HIH⟩⟨HIH⟩	⟨HIH⟩⟨HIH⟩⟨HIH⟩	⟨MOT⟩⟨MOT⟩⟨MOT⟩	⟨EXG⟩⟨EXG⟩⟨EXG⟩	⟨EXG⟩⟨EXG⟩⟨EXG⟩	⟨EXG⟩⟨EXG⟩⟨EXG⟩
City$_7$	⟨ETL⟩⟨ETL⟩⟨ETL⟩	⟨LLO⟩⟨LLO⟩⟨LLO⟩	⟨LLO⟩⟨LLO⟩⟨LLO⟩	⟨MOT⟩⟨MOT⟩⟨MOT⟩	⟨MOT⟩⟨MOT⟩⟨MOT⟩	⟨MOT⟩⟨MOT⟩⟨MOT⟩
City$_8$	⟨ETL⟩⟨ETL⟩⟨ETL⟩	⟨LLO⟩⟨LLO⟩⟨LLO⟩	⟨LLO⟩⟨LLO⟩⟨LLO⟩	⟨ETL⟩⟨ETL⟩⟨ETL⟩	⟨ETL⟩⟨ETL⟩⟨ETL⟩	⟨MOT⟩⟨MOT⟩⟨MOT⟩
City$_9$	⟨EXG⟩⟨EXG⟩⟨EXG⟩	⟨EXG⟩⟨EXG⟩⟨EXG⟩	⟨EHH⟩⟨EHH⟩⟨EHH⟩	⟨EXG⟩⟨EXG⟩⟨EXG⟩	⟨EXG⟩⟨EXG⟩⟨EXG⟩	⟨EXG⟩⟨EXG⟩⟨EXG⟩
City$_{10}$	⟨MOT⟩⟨MOT⟩⟨MOT⟩	⟨HIH⟩⟨HIH⟩⟨HIH⟩	⟨MOT⟩⟨MOT⟩⟨MOT⟩	⟨MOT⟩⟨MOT⟩⟨MOT⟩	⟨ETL⟩⟨ETL⟩⟨ETL⟩	⟨HIH⟩⟨HIH⟩⟨HIH⟩

TABLE 1.37

Combined Decision Matrix of Ten Cities According to Smart Economy's Criteria Using TFNs

Expert$_s$	ISC$_{2\_1}$	ENC$_{2\_2}$	PRC$_{2\_3}$	ETC$_{2\_4}$	FLC$_{2\_5}$	IEC$_{2\_6}$
City$_1$	$\langle 3, 5, 7\rangle$	$\langle 1, 3, 5\rangle$	$\langle 1, 3, 5\rangle$	$\langle 1, 1, 3\rangle$	$\langle 1, 1, 3\rangle$	$\langle 5, 7, 9\rangle$
City$_2$	$\langle 3, 7, 11\rangle$	$\langle 1, 3, 5\rangle$	$\langle 1, 3, 5\rangle$	$\langle 1, 3.67, 7\rangle$	$\langle 1, 1, 3\rangle$	$\langle 7, 9, 11\rangle$
City$_3$	$\langle 3, 5, 7\rangle$	$\langle 5, 7, 9\rangle$	$\langle 7, 9, 11\rangle$	$\langle 3, 5, 7\rangle$	$\langle 1, 3, 5\rangle$	$\langle 5, 7, 9\rangle$
City$_4$	$\langle 1, 1, 3\rangle$	$\langle 1, 3, 5\rangle$	$\langle 1, 3, 5\rangle$	$\langle 1, 1, 3\rangle$	$\langle 1, 1, 3\rangle$	$\langle 5, 7, 9\rangle$
City$_5$	$\langle 1, 3, 5\rangle$	$\langle 1, 3, 7\rangle$	$\langle 1, 1, 3\rangle$	$\langle 1, 1, 3\rangle$	$\langle 3, 5, 7\rangle$	$\langle 3, 5, 7\rangle$
City$_6$	$\langle 5, 7, 9\rangle$	$\langle 5, 7, 9\rangle$	$\langle 3, 5, 7\rangle$	$\langle 7, 9, 11\rangle$	$\langle 7, 9, 11\rangle$	$\langle 7, 9, 11\rangle$
City$_7$	$\langle 1, 1, 3\rangle$	$\langle 1, 3, 5\rangle$	$\langle 1, 3, 5\rangle$	$\langle 3, 5, 7\rangle$	$\langle 3, 5, 7\rangle$	$\langle 3, 5, 7\rangle$
City$_8$	$\langle 1, 1, 3\rangle$	$\langle 1, 3, 5\rangle$	$\langle 1, 3, 5\rangle$	$\langle 1, 1, 3\rangle$	$\langle 1, 1, 3\rangle$	$\langle 3, 5, 7\rangle$
City$_9$	$\langle 7, 9, 11\rangle$	$\langle 7, 9, 11\rangle$	$\langle 7, 9, 11\rangle$	$\langle 7, 9, 11\rangle$	$\langle 7, 9, 11\rangle$	$\langle 7, 9, 11\rangle$
City$_{10}$	$\langle 3, 5, 7\rangle$	$\langle 5, 7, 9\rangle$	$\langle 3, 5, 7\rangle$	$\langle 3, 5, 7\rangle$	$\langle 1, 1, 3\rangle$	$\langle 5, 7, 9\rangle$

TABLE 1.38

Normalized Decision Matrix of Ten Cities According to Smart Economy's Criteria

Expert$_s$	ISC$_{2\_1}$			ENC$_{2\_2}$			PRC$_{2\_3}$			ETC$_{2\_4}$			FLC$_{2\_5}$			IEC$_{2\_6}$		
City$_1$	0.27	0.45	0.64	0.09	0.27	0.45	0.09	0.27	0.45	0.09	0.09	0.27	0.09	0.09	0.27	0.45	0.64	0.82
City$_2$	0.27	0.64	1.00	0.09	0.27	0.45	0.09	0.27	0.45	0.09	0.33	0.64	0.09	0.09	0.27	0.64	0.82	1.00
City$_3$	0.27	0.45	0.64	0.45	0.64	0.82	0.64	0.82	1.00	0.27	0.45	0.64	0.09	0.27	0.45	0.45	0.64	0.82
City$_4$	0.09	0.09	0.27	0.09	0.27	0.45	0.09	0.27	0.45	0.09	0.09	0.27	0.09	0.09	0.27	0.45	0.64	0.82
City$_5$	0.09	0.27	0.45	0.09	0.27	0.64	0.09	0.09	0.27	0.09	0.09	0.27	0.27	0.45	0.64	0.27	0.45	0.64
City$_6$	0.45	0.64	0.82	0.45	0.64	0.82	0.27	0.45	0.64	0.64	0.82	1.00	0.64	0.82	1.00	0.64	0.82	1.00
City$_7$	0.09	0.09	0.27	0.09	0.27	0.45	0.09	0.27	0.45	0.27	0.45	0.64	0.27	0.45	0.64	0.27	0.45	0.64
City$_8$	0.09	0.09	0.27	0.09	0.27	0.45	0.09	0.27	0.45	0.09	0.09	0.27	0.09	0.09	0.27	0.27	0.45	0.64
City$_9$	0.64	0.82	1.00	0.64	0.82	1.00	0.64	0.82	1.00	0.64	0.82	1.00	0.64	0.82	1.00	0.64	0.82	1.00
City$_{10}$	0.27	0.45	0.64	0.45	0.64	0.82	0.27	0.45	0.64	0.27	0.45	0.64	0.09	0.09	0.27	0.45	0.64	0.82

between each city and either FPIS or FNIS is computed by using Eqs. (1.30) and (1.31).

Step 29: The closeness coefficient for each city is computed by applying Eq. (1.32) as presented in Table 1.40. Finally, all cities are ranked in ascending order as in Table 1.40 and in Figure 1.8.

Step 30: At this phase, the cities identified in the evaluation process are evaluated according to the sub-criteria for each main criterion. Thirdly, cities are evaluated according to the smart mobility criterion's sub-criteria.

Step 31: The decision matrix was constructed among the smart mobility criterion's sub-criteria and the selected cities by the experts using verbal

TABLE 1.39

Weighted Normalized Decision Matrix of Ten Cities According to Smart Economy's Criteria

Expert$_s$	ISC_{2_1}			ENC_{2_2}			PRC_{2_3}			ETC_{2_4}			FLC_{2_5}			IEC_{2_6}		
City$_1$	0.03	0.04	0.06	0.01	0.03	0.05	0.02	0.06	0.10	0.01	0.01	0.04	0.02	0.02	0.07	0.09	0.12	0.16
City$_2$	0.03	0.06	0.10	0.01	0.03	0.05	0.02	0.06	0.10	0.01	0.05	0.09	0.02	0.02	0.07	0.12	0.16	0.19
City$_3$	0.03	0.04	0.06	0.05	0.06	0.08	0.14	0.18	0.21	0.04	0.06	0.09	0.02	0.07	0.12	0.09	0.12	0.16
City$_4$	0.01	0.01	0.03	0.01	0.03	0.05	0.02	0.06	0.10	0.01	0.01	0.04	0.02	0.02	0.07	0.09	0.12	0.16
City$_5$	0.01	0.03	0.04	0.01	0.03	0.06	0.02	0.02	0.06	0.01	0.01	0.04	0.07	0.12	0.16	0.05	0.09	0.12
City$_6$	0.04	0.06	0.08	0.05	0.06	0.08	0.06	0.10	0.14	0.09	0.11	0.14	0.16	0.21	0.26	0.12	0.16	0.19
City$_7$	0.01	0.01	0.03	0.01	0.03	0.05	0.02	0.06	0.10	0.04	0.06	0.09	0.07	0.12	0.16	0.05	0.09	0.12
City$_8$	0.01	0.01	0.03	0.01	0.03	0.05	0.02	0.06	0.10	0.01	0.01	0.04	0.02	0.02	0.07	0.05	0.09	0.12
City$_9$	0.06	0.08	0.10	0.06	0.08	0.10	0.14	0.18	0.21	0.09	0.11	0.14	0.16	0.21	0.26	0.12	0.16	0.19
City$_{10}$	0.03	0.04	0.06	0.05	0.06	0.08	0.06	0.10	0.14	0.04	0.06	0.09	0.02	0.02	0.07	0.09	0.12	0.16
A*	0.06	0.08	0.10	0.06	0.08	0.10	0.14	0.18	0.21	0.09	0.11	0.14	0.16	0.21	0.26	0.12	0.16	0.19
A$^-$	0.01	0.01	0.03	0.01	0.03	0.05	0.02	0.02	0.06	0.01	0.01	0.04	0.02	0.02	0.07	0.05	0.09	0.12

TABLE 1.40

Distance from Each Alternative to the FPIS and to the FNIS of Smart Economy's Criteria

Expert$_s$	$\sum_{j=1}^{n} p\left(\breve{r}_{ij}, \breve{r}_j^*\right)$	$\sum_{j=1}^{n} p\left(\breve{r}_{ij}, \breve{r}_j^-\right)$	C_i	Rank
City$_1$	0.508	0.097	0.1601	8
City$_2$	0.433	0.188	0.3028	5
City$_3$	0.279	0.328	0.5403	3
City$_4$	0.538	0.067	0.1103	9
City$_5$	0.503	0.106	0.1739	7
City$_6$	0.114	0.488	0.8108	2
City$_7$	0.451	0.156	0.2577	6
City$_8$	0.573	0.032	0.0525	10
City$_9$	0.000	0.600	1.0000	1
City$_{10}$	0.389	0.213	0.3540	4

vocabularies according to Eq. (1.20) as presented in Table 1.41 and using TFNs according to Eq. (1.21).

Step 32: The final combined decision matrix between the smart mobility criterion's sub-criteria and the selected cities by the experts is presented in Table 1.42 according to Eq. (1.22).

Step 33: The standardized decision matrix was computed according to Eq. (1.23) for the beneficial criteria by using Eq. (1.24) and for the non-beneficial criteria by applying Eq. (1.25) as exhibited in Table 1.43.

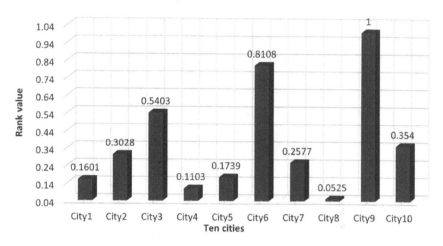

FIGURE 1.8
Final ranking of ten cities according to smart economy's criteria.

Step 34: The weighted standardized decision matrix is computed as shown in Eq. (1.26) by applying Eq. (1.27), and the results are created in Table 1.44.

Step 35: The FPIS and the FNIS are calculated by applying Eqs. (1.28) and (1.29) as presented in Table 1.44.

Step 36: The distance from each city to the FPIS and the FNIS is computed by applying Eq. (1.11) as exhibited in Table 1.45. Also, the distance between each city and either FPIS or FNIS is computed by using Eqs. (1.30) and (1.31).

Step 37: The closeness coefficient for each city is computed by applying Eq. (1.32) as presented in Table 1.45. Finally, all cities are ranked in ascending order as in Table 1.45 and in Figure 1.9.

Step 38: At this phase, the cities identified in the evaluation process are evaluated according to the sub-criteria for each main criterion. Fourthly, cities are evaluated according to the smart living criterion's sub-criteria.

Step 39: The decision matrix was constructed among the smart living criterion's sub-criteria and the selected cities by the experts using verbal vocabularies according to Eq. (1.20) as presented in Table 1.46 and using TFNs according to Eq. (1.21).

Step 40: The final combined decision matrix between the smart living criterion's sub-criteria and the selected cities by the experts is presented in Table 1.47 according to Eq. (1.22).

Step 41: The standardized decision matrix was computed according to Eq. (1.23) for the beneficial criteria by using Eq. (1.24) and for the non-beneficial criteria by applying Eq. (1.25) as exhibited in Table 1.48.

TABLE 1.41

Decision Matrices of Ten Cities According to Smart Mobility Criteria Using Verbal Vocabularies

Expert$_s$	LAC$_{3\_1}$	SNC$_{3\_2}$	IAC$_{3\_3}$	AVC$_{3\_4}$
City$_1$	⟨EXG⟩⟨EXG⟩⟨EXG⟩	⟨HIH⟩⟨HIH⟩⟨HIH⟩	⟨HIH⟩⟨HIH⟩⟨HIH⟩	⟨EXG⟩⟨EXG⟩⟨EXG⟩
City$_2$	⟨EXG⟩⟨EXG⟩⟨EXG⟩	⟨LOW⟩⟨LOW⟩⟨LOW⟩	⟨LLO⟩⟨MOT⟩⟨MOT⟩	⟨MOT⟩⟨MOT⟩⟨MOT⟩
City$_3$	⟨MOT⟩⟨MOT⟩⟨MOT⟩	⟨HIH⟩⟨HIH⟩⟨HIH⟩	⟨EXG⟩⟨EXG⟩⟨EXG⟩	⟨LLO⟩⟨MOT⟩⟨MOT⟩
City$_4$	⟨LLO⟩⟨MOT⟩⟨MOT⟩	⟨EXG⟩⟨EXG⟩⟨EXG⟩	⟨MOT⟩⟨MOT⟩⟨MOT⟩	⟨MOT⟩⟨MOT⟩⟨MOT⟩
City$_5$	⟨EXG⟩⟨EXG⟩⟨EXG⟩	⟨MOT⟩⟨MOT⟩⟨MOT⟩	⟨EXG⟩⟨EXG⟩⟨EXG⟩	⟨MOT⟩⟨MOT⟩⟨MOT⟩
City$_6$	⟨LLO⟩⟨LLO⟩⟨LLO⟩	⟨EXG⟩⟨EXG⟩⟨EXG⟩	⟨MOT⟩⟨MOT⟩⟨MOT⟩	⟨LOW⟩⟨LOW⟩⟨LOW⟩
City$_7$	⟨EXG⟩⟨EXG⟩⟨EXG⟩	⟨HIH⟩⟨HIH⟩⟨HIH⟩	⟨HIH⟩⟨HIH⟩⟨HIH⟩	⟨EXG⟩⟨EXG⟩⟨EXG⟩
City$_8$	⟨EXG⟩⟨EXG⟩⟨EXG⟩	⟨LLO⟩⟨LLO⟩⟨LLO⟩	⟨LLO⟩⟨MOT⟩⟨MOT⟩	⟨MOT⟩⟨MOT⟩⟨MOT⟩
City$_9$	⟨EXG⟩⟨EXG⟩⟨EXG⟩	⟨MOT⟩⟨MOT⟩⟨MOT⟩	⟨EXG⟩⟨EXG⟩⟨EXG⟩	⟨MOT⟩⟨MOT⟩⟨MOT⟩
City$_{10}$	⟨LLO⟩⟨LLO⟩⟨LLO⟩	⟨EXG⟩⟨EXG⟩⟨EXG⟩	⟨MOT⟩⟨MOT⟩⟨MOT⟩	⟨LLO⟩⟨LLO⟩⟨LLO⟩

TABLE 1.42

Combined Decision Matrix of Ten Cities According to Smart Mobility's Criteria Using TFNs

Expert$_s$	LAC$_{3\_1}$	SNC$_{3\_2}$	IAC$_{3\_3}$	AVC$_{3\_4}$
City$_1$	$\langle 7, 9, 11 \rangle$	$\langle 5, 7, 9 \rangle$	$\langle 5, 7, 9 \rangle$	$\langle 7, 9, 11 \rangle$
City$_2$	$\langle 7, 9, 11 \rangle$	$\langle 1, 3, 5 \rangle$	$\langle 1, 4.33, 7 \rangle$	$\langle 3, 5, 7 \rangle$
City$_3$	$\langle 1, 4.33, 7 \rangle$	$\langle 7, 9, 11 \rangle$	$\langle 3, 5, 7 \rangle$	$\langle 3, 5, 7 \rangle$
City$_4$	$\langle 7, 9, 11 \rangle$	$\langle 3, 5, 7 \rangle$	$\langle 7, 9, 11 \rangle$	$\langle 3, 5, 7 \rangle$
City$_5$	$\langle 1, 3, 5 \rangle$	$\langle 7, 9, 11 \rangle$	$\langle 3, 5, 7 \rangle$	$\langle 1, 3, 5 \rangle$
City$_6$	$\langle 3, 5, 7 \rangle$	$\langle 3, 5, 7 \rangle$	$\langle 5, 7, 9 \rangle$	$\langle 5, 7, 9 \rangle$
City$_7$	$\langle 7, 9, 11 \rangle$	$\langle 5, 7, 9 \rangle$	$\langle 5, 7, 9 \rangle$	$\langle 7, 9, 11 \rangle$
City$_8$	$\langle 7, 9, 11 \rangle$	$\langle 1, 3, 5 \rangle$	$\langle 1, 4.33, 7 \rangle$	$\langle 3, 5, 7 \rangle$
City$_9$	$\langle 1, 3, 5 \rangle$	$\langle 7, 9, 11 \rangle$	$\langle 3, 5, 7 \rangle$	$\langle 1, 3, 5 \rangle$
City$_{10}$	$\langle 3, 5, 7 \rangle$	$\langle 3, 5, 7 \rangle$	$\langle 5, 7, 9 \rangle$	$\langle 5, 7, 9 \rangle$

TABLE 1.43

Normalized Decision Matrix of Ten Cities According to Smart Mobility's Criteria

Expert$_s$	LAC$_{3\_1}$			SNC$_{3\_2}$			IAC$_{3\_3}$			AVC$_{3\_4}$		
City$_1$	0.636	0.818	1.000	0.455	0.636	0.818	0.455	0.636	0.818	0.636	0.818	1.000
City$_2$	0.636	0.818	1.000	0.091	0.273	0.455	0.091	0.394	0.636	0.273	0.455	0.636
City$_3$	0.091	0.394	0.636	0.636	0.818	1.000	0.273	0.455	0.636	0.273	0.455	0.636
City$_4$	0.636	0.818	1.000	0.273	0.455	0.636	0.636	0.818	1.000	0.273	0.455	0.636
City$_5$	0.091	0.273	0.455	0.636	0.818	1.000	0.273	0.455	0.636	0.091	0.273	0.455
City$_6$	0.273	0.455	0.636	0.273	0.455	0.636	0.455	0.636	0.818	0.455	0.636	0.818
City$_7$	0.636	0.818	1.000	0.455	0.636	0.818	0.455	0.636	0.818	0.636	0.818	1.000
City$_8$	0.636	0.818	1.000	0.091	0.273	0.455	0.091	0.394	0.636	0.273	0.455	0.636
City$_9$	0.091	0.273	0.455	0.636	0.818	1.000	0.273	0.455	0.636	0.091	0.273	0.455
City$_{10}$	0.273	0.455	0.636	0.273	0.455	0.636	0.455	0.636	0.818	0.455	0.636	0.818

Step 42: The weighted standardized decision matrix is computed as shown in Eq. (1.26) by applying Eq. (1.27), and the results are created in Table 1.49.

Step 43: The FPIS and the FNIS are calculated by applying Eq. (1.28) and Eq. (1.29) as presented in Table 1.49.

Step 44: The distance from each city to the FPIS and the FNIS is computed by applying Eq. (1.11) as exhibited in Table 1.50. Also, the distance between each city and either FPIS or FNIS is computed by using Eq. (1.30) and (1.31).

Step 45: The closeness coefficient for each city is computed by applying Eq. (1.32) as presented in Table 1.50. Finally, all cities are ranked in ascending order as in Table 1.50 and in Figure 1.10.

TABLE 1.44

Weighted Normalized Decision Matrix of Ten Cities According to Smart Mobility's Criteria

Expert$_s$	LAC$_{3\_1}$			SNC$_{3\_2}$			IAC$_{3\_3}$			AVC$_{3\_4}$		
City$_1$	0.135	0.173	0.212	0.115	0.161	0.207	0.082	0.115	0.148	0.225	0.290	0.354
City$_2$	0.135	0.173	0.212	0.023	0.069	0.115	0.016	0.071	0.115	0.097	0.161	0.225
City$_3$	0.019	0.083	0.135	0.161	0.207	0.253	0.049	0.082	0.115	0.097	0.161	0.225
City$_4$	0.135	0.173	0.212	0.069	0.115	0.161	0.115	0.148	0.181	0.097	0.161	0.225
City$_5$	0.019	0.058	0.096	0.161	0.207	0.253	0.049	0.082	0.115	0.032	0.097	0.161
City$_6$	0.058	0.096	0.135	0.069	0.115	0.161	0.082	0.115	0.148	0.161	0.225	0.290
City$_7$	0.135	0.173	0.212	0.115	0.161	0.207	0.082	0.115	0.148	0.225	0.290	0.354
City$_8$	0.135	0.173	0.212	0.023	0.069	0.115	0.016	0.071	0.115	0.097	0.161	0.225
City$_9$	0.019	0.058	0.096	0.161	0.207	0.253	0.049	0.082	0.115	0.032	0.097	0.161
City$_{10}$	0.058	0.096	0.135	0.069	0.115	0.161	0.082	0.115	0.148	0.161	0.225	0.290
A*	0.135	0.173	0.212	0.161	0.207	0.253	0.115	0.148	0.181	0.225	0.290	0.354
A⁻	0.019	0.058	0.096	0.023	0.069	0.115	0.016	0.071	0.115	0.032	0.097	0.161

Step 46: At this phase, the cities identified in the evaluation process are evaluated according to the sub-criteria for each main criterion. Fifthly, cities are evaluated according to the smart people criterion's sub-criteria.

Step 47: The decision matrix was constructed among the smart people criterion's sub-criteria and the selected cities by the experts using verbal vocabularies according to Eq. (1.20) as presented in Table 1.51 and using TFNs according to Eq. (1.21).

Step 48: The final combined decision matrix between the smart people criterion's sub-criteria and the selected cities by the experts is presented in Table 1.52 according to Eq. (1.22).

Step 49: The standardized decision matrix was computed according to Eq. (1.23) for the beneficial criteria by using Eq. (1.24) and for the non-beneficial criteria by applying Eq. (1.25) as exhibited in Table 1.53.

Step 50: The weighted standardized decision matrix is computed as shown in Eq. (1.26) by applying Eq. (1.27), and the results are created in Table 1.54.

Step 51: The FPIS and the FNIS are calculated by applying Eqs. (1.28) and (1.29) as presented in Table 1.54.

Step 52: The distance from each city to the FPIS and the FNIS is computed by applying Eq. (1.11) as exhibited in Table 1.55. Also, the distance between each city and either FPIS or FNIS is computed by using Eqs. (1.30) and (1.31).

Step 53: The closeness coefficient for each city is computed by applying Eq. (1.32) as presented in Table 1.55. Finally, all cities are ranked in ascending order as in Table 1.55 and in Figure 1.11.

TABLE 1.45

Distance from Each Alternative to the FPIS and to the FNIS of Smart Mobility's Criteria

Experts	p_i^*				$\sum_{j=1}^{n} p\left(\tilde{r}_{ij}, \tilde{r}_j^*\right)$	p_i^-				$\sum_{j=1}^{n} p\left(\tilde{r}_{ij}, \tilde{r}_j^-\right)$	C_i	Rank
	$LAC_{3.1}$	$SNC_{3.2}$	$IAC_{3.3}$	$AVC_{3.4}$		$LAC_{3.1}$	$SNC_{3.2}$	$IAC_{3.3}$	$AVC_{3.4}$			
City$_1$	0.000	0.046	0.033	0.000	0.079	0.116	0.092	0.049	0.193	0.450	0.851	1
City$_2$	0.000	0.138	0.082	0.129	0.348	0.116	0.000	0.000	0.064	0.180	0.341	5
City$_3$	0.096	0.000	0.066	0.129	0.290	0.027	0.138	0.020	0.064	0.249	0.462	4
City$_4$	0.000	0.092	0.000	0.129	0.221	0.116	0.046	0.082	0.064	0.308	0.582	2
City$_5$	0.116	0.000	0.066	0.193	0.375	0.000	0.138	0.020	0.000	0.158	0.297	6
City$_6$	0.077	0.092	0.033	0.064	0.266	0.039	0.046	0.049	0.129	0.263	0.497	3
City$_7$	0.000	0.046	0.033	0.000	0.079	0.116	0.092	0.049	0.193	0.450	0.851	1
City$_8$	0.000	0.138	0.082	0.129	0.348	0.116	0.000	0.000	0.064	0.180	0.341	5
City$_9$	0.116	0.000	0.066	0.193	0.375	0.000	0.138	0.020	0.000	0.158	0.297	6
City$_{10}$	0.077	0.092	0.033	0.064	0.266	0.039	0.046	0.049	0.129	0.263	0.497	3

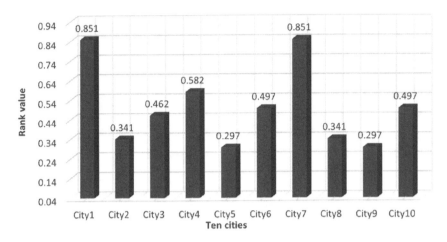

FIGURE 1.9
Final ranking of ten cities according to smart mobility criteria.

Step 54: At this phase, the cities identified in the evaluation process are evaluated according to the sub-criteria for each main criterion. Sixthly, cities are evaluated according to the smart environment criterion's sub-criteria.

Step 55: The decision matrix was constructed among the smart environment criterion's sub-criteria and the selected cities by the experts using verbal vocabularies according to Eq. (1.20) as presented in Table 1.56 and using TFNs according to Eq. (1.21).

Step 56: The final combined decision matrix between the smart environment criterion's sub-criteria and the selected cities by the experts is presented in Table 1.57 according to Eq. (1.22).

Step 57: The standardized decision matrix was computed according to Eq. (1.23) for the beneficial criteria by using Eq. (1.24) and for the non-beneficial criteria by applying Eq. (1.25) as exhibited in Table 1.58.

Step 58: The weighted standardized decision matrix is computed as shown in Eq. (1.26) by applying Eq. (1.27), and the results are created in Table 1.59.

Step 59: The FPIS and the FNIS are calculated by applying Eqs. (1.28) and (1.29) as presented in Table 1.59.

Step 60: The distance from each city to the FPIS and the FNIS is computed by applying Eq. (1.11) as exhibited in Table 1.60. Also, the distance between each city and either FPIS or FNIS is computed by using Eqs. (1.30) and (1.31).

Step 61: The closeness coefficient for each city is computed by applying Eq. (1.32) as presented in Table 1.60. Finally, all cities are ranked in ascending order as in Table 1.60 and in Figure 1.12.

TABLE 1.46

Decision Matrices of Ten Cities According to Smart Living's Criteria Using Verbal Vocabularies

Expert_s	$\text{CFC}_{4,1}$	$\text{HCC}_{4,2}$	$\text{ISC}_{4,3}$	$\text{HQC}_{4,4}$	$\text{EFC}_{4,5}$	$\text{TAC}_{4,6}$	$\text{SCC}_{4,7}$
City_1	⟨EXG⟩⟨EXG⟩⟨EXG⟩	⟨MOT⟩⟨MOT⟩⟨MOT⟩	⟨MOT⟩⟨MOT⟩⟨MOT⟩	⟨HIH⟩⟨HIH⟩⟨HIH⟩	⟨MOT⟩⟨MOT⟩⟨MOT⟩	⟨HIH⟩⟨HIH⟩⟨HIH⟩	⟨MOT⟩⟨MOT⟩⟨MOT⟩
City_2	⟨ETL⟩⟨MOT⟩⟨MOT⟩	⟨EXG⟩⟨EXG⟩⟨EXG⟩	⟨EXG⟩⟨EXG⟩⟨EXG⟩	⟨EXG⟩⟨EXG⟩⟨EXG⟩	⟨EXG⟩⟨EXG⟩⟨EXG⟩	⟨HIH⟩⟨HIH⟩⟨HIH⟩	⟨EXG⟩⟨EXG⟩⟨EXG⟩
City_3	⟨ETL⟩⟨ETL⟩⟨ETL⟩	⟨ETL⟩⟨ETL⟩⟨ETL⟩	⟨EXG⟩⟨EXG⟩⟨EXG⟩	⟨HIH⟩⟨HIH⟩⟨HIH⟩	⟨EXG⟩⟨EXG⟩⟨EXG⟩	⟨EXG⟩⟨EXG⟩⟨EXG⟩	⟨EXG⟩⟨EXG⟩⟨EXG⟩
City_4	⟨ETL⟩⟨ETL⟩⟨ETL⟩	⟨HIH⟩⟨HIH⟩⟨HIH⟩	⟨MOE⟩⟨MOE⟩⟨MOE⟩	⟨MOT⟩⟨MOT⟩⟨MOT⟩	⟨HIH⟩⟨HIH⟩⟨HIH⟩	⟨MOT⟩⟨MOT⟩⟨MOT⟩	⟨MOT⟩⟨MOT⟩⟨MOT⟩
City_5	⟨EXG⟩⟨EXG⟩⟨EXG⟩	⟨HIH⟩⟨HIH⟩⟨HIH⟩	⟨LLO⟩⟨LLO⟩⟨LLO⟩	⟨ETL⟩⟨ETL⟩⟨ETL⟩	⟨MOT⟩⟨MOT⟩⟨MOT⟩	⟨MOT⟩⟨MOT⟩⟨MOT⟩	⟨LLO⟩⟨LLO⟩⟨LLO⟩
City_6	⟨MOT⟩⟨MOT⟩⟨MOT⟩	⟨LLO⟩⟨LLO⟩⟨LLO⟩	⟨MOT⟩⟨MOT⟩⟨MOT⟩	⟨HIH⟩⟨HIH⟩⟨HIH⟩	⟨MOT⟩⟨MOT⟩⟨MOT⟩	⟨HIH⟩⟨HIH⟩⟨HIH⟩	⟨MOT⟩⟨MOT⟩⟨MOT⟩
City_7	⟨HIH⟩⟨HIH⟩⟨HIH⟩	⟨ETL⟩⟨ETL⟩⟨ETL⟩	⟨MOT⟩⟨MOT⟩⟨MOT⟩	⟨EXG⟩⟨EXG⟩⟨EXG⟩	⟨ETL⟩⟨ETL⟩⟨ETL⟩	⟨HIH⟩⟨HIH⟩⟨HIH⟩	⟨MOT⟩⟨MOT⟩⟨MOT⟩
City_8	⟨LLO⟩⟨LLO⟩⟨LLO⟩	⟨MOT⟩⟨MOT⟩⟨MOT⟩	⟨MOT⟩⟨MOT⟩⟨MOT⟩	⟨EXG⟩⟨EXG⟩⟨EXG⟩	⟨HIH⟩⟨HIH⟩⟨HIH⟩	⟨HIH⟩⟨HIH⟩⟨HIH⟩	⟨MOT⟩⟨MOT⟩⟨MOT⟩
City_9	⟨ETL⟩⟨ETL⟩⟨ETL⟩	⟨HIH⟩⟨HIH⟩⟨HIH⟩	⟨MOT⟩⟨MOT⟩⟨MOT⟩	⟨MOT⟩⟨MOT⟩⟨MOT⟩	⟨HIH⟩⟨HIH⟩⟨HIH⟩	⟨MOT⟩⟨MOT⟩⟨MOT⟩	⟨MOT⟩⟨MOT⟩⟨MOT⟩
City_{10}	⟨EXG⟩⟨EXG⟩⟨EXG⟩	⟨HIH⟩⟨HIH⟩⟨HIH⟩	⟨LLO⟩⟨LLO⟩⟨LLO⟩	⟨ETL⟩⟨ETL⟩⟨ETL⟩	⟨MOT⟩⟨MOT⟩⟨MOT⟩	⟨MOT⟩⟨MOT⟩⟨MOT⟩	⟨LLO⟩⟨LLO⟩⟨LLO⟩

TABLE 1.47

Combined Decision Matrix of Ten Cities According to Smart Living's Criteria Using TFNs

Expert$_s$	CFC$_{4\_1}$	HCC$_{4\_2}$	ISC$_{4\_3}$	HQC$_{4\_4}$	EFC$_{4\_5}$	TAC$_{4\_6}$	SCC$_{4\_7}$
City$_1$	$\langle 7, 9, 11\rangle$	$\langle 3, 5, 7\rangle$	$\langle 3, 5, 7\rangle$	$\langle 5, 7, 9\rangle$	$\langle 3, 5, 7\rangle$	$\langle 5, 7, 9\rangle$	$\langle 3, 5, 7\rangle$
City$_2$	$\langle 1, 3.67, 5\rangle$	$\langle 7, 9, 11\rangle$	$\langle 7, 9, 11\rangle$	$\langle 7, 9, 11\rangle$	$\langle 7, 9, 11\rangle$	$\langle 5, 7, 9\rangle$	$\langle 7, 9, 11\rangle$
City$_3$	$\langle 1, 1, 3\rangle$	$\langle 1, 1, 3\rangle$	$\langle 7, 9, 11\rangle$	$\langle 5, 7, 9\rangle$	$\langle 7, 9, 11\rangle$	$\langle 7, 9, 11\rangle$	$\langle 7, 9, 11\rangle$
City$_4$	$\langle 1, 1, 3\rangle$	$\langle 5, 7, 9\rangle$	$\langle 3, 5, 7\rangle$	$\langle 3, 5, 7\rangle$	$\langle 5, 7, 9\rangle$	$\langle 3, 5, 7\rangle$	$\langle 3, 5, 7\rangle$
City$_5$	$\langle 7, 9, 11\rangle$	$\langle 5, 7, 9\rangle$	$\langle 1, 3, 5\rangle$	$\langle 1, 1, 3\rangle$	$\langle 3, 5, 7\rangle$	$\langle 3, 5, 7\rangle$	$\langle 1, 3, 5\rangle$
City$_6$	$\langle 3, 5, 7\rangle$	$\langle 1, 3, 5\rangle$	$\langle 3, 5, 7\rangle$	$\langle 5, 7, 9\rangle$	$\langle 1, 4.33, 7\rangle$	$\langle 5, 7, 9\rangle$	$\langle 3, 5, 7\rangle$
City$_7$	$\langle 5, 7, 9\rangle$	$\langle 1, 1.67, 5\rangle$	$\langle 3, 5, 7\rangle$	$\langle 7, 9, 11\rangle$	$\langle 1, 1, 3\rangle$	$\langle 5, 7, 9\rangle$	$\langle 3, 5, 7\rangle$
City$_8$	$\langle 1, 3, 5\rangle$	$\langle 3, 5, 7\rangle$	$\langle 3, 5, 7\rangle$	$\langle 7, 9, 11\rangle$	$\langle 5, 7, 9\rangle$	$\langle 5, 7, 9\rangle$	$\langle 3, 5, 7\rangle$
City$_9$	$\langle 1, 1, 3\rangle$	$\langle 5, 7, 9\rangle$	$\langle 3, 5, 7\rangle$	$\langle 3, 5, 7\rangle$	$\langle 5, 7, 9\rangle$	$\langle 3, 5, 7\rangle$	$\langle 3, 5, 7\rangle$
City$_{10}$	$\langle 7, 9, 11\rangle$	$\langle 5, 7, 9\rangle$	$\langle 1, 3, 5\rangle$	$\langle 1, 1, 3\rangle$	$\langle 3, 5, 7\rangle$	$\langle 3, 5, 7\rangle$	$\langle 1, 3, 5\rangle$

Step 62: At this phase, cities are evaluated according to all sub-criteria, and the final results are presented in Table 1.61 and in Figure 1.13.

1.5 Results and Discussion

In this part, the results obtained from applying the proposed approach to a case study to assess several smart sustainable cities are discussed. Initially, six main criteria and thirty-one sub-criteria were identified to evaluate smart and sustainable cities. According to the results of the six main criteria, it is clear that the smart mobility criterion ranks first, with a weight of 0.236, followed by the smart economy criteria with a weight of 0.226. On the contrary, the smart people criterion ranks last with a weight of 0.040.

Secondly, sub-criteria were evaluated for each main criteria, and the results are constructed in Table 1.30. According to the sub-criteria of the smart governance criterion, it is clear that the public and social services criterion tops the ranking of criteria with a weight of 0.372, while the transparent governance criterion is at the bottom of the ranking with a weight of 0.289. According to the sub-criteria of the smart economy criterion, it is clear that the flexibility of labor market criterion tops the ranking of criteria with a weight of 0.257, while the innovative spirit criterion is at the bottom of the ranking with a weight of 0.096. According to the sub-criteria of the smart mobility criterion, it is clear that the availability

TABLE 1.48

Normalized Decision Matrix of Ten Cities According to Smart Living's Criteria

Experts	CFC$_{4.1}$			HCC$_{4.2}$			ISC$_{4.3}$			HQC$_{4.4}$			EFC$_{4.5}$			TAC$_{4.6}$			SCC$_{4.7}$		
City$_1$	0.64	0.82	1.00	0.27	0.45	0.64	0.27	0.45	0.64	0.45	0.64	0.82	0.27	0.45	0.64	0.45	0.64	0.82	0.27	0.45	0.64
City$_2$	0.09	0.33	0.45	0.64	0.82	1.00	0.64	0.82	1.00	0.64	0.82	1.00	0.64	0.82	1.00	0.45	0.64	0.82	0.64	0.82	1.00
City$_3$	0.09	0.09	0.27	0.09	0.09	0.27	0.64	0.82	1.00	0.45	0.64	0.82	0.64	0.82	1.00	0.64	0.82	1.00	0.64	0.82	1.00
City$_4$	0.09	0.09	0.27	0.45	0.64	0.82	0.27	0.45	0.64	0.27	0.45	0.64	0.45	0.64	0.82	0.27	0.45	0.64	0.27	0.45	0.64
City$_5$	0.64	0.82	1.00	0.45	0.64	0.82	0.09	0.27	0.45	0.09	0.09	0.27	0.27	0.45	0.64	0.27	0.45	0.64	0.09	0.27	0.45
City$_6$	0.27	0.45	0.64	0.09	0.27	0.45	0.27	0.45	0.64	0.45	0.64	0.82	0.09	0.39	0.64	0.45	0.64	0.82	0.27	0.45	0.64
City$_7$	0.45	0.64	0.82	0.09	0.15	0.45	0.27	0.45	0.64	0.64	0.82	1.00	0.09	0.09	0.27	0.45	0.64	0.82	0.27	0.45	0.64
City$_8$	0.09	0.27	0.45	0.27	0.45	0.64	0.27	0.45	0.64	0.64	0.82	1.00	0.45	0.64	0.82	0.45	0.64	0.82	0.27	0.45	0.64
City$_9$	0.09	0.09	0.27	0.45	0.64	0.82	0.27	0.45	0.64	0.27	0.45	0.64	0.45	0.64	0.82	0.27	0.45	0.64	0.27	0.45	0.64
City$_{10}$	0.64	0.82	1.00	0.45	0.64	0.82	0.09	0.27	0.45	0.09	0.09	0.27	0.27	0.45	0.64	0.27	0.45	0.64	0.09	0.27	0.45

TABLE 1.49

Weighted Normalized Decision Matrix of Ten Cities According to Smart Living's Criteria

Experts	CFC_{4_1}			HCC_{4_2}			ISC_{4_3}			HQC_{4_4}			EFC_{4_5}			TAC_{4_6}			SCC_{4_7}		
$City_1$	0.05	0.06	0.08	0.04	0.07	0.09	0.05	0.08	0.12	0.06	0.09	0.12	0.04	0.07	0.10	0.05	0.08	0.10	0.05	0.08	0.11
$City_2$	0.01	0.03	0.03	0.09	0.12	0.15	0.12	0.15	0.19	0.09	0.12	0.14	0.10	0.13	0.16	0.05	0.08	0.10	0.11	0.14	0.18
$City_3$	0.01	0.01	0.02	0.01	0.01	0.04	0.12	0.15	0.19	0.06	0.09	0.12	0.10	0.13	0.16	0.08	0.10	0.12	0.11	0.14	0.18
$City_4$	0.01	0.01	0.02	0.07	0.09	0.12	0.05	0.08	0.12	0.04	0.06	0.09	0.07	0.10	0.13	0.03	0.05	0.08	0.05	0.08	0.11
$City_5$	0.05	0.06	0.08	0.07	0.09	0.12	0.02	0.05	0.08	0.01	0.01	0.04	0.04	0.07	0.10	0.03	0.05	0.08	0.02	0.05	0.08
$City_6$	0.02	0.03	0.05	0.01	0.04	0.07	0.05	0.08	0.12	0.06	0.09	0.12	0.01	0.06	0.10	0.05	0.08	0.10	0.05	0.08	0.11
$City_7$	0.03	0.05	0.06	0.01	0.02	0.07	0.05	0.08	0.12	0.09	0.12	0.14	0.01	0.01	0.04	0.05	0.08	0.10	0.05	0.08	0.11
$City_8$	0.01	0.02	0.03	0.04	0.07	0.09	0.05	0.08	0.12	0.09	0.12	0.14	0.07	0.10	0.13	0.05	0.08	0.10	0.05	0.08	0.11
$City_9$	0.01	0.01	0.02	0.07	0.09	0.12	0.05	0.08	0.12	0.04	0.06	0.09	0.07	0.10	0.13	0.03	0.05	0.08	0.05	0.08	0.11
$City_{10}$	0.05	0.06	0.08	0.07	0.09	0.12	0.02	0.05	0.08	0.01	0.01	0.04	0.04	0.07	0.10	0.03	0.05	0.08	0.02	0.05	0.08
A^*	0.05	0.06	0.08	0.04	0.07	0.09	0.05	0.08	0.12	0.06	0.09	0.12	0.04	0.07	0.10	0.05	0.08	0.10	0.05	0.08	0.11
A^-	0.01	0.03	0.03	0.09	0.12	0.15	0.12	0.15	0.19	0.09	0.12	0.14	0.10	0.13	0.16	0.08	0.10	0.10	0.11	0.14	0.18

TABLE 1.50

Distance from Each Alternative to the FPIS and to the FNIS of Smart Living's Criteria

Expert$_s$	$\sum_{j=1}^{n} p\left(\breve{r}_{ij}, \breve{r}_{j}^{*}\right)$	$\sum_{j=1}^{n} p\left(\breve{r}_{ij}, \breve{r}_{j}^{-}\right)$	C_i	Rank
City$_1$	0.289	0.303	0.512	4
City$_2$	0.062	0.530	0.896	1
City$_3$	0.174	0.416	0.705	2
City$_4$	0.332	0.259	0.438	5
City$_5$	0.419	0.172	0.291	8
City$_6$	0.357	0.245	0.408	6
City$_7$	0.358	0.236	0.397	7
City$_8$	0.276	0.317	0.535	3
City$_9$	0.332	0.259	0.438	5
City$_{10}$	0.419	0.172	0.291	8

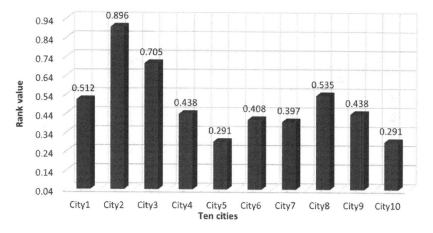

FIGURE 1.10

Final ranking of ten cities according to smart living criteria.

of ICT-infrastructure criterion tops the ranking of criteria with a weight of 0.354, while the (inter)national accessibility criterion is at the bottom of the ranking with a weight of 0.181. According to the sub-criteria of the smart living criterion, it is clear that the individual safety criterion tops the ranking of criteria with a weight of 0.185, while the cultural facilities criterion is at the bottom of the ranking with a weight of 0.076. According to the sub-criteria of the smart people criterion, it is clear that the participation in public life criterion tops the ranking of criteria with a weight of 0.135, while the level of qualification criterion is at the bottom of the

TABLE 1.51

Decision Matrices of Ten Cities According to Smart People's Criteria Using Verbal Vocabularies

Expert$_s$	LQC$_{5\_1}$	FLC$_{5\_2}$	PPC$_{5\_3}$	ALC$_{5\_4}$	COC$_{5\_5}$	SPC$_{5\_6}$	CRC$_{5\_7}$
City$_1$	⟨MOT⟩⟨MOT⟩⟨MOT⟩	⟨LLO⟩⟨LLO⟩⟨LLO⟩	⟨MOT⟩⟨MOT⟩⟨MOT⟩	⟨HIH⟩⟨HIH⟩⟨HIH⟩	⟨HIH⟩⟨HIH⟩⟨HIH⟩	⟨HIH⟩⟨HIH⟩⟨HIH⟩	⟨EXG⟩⟨EXG⟩⟨EXG⟩
City$_2$	⟨EXG⟩⟨EXG⟩⟨EXG⟩	⟨ETL⟩⟨ETL⟩⟨LOW⟩	⟨EXG⟩⟨EXG⟩⟨EXG⟩	⟨EXG⟩⟨EXG⟩⟨EXG⟩	⟨EXG⟩⟨EXG⟩⟨EXG⟩	⟨HIH⟩⟨HIH⟩⟨HIH⟩	⟨ETL⟩⟨MOT⟩⟨MOT⟩
City$_3$	⟨EXG⟩⟨EXG⟩⟨EXG⟩	⟨MOT⟩⟨MOT⟩⟨MOT⟩	⟨EXG⟩⟨EXG⟩⟨EXG⟩	⟨HIH⟩⟨HIH⟩⟨HIH⟩	⟨EXG⟩⟨EXG⟩⟨EXG⟩	⟨EXG⟩⟨EXG⟩⟨EXG⟩	⟨ETL⟩⟨ETL⟩⟨ETL⟩
City$_4$	⟨MOT⟩⟨MOT⟩⟨MOT⟩	⟨HIH⟩⟨HIH⟩⟨HIH⟩	⟨MOE⟩⟨MOE⟩⟨MOE⟩	⟨MOT⟩⟨MOT⟩⟨MOT⟩	⟨MOT⟩⟨MOT⟩⟨MOT⟩	⟨MOT⟩⟨MOT⟩⟨MOT⟩	⟨ETL⟩⟨ETL⟩⟨ETL⟩
City$_5$	⟨LLO⟩⟨LLO⟩⟨LLO⟩	⟨HIH⟩⟨HIH⟩⟨HIH⟩	⟨LLO⟩⟨LLO⟩⟨LLO⟩	⟨ETL⟩⟨ETL⟩⟨ETL⟩	⟨ETL⟩⟨ETL⟩⟨ETL⟩	⟨MOT⟩⟨MOT⟩⟨MOT⟩	⟨EXG⟩⟨EXG⟩⟨EXG⟩
City$_6$	⟨MOT⟩⟨MOT⟩⟨MOT⟩	⟨MOT⟩⟨MOT⟩⟨MOT⟩	⟨HIH⟩⟨HIH⟩⟨HIH⟩	⟨MOT⟩⟨MOT⟩⟨MOT⟩	⟨MOT⟩⟨MOT⟩⟨MOT⟩	⟨MOT⟩⟨MOT⟩⟨MOT⟩	⟨MOT⟩⟨MOT⟩⟨MOT⟩
City$_7$	⟨HIH⟩⟨HIH⟩⟨HIH⟩	⟨EXG⟩⟨EXG⟩⟨EXG⟩	⟨HIH⟩⟨HIH⟩⟨HIH⟩	⟨EXG⟩⟨EXG⟩⟨EXG⟩	⟨ETL⟩⟨ETL⟩⟨ETL⟩	⟨MOT⟩⟨MOT⟩⟨MOT⟩	⟨MOT⟩⟨MOT⟩⟨MOT⟩
City$_8$	⟨LLO⟩⟨LLO⟩⟨LLO⟩	⟨ETL⟩⟨ETL⟩⟨ETL⟩	⟨HIH⟩⟨HIH⟩⟨HIH⟩	⟨EXG⟩⟨EXG⟩⟨EXG⟩	⟨HIH⟩⟨HIH⟩⟨HIH⟩	⟨MOT⟩⟨MOT⟩⟨MOT⟩	⟨MOT⟩⟨MOT⟩⟨MOT⟩
City$_9$	⟨ETL⟩⟨ETL⟩⟨ETL⟩	⟨HIH⟩⟨HIH⟩⟨HIH⟩	⟨MOT⟩⟨MOT⟩⟨MOT⟩	⟨HIH⟩⟨HIH⟩⟨HIH⟩	⟨HIH⟩⟨HIH⟩⟨HIH⟩	⟨MOT⟩⟨MOT⟩⟨MOT⟩	⟨MOT⟩⟨MOT⟩⟨MOT⟩
City$_{10}$	⟨EXG⟩⟨EXG⟩⟨EXG⟩	⟨HIH⟩⟨HIH⟩⟨HIH⟩	⟨MOT⟩⟨MOT⟩⟨MOT⟩	⟨MOT⟩⟨MOT⟩⟨MOT⟩	⟨MOT⟩⟨MOT⟩⟨MOT⟩	⟨LLO⟩⟨LLO⟩⟨LLO⟩	⟨LLO⟩⟨LLO⟩⟨LLO⟩

TABLE 1.52

Combined Decision Matrix of Ten Cities According to Smart People's Criteria Using TFNs

Experts	CFC_{4_1}	HCC_{4_2}	ISC_{4_3}	HQC_{4_4}	EFC_{4_5}	TAC_{4_6}	SCC_{4_7}
City$_1$	⟨3, 5, 7⟩	⟨1, 3, 5⟩	⟨3, 5, 7⟩	⟨5, 7, 9⟩	⟨5, 7, 9⟩	⟨5, 7, 9⟩	⟨7, 9, 11⟩
City$_2$	⟨7, 9, 11⟩	⟨1, 1.67, 5⟩	⟨7, 9, 11⟩	⟨7, 9, 11⟩	⟨7, 9, 11⟩	⟨5, 7, 9⟩	⟨1, 3.67, 5⟩
City$_3$	⟨7, 9, 11⟩	⟨3, 5, 7⟩	⟨7, 9, 11⟩	⟨5, 7, 9⟩	⟨7, 9, 11⟩	⟨7, 9, 11⟩	⟨1, 1, 3⟩
City$_4$	⟨3, 5, 7⟩	⟨5, 7, 9⟩	⟨3, 5, 7⟩	⟨3, 5, 7⟩	⟨3, 5, 7⟩	⟨3, 5, 7⟩	⟨1, 1, 3⟩
City$_5$	⟨1, 3, 5⟩	⟨5, 7, 9⟩	⟨1, 3, 5⟩	⟨1, 1, 3⟩	⟨1, 1, 3⟩	⟨3, 5, 7⟩	⟨7, 9, 11⟩
City$_6$	⟨3, 5, 7⟩	⟨3, 5, 7⟩	⟨7, 9, 11⟩	⟨3, 5, 7⟩	⟨1, 4.33, 7⟩	⟨3, 5, 7⟩	⟨3, 5, 7⟩
City$_7$	⟨5, 7, 9⟩	⟨7, 9, 11⟩	⟨1, 3.67, 5⟩	⟨7, 9, 11⟩	⟨1, 1, 3⟩	⟨3, 5, 7⟩	⟨3, 5, 7⟩
City$_8$	⟨1, 3, 5⟩	⟨1, 1, 3⟩	⟨1, 1, 3⟩	⟨7, 9, 11⟩	⟨5, 7, 9⟩	⟨3, 5, 7⟩	⟨3, 5, 7⟩
City$_9$	⟨1, 1, 3⟩	⟨5, 7, 9⟩	⟨1, 1, 3⟩	⟨5, 7, 9⟩	⟨5, 7, 9⟩	⟨3, 5, 7⟩	⟨3, 5, 7⟩
City$_{10}$	⟨7, 9, 11⟩	⟨5, 7, 9⟩	⟨7, 9, 11⟩	⟨3, 5, 7⟩	⟨3, 5, 7⟩	⟨1, 3, 5⟩	⟨1, 3, 5⟩

TABLE 1.53

Normalized Decision Matrix of Ten Cities According to Smart People's Criteria

Experts	CFC_4_1			HCC_4_2			ISC_4_3			HQC_4_4			EFC_4_5			TAC_4_6			SCC_4_7		
City$_1$	0.27	0.45	0.09	0.27	0.45	0.64	0.27	0.45	0.64	0.45	0.64	0.82	0.45	0.64	0.82	0.45	0.64	0.82	0.64	0.82	1.00
City$_2$	0.64	0.82	0.09	0.15	0.45	1.00	0.64	0.82	1.00	0.64	0.82	1.00	0.64	0.82	1.00	0.45	0.64	0.82	0.09	0.33	0.45
City$_3$	0.64	0.82	0.27	0.45	0.64	0.27	0.64	0.82	1.00	0.45	0.64	0.82	0.64	0.82	1.00	0.64	0.82	1.00	0.09	0.09	0.27
City$_4$	0.27	0.45	0.45	0.64	0.82	0.82	0.27	0.45	0.64	0.27	0.45	0.64	0.27	0.45	0.64	0.27	0.45	0.64	0.09	0.09	0.27
City$_5$	0.09	0.27	0.45	0.64	0.82	0.82	0.09	0.27	0.45	0.09	0.09	0.27	0.09	0.09	0.27	0.27	0.45	0.64	0.64	0.82	1.00
City$_6$	0.27	0.45	0.27	0.45	0.64	0.45	0.64	0.82	1.00	0.27	0.45	0.64	0.09	0.39	0.64	0.27	0.45	0.64	0.27	0.45	0.64
City$_7$	0.45	0.64	0.64	0.82	1.00	0.45	0.09	0.33	0.45	0.64	0.82	1.00	0.09	0.09	0.27	0.27	0.45	0.64	0.27	0.45	0.64
City$_8$	0.09	0.27	0.09	0.09	0.27	0.64	0.09	0.09	0.27	0.64	0.82	1.00	0.45	0.64	0.82	0.27	0.45	0.64	0.27	0.45	0.64
City$_9$	0.09	0.09	0.45	0.64	0.82	0.82	0.09	0.09	0.27	0.45	0.64	0.82	0.45	0.64	0.82	0.27	0.45	0.64	0.27	0.45	0.64
City$_{10}$	0.64	0.82	0.45	0.64	0.82	0.82	0.64	0.82	1.00	0.27	0.45	0.64	0.27	0.45	0.64	0.09	0.27	0.45	0.09	0.27	0.45

TABLE 1.54

Weighted Normalized Decision Matrix of Ten Cities According to Smart People's Criteria

Expert_s	$CFC_{4.1}$			$HCC_{4.2}$			$ISC_{4.3}$			$HQC_{4.4}$			$EFC_{4.5}$			$TAC_{4.6}$			$SCC_{4.7}$		
City$_1$	0.03	0.05	0.01	0.04	0.06	0.09	0.05	0.09	0.12	0.07	0.10	0.13	0.06	0.08	0.11	0.06	0.08	0.11	0.09	0.12	0.15
City$_2$	0.07	0.09	0.01	0.02	0.06	0.14	0.12	0.16	0.20	0.10	0.13	0.15	0.08	0.11	0.13	0.06	0.08	0.11	0.01	0.05	0.07
City$_3$	0.07	0.09	0.03	0.06	0.09	0.04	0.12	0.16	0.20	0.07	0.10	0.13	0.08	0.11	0.13	0.08	0.11	0.13	0.01	0.01	0.04
City$_4$	0.03	0.05	0.05	0.09	0.11	0.11	0.05	0.09	0.12	0.04	0.07	0.10	0.04	0.06	0.08	0.04	0.06	0.08	0.01	0.01	0.04
City$_5$	0.01	0.03	0.05	0.09	0.11	0.11	0.02	0.05	0.09	0.01	0.01	0.04	0.01	0.01	0.04	0.04	0.06	0.08	0.09	0.12	0.15
City$_6$	0.03	0.05	0.03	0.06	0.09	0.06	0.12	0.16	0.20	0.04	0.07	0.10	0.05	0.05	0.08	0.04	0.06	0.08	0.04	0.07	0.09
City$_7$	0.05	0.07	0.07	0.11	0.14	0.06	0.02	0.07	0.09	0.10	0.13	0.15	0.01	0.01	0.04	0.04	0.06	0.08	0.04	0.07	0.09
City$_8$	0.01	0.03	0.01	0.01	0.04	0.09	0.02	0.02	0.05	0.10	0.13	0.15	0.06	0.08	0.11	0.04	0.06	0.08	0.04	0.07	0.09
City$_9$	0.01	0.01	0.05	0.09	0.11	0.11	0.02	0.02	0.05	0.07	0.10	0.13	0.06	0.08	0.11	0.04	0.06	0.08	0.04	0.07	0.09
City$_{10}$	0.07	0.09	0.05	0.09	0.11	0.11	0.12	0.16	0.20	0.04	0.07	0.10	0.04	0.06	0.08	0.01	0.04	0.06	0.01	0.04	0.07
A^*	0.07	0.09	0.07	0.11	0.14	0.14	0.12	0.16	0.20	0.10	0.13	0.15	0.08	0.11	0.13	0.08	0.11	0.13	0.09	0.12	0.15
A^-	0.01	0.03	0.01	0.01	0.04	0.04	0.02	0.02	0.05	0.01	0.01	0.04	0.01	0.01	0.04	0.04	0.06	0.08	0.01	0.01	0.04

TABLE 1.55

Distance from Each Alternative to the FPIS and to the FNIS of Smart People's Criteria

Expert$_s$	$\sum_{j=1}^{n} p\left(\tilde{r}_{ij}, \tilde{r}_j^*\right)$	$\sum_{j=1}^{n} p\left(\tilde{r}_{ij}, \tilde{r}_j^-\right)$	C_i	Rank
City$_1$	0.259	0.376	0.592	3
City$_2$	0.202	0.479	0.703	1
City$_3$	0.220	0.431	0.662	2
City$_4$	0.379	0.253	0.400	8
City$_5$	0.418	0.225	0.350	10
City$_6$	0.314	0.324	0.508	5
City$_7$	0.351	0.312	0.471	6
City$_8$	0.399	0.244	0.379	9
City$_9$	0.365	0.287	0.440	7
City$_{10}$	0.291	0.393	0.575	4

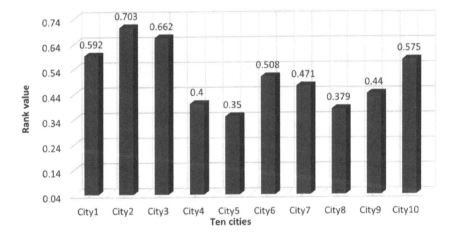

FIGURE 1.11

Final ranking of ten cities according to smart people's criteria.

ranking with a weight of 0.105. According to the sub-criteria of the smart environment criterion, it is clear that the attractivity of natural conditions criterion tops the ranking of criteria with a weight of 0.298, while the sustainable resource management criterion is at the bottom of the ranking with a weight of 0.192.

Thirdly, the global weights of all sub-criteria were calculated according to their effect on the weights of the main criteria. It is clear that the availability of the ICT-infrastructure criterion has the highest weight with a

TABLE 1.56

Decision Matrices of Ten Cities According to Smart Environment's Criteria Using Verbal Vocabularies

$Expert_s$	$ANC_{6.1}$	$POC_{6.2}$	$ENC_{6.3}$	$SRC_{6.4}$
$City_1$	⟨HIH⟩⟨HIH⟩⟨HIH⟩	⟨HIH⟩⟨HIH⟩⟨HIH⟩	⟨EXG⟩⟨EXG⟩⟨EXG⟩	⟨EXG⟩⟨EXG⟩⟨EXG⟩
$City_2$	⟨LLO⟩⟨LLO⟩⟨LLO⟩	⟨LOW⟩⟨LOW⟩⟨LOW⟩	⟨MOT⟩⟨MOT⟩⟨MOT⟩	⟨MOT⟩⟨MOT⟩⟨MOT⟩
$City_3$	⟨MOT⟩⟨MOT⟩⟨MOT⟩	⟨HIH⟩⟨HIH⟩⟨HIH⟩	⟨LLO⟩⟨MOT⟩⟨MOT⟩	⟨LLO⟩⟨MOT⟩⟨MOT⟩
$City_4$	⟨EXG⟩⟨EXG⟩⟨EXG⟩	⟨EXG⟩⟨EXG⟩⟨EXG⟩	⟨MOT⟩⟨MOT⟩⟨MOT⟩	⟨MOT⟩⟨MOT⟩⟨MOT⟩
$City_5$	⟨EXG⟩⟨EXG⟩⟨EXG⟩	⟨MOT⟩⟨MOT⟩⟨MOT⟩	⟨EXG⟩⟨EXG⟩⟨EXG⟩	⟨MOT⟩⟨MOT⟩⟨MOT⟩
$City_6$	⟨LLO⟩⟨LLO⟩⟨LLO⟩	⟨EXG⟩⟨EXG⟩⟨EXG⟩	⟨MOT⟩⟨MOT⟩⟨MOT⟩	⟨LOW⟩⟨LOW⟩⟨LOW⟩
$City_7$	⟨EXG⟩⟨EXG⟩⟨EXG⟩	⟨EXG⟩⟨EXG⟩⟨EXG⟩	⟨HIH⟩⟨HIH⟩⟨HIH⟩	⟨HIH⟩⟨HIH⟩⟨HIH⟩
$City_8$	⟨EXG⟩⟨EXG⟩⟨EXG⟩	⟨EXG⟩⟨EXG⟩⟨EXG⟩	⟨LLO⟩⟨MOT⟩⟨MOT⟩	⟨LLO⟩⟨MOT⟩⟨MOT⟩
$City_9$	⟨EXG⟩⟨EXG⟩⟨EXG⟩	⟨MOT⟩⟨MOT⟩⟨MOT⟩	⟨EXG⟩⟨EXG⟩⟨EXG⟩	⟨EXG⟩⟨EXG⟩⟨EXG⟩
$City_{10}$	⟨LLO⟩⟨LLO⟩⟨LLO⟩	⟨LLO⟩⟨MOT⟩⟨MOT⟩	⟨MOT⟩⟨MOT⟩⟨MOT⟩	⟨MOT⟩⟨MOT⟩⟨MOT⟩

TABLE 1.57

Combined Decision Matrix of Ten Cities According to Smart Environment's Criteria Using TFNs

Expert$_s$	ANC$_{6\_1}$	POC$_{6\_2}$	ENC$_{6\_3}$	SRC$_{6\_4}$
City$_1$	⟨5, 7, 9⟩	⟨5, 7, 9⟩	⟨7, 9, 11⟩	⟨7, 9, 11⟩
City$_2$	⟨1, 3, 5⟩	⟨1, 3, 5⟩	⟨3, 5, 7⟩	⟨3, 5, 7⟩
City$_3$	⟨7, 9, 11⟩	⟨7, 9, 11⟩	⟨1, 3, 5⟩	⟨3, 5, 7⟩
City$_4$	⟨3, 5, 7⟩	⟨3, 5, 7⟩	⟨5, 7, 9⟩	⟨3, 5, 7⟩
City$_5$	⟨1, 3, 5⟩	⟨7, 9, 11⟩	⟨3, 5, 7⟩	⟨1, 3, 5⟩
City$_6$	⟨3, 5, 7⟩	⟨3, 5, 7⟩	⟨5, 7, 9⟩	⟨5, 7, 9⟩
City$_7$	⟨7, 9, 11⟩	⟨7, 9, 11⟩	⟨5, 7, 9⟩	⟨5, 7, 9⟩
City$_8$	⟨7, 9, 11⟩	⟨7, 9, 11⟩	⟨1, 4.33, 7⟩	⟨1, 4.33, 7⟩
City$_9$	⟨1, 3, 5⟩	⟨1, 4.33, 7⟩	⟨3, 5, 7⟩	⟨3, 5, 7⟩
City$_{10}$	⟨3, 5, 7⟩	⟨7, 9, 11⟩	⟨5, 7, 9⟩	⟨7, 9, 11⟩

TABLE 1.58

Normalized Decision Matrix of Ten Cities According to Smart Environment's Criteria

Expert$_s$	ANC$_{6\_1}$			POC$_{6\_2}$			ENC$_{6\_3}$			SRC$_{6\_4}$		
City$_1$	0.455	0.636	0.818	0.455	0.636	0.818	0.636	0.818	1.000	0.636	0.818	1.000
City$_2$	0.091	0.273	0.455	0.091	0.273	0.455	0.273	0.455	0.636	0.273	0.455	0.636
City$_3$	0.636	0.818	1.000	0.636	0.818	1.000	0.091	0.273	0.455	0.273	0.455	0.636
City$_4$	0.273	0.455	0.636	0.273	0.455	0.636	0.455	0.636	0.818	0.273	0.455	0.636
City$_5$	0.091	0.273	0.455	0.636	0.818	1.000	0.273	0.455	0.636	0.091	0.273	0.455
City$_6$	0.273	0.455	0.636	0.273	0.455	0.636	0.455	0.636	0.818	0.455	0.636	0.818
City$_7$	0.636	0.818	1.000	0.636	0.818	1.000	0.455	0.636	0.818	0.455	0.636	0.818
City$_8$	0.636	0.818	1.000	0.636	0.818	1.000	0.091	0.394	0.636	0.091	0.394	0.636
City$_9$	0.091	0.273	0.455	0.091	0.394	0.636	0.273	0.455	0.636	0.273	0.455	0.636
City$_{10}$	0.273	0.455	0.636	0.636	0.818	1.000	0.455	0.636	0.818	0.636	0.818	1.000

value of 0.083, followed by the public and social services criterion with a weight of 0.073, while the level of qualification criterion comes in the last rank with a weight of 0.004.

Finally, smart and sustainable cities were ranked according to the local weights of all sub-criteria of each main criterion. According to the local weights of the sub-criteria of the smart governance criterion, it is clear that the city of Dubai is the highest in the ranking with a weight of 1.000, followed by the city of Berlin with a weight of 0.6956, while the cities of Moscow, Sydney, and Los Angeles come last with a weight of 0.068 as presented in Table 1.35 and Figure 1.7. Also, according to the local weights of

TABLE 1.59

Weighted Normalized Decision Matrix of Ten Cities According to Smart Environment's Criteria

Expert$_s$	ANC$_{6.1}$			POC$_{6.2}$			ENC$_{6.3}$			SRC$_{6.4}$		
City$_1$	0.135	0.190	0.244	0.121	0.170	0.218	0.155	0.199	0.243	0.122	0.157	0.192
City$_2$	0.027	0.081	0.135	0.024	0.073	0.121	0.066	0.110	0.155	0.052	0.087	0.122
City$_3$	0.190	0.244	0.298	0.170	0.218	0.267	0.022	0.066	0.110	0.052	0.087	0.122
City$_4$	0.081	0.135	0.190	0.073	0.121	0.170	0.110	0.155	0.199	0.052	0.087	0.122
City$_5$	0.027	0.081	0.135	0.170	0.218	0.267	0.066	0.110	0.155	0.017	0.052	0.087
City$_6$	0.081	0.135	0.190	0.073	0.121	0.170	0.110	0.155	0.199	0.087	0.122	0.157
City$_7$	0.190	0.244	0.298	0.170	0.218	0.267	0.110	0.155	0.199	0.087	0.122	0.157
City$_8$	0.190	0.244	0.298	0.170	0.218	0.267	0.022	0.096	0.155	0.017	0.076	0.122
City$_9$	0.027	0.081	0.135	0.024	0.105	0.170	0.066	0.110	0.155	0.052	0.087	0.087
City$_{10}$	0.081	0.135	0.190	0.170	0.218	0.267	0.110	0.155	0.199	0.122	0.157	0.192
A*	0.190	0.244	0.298	0.170	0.218	0.267	0.155	0.199	0.243	0.122	0.157	0.192
A⁻	0.027	0.081	0.135	0.024	0.073	0.121	0.022	0.066	0.110	0.017	0.052	0.087

TABLE 1.60

Distance from Each Alternative to the FPIS and to the FNIS of Smart Environment's Criteria

Experts	p_i^*				$\sum_{j=1}^{n} p\left(\tilde{r}_{ij}, \tilde{r}_j^*\right)$	p_i^-				$\sum_{j=1}^{n} p\left(\tilde{r}_{ij}, \tilde{r}_j^-\right)$	C_i	Rank
	ANC_{6_1}	POC_{6_2}	ENC_{6_3}	SRC_{6_4}		ANC_{6_1}	POC_{6_2}	ENC_{6_3}	SRC_{6_4}			
$City_1$	0.054	0.049	0.000	0.000	0.103	0.108	0.097	0.133	0.105	0.443	0.812	2
$City_2$	0.163	0.146	0.088	0.070	0.466	0.000	0.000	0.044	0.035	0.079	0.145	10
$City_3$	0.000	0.000	0.133	0.070	0.202	0.163	0.146	0.000	0.035	0.343	0.629	5
$City_4$	0.108	0.097	0.044	0.070	0.319	0.054	0.049	0.088	0.035	0.226	0.414	7
$City_5$	0.163	0.000	0.088	0.105	0.356	0.000	0.146	0.044	0.000	0.190	0.348	8
$City_6$	0.108	0.097	0.044	0.035	0.285	0.054	0.049	0.088	0.070	0.261	0.478	6
$City_7$	0.000	0.000	0.044	0.035	0.079	0.163	0.146	0.088	0.070	0.466	0.855	1
$City_8$	0.000	0.000	0.110	0.087	0.196	0.163	0.146	0.031	0.024	0.363	0.649	4
$City_9$	0.163	0.120	0.088	0.070	0.441	0.000	0.034	0.044	0.035	0.113	0.204	9
$City_{10}$	0.108	0.000	0.044	0.000	0.153	0.054	0.146	0.088	0.105	0.393	0.720	3

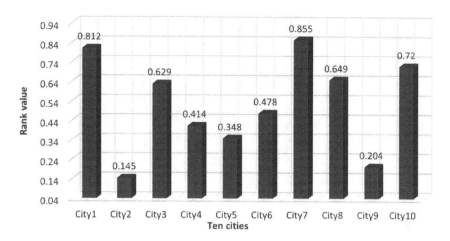

FIGURE 1.12
Final ranking of ten cities according to smart environment's criteria.

TABLE 1.61

Distance from Each Alternative to the FPIS and to the FNIS According to All Sub-Criteria

Expert$_s$	$\sum_{j=1}^{n} p\left(\breve{r}_{ij},\breve{r}_j^*\right)$	$\sum_{j=1}^{n} p\left(\breve{r}_{ij},\breve{r}_j^-\right)$	C_i	Rank
City$_1$	0.284	0.294	0.509	10
City$_2$	0.379	3.092	0.891	5
City$_3$	0.235	4.383	0.949	2
City$_4$	0.400	3.062	0.885	6
City$_5$	0.439	1.876	0.810	8
City$_6$	0.238	0.915	0.794	9
City$_7$	0.296	2.011	0.872	7
City$_8$	0.407	4.211	0.912	4
City$_9$	0.226	4.391	0.951	1
City$_{10}$	0.287	3.174	0.917	3

the sub-criteria of the smart economy criterion, it is clear that the city of Dubai is the highest in the ranking with a weight of 1.000, followed by the city of Tokyo with a weight of 0.8108, while the city of Los Angeles comes last with a weight of 0.0525 as presented in Table 1.40 and Figure 1.8. Then, according to the local weights of the sub-criteria of the smart mobility criterion, it is clear that the cities of Madrid and Sydney are the highest in

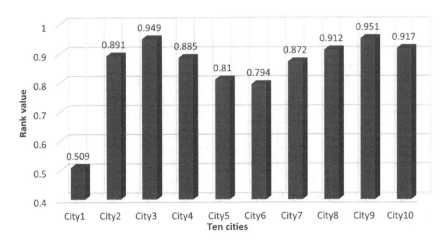

FIGURE 1.13
Final ranking of ten cities according to all sub-criteria.

the ranking with a weight of 0.851, followed by the city of Moscow with a weight of 0.582, while the cities of Hong Kong and Dubai come last with a weight of 0.297 as presented in Table 1.45 and Figure 1.9. In this regard, according to the local weights of the sub-criteria of the smart living criterion, it is clear that the city of Paris is the highest in the ranking with a weight of 0.896, followed by the city of Berlin with a weight of 0.705, while the cities of Hong Kong and New York come last with a weight of 0.291 as presented in Table 1.50 and Figure 1.10. After that, according to the local weights of the sub-criteria of the smart people criterion, it is clear that the city of Paris is the highest in the ranking with a weight of 0.703, followed by the city of Berlin with a weight of 0.662, while the city of Hong Kong comes last with a weight of 0.350 as presented in Table 1.55 and Figure 1.11. Eventually, according to the local weights of the sub-criteria of the smart environment criterion, it is clear that the city of Sydney is the highest in the ranking with a weight of 0.855, followed by the city of Madrid with a weight of 0.812, while the city of Paris comes last with a weight of 0.145 as presented in Table 1.60 and Figure 1.12.

In conclusion, according to the assessment of the cities selected according to the 31 sub-criteria, it is clear that the city of Dubai is the most sustainable and smart city with a weight value of 0.951, followed by the city of Berlin with a weight of 0.949. On the contrary, Madrid is the least sustainable and least smart city with a weight of 0.509 as exhibited in Table 1.61 and Figure 1.13.

1.6 Summary

- This chapter provides a comprehensive description of smart cities.
- This chapter reviews the features of the smart city in terms of the characteristics and formation of smart cities.
- This chapter presents the most important criteria used in evaluating smart and sustainable cities after a comprehensive analysis of a number of research articles.
- This chapter presents a proposed hybrid approach to multi-criteria decision-making consisting of two fuzzy ANP-fuzzy TOPSIS methods.
- This chapter presents a real case study evaluating a number of cities around the world.

References

Ghosh, Subrata, Nilanjana Das Chatterjee, and Santanu Dinda. 2021. "Urban Ecological Security Assessment and Forecasting Using Integrated DEMATEL-ANP and CA-Markov Models: A Case Study on Kolkata Metropolitan Area, India." *Sustainable Cities and Society* 68: 102773. https://doi.org/https://doi.org/10.1016/j.scs.2021.102773.

Kumar, Shashank, Rakesh D. Raut, Kirti Nayal, Sascha Kraus, Vinay Surendra Yadav, and Balkrishna E. Narkhede. 2021. "To Identify Industry 4.0 and Circular Economy Adoption Barriers in the Agriculture Supply Chain by Using ISM-ANP." *Journal of Cleaner Production* 293: 126023. https://doi.org/https://doi.org/10.1016/j.jclepro.2021.126023.

Liu, Xiahui, Qianwang Deng, Guiliang Gong, Xingdong Zhao, and Kexin Li. 2021. "Evaluating the Interactions of Multi-Dimensional Value for Sustainable Product-Service System with Grey DEMATEL-ANP Approach." *Journal of Manufacturing Systems* 60: 449–58. https://doi.org/https://doi.org/10.1016/j.jmsy.2021.07.006.

Mardani Shahri, Majid, Abdolhamid Eshraghniaye Jahromi, and Mahmoud Houshmand. 2021. "Failure Mode and Effect Analysis Using an Integrated Approach of Clustering and MCDM under Pythagorean Fuzzy Environment." *Journal of Loss Prevention in the Process Industries* 72: 104591. https://doi.org/https://doi.org/10.1016/j.jlp.2021.104591.

Patil, Sachin K, and Ravi Kant. 2014. "A Hybrid Approach Based on Fuzzy DEMATEL and FMCDM to Predict Success of Knowledge Management Adoption in Supply Chain." *Applied Soft Computing* 18: 126–35. https://doi.org/https://doi.org/10.1016/j.asoc.2014.01.027.

Saaty, Thomas L. 2001. *"Decision Making with Dependence and Feedback: The Analytic Network Process : The Organization and Prioritization of Complexity,"* 370. http://books.google.com/books?id=MGpaAAAAYAAJ&pgis=1.

Solangi, Yasir Ahmed, Cheng Longsheng, and Syed Ahsan Ali Shah. 2021. "Assessing and Overcoming the Renewable Energy Barriers for Sustainable Development in Pakistan: An Integrated AHP and Fuzzy TOPSIS Approach." *Renewable Energy* 173: 209–22. https://doi.org/https://doi.org/10.1016/j.renene.2021.03.141.

Yoon, Kwangsun, and Ching-Lai Hwang. 1985. "Manufacturing Plant Location Analysis by Multiple Attribute Decision Making: Part I—Single-Plant Strategy." *International Journal of Production Research* 23 (2): 345–59. https://doi.org/10.1080/00207548508904712.

Zadeh, Lotfi Asker. 1975. "The Concept of a Linguistic Variable and Its Application to Approximate Reasoning—I." *Information Sciences* 8 (3): 199–249. https://doi.org/https://doi.org/10.1016/0020-0255(75)90036-5.

2

A Conceptual Design and Evaluation Framework for Assessing Smart Health Technologies

2.1 Introduction

Personal and social health is very important. It is at the heart of happiness. From an economic standpoint, healthcare is one of the world's most important industries. With new digital technology, modern healthcare is developing quickly, and more ailments are being cured. Smart technologies, such as broadband Internet and mobile communication technologies, wearable electronics, the Internet of Things, cloud computing, robotics, and others, provide new improvements to treatment approaches, and the health industry is altering as a result. Smart health refers to the provision of healthcare using smart technology to monitor residents' health. Artificial intelligence and machine learning are becoming crucial assistants for health professionals in illness prevention, diagnosis, treatment, and post-treatment services, thanks to the capabilities of these smart technologies. As a result, smart technologies are at the forefront of health-tech research and development. This area is where universities, health institutions, and health technology corporations earn handsomely. Every day, the number of smart technology applications in healthcare grows. One of the goals of this chapter is to give advice and information on the usage of smart technology in the healthcare industry.

Through improved health applications, the adoption and implementation of developing smart health technology may improve living circumstances. The most important accomplishment in smart health solutions is the balanced application of technology and engagement in human-based systems. Effective healthcare services such as customization of medicines via big data, robots in cure and care, and artificial intelligence help for physicians, and others are offered using smart health technology. Furthermore, smart health helps individuals with preventative care

DOI: 10.1201/9781003357681-2

and therapeutic services while also improving their living situations. Individuals who may have limited access to health services now have access to these services because of smart health solutions.

Health is one of the most important areas where new digital technologies give these benefits. This area employs a variety of technologies, including cloud computing, the Internet of Things (IoT), big data, artificial intelligence (AI), and robots. The amount of data gathered in the area of health is quickly expanding because of the Internet of Things and the adoption of wearable health devices. Decision support systems that leverage big data analytics assist healthcare practitioners in making rapid and efficient judgments. Big data analytic tools and apps trigger new advances in patient behavior, treatment costs, and R&D. AI is also becoming one of the most widely employed technologies in the area of medicine. For instance, AI is used to analyze pathology data. With its capacity to access massive databases, AI assists clinicians in making therapy choices by scanning identical symptoms and their analysis findings in any nation across the globe.

Poor healthcare technology has the potential to kill people. As a result, the region in which smart health technology will be implemented should be thoroughly analyzed before the most appropriate technology is chosen. Because these assessments are based on people's desires and expectations, they might sometimes be hazy and imprecise. As a result, smart health solutions may be chosen based on carefully chosen parameters. This chapter also aims to present a paradigm for the healthcare industry in terms of smart health technology selection and assessment. As a result, smart health technology assessment is treated as a multicriteria decision-making (MCDM) issue. The MCDM area comprises ideas and methods for achieving the "best suitable" answer for a decision scenario that fulfills several competing criteria. It is both a strategy and a set of procedures or approaches for assisting individuals who are confronted with various, non-uniform, and sometimes competing challenges in making choices that are acceptable to their own value judgments.

The mixed structure of smart health technology assessment includes a set of contradicting criteria. It is tough to decide on and assess the material that is of an unclear nature. A fuzzy linguistic term set technique is used to deal with the ambiguity in this MCDM situation. This method may be used to help professionals make better decisions in difficult and ambiguous circumstances. It enables professionals to quickly convey their thoughts using words rather than figures, allowing them to pick the best option. It provides more realistic outcomes. This chapter suggests an integrated fuzzy linguistic MCDM framework to assess smart health technologies. The fuzzy Analytic Hierarchy Process weights the criteria (AHP), and alternatives are ranked with the fuzzy VIseKriterijumska Optimizacija I Kompromisno Resenje (VIKOR) method.

2.2 MCDM Model

In this part, a hybrid MCDM approach to evaluating smart health technologies has been presented. For the purpose of this task, we find fuzzy AHP and fuzzy VIKOR methods to be the best approach to solve this problem, prioritize criteria, and rank selected alternatives. Figure 2.1 indicates the research approach guiding this study, where the AHP method is used as an initial development level of the analysis, which is then completed with the help of experts to compute the weights of the key criteria and their sub-criteria for the pairwise comparison matrix. Then, the fuzzy VIKOR method is used to select the best alternative to smart health technologies based on the available criteria. To take scholars, undergraduates, interested parties, and researchers through our analysis process and attempt to provide a comprehensive context for our work, we then provide a detailed description of the fuzzy AHP and fuzzy VIKOR methods used in this study.

2.2.1 Fuzzy Set Theory

Zadeh (1975) began by outlining the theory's central concept. Each element in a fuzzy set must be given a membership degree based on fuzzy set theory. Each element's membership degree is inside a particular interval, which is often [0, 1]. The most frequent fuzzy membership functions are monotone, triangular, and trapezoidal (Abdel-Basset, Gamal, and Teleb 2022). A triangular fuzzy number (TFN) is employed in most fuzzy settings owing to its ease of computation. TFN is also often used in most studies to represent a fuzzy number (Du and Li 2021). The membership grade function of a TFN $\tilde{B} = \left(B^l, B^m, B^u\right)$ is introduced as follows:

$$\mu_{\tilde{B}}(x) = \begin{cases} \left(x - B^l\right)/\left(B^m - B^l\right) \\ \left(B^u - x\right)/\left(B^u - B^m\right) \\ 0 \end{cases}$$

2.2.2 Fuzzy AHP

In the 1970s, T.L. Saaty created the AHP approach (Liu, Eckert, and Earl 2020). The AHP that Saaty represents is known as a traditional AHP. AHP is a great strategy since it uses consistency measure to improve decision-making learning. The AHP technique is an MCDM methodology that examines the issue at many levels of hierarchy. Using a pairwise comparison matrix, this approach has the ability to identify quantitative and qualitative variables (Solangi, Longsheng, and Shah 2021). The pairwise comparison is the foundation of the AHP approach. The preferences are

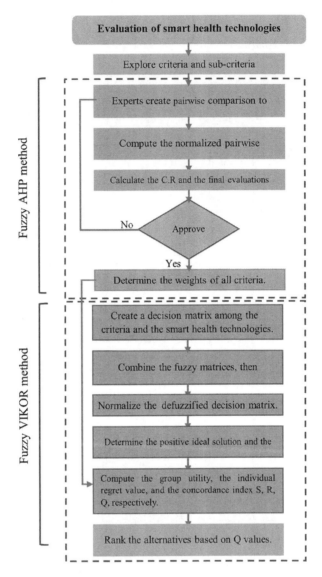

FIGURE 2.1
Suggested scheme of the problem.

entered in order to compare reasonably. It offers a practical answer. However, there is a rigorous consistency criterion to maintain the reasonableness of preference intensities between the compared items. In actual life, this condition for Saaty's matrix is difficult to meet. Instead of the consistency criterion, Jandová and Talasová (2013) portrayed a weak consistency condition. The weak consistency criteria are quite natural and appropriate for Saaty's scale linguistic descriptions. Another difficulty with the AHP is that it makes judgments based on true attributes. For example, in certain circumstances, human emotions are unreliable, and the analyst may be unable to apply accurate numerical values to examination judgments.

2.2.3 Fuzzy VIKOR

In MCDM, the VIKOR strategy is a more often used method for handling issues with many competing criteria. The low and simple computational steps are one of the reasons for this method's high use for ranking alternatives compared to other MCDM approaches. The VIKOR technique offers and employs compromise solutions to rank alternatives based on incompatible and incompatible criteria. According to some writers, using a compromise solution is the method's greatest benefit and strength compared to other techniques. The VIKOR technique is a compromise approach for ranking alternatives based on incompatible and incommensurable criteria (Opricovic and Tzeng 2004). The compromise solution refers to an approach that seeks a ranking order by balancing anticipated and pessimistic alternatives. Like other MCDM techniques, the VIKOR method may be integrated with fuzzy set theory (Hosseini, Paydar, and Hajiaghaei-Keshteli 2021). In the present chapter, we apply this technique to rank some of the smart health technologies.

2.2.4 The Mathematical Steps of the Hybrid MCDM Framework

The main steps of the hybrid approach, which combines the fuzzy AHP and fuzzy VIKOR methods, are briefly introduced as follows:

Step 1: A group of specialists is selected to share the basic information on the chosen problem of evaluating smart health technologies with the authors. Before all that, basic criteria must be established for the selection of specialists. First, the number of years of experience must not be less than 5 years in the field under study. Secondly, the academic degree of the participating specialists shall not be less than a master's degree.

Step 2: The problem is carefully studied to determine the study's main objective. Also, the main and sub-criteria affecting the problem are identified. Next, a range of smart health technologies is identified as alternatives.

Step 3: The problem is divided into several levels. The first level represents the main objective of the problem. The second level represents the basic criteria and their sub-factors that affect the selection of the best alternative. The third level represents the alternatives used, which are determined according to the problem.

Step 4: Linguistic terms and corresponding TFNs are identified for evaluating the main criteria and their sub-criteria as in Table 2.1. Also, linguistic terms and corresponding TFNs are selected to rank the selected alternatives as in Table 2.2.

TABLE 2.1

Linguistic Terms and Their Corresponding TFNs for Weighting Criteria

Linguistic Terms	Connotation	Acronyms	TFN $\langle l_{ij}, m_{ij}, u_{ij} \rangle$	Reciprocals $\langle 1/u_{ij}, 1/m_{ij}, 1/l_{ij} \rangle$
Equally important	1	$\langle$LMP$\rangle$	$\langle 1, 1, 1 \rangle$	$\langle 1, 1, 1 \rangle$
Equally to moderately more important	2	$\langle$EMP$\rangle$	$\langle 1, 2, 3 \rangle$	$\langle 1/3, 1/2, 1 \rangle$
Moderately more important	3	$\langle$MPM$\rangle$	$\langle 2, 3, 4 \rangle$	$\langle 1/4, 1/3, 1/2 \rangle$
Justly more important to very important	4	$\langle$JVM$\rangle$	$\langle 3, 4, 5 \rangle$	$\langle 1/5, 1/4, 1/3 \rangle$
Extremely important	5	$\langle$XMM$\rangle$	$\langle 4, 5, 6 \rangle$	$\langle 1/6, 1/5, 1/4 \rangle$
Extremely important to vary very important	6	$\langle$XMV$\rangle$	$\langle 5, 6, 7 \rangle$	$\langle 1/7, 1/6, 1/5 \rangle$
Very extremely important	7	$\langle$VXM$\rangle$	$\langle 6, 7, 8 \rangle$	$\langle 1/8, 1/7, 1/6 \rangle$
Very extremely important to perfectly more important	8	$\langle$VVP$\rangle$	$\langle 7, 8, 9 \rangle$	$\langle 1/9, 1/8, 1/7 \rangle$
Perfectly more important	9	$\langle$PFM$\rangle$	$\langle 8, 9, 10 \rangle$	$\langle 1/10, 1/9, 1/8 \rangle$

TABLE 2.2

Linguistic Terms and Their Corresponding TFNs for Assessing Alternatives

Linguistic Terms	Acronyms	TFN $\langle l_{ij}, m_{ij}, u_{ij} \rangle$
Extremely low	$\langle$XLL$\rangle$	$\langle 1, 1, 3 \rangle$
Low	$\langle$LOO$\rangle$	$\langle 1, 3, 5 \rangle$
Moderate	$\langle$MDE$\rangle$	$\langle 3, 5, 7 \rangle$
High	$\langle$HHH$\rangle$	$\langle 5, 7, 9 \rangle$
Extremely high	$\langle$EHH$\rangle$	$\langle 7, 9, 11 \rangle$

Step 5: Generate a pairwise comparison matrix (G) among the criteria and itself by each professional as in Eq. (2.1) by using the linguistic terms in Table 1.1 and then by using TFNs as demonstrated in Eq. (2.2).

$$G = \begin{array}{c} \\ CC_1 \\ CC_2 \\ \vdots \\ CC_n \end{array} \begin{array}{cccc} CC_1 & CC_2 & \dots & CC_n \\ \left(\begin{array}{cccc} - & x_{12} & \dots & x_{1i} \\ 1/x_{21} & - & \dots & x_{2i} \\ 1/x_{31} & 1/x_{32} & - & \dots \\ 1/x_{j1} & 1/x_{j2} & 1/x_{j3} & - \end{array} \right) \end{array} \qquad (2.1)$$

where (x_{ij}), i, j=1, 2... n, and x_{ij} is the assessment of the criteria of the ith element CC_1, CC_2, ..., CC_i regarding the jth element CC_1, CC_2, ..., CC_j. Also, the main diagonal of the matrix equals 1 such that x_{ij} equals 1.

$$G = \begin{array}{c} \\ CC_1 \\ CC_2 \\ \vdots \\ CC_n \end{array} \begin{array}{cccc} CC_1 & CC_2 & \cdots & CC_n \\ \left(\begin{array}{cccc} - & \langle l_{12}, m_{12}, u_{12} \rangle & \cdots & \langle l_{1i}, m_{1i}, u_{1i} \rangle \\ 1/\langle u_{21}, m_{21}, l_{21} \rangle & - & \cdots & \langle l_{2i}, m_{2i}, u_{2i} \rangle \\ 1/\langle u_{31}, m_{31}, l_{31} \rangle & 1/\langle u_{32}, m_{32}, l_{32} \rangle & - & \cdots \\ 1/\langle u_{j1}, m_{j1}, l_{j1} \rangle & 1/\langle u_{j2}, m_{j2}, l_{j2} \rangle & 1/\langle u_{j3}, m_{j3}, l_{j3} \rangle & - \end{array} \right) \end{array}$$

(2.2)

where l, m, and u, characterize lower, medium, and upper limit, respectively.

Step 6: Calculate the geometric mean of the comparisons for criterion ith in contradiction to other criteria using Eq. (2.3).

$$xe_i = \left(\prod_{j-1}^{N} x_{ij} \right)^{1/n} \quad i = 1, 2, 3, \dots, N$$

(2.3)

Step 7: Calculate the fuzzy weight of the ith criterion as a TFN by applying Eq. (2.4). Also, the fuzzy weights are standardized by dividing each fuzzy weight by the sum of the fuzzy weights as in Eq. (2.4).

$$w_i = xe_i \times (xe_1 + xe_2 + xe_3 + \cdots + xe_N)^{-1}$$

(2.4)

Step 8: Compute the crisp weights by converting the fuzzy numbers to crisp numbers by removing the fuzzy numbers by using the Center of Area (CoA) technique (Abdel-Basset, Gamal, and Teleb 2022) as exhibited in Eq. (2.5).

$$w_{crisp} = \frac{l + m + u}{3}$$

(2.5)

Step 9: Calculate the consistency ratio (CR) for each matrix generated by each specialist distinctly to approve the dependability of the comparison matrix as exhibited in Eq. (2.6), where $CI = \frac{\lambda_{max-n}}{n-1}$, λ_{max} is the average of the weighted sum vector divided by the corresponding criterion, and n is the number of criteria. RI is a random index defined by a number of criteria (Saaty 2001).

$$CR = \frac{CI}{RI}$$

(2.6)

Step 10: Compute the ultimate weights of the criteria by applying the ordered weighted aggregation (OWA) operator of the final weights of all specialists.

Step 11: Generate a decision matrix (D) among the criteria identified and the smart health technologies designated by the specialists as presented in Eqs. (2.7) and (2.8), using linguistic terms and TFNs, respectively, as in Table 2.2.

$$
D = \left(x_{ij}\right)_{m \times n} =
\begin{array}{c}
 \\
A_1 \\
A_2 \\
\vdots \\
A_m
\end{array}
\begin{array}{cccc}
CC_1 & CC_2 & \cdots & CC_n \\
\left(\begin{array}{cccc}
x_{11} & x_{12} & \cdots & x_{1n} \\
x_{21} & x_{22} & \cdots & x_{2n} \\
\cdots & \cdots & \cdots & \cdots \\
x_{m1} & x_{m2} & \cdots & x_{mn}
\end{array}\right)
\end{array}
\tag{2.7}
$$

$$
D = \left(x_{ij}\right)_{m \times n} =
\begin{array}{c}
 \\
A_1 \\
A_2 \\
\vdots \\
A_m
\end{array}
\begin{array}{cccc}
CC_1 & CC_2 & \cdots & CC_n \\
\left[\begin{array}{cccc}
\langle l_{11}, m_{11}, u_{11} \rangle & \langle l_{12}, m_{12}, u_{12} \rangle & \cdots & \langle l_{1n}, m_{1n}, u_{1n} \rangle \\
\langle l_{21}, m_{21}, u_{21} \rangle & \langle l_{22}, m_{22}, u_{22} \rangle & \cdots & \langle l_{2n}, m_{2n}, u_{2n} \rangle \\
\cdots & \cdots & \cdots & \cdots \\
\langle l_{m1}, m_{m1}, u_{m1} \rangle & \langle l_{m2}, m_{m2}, u_{m2} \rangle & \cdots & \langle l_{mn}, m_{mn}, u_{mn} \rangle
\end{array}\right]
\end{array}
$$

$$\tag{2.8}$$

where n is the number of criteria, m is the number of smart health technologies, and x_{ij} is the performance evaluation of the ith alternative A_1, $A_2, ..., A_n$ regarding the jth criterion $CC_1, CC_2, ..., CC_m$.

Step 12: Calculate the combined decision matrix among the selected criteria and alternatives by combining the estimations of all specialists, by using Eq. (2.9).

$$
l_{ij} = \min_e \left\{ l_{ije} \right\}, \quad m_{ij} = \frac{1}{e} \sum_{e=1}^{e} \left\{ m_{ije} \right\}, \quad u_{ij} = \max_e \left\{ u_{ije} \right\}
\tag{2.9}
$$

where e is the number of participating specialists.

Step 13: Defuzzify the fuzzy combined decision matrix into the crisp combined decision matrix by removing the fuzzy numbers by applying the CoA technique as presented in Eq. (2.5).

Step 14: Calculate the normalized decision matrix among the selected criteria and alternatives by applying Eq. (2.10).

$$
\left(T_{ij}\right)_{m \times n} = \left. x_{ij} \middle/ \left(\sqrt{\sum_{j=1}^{m} x_{ij}^2} \right) \right.
\tag{2.10}
$$

Step 15: Determine the positive and negative ideal solution A_j^* and A_j^-, respectively. If A_j are advantageous criteria, then $A_j^* = \max(A_{ij})$ and $A_j^- = \min(A_{ij})$. Then, if A_j are non-advantageous criteria, then

$$A_j^* = \min(A_{ij}) \text{ and } A_j^- = \max(A_{ij}) \tag{2.11}$$

Step 16: Compute the group utility S_i by applying Eq. (2.12) and individual regret values R_i by applying Eq. (2.13) as follows:

$$S_i = \sum_{j=1}^{n} w_j * \frac{A_j^* - A_{ij}}{A_j^* - A_j^-} \tag{2.12}$$

$$R_i = \max\left[w_j * \frac{A_j^* - A_{ij}}{a_j^* - A_j^-} \right] \tag{2.13}$$

w_j is the weight of all sub-criteria.

Step 17: Compute the concordance index Q_j among the selected criteria and alternatives by applying Eq. (2.14).

$$Q_j = v\left[\frac{S_j - S^*}{S^- - S^*} \right] + (1-v)\left[\frac{R_j - R^*}{R^- - R^*} \right] \tag{2.14}$$

where $S^- = \max_j S_j$, $S^* = \min_j S_j$, $R^- = \max_j R_j$, $R^* = \min_j R_j$, and $v \in [0, 1]$ is generally 0.5.

Step 18: Rank the smart health technologies in descending order according to the value Q_j computed by applying Eq. (2.14).

Step 19: Conduct the two final necessities in the evaluation process of the smart health technologies by the VIKOR technique. Situation 1: (adequate advantage) by using Eq. (2.15):

$$Q(A^2) - Q(A^1) \geq \frac{1}{m-1} \tag{2.15}$$

where A^1 is rated as the top alternative rendering to Q and A^2 is rated second, and m is the count of substitutes. Situation 2 (appropriate stability): as the classification of Q, A^1 must be the maximum in the ranking of S and R. If one of the conditions is not changed, there is a set of explanations as follows:

- If situation 2 is not chanced, then A^1 and A^2 are a compromise solution.

- If situation 1 is not chanced, then A^1, A^2,..., A^m are a compromise solution, where A^m is computed by Eq. (2.16).

$$Q(A^m) - Q(A^1) < \frac{1}{m-1} \qquad (2.16)$$

2.3 An Illustrated Example

The health industry has been one of the most influenced by technological advancements. Smart health apps are being introduced in several nations throughout the globe to keep up with this trend. In the sphere of health-care, integrating the appropriate smart technology is critical. A mistake in this area might result in major issues. In this regard, one business intends to invest in the area of smart technology in the healthcare industry. They are aware, however, that there are several sorts of smart health technology on the market. They aim to figure out which smart technology is best for health. The organization examines several smart technologies on the market to obtain the greatest smart health technology product. They resolve to pursue their efforts scientifically. As a result, the smart health technology assessment model is built. Academic research and expert views are used to determine the criteria and alternatives. There are six options to choose from when it comes to smart health technology: H_1 stands for "cloud computing." "Smart Sensors and the Internet of Things (IoT)" is the topic of H_2. H_3 stands for "big data." H_4 stands for "3D printers." H_5 stands for "artificial intelligence." H_6 stands for "robotics."

- **Cloud Computing**: It is possible for health professionals to remotely monitor individuals with chronic diseases by scanning their life data with tricorder devices and recording it in information systems using cloud information solutions. The main goal of cloud computing health applications is to be able to alert health institutions in the event of an emergency within minutes.
- **Smart Sensors and the Internet of Things (IoT)**: Sensors connected to mobile devices accurately read and interpret numerous parameters, which are then relayed to medical institutes. Healthcare practitioners may regulate the patient's treatment and monitor health status outside of the hospital in this fashion. Biosensors are used to send medical data to online and mobile apps.
- **Big Data**: Health service providers, health policymakers, software and hardware developers, and private sector service businesses

are all concerned about the application of big data analytics via health decision support mechanisms. Wi-Fi or Bluetooth may be used to send the acquired data to the centers. Hospital infections may be diagnosed significantly sooner with this technology, and treatment can begin 24 hours before standard approaches.

- **3D Printers:** The diagnostic tool, which is printed on a 3D printer and assembled on a smartphone, can identify illnesses including malaria, HIV, *E. coli* bacteria, and allergies in ready meals.

- **Artificial Intelligence:** Applications of artificial intelligence are employed in many different domains, including the automation of hospitals and the monitoring of public health. In addition, several commercial and governmental hospitals, as well as academic medical centers, have implemented cutting-edge technological solutions, such as surgical robots. There has been a gradual increase in the participation of domestic enterprises in the market for health technology. When it comes to data analysis, AI may assist in choosing the appropriate, individually tailored treatment plan.

- **Robotics:** Because of advances in medical nanotechnology, the goal is to have the Nanorobots function at the cellular level of the patients' bodies once they have been administered. With the help of wireless technology, the ingestible and built-in gadgets make it possible to monitor how the body reacts to the smart pills that are taken inside. Robotic surgery is used in the healthcare industry to conduct clinical applications, prosthetics are utilized to provide medical solutions for amputated limbs, automated robots are used to decrease expenses associated with employees, and delivery robots and cleaning robots are also employed.

2.3.1 Determination of Basic Information about the Problem

Step 1: A group of three specialists were selected to share with the authors the problem and to identify the main dimensions of the problem. Also, specialists fill out questionnaires to collect information about criteria and their sub-criteria. In the end, the experts were selected according to the criteria that were set.

Step 2: The problem has been studied from all sides very carefully, and the main objective is to evaluate smart health technologies. Also, six main criteria that have been identified are technology-based criterion (TBC_1), human-based criterion (HBC_2), system-based criterion (SBC_3), and organization-based criterion (OBC_4). In addition, twelve sub-criteria have been defined, namely, hardware technology (HTC_{1_1}), software technology (STC_{1_2}), network security (NSC_{1_3}), the privacy of user's information

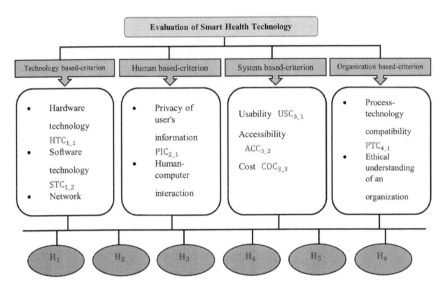

FIGURE 2.2
Final hierarchy of the problem.

(PIC_{2_1}), human-computer interaction (HCC_{2_2}), protection of human health (PHC_{2_3}), usability (USC_{3_1}), accessibility (ACC_{3_2}), cost (COC_{3_3}), process-technology compatibility (PTC_{4_1}), ethical understanding of an organization (EUC_{4_2}), and legal v. social factors (LSC_{4_3}). In the end, six smart health technologies were identified as alternatives, which are H_1, H_2, H_3, H_4, H_5, and H_6.

Step 3: The problem was divided into a hierarchical problem consisting of three levels, where the first level represents the goal, the second level represents the criteria and their sub-criteria, and the third level represents the alternatives used as in Figure 2.2.

Step 4: Linguistic variables and corresponding TFNs used in evaluating criteria and ranking alternatives are identified as presented in Tables 2.1 and 2.2.

2.3.2 Computation of Criterion Weights with the Fuzzy AHP Method

Step 5: The pairwise comparison matrices have been generated between the criteria and itself by three specialists using linguistic terms by applying Eq. (2.1) as presented in Table 2.3 and then using TFNs by applying Eq. (2.2) as presented in Table 2.4.

Step 6: The geometric mean of the comparisons for criterion ith in contradiction to other criteria has been calculated by applying Eq. (2.3) as presented in Table 2.5.

TABLE 2.3

Evaluation of Main Criteria Using Linguistic Terms by All Specialists

Specialists	TBC$_1$	HBC$_2$	SBC$_3$	OBC$_4$
TBC$_1$	$\langle$LMP$\rangle$	$\langle$XMM$\rangle$	$1/\langle$VXM$\rangle$	$\langle$XMM$\rangle$
HBC$_2$	$1/\langle$XMM$\rangle$	$\langle$LMP$\rangle$	$\langle$XMM$\rangle$	$1/\langle$VVP$\rangle$
SBC$_3$	$\langle$VXM$\rangle$	$1/\langle$XMM$\rangle$	$\langle$LMP$\rangle$	$1/\langle$MPM$\rangle$
OBC$_4$	$1/\langle$XMM$\rangle$	$\langle$VVP$\rangle$	$\langle$MPM$\rangle$	$\langle$LMP$\rangle$

Specialists$_2$	TBC$_1$	HBC$_2$	SBC$_3$	OBC$_4$
TBC$_1$	$\langle$LMP$\rangle$	$\langle$XMM$\rangle$	$\langle$PFM$\rangle$	$\langle$XMM$\rangle$
HBC$_2$	$1/\langle$XMM$\rangle$	$\langle$LMP$\rangle$	$\langle$XMM$\rangle$	$1/\langle$VVP$\rangle$
SBC$_3$	$1/\langle$PFM$\rangle$	$1/\langle$XMM$\rangle$	$\langle$LMP$\rangle$	$1/\langle$MPM$\rangle$
OBC$_4$	$1/\langle$XMM$\rangle$	$\langle$VVP$\rangle$	$\langle$MPM$\rangle$	$\langle$LMP$\rangle$

Specialists$_3$	TBC$_1$	HBC$_2$	SBC$_3$	OBC$_4$
TBC$_1$	$\langle$LMP$\rangle$	$\langle$XMM$\rangle$	$1/\langle$VXM$\rangle$	$\langle$XMM$\rangle$
HBC$_2$	$1/\langle$XMM$\rangle$	$\langle$LMP$\rangle$	$\langle$XMV$\rangle$	$1/\langle$VVP$\rangle$
SBC$_3$	$\langle$VXM$\rangle$	$1/\langle$XMV$\rangle$	$\langle$LMP$\rangle$	$1/\langle$MPM$\rangle$
OBC$_4$	$1/\langle$XMM$\rangle$	$\langle$VVP$\rangle$	$\langle$MPM$\rangle$	$\langle$LMP$\rangle$

TABLE 2.4

Evaluation of Main Criteria Using TFNs by All Specialists

Specialists$_1$	TBC$_1$	HBC$_2$	SBC$_3$	OBC$_4$
TBC$_1$	$\langle 1, 1, 1 \rangle$	$\langle 4, 5, 6 \rangle$	$\langle 1/8, 1/7, 1/6 \rangle$	$\langle 4, 5, 6 \rangle$
HBC$_2$	$\langle 1/6, 1/5, 1/4 \rangle$	$\langle 1, 1, 1 \rangle$	$\langle 4, 5, 6 \rangle$	$\langle 1/9, 1/8, 1/7 \rangle$
SBC$_3$	$\langle 6, 7, 8 \rangle$	$\langle 1/6, 1/5, 1/4 \rangle$	$\langle 1, 1, 1 \rangle$	$\langle 1/4, 1/3, 1/2 \rangle$
OBC$_4$	$\langle 1/6, 1/5, 1/4 \rangle$	$\langle 7, 8, 9 \rangle$	$\langle 2, 3, 4 \rangle$	$\langle 1, 1, 1 \rangle$

Specialists$_2$	TBC$_1$	HBC$_2$	SBC$_:$	OBC$_4$
TBC$_1$	$\langle 1, 1, 1 \rangle$	$\langle 4, 5, 6 \rangle$	$\langle 8, 9, 10 \rangle$	$\langle 4, 5, 6 \rangle$
HBC$_2$	$\langle 1/6, 1/5, 1/4 \rangle$	$\langle 1, 1, 1 \rangle$	$\langle 4, 5, 6 \rangle$	$\langle 1/9, 1/8, 1/7 \rangle$
SBC$_3$	$\langle 1/10, 1/9, 1/8 \rangle$	$\langle 1/6, 1/5, 1/4 \rangle$	$\langle 1, 1, 1 \rangle$	$\langle 1/4, 1/3, 1/2 \rangle$
OBC$_4$	$\langle 1/6, 1/5, 1/4 \rangle$	$\langle 7, 8, 9 \rangle$	$\langle 2, 3, 4 \rangle$	$\langle 1, 1, 1 \rangle$

Specialists$_3$	TBC$_1$	HBC$_2$	SBC$_3$	OBC$_4$
TBC$_1$	$\langle 1, 1, 1 \rangle$	$\langle 4, 5, 6 \rangle$	$\langle 1/8, 1/7, 1/6 \rangle$	$\langle 4, 5, 6 \rangle$
HBC$_2$	$\langle 1/6, 1/5, 1/4 \rangle$	$\langle 1, 1, 1 \rangle$	$\langle 5, 6, 7 \rangle$	$\langle 1/9, 1/8, 1/7 \rangle$
SBC$_3$	$\langle 6, 7, 8 \rangle$	$\langle 1/7, 1/6, 1/5 \rangle$	$\langle 1, 1, 1 \rangle$	$\langle 1/4, 1/3, 1/2 \rangle$
OBC$_4$	$\langle 1/6, 1/5, 1/4 \rangle$	$\langle 7, 8, 9 \rangle$	$\langle 2, 3, 4 \rangle$	$\langle 1, 1, 1 \rangle$

TABLE 2.5

Final Weights of Main Criteria Using the AHP Technique by All Specialists

Specialists$_1$	$\left(\prod_{j-1}^{N} E_{ij}\right)^{1/n}$			Fuzzy Weight			Crisp Weight	Normalized Weight	Rank	C.R.	Final Weight
TBC$_1$	1.189	1.375	1.566	0.239	0.337	0.428	0.335	0.325	2		0.319
HBC$_2$	0.522	0.595	0.670	0.105	0.146	0.183	0.145	0.140	4		0.143
SBC$_3$	0.707	0.628	1.000	0.142	0.154	0.274	0.190	0.184	3	≤ 0.1	0.186
OBC$_4$	1.237	1.480	1.732	0.249	0.363	0.474	0.362	0.351	1		0.352

Specialists$_2$	$\left(\prod_{j-1}^{N} E_{ij}\right)^{1/n}$			Fuzzy Weight			Crisp Weight	Normalized Weight	Rank	C.R.	Final Weight
TBC$_1$	1.125	1.291	1.456	0.229	0.320	0.400	0.316	0.307	2		0.319
HBC$_2$	0.522	0.595	0.670	0.106	0.147	0.184	0.146	0.142	4		0.143
SBC$_3$	0.760	0.669	1.057	0.155	0.166	0.290	0.204	0.198	3	≤ 0.1	0.186
OBC$_4$	1.237	1.480	1.732	0.252	0.367	0.475	0.365	0.354	1		0.352

Specialists$_3$	$\left(\prod_{j-1}^{N} E_{ij}\right)^{1/n}$			Fuzzy Weight			Crisp Weight	Normalized Weight	Rank	C.R.	Final Weight
TBC$_1$	1.189	1.375	1.566	0.241	0.337	0.428	0.335	0.325	2		0.319
HBC$_2$	0.552	0.622	0.696	0.112	0.153	0.190	0.152	0.147	4		0.143
SBC$_3$	0.681	0.600	0.946	0.138	0.147	0.259	0.181	0.176	3	≤ 0.1	0.186
OBC$_4$	1.237	1.480	1.732	0.250	0.363	0.473	0.362	0.352	1		0.352

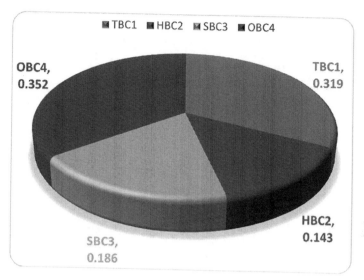

FIGURE 2.3
Final weights of main criteria.

Step 7: The fuzzy weight of each criterion has been computed by applying Eq. (2.4) as exhibited in Table 2.5. Also, the fuzzy weights of all criteria have been normalized by the sum of the fuzzy weight as exhibited in Table 2.5. In this regard, the fuzzy weights are converted to the crisp values by applying the CoA technique as in Eq. (2.5) as shown in Table 2.5.

Step 8: The CR for each matrix created by each specialist has been checked by applying Eq. (2.6) as shown in Table 2.5.

Step 9: The final weights for the main criteria by three specialists were aggregated by using the OWA operator as presented in Table 2.5 and Figure 2.3.

Step 10: The previous steps (5–9) are applied to the technology criterion's sub-criteria, and the results are mentioned in Tables 2.6–2.8. Also, the final weights of the technology criterion's sub-criteria are charted in Figure 2.4.

Step 11: The previous steps (5–9) are applied to the human criterion's sub-criteria, and the results are mentioned in Tables 2.9–2.11. Also, the final weights of the human criterion's sub-criteria are charted in Figure 2.5.

Step 12: The previous steps (5–9) are applied to the system criterion's sub-criteria, and the results are mentioned in Tables 2.12–2.14. Also, the final weights of the system criterion's sub-criteria are charted in Figure 2.6.

TABLE 2.6

Evaluation of the Technology Criterion's Sub-Criteria Using Linguistic Terms by All Specialists

Specialists$_1$	HTC$_{1\_1}$	STC$_{1\_2}$	NSC$_{1\_3}$
HTC$_{1\_1}$	$\langle$LMP$\rangle$	$\langle$XMM$\rangle$	$1/\langle$EMP$\rangle$
STC$_{1\_2}$	$1/$XMM	$\langle$LMP$\rangle$	$\langle$VVP$\rangle$
NSC$_{1\_3}$	$\langle$EMP$\rangle$	$1/\langle$VVP$\rangle$	$\langle$LMP$\rangle$
Specialists$_2$	**HTC$_{1\_1}$**	**STC$_{1\_2}$**	**NSC$_{1\_:}$**
HTC$_{1\_1}$	$\langle$LMP$\rangle$	$\langle$MPM$\rangle$	$1/$XMM
STC$_{1\_2}$	$1/\langle$MPM$\rangle$	$\langle$LMP$\rangle$	$\langle$VXM$\rangle$
NSC$_{1\_3}$	$\langle$XMM$\rangle$	$1/\langle$VXM$\rangle$	$\langle$LMP$\rangle$
Specialists$_3$	**HTC$_{1\_1}$**	**STC$_{1\_2}$**	**NSC$_{1\_3}$**
HTC$_{1\_1}$	$\langle$LMP$\rangle$	$1/\langle$XMM$\rangle$	$\langle$VVP$\rangle$
STC$_{1\_2}$	$\langle$XMM$\rangle$	$\langle$LMP$\rangle$	$1/\langle$VXM$\rangle$
NSC$_{1\_3}$	$1/\langle$VVP$\rangle$	$\langle$VXM$\rangle$	$\langle$LMP$\rangle$

TABLE 2.7

Evaluation of the Technology Criterion's Sub-Criteria Using TFNs by All Specialists

Specialists$_1$	HTC$_{1\_1}$	STC$_{1\_2}$	NSC$_{1\_3}$
HTC$_{1\_1}$	$\langle 1, 1, 1 \rangle$	$\langle 4, 5, 6 \rangle$	$\langle 1/3, 1/2, 1 \rangle$
STC$_{1\_2}$	$\langle 1/6, 1/5, 1/4 \rangle$	$\langle 1, 1, 1 \rangle$	$\langle 7, 8, 9 \rangle$
NSC$_{1\_3}$	$\langle 1, 2, 3 \rangle$	$\langle 1/9, 1/8, 1/7 \rangle$	$\langle 1, 1, 1 \rangle$
Specialists$_2$	**HTC$_{1\_1}$**	**STC$_{1\_2}$**	**NSC$_{1\_3}$**
HTC$_{1\_1}$	$\langle 1, 1, 1 \rangle$	$\langle 2, 3, 4 \rangle$	$\langle 1/6, 1/5, 1/4 \rangle$
STC$_{1\_2}$	$\langle 1/4, 1/3, 1/2 \rangle$	$\langle 1, 1, 1 \rangle$	$\langle 6, 7, 8 \rangle$
NSC$_{1\_3}$	$\langle 4, 5, 6 \rangle$	$\langle 1/8, 1/7, 1/6 \rangle$	$\langle 1, 1, 1 \rangle$
Specialists$_3$	**HTC$_{1\_1}$**	**STC$_{1\_2}$**	**NSC$_{1\_3}$**
HTC$_{1\_1}$	$\langle 1, 1, 1 \rangle$	$\langle 1/6, 1/5, 1/4 \rangle$	$\langle 7, 8, 9 \rangle$
STC$_{1\_2}$	$\langle 4, 5, 6 \rangle$	$\langle 1, 1, 1 \rangle$	$\langle 1/8, 1/7, 1/6 \rangle$
NSC$_{1\_3}$	$\langle 1/9, 1/8, 1/7 \rangle$	$\langle 6, 7, 8 \rangle$	$\langle 1, 1, 1 \rangle$

TABLE 2.8

Final Weights of the Technology Criterion's Sub-Criteria Using the AHP Technique by All Specialists

Specialists$_1$	$\left(\prod_{j=1}^{N} E_{ij}\right)^{1/n}$			Fuzzy Weight			Crisp Weight	Normalized Weight	Rank	Final Weight
HTC$_{1\_1}$	1.100	1.357	1.816	0.284	0.430	0.689	0.468	0.445	1	0.370
STC$_{1\_2}$	1.053	1.169	1.310	0.271	0.370	0.497	0.380	0.361	2	0.364
NSC$_{1\_3}$	0.481	0.630	0.754	0.124	0.200	0.286	0.203	0.194	3	0.266

Specialists$_2$	$\left(\prod_{j=1}^{N} E_{ij}\right)^{1/n}$			Fuzzy Weight			Crisp Weight	Normalized Weight	Rank	Final Weight
HTC$_{1\_1}$	0.694	0.844	1.000	0.193	0.275	0.380	0.283	0.274	3	0.370
STC$_{1\_2}$	1.145	1.326	1.587	0.319	0.433	0.603	0.451	0.437	1	0.364
NSC$_{1\_3}$	0.794	0.894	1.001	0.221	0.292	0.380	0.298	0.288	2	0.266

Specialists$_3$	$\left(\prod_{j=1}^{N} E_{ij}\right)^{1/n}$			Fuzzy Weight			Crisp Weight	Normalized Weight	Rank	Final Weight
HTC$_{1\_1}$	1.053	1.169	1.310	0.314	0.387	0.482	0.394	0.388	1	0.370
STC$_{1\_2}$	0.794	0.894	1.001	0.237	0.296	0.368	0.300	0.296	3	0.364
NSC$_{1\_3}$	0.873	0.957	1.046	0.260	0.317	0.384	0.320	0.316	2	0.266

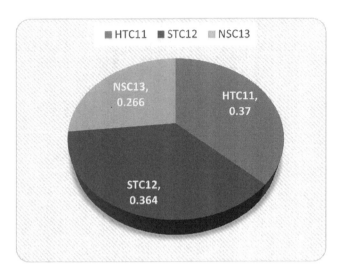

FIGURE 2.4
Weights of technology criterion's sub-criteria.

Step 13: The previous steps (5–9) are applied to the organization criterion's sub-criteria, and the results are mentioned in Tables 2.15–2.17. Also, the final weights of the organization criterion's sub-criteria are charted in Figure 2.7.

Step 14: Based on the final weights of the main criteria and the local weights of the sub-criteria, the global weights of the sub-criteria are calculated in Table 2.18 and Figure 2.8.

2.3.3 Ranking of the Smart Health Technologies with the Fuzzy VIKOR Method

Step 15: The decision matrices among the criteria identified and the smart health technologies designated by the specialists are generated using linguistic terms according to Eq. (2.7) as presented in Table 2.19.

Step 16: The combined decision matrix among the selected criteria and the smart health technologies designated is computed by applying Eq. (2.9) as presented in Table 2.20.

Step 17: The fuzzy combined decision matrix is defuzzified by applying the CoA method in Eq. (2.5) as presented in Table 2.21.

Step 18: The normalized decision matrix among the selected criteria and the smart health technologies is computed by applying Eq. (2.10) as exhibited in Table 2.22.

Step 19: The positive and negative ideal solutions are identified according to Eq. (2.11) as presented in Table 2.22.

TABLE 2.9

Evaluation of the Human Criterion's Sub-Criteria Using Linguistic Terms by All Specialists

Specialists[1]	PIC_{2_1}	HCC_{2_2}	PHC_{2_3}
PIC_{2_1}	$\langle LMP \rangle$	$\langle JVM \rangle$	$1/\langle MPM \rangle$
HCC_{2_2}	$1/\langle JVM \rangle$	$\langle LMP \rangle$	$\langle VXM \rangle$
PHC_{2_3}	$\langle MPM \rangle$	$1/\langle VXM \rangle$	$\langle LMP \rangle$
Specialists[2]	PIC_{2_1}	HCC_{2_2}	PHC_{2_3}
PIC_{2_1}	$\langle LMP \rangle$	$\langle XMM \rangle$	$1/\langle XMM \rangle$
HCC_{2_2}	$1/\langle XMM \rangle$	$\langle LMP \rangle$	$\langle PFM \rangle$
PHC_{2_3}	$\langle XMM \rangle$	$1/\langle PFM \rangle$	$\langle LMP \rangle$
Specialists[3]	PIC_{2_1}	HCC_{2_2}	PHC_{2_3}
PIC_{2_1}	$\langle LMP \rangle$	$\langle XMM \rangle$	$1/\langle VVP \rangle$
HCC_{2_2}	$1/\langle XMM \rangle$	$\langle LMP \rangle$	$\langle PFM \rangle$
PHC_{2_3}	$\langle VVP \rangle$	$1/\langle PFM \rangle$	$\langle LMP \rangle$

TABLE 2.10

Evaluation of the Human Criterion's Sub-Criteria Using TFNs by All Specialists

Specialists[1]	PIC_{2_1}	HCC_{2_2}	PHC_{2_3}
PIC_{2_1}	$\langle 1, 1, 1 \rangle$	$\langle 3, 4, 5 \rangle$	$\langle 1/4, 1/3, 1/2 \rangle$
HCC_{2_2}	$\langle 1/5, 1/4, 1/3 \rangle$	$\langle 1, 1, 1 \rangle$	$\langle 6, 7, 8 \rangle$
PHC_{2_3}	$\langle 2, 3, 4 \rangle$	$\langle 1/8, 1/7, 1/6 \rangle$	$\langle 1, 1, 1 \rangle$
Specialists[2]	PIC_{2_1}	HCC_{2_2}	PHC_{2_3}
PIC_{2_1}	$\langle 1, 1, 1 \rangle$	$\langle 4, 5, 6 \rangle$	$\langle 1/6, 1/5, 1/4 \rangle$
HCC_{2_2}	$\langle 1/6, 1/5, 1/4 \rangle$	$\langle 1, 1, 1 \rangle$	$\langle 8, 9, 10 \rangle$
PHC_{2_3}	$\langle 4, 5, 6 \rangle$	$\langle 1/10, 1/9, 1/8 \rangle$	$\langle 1, 1, 1 \rangle$
Specialists[3]	PIC_{2_1}	HCC_{2_2}	PHC_{2_3}
PIC_{2_1}	$\langle 1, 1, 1 \rangle$	$\langle 4, 5, 6 \rangle$	$\langle 1/9, 1/8, 1/7 \rangle$
HCC_{2_2}	$\langle 1/6, 1/5, 1/4 \rangle$	$\langle 1, 1, 1 \rangle$	$\langle 8, 9, 10 \rangle$
PHC_{2_3}	$\langle 7, 8, 9 \rangle$	$\langle 1/10, 1/9, 1/8 \rangle$	$\langle 1, 1, 1 \rangle$

TABLE 2.11

Final Weights of the Human Criterion's Sub-Criteria Using the AHP Technique by All Specialists

Specialists$_1$	$\left(\prod\limits_{j=1}^{N} E_{ij}\right)^{1/n}$			Fuzzy Weight			Crisp Weight	Normalized Weight	Rank	Final Weight
PIC$_{2\_1}$	0.909	1.100	1.357	0.251	0.360	0.522	0.377	0.364	2	0.325
HCC$_{2\_2}$	1.063	1.205	1.386	0.294	0.394	0.533	0.407	0.392	1	0.398
PHC$_{2\_3}$	0.630	0.754	0.874	0.174	0.247	0.336	0.252	0.243	3	0.277

Specialists$_2$	$\left(\prod\limits_{j=1}^{N} E_{ij}\right)^{1/n}$			Fuzzy Weight			Crisp Weight	Normalized Weight	Rank	Final Weight
PIC$_{2\_1}$	0.874	1.000	1.145	0.256	0.329	0.422	0.336	0.330	2	0.325
HCC$_{2\_2}$	1.101	1.216	1.357	0.323	0.400	0.500	0.408	0.401	1	0.398
PHC$_{2\_3}$	0.737	0.822	0.909	0.216	0.271	0.335	0.274	0.269	3	0.277

Specialists$_3$	$\left(\prod\limits_{j=1}^{N} E_{ij}\right)^{1/n}$			Fuzzy Weight			Crisp Weight	Normalized Weight	Rank	Final Weight
PIC$_{2\_1}$	0.763	0.855	0.950	0.228	0.282	0.345	0.285	0.281	3	0.325
HCC$_{2\_2}$	1.101	1.216	1.357	0.329	0.401	0.493	0.408	0.403	1	0.398
PHC$_{2\_3}$	0.888	0.961	1.040	0.265	0.317	0.378	0.320	0.316	2	0.277

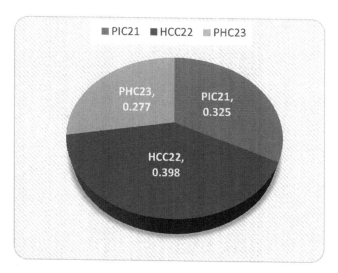

FIGURE 2.5

Weights of human criterion's sub-criteria.

TABLE 2.12

Evaluation of the System Criterion's Sub-Criteria Using Linguistic Terms by All Specialists

Specialists$_1$	USC$_{3\_1}$	ACC$_{3\_2}$	COC$_{3\_3}$
USC$_{3\_1}$	$\langle$LMP$\rangle$	$\langle$JVM$\rangle$	$\langle$EMP$\rangle$
ACC$_{3\_2}$	$1/\langle$JVM$\rangle$	$\langle$LMP$\rangle$	$\langle$VXM$\rangle$
COC$_{3\_3}$	$1/\langle$EMP$\rangle$	$1/\langle$VXM$\rangle$	$\langle$LMP$\rangle$
Specialists$_2$	**USC$_{3\_1}$**	**ACC$_{3\_2}$**	**COC$_{3\_3}$**
USC$_{3\_1}$	$\langle$LMP$\rangle$	$\langle$MPM$\rangle$	$\langle$EMP$\rangle$
ACC$_{3\_2}$	$1/\langle$MPM$\rangle$	$\langle$LMP$\rangle$	$\langle$VXM$\rangle$
COC$_{3\_3}$	$1/\langle$EMP$\rangle$	$1/\langle$VXM$\rangle$	$\langle$LMP$\rangle$
Specialists$_3$	**USC$_{3\_1}$**	**ACC$_{3\_2}$**	**COC$_{3\_3}$**
USC$_{3\_1}$	$\langle$LMP$\rangle$	$\langle$MPM$\rangle$	$\langle$EMP$\rangle$
ACC$_{3\_2}$	$1/\langle$MPM$\rangle$	$\langle$LMP$\rangle$	$\langle$PFM$\rangle$
COC$_{3\_3}$	$1/\langle$EMP$\rangle$	$1/\langle$PFM$\rangle$	$\langle$LMP$\rangle$

TABLE 2.13

Evaluation of the System Criterion's Sub-Criteria Using TFNs by All Specialists

Specialists$_1$	USC$_{3\_1}$	ACC$_{3\_2}$	COC$_{3\_3}$
USC$_{3\_1}$	$\langle 1, 1, 1 \rangle$	$\langle 3, 4, 5 \rangle$	$\langle 1, 2, 3 \rangle$
ACC$_{3\_2}$	$\langle 1/5, 1/4, 1/3 \rangle$	$\langle 1, 1, 1 \rangle$	$\langle 6, 7, 8 \rangle$
COC$_{3\_3}$	$\langle 1/3, 1/1, 1/1 \rangle$	$\langle 1/8, 1/7, 1/6 \rangle$	$\langle 1, 1, 1 \rangle$
Specialists$_2$	**USC$_{3\_1}$**	**ACC$_{3\_2}$**	**COC$_{3\_3}$**
USC$_{3\_1}$	$\langle 1, 1, 1 \rangle$	$\langle 2, 3, 4 \rangle$	$\langle 1, 2, 3 \rangle$
ACC$_{3\_2}$	$\langle 1/4, 1/3, 1/2 \rangle$	$\langle 1, 1, 1 \rangle$	$\langle 6, 7, 8 \rangle$
COC$_{3\_3}$	$\langle 1/3, 1/1, 1/1 \rangle$	$\langle 1/8, 1/7, 1/6 \rangle$	$\langle 1, 1, 1 \rangle$
Specialists$_3$	**USC$_{3\_1}$**	**ACC$_{3\_2}$**	**COC$_{3\_3}$**
USC$_{3\_1}$	$\langle 1, 1, 1 \rangle$	$\langle 2, 3, 4 \rangle$	$\langle 1, 2, 3 \rangle$
ACC$_{3\_2}$	$\langle 1/4, 1/3, 1/2 \rangle$	$\langle 1, 1, 1 \rangle$	$\langle 8, 9, 10 \rangle$
COC$_{3\_3}$	$\langle 1/3, 1/1, 1/1 \rangle$	$\langle 1/10, 1/9, 1/8 \rangle$	$\langle 1, 1, 1 \rangle$

Step 20: The group utility S_j and individual regret values R_j are computed by applying Eq. (2.12) and Eq. (2.13) as presented in Tables 2.23 and 2.24.

Step 21: The concordance index Q_j among the selected criteria and the smart health technologies is computed according to Eq. (2.14) as presented in Table 2.24.

Step 22: The smart health technologies are ranked in descending order according to the value Q_j as presented in Table 2.24 and Figure 2.9. Also, the two final conditions are checked according to Eqs. (2.15) and (2.16).

2.4 Results and Discussion

This part discusses the results obtained from applying the proposed model to the identified case study evaluating smart health technologies. At the outset, the weights of the six main criteria were determined, which were selected according to the opinions of the three specialists. The results show that the organization criterion is the highest in the ranking with a weight of 0.352, followed by the technology criterion with a weight of 0.319, while the human criterion is the last in the ranking with a weight of 0.143. After that, the weights of the technology criterion's sub-criteria were determined, which were identified according to the opinions of the three specialists. The findings show that the HTC$_{1\_1}$ is the highest in the

TABLE 2.14

Final Weights of the System Criterion's Sub-Criteria Using the AHP Technique by All Specialists

Specialists$_1$	$\left(\prod_{j=1}^{N} E_{ij}\right)^{1/n}$			Fuzzy Weight			Crisp Weight	Normalized Weight	Rank	Final Weight
USC$_{3\_1}$	1.442	1.999	2.464	0.328	0.552	0.864	0.581	0.546	1	0.514
ACC$_{3\_2}$	1.063	1.205	1.386	0.241	0.333	0.486	0.353	0.332	2	0.367
COC$_{3\_3}$	0.347	0.415	0.551	0.079	0.115	0.193	0.129	0.121	3	0.119

Specialists$_2$	$\left(\prod_{j=1}^{N} E_{ij}\right)^{1/n}$			Fuzzy Weight			Crisp Weight	Normalized Weight	Rank	Final Weight
USC$_{3\_1}$	1.260	1.816	2.288	0.285	0.511	0.831	0.542	0.504	1	0.514
ACC$_{3\_2}$	1.145	1.326	1.587	0.259	0.373	0.577	0.403	0.374	2	0.367
COC$_{3\_3}$	0.347	0.415	0.551	0.078	0.117	0.200	0.132	0.122	3	0.119

Specialists$_3$	$\left(\prod_{j=1}^{N} E_{ij}\right)^{1/n}$			Fuzzy Weight			Crisp Weight	Normalized Weight	Rank	Final Weight
USC$_{3\_1}$	1.260	1.816	2.288	0.280	0.499	0.805	0.528	0.493	1	0.514
ACC$_{3\_2}$	1.260	1.441	1.709	0.280	0.396	0.601	0.426	0.397	2	0.367
COC$_{3\_3}$	0.322	0.382	0.500	0.072	0.105	0.176	0.118	0.110	3	0.119

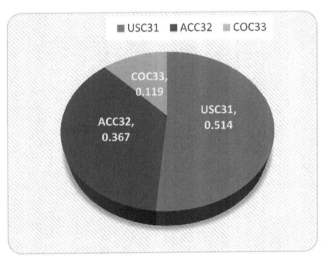

FIGURE 2.6

Weights of system criterion's sub-criteria.

TABLE 2.15

Evaluation of the Organization Criterion's Sub-Criteria Using Linguistic Terms by All Specialists

Specialists$_1$	PTC$_{4\_1}$	EUC$_{4\_2}$	LSC$_{4\_3}$
PTC$_{4\_1}$	$\langle$LMP$\rangle$	$\langle$EMP$\rangle$	$1/\langle$MPM$\rangle$
EUC$_{4\_2}$	$1/\langle$EMP$\rangle$	$\langle$LMP$\rangle$	$\langle$VXM$\rangle$
LSC$_{4\_3}$	$\langle$MPM$\rangle$	$1/\langle$VXM$\rangle$	$\langle$LMP$\rangle$
Specialists$_2$	**PTC$_{4\_1}$**	**EUC$_{4\_2}$**	**LSC$_{4\_3}$**
PTC$_{4\_1}$	$\langle$LMP$\rangle$	$\langle$XMM$\rangle$	
EUC$_{4\_2}$	$1/\langle$XMM$\rangle$	$\langle$LMP$\rangle$	$\langle$VXM$\rangle$
LSC$_{4\_3}$	$\langle$XMM$\rangle$	$1/\langle$VXM$\rangle$	$\langle$LMP$\rangle$
Specialists$_3$	**PTC$_{4\_1}$**	**EUC$_{4\_2}$**	**LSC$_{4\_3}$**
PTC$_{4\_1}$	$\langle$LMP$\rangle$	$\langle$XMM$\rangle$	$1/$XMV
EUC$_{4\_2}$	$1/\langle$XMM$\rangle$	$\langle$LMP$\rangle$	$\langle$PFM$\rangle$
LSC$_{4\_3}$	$\langle$XMV$\rangle$	$1/\langle$PFM$\rangle$	$\langle$LMP$\rangle$

TABLE 2.16

Evaluation of the Organization Criterion's Sub-Criteria Using TFNs by All Specialists

Specialists₁	PTC_{4_1}	EUC_{4_2}	LSC_{4_3}
PTC_{4_1}	$\langle 1, 1, 1 \rangle$	$\langle 1, 2, 3 \rangle$	$\langle 1/4, 1/3, 1/2 \rangle$
EUC_{4_2}	$\langle 1/3, 1/2, 1/1 \rangle$	$\langle 1, 1, 1 \rangle$	$\langle 6, 7, 8 \rangle$
LSC_{4_3}	$\langle 2, 3, 4 \rangle$	$\langle 1/8, 1/7, 1/6 \rangle$	$\langle 1, 1, 1 \rangle$
Specialists₂	PTC_{4_1}	EUC_{4_2}	LSC_{4_3}
PTC_{4_1}	$\langle 1, 1, 1 \rangle$	$\langle 4, 5, 6 \rangle$	$\langle 1/6, 1/5, 1/4 \rangle$
EUC_{4_2}	$\langle 1/6, 1/5, 1/4 \rangle$	$\langle 1, 1, 1 \rangle$	$\langle 6, 7, 8 \rangle$
LSC_{4_3}	$\langle 4, 5, 6 \rangle$	$\langle 1/8, 1/7, 1/6 \rangle$	$\langle 1, 1, 1 \rangle$
Specialists₃	PTC_{4_1}	EUC_{4_2}	LSC_{4_3}
PTC_{4_1}	$\langle 1, 1, 1 \rangle$	$\langle 4, 5, 6 \rangle$	$1/7, 1/6, 1/5$
EUC_{4_2}	$\langle 1/6, 1/5, 1/4 \rangle$	$\langle 1, 1, 1 \rangle$	$\langle 8, 9, 10 \rangle$
LSC_{4_3}	$\langle 5, 6, 7 \rangle$	$\langle 1/10, 1/9, 1/8 \rangle$	$\langle 1, 1, 1 \rangle$

ranking with a weight of 0.370, followed by the STC_{1_2} with a weight of 0.364, while the NSC_{1_3} is the last in the ranking with a weight of 0.266. Also, the weights of the human criterion's sub-criteria were determined, which were identified according to the opinions of the three specialists. The findings show that the HCC_{2_2} is the highest in the ranking with a weight of 0.398, followed by the PIC_{2_1} with a weight of 0.325, while the PHC_{2_3} is the last in the ranking with a weight of 0.277. In this regard, the weights of the system criterion's sub-criteria were determined, which were identified according to the opinions of the three specialists. The findings show that the USC_{3_1} is the maximum in the ranking with a weight of 0.514, followed by the ACC_{3_2} with a weight of 0.367, while the COC_{3_3} is the last in the ranking with a weight of 0.119. Eventually, the weights of the organization criterion's sub-criteria were determined, which were identified according to the opinions of the three specialists. The findings show that the EUC_{4_2} is the uppermost in the ranking with a weight of 0.422, followed by the PTC_{4_1} with a weight of 0.306, while the LSC_{4_3} is the last in the ranking with a weight of 0.272.

According to the global sub-criteria weights in Table 2.18, the EUC_{4_2} comes first with a weight of 0.148, followed by the HTC_{1_1} with a weight of 0.118, while the COC_{3_3} ranks last with a weight of 0.026.

Finally, the results of the ranking of the six selected alternatives (smart health technologies) are analyzed according to the fuzzy VIKOR method, as presented in Table 2.24. The results show that H_2 is the highest alternative in the ranking, followed by H_1, while H_4 is the last one.

TABLE 2.17

Final Weights of the Organization Criterion's Sub-Criteria Using the AHP Technique by All Specialists

Specialists$_1$	$\left(\prod\limits_{j-1}^{N} E_{ij}\right)^{1/n}$			Fuzzy Weight			Crisp Weight	Normalized Weight	Rank	Final Weight
PTC$_{4\_1}$	0.630	0.873	1.145	0.157	0.278	0.454	0.296	0.276	2	0.306
EUC$_{4\_2}$	1.259	1.518	1.999	0.313	0.482	0.793	0.530	0.493	1	0.422
LSC$_{4\_3}$	0.630	0.754	0.874	0.157	0.240	0.347	0.248	0.231	3	0.272

Specialists$_2$	$\left(\prod\limits_{j-1}^{N} E_{ij}\right)^{1/n}$			Fuzzy Weight			Crisp Weight	Normalized Weight	Rank	Final Weight
PTC$_{4\_1}$	0.874	1.000	1.145	0.257	0.332	0.429	0.339	0.333	2	0.306
EUC$_{4\_2}$	1.001	1.119	1.260	0.294	0.371	0.472	0.379	0.372	1	0.422
LSC$_{4\_3}$	0.794	0.894	1.001	0.233	0.297	0.375	0.302	0.296	3	0.272

Specialists$_3$	$\left(\prod\limits_{j-1}^{N} E_{ij}\right)^{1/n}$			Fuzzy Weight			Crisp Weight	Normalized Weight	Rank	Final Weight
PTC$_{4\_1}$	0.830	0.942	1.063	0.246	0.311	0.390	0.315	0.311	2	0.306
EUC$_{4\_2}$	1.101	1.216	1.357	0.326	0.401	0.498	0.408	0.402	1	0.422
LSC$_{4\_3}$	0.794	0.873	0.957	0.235	0.288	0.351	0.291	0.287	3	0.272

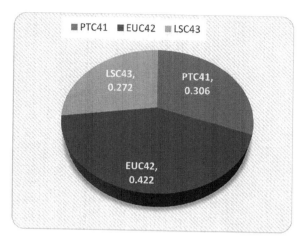

FIGURE 2.7
Weights of organization criterion's sub-criteria.

TABLE 2.18

Final Local and Global Weights of Criteria and Their Sub-Criteria Using the AHP Method

Criteria	Technology-Based Criterion TBC$_1$			Human-Based Criterion HBC$_2$		
weight	0.319			0.143		
Sub-criteria	HTC$_{1\_1}$	STC$_{1\_2}$	NSC$_{1\_3}$	PIC$_{2\_1}$	HCC$_{2\_2}$	PHC$_{2\_3}$
Local weights	0.370	0.364	0.266	0.325	0.398	0.277
Global weights	0.118	0.116	0.085	0.046	0.057	0.039

Criteria	System-Based Criterion SBC$_3$			Organization-Based Criterion OBC$_4$		
weight	0.186			0.352		
Sub-criteria	USC$_{3\_1}$	ACC$_{3\_2}$	COC$_{3\_3}$	PTC$_{4\_1}$	EUC$_{4\_2}$	LSC$_{4\_3}$
Local weights	0.514	0.367	0.119	0.306	0.422	0.272
Global weights	0.095	0.068	0.026	0.107	0.148	0.095

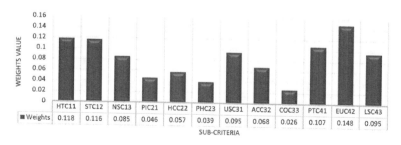

FIGURE 2.8
Final global weights of sub-criteria through the AHP method.

TABLE 2.19

Decision Matrices of Six Smart Health Technologies according to All Sub-Criteria Using Linguistic Terms

Specialists$_s$	HTC$_{1\_1}$	STC$_{1\_2}$	NSC$_{1\_3}$	PIC$_{2\_1}$	HCC$_{2\_2}$	PHC$_{2\_3}$
H$_1$	⟨EHH⟩⟨EHH⟩⟨EHH⟩	⟨MDE⟩⟨MDE⟩⟨MDE⟩	⟨MDE⟩⟨MDE⟩⟨MDE⟩	⟨HHH⟩⟨HHH⟩⟨HHH⟩	⟨MDE⟩⟨MDE⟩⟨MDE⟩	⟨HHH⟩⟨HHH⟩⟨HHH⟩
H$_2$	⟨XLL⟩⟨MDE⟩⟨MDE⟩	⟨EHH⟩⟨EHH⟩⟨EHH⟩	⟨EHH⟩⟨EHH⟩⟨EHH⟩	⟨EHH⟩⟨EHH⟩⟨EHH⟩	⟨EHH⟩⟨EHH⟩⟨EHH⟩	⟨HHH⟩⟨HHH⟩⟨HHH⟩
H$_3$	⟨XLL⟩⟨XLL⟩⟨XLL⟩	⟨XLL⟩⟨XLL⟩⟨XLL⟩	⟨EHH⟩⟨EHH⟩⟨EHH⟩	⟨HHH⟩⟨HHH⟩⟨HHH⟩	⟨EHH⟩⟨EHH⟩⟨EHH⟩	⟨EHH⟩⟨EHH⟩⟨EHH⟩
H$_4$	⟨XLL⟩⟨XLL⟩⟨XLL⟩	⟨HHH⟩⟨HHH⟩⟨HHH⟩	⟨MOE⟩⟨MOE⟩⟨MOE⟩	⟨MDE⟩⟨MDE⟩⟨MDE⟩	⟨HHH⟩⟨HHH⟩⟨HHH⟩	⟨MDE⟩⟨MDE⟩⟨MDE⟩
H$_5$	⟨EHH⟩⟨EHH⟩⟨EHH⟩	⟨HHH⟩⟨HHH⟩⟨HHH⟩	⟨LOO⟩⟨LOO⟩⟨LOO⟩	⟨XLL⟩⟨XLL⟩⟨XLL⟩	⟨MDE⟩⟨MDE⟩⟨MDE⟩	⟨MDE⟩⟨MDE⟩⟨MDE⟩
H$_6$	⟨MDE⟩⟨MDE⟩⟨MDE⟩	⟨LOO⟩⟨LOO⟩⟨LOO⟩	⟨MDE⟩⟨MDE⟩⟨MDE⟩	⟨HHH⟩⟨HHH⟩⟨HHH⟩	⟨MDE⟩⟨MDE⟩⟨MDE⟩	⟨HHH⟩⟨HHH⟩⟨HHH⟩

Specialists$_s$	USC$_{3\_1}$	ACC$_{3\_2}$	COC$_{3\_3}$	PTC$_{4\_1}$	EUC$_{4\_2}$	LSC$_{4\_3}$
H$_1$	⟨MDE⟩⟨MDE⟩⟨MDE⟩	⟨HHH⟩⟨HHH⟩⟨HHH⟩	⟨XLL⟩⟨XLL⟩⟨LOW⟩	⟨MDE⟩⟨MDE⟩⟨MDE⟩	⟨EHH⟩⟨EHH⟩⟨EHH⟩	⟨XLL⟩⟨XLL⟩⟨XLL⟩
H$_2$	⟨EHH⟩⟨EHH⟩⟨EHH⟩	⟨LOO⟩⟨LOO⟩⟨LOO⟩	⟨MDE⟩⟨MDE⟩⟨MDE⟩	⟨MDE⟩⟨MDE⟩⟨MDE⟩	⟨EHH⟩⟨EHH⟩⟨EHH⟩	⟨HHH⟩⟨HHH⟩⟨HHH⟩
H$_3$	⟨EHH⟩⟨EHH⟩⟨EHH⟩	⟨XLL⟩⟨XLL⟩⟨XLL⟩	⟨HHH⟩⟨HHH⟩⟨HHH⟩	⟨MDE⟩⟨MDE⟩⟨MDE⟩	⟨MDE⟩⟨MDE⟩⟨MDE⟩	⟨HHH⟩⟨HHH⟩⟨HHH⟩
H$_4$	⟨MDE⟩⟨MDE⟩⟨MDE⟩	⟨EHH⟩⟨EHH⟩⟨EHH⟩	⟨HHH⟩⟨HHH⟩⟨HHH⟩	⟨LOO⟩⟨LOO⟩⟨LOO⟩	⟨XLL⟩⟨XLL⟩⟨XLL⟩	⟨MDE⟩⟨MDE⟩⟨MDE⟩
H$_5$	⟨LOO⟩⟨LOO⟩⟨LOO⟩	⟨HHH⟩⟨HHH⟩⟨HHH⟩	⟨MDE⟩⟨MDE⟩⟨MDE⟩	⟨MDE⟩⟨MDE⟩⟨MDE⟩	⟨MDE⟩⟨MDE⟩⟨MDE⟩	⟨HHH⟩⟨HHH⟩⟨HHH⟩
H$_6$	⟨MDE⟩⟨MDE⟩⟨MDE⟩	⟨HHH⟩⟨HHH⟩⟨HHH⟩	⟨MDE⟩⟨MDE⟩⟨MDE⟩	⟨MDE⟩⟨MDE⟩⟨MDE⟩	⟨LOO⟩⟨LOO⟩⟨LOO⟩	⟨EHH⟩⟨EHH⟩⟨EHH⟩

TABLE 2.20

Combined Decision Matrix of Six Smart Health Technologies According to All Sub-Criteria Using TFNs

Specialists$_s$	HTC$_{1\_1}$	STC$_{1\_2}$	NSC$_{1\_3}$	PIC$_{2\_1}$	HCC$_{2\_2}$	PHC$_{2\_3}$
H$_1$	$\langle 7, 9, 11 \rangle$	$\langle 3, 5, 7 \rangle$	$\langle 3, 5, 7 \rangle$	$\langle 5, 7, 9 \rangle$	$\langle 3, 5, 7 \rangle$	$\langle 5, 7, 9 \rangle$
H$_2$	$\langle 1, 3.67, 5 \rangle$	$\langle 7, 9, 11 \rangle$	$\langle 7, 9, 11 \rangle$	$\langle 7, 9, 11 \rangle$	$\langle 7, 9, 11 \rangle$	$\langle 5, 7, 9 \rangle$
H$_3$	$\langle 1, 1, 3 \rangle$	$\langle 1, 1, 3 \rangle$	$\langle 7, 9, 11 \rangle$	$\langle 5, 7, 9 \rangle$	$\langle 7, 9, 11 \rangle$	$\langle 7, 9, 11 \rangle$
H$_4$	$\langle 1, 1, 3 \rangle$	$\langle 5, 7, 9 \rangle$	$\langle 3, 5, 7 \rangle$	$\langle 3, 5, 7 \rangle$	$\langle 5, 7, 9 \rangle$	$\langle 3, 5, 7 \rangle$
H$_5$	$\langle 7, 9, 11 \rangle$	$\langle 5, 7, 9 \rangle$	$\langle 1, 3, 5 \rangle$	$\langle 1, 1, 3 \rangle$	$\langle 3, 5, 7 \rangle$	$\langle 3, 5, 7 \rangle$
H$_6$	$\langle 3, 5, 7 \rangle$	$\langle 1, 3, 5 \rangle$	$\langle 3, 5, 7 \rangle$	$\langle 5, 7, 9 \rangle$	$\langle 1, 4.33, 7 \rangle$	$\langle 5, 7, 9 \rangle$

Specialists$_s$	USC$_{3\_1}$	ACC$_{3\_2}$	COC$_{3\_3}$	PTC$_{4\_1}$	EUC$_{4\_2}$	LSC$_{4\_3}$
H$_1$	$\langle 3, 5, 7 \rangle$	$\langle 5, 7, 9 \rangle$	$\langle 1, 1.67, 5 \rangle$	$\langle 3, 5, 7 \rangle$	$\langle 7, 9, 11 \rangle$	$\langle 1, 1, 3 \rangle$
H$_2$	$\langle 7, 9, 11 \rangle$	$\langle 1, 3, 5 \rangle$	$\langle 3, 5, 7 \rangle$	$\langle 3, 5, 7 \rangle$	$\langle 7, 9, 11 \rangle$	$\langle 5, 7, 9 \rangle$
H$_3$	$\langle 7, 9, 11 \rangle$	$\langle 1, 1, 3 \rangle$	$\langle 5, 7, 9 \rangle$	$\langle 3, 5, 7 \rangle$	$\langle 3, 5, 7 \rangle$	$\langle 5, 7, 9 \rangle$
H$_4$	$\langle 3, 5, 7 \rangle$	$\langle 7, 9, 11 \rangle$	$\langle 5, 7, 9 \rangle$	$\langle 1, 3, 5 \rangle$	$\langle 1, 1, 3 \rangle$	$\langle 3, 5, 7 \rangle$
H$_5$	$\langle 1, 3, 5 \rangle$	$\langle 5, 7, 9 \rangle$	$\langle 3, 5, 7 \rangle$	$\langle 3, 5, 7 \rangle$	$\langle 3, 5, 7 \rangle$	$\langle 5, 7, 9 \rangle$
H$_6$	$\langle 3, 5, 7 \rangle$	$\langle 5, 7, 9 \rangle$	$\langle 3, 5, 7 \rangle$	$\langle 3, 5, 7 \rangle$	$\langle 1, 3, 5 \rangle$	$\langle 7, 9, 11 \rangle$

2.5 Summary

- This chapter provides a comprehensive description of smart health technologies.
- This chapter reviews the importance and needs of assessing smart health technologies.
- This chapter presents the most important criteria used in evaluating smart and sustainable health technologies after a comprehensive analysis of a number of research articles.
- This chapter suggests an integrated fuzzy linguistic MCDM framework to assess smart health technologies. The fuzzy Analytic Hierarchy Process weights the criteria (AHP), and alternatives are ranked with the fuzzy VIseKriterijumska Optimizacija I Kompromisno Resenje (VIKOR) method.
- This chapter presents a real case study evaluating a number of smart health technologies around the world.

TABLE 2.21

Defuzzified Decision Matrix of Smart Health Technologies According to All Sub-Criteria Using the CoA Method

Specialists	HTC_{1_1}	STC_{1_2}	NSC_{1_3}	PIC_{2_1}	HCC_{2_2}	PHC_{2_3}	USC_{3_1}	ACC_{3_2}	COC_{3_3}	PTC_{4_1}	EUC_{4_2}	LSC_{4_3}
H_1	9.000	5.00	5.000	7.00	5.000	7.000	5.000	7.000	2.560	5.000	9.000	1.67
H_2	3.220	9.00	9.000	9.00	9.000	7.000	9.000	3.000	5.000	5.000	9.000	7.00
H_3	1.670	1.67	9.000	7.00	9.000	9.000	9.000	1.670	7.000	5.000	5.000	7.00
H_4	1.670	7.00	5.000	5.00	7.000	5.000	5.000	9.000	7.000	3.000	1.670	5.00
H_5	9.000	7.00	3.000	1.67	5.000	5.000	3.000	7.000	5.000	5.000	5.000	7.00
H_6	5.000	3.00	5.000	7.00	4.110	7.000	5.000	7.000	5.000	5.000	3.000	9.00

TABLE 2.22

Normalized Decision Matrix of Smart Health Technologies According to All Sub-Criteria

Specialists	HTC_{1_1}	STC_{1_2}	NSC_{1_3}	PIC_{2_1}	HCC_{2_2}	PHC_{2_3}	USC_{3_1}	ACC_{3_2}	COC_{3_3}	PTC_{4_1}	EUC_{4_2}	LSC_{4_3}
H_1	0.632	0.340	0.319	0.438	0.300	0.420	0.319	0.452	0.191	0.432	0.602	0.104
H_2	0.226	0.613	0.574	0.563	0.540	0.420	0.574	0.194	0.373	0.432	0.602	0.438
H_3	0.117	0.114	0.574	0.438	0.540	0.540	0.574	0.108	0.522	0.432	0.334	0.438
H_4	0.117	0.477	0.319	0.313	0.420	0.300	0.319	0.581	0.522	0.259	0.112	0.313
H_5	0.632	0.477	0.191	0.104	0.300	0.300	0.191	0.452	0.373	0.432	0.334	0.438
H_6	0.351	0.204	0.319	0.438	0.247	0.420	0.319	0.452	0.373	0.432	0.201	0.563
Best A_j^*	0.632	0.613	0.574	0.563	0.540	0.540	0.574	0.581	0.522	0.432	0.602	0.563
Worst A_j^-	0.117	0.114	0.191	0.104	0.247	0.300	0.191	0.108	0.191	0.259	0.112	0.104

TABLE 2.23

Decision Matrix for Calculating Group Utility and Individual Regret of Six Smart Health Technologies

Specialists$_s$	HTC$_{1\_1}$	STC$_{1\_2}$	NSC$_{1\_3}$	PIC$_{2\_1}$	HCC$_{2\_2}$	PHC$_{2\_3}$	USC$_{3\_1}$	ACC$_{3\_2}$	COC$_{3\_3}$	PTC$_{4\_1}$	EUC$_{4\_2}$	LSC$_{4\_3}$
H$_1$	0.000	0.063	0.057	0.013	0.047	0.020	0.063	0.019	0.026	0.000	0.000	0.095
H$_2$	0.093	0.000	0.000	0.000	0.000	0.020	0.000	0.056	0.012	0.000	0.000	0.026
H$_3$	0.118	0.116	0.000	0.013	0.000	0.000	0.000	0.068	0.000	0.000	0.081	0.026
H$_4$	0.118	0.032	0.057	0.025	0.023	0.039	0.063	0.000	0.000	0.107	0.148	0.052
H$_5$	0.000	0.032	0.085	0.046	0.047	0.039	0.095	0.019	0.012	0.000	0.081	0.026
H$_6$	0.064	0.095	0.057	0.013	0.057	0.020	0.063	0.019	0.012	0.000	0.121	0.000

TABLE 2.24

Calculating of S_j, R_j, and Q_j and Ranking of Alternatives

Alternatives	S_j	Rank (S_j)	R_j	Rank (R_j)	Q_j (v = 0.5)	Rank (Q_j)
H$_1$	0.4015	2	0.0950	2	0.2314	2
H$_2$	0.2058	1	0.0930	1	0.0000	1
H$_3$	0.4212	3	0.1180	4	0.4621	4
H$_4$	0.6639	6	0.1480	6	1.0000	6
H$_5$	0.4802	4	0.0950	3	0.3173	3
H$_6$	0.5198	5	0.1211	5	0.5984	5

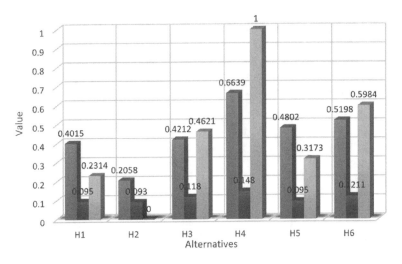

FIGURE 2.9
Final chart of S, R, and Q for each alternative.

2.6 Exercises

a. How do you define "smart health technologies"? Why is an evaluation of smart and sustainable health technology important?

b. What are the differences between VIKOR and AHP methods? Discuss their relative advantages while making a decision.

c. Discuss the features of smart health technology in terms of the characteristics and formation of smart healthcare.

d. What are the key steps to embedding fuzzy linguistics in an MCDM framework?

e. Discuss the differences between fuzzy VIKOR and fuzzy AHP methods.

References

Abdel-Basset, Mohamed, Abduallah Gamal, and Samir S. Teleb. 2022. "Intelligent Fuzzy Decision-making System of Afforestation in New Cities: A Case Study of the New Administrative Capital, Egypt." *Intelligent Systems with Applications* 14: 200085. https://doi.org/https://doi.org/10.1016/j.iswa.2022.200085.

Du, Yuan-Wei, and Xiao-Xue Li. 2021. "Hierarchical DEMATEL Method for Complex Systems." *Expert Systems with Applications* 167: 113871. https://doi.org/https://doi.org/10.1016/j.eswa.2020.113871.

Hosseini, Seyyed Mehdi, Mohammad Mahdi Paydar, and Mostafa Hajiaghaei-Keshteli. 2021. "Recovery Solutions for Ecotourism Centers during the Covid-19 Pandemic: Utilizing Fuzzy DEMATEL and Fuzzy VIKOR Methods." *Expert Systems with Applications* 185: 115594. https://doi.org/https://doi.org/10.1016/j.eswa.2021.115594.

Jandová, Vera, and Jana Talasová. 2013. "Weak Consistency : A New Approach to Consistency in the Saaty ' s Analytic Hierarchy." *Mathematica* 52 (2): 71–83.

Liu, Yan, Claudia M. Eckert, and Christopher Earl. 2020. "A Review of Fuzzy AHP Methods for Decision-Making with Subjective Judgements." *Expert Systems with Applications* 161: 113738. https://doi.org/https://doi.org/10.1016/j.eswa.2020.113738.

Opricovic, Serafim, and Gwo-Hshiung Tzeng. 2004. "Compromise Solution by MCDM Methods: A Comparative Analysis of VIKOR and TOPSIS." *European Journal of Operational Research* 156 (2): 445–55. https://doi.org/https://doi.org/10.1016/S0377-2217(03)00020-1.

Saaty, Thomas L. 2001. "*Decision Making with Dependence and Feedback: The Analytic Network Process : The Organization and Prioritization of Complexity,*" 370. http://books.google.com/books?id=MGpaAAAAYAAJ&pgis=1.

Solangi, Yasir Ahmed, Cheng Longsheng, and Syed Ahsan Ali Shah. 2021. "Assessing and Overcoming the Renewable Energy Barriers for Sustainable Development in Pakistan: An Integrated AHP and Fuzzy TOPSIS Approach." *Renewable Energy* 173: 209–22. https://doi.org/https://doi.org/10.1016/j.renene.2021.03.141.

Zadeh, Lotfi Asker. 1975. "The Concept of a Linguistic Variable and Its Application to Approximate Reasoning—I." *Information Sciences* 8 (3): 199–249. https://doi.org/https://doi.org/10.1016/0020-0255(75)90036-5.

3

An Intelligent Approach for Assessing Smart Disaster Response Systems

3.1 Introduction

Disaster management is one of the most significant fields of study since it directly affects the quality of human life. One of the most important foundations of disaster management is responding to catastrophes in a way consistent with the protection of residents' lives from their effects. Consequently, the study of disaster response systems is regarded as one of the essential issues that must be researched and improved. Failure to respond appropriately to natural disasters is detrimental to human and economic life. The number of persons impacted by catastrophes who do not get enough aid is enormous. As a result of the world's technical advancement, it was not possible to warn citizens of the impending disaster before it happened. Also, one of the most significant reasons for nation development retardation is the aftermath of catastrophes that have not been adequately addressed. Due to the escalation of natural catastrophes throughout time, academics are becoming more interested in ideas and innovations to avoid disasters and mitigate their negative impact on inhabitants' lives.

The Internet of Things (IoT) is one of the most influential parts of technology growth in the modern period since it has significantly contributed to several disciplines, including economics, healthcare, politics, industry, agriculture, and many more. Wireless Sensor Network (WSN) is one of the most commonly used technological solutions in the area of catastrophe detection; therefore, it has several socio-technical and economic flaws. WSNs aid specialized agencies (police, firefighters, and physicians) in responding to and managing catastrophes by gathering data from the disaster scene. Numerous technology technologies, such as social media, location-based systems, radiofrequency identification, and big data analytics (BDA), assist stakeholders in disaster management. The Internet of Things has proved its capacity to deliver more effective, intelligent, and adaptable disaster response solutions for varying circumstances.

DOI: 10.1201/9781003357681-3

In addition, it has become a very effective solution for decision-making difficulties and a support system for other disciplines, such as data mining science. Therefore, it is essential to focus on intelligent disaster response systems based on IoT capabilities.

3.2 Smart Disaster Response Systems

The destructive consequences of natural catastrophes prompted academics to assess response measures and create efficient techniques for maintaining the most effective response. Due to the recurrence of natural catastrophes, there is a growing interest in examining their consequences on the economic and social levels. This has led to an increased focus on investigating the identification of these catastrophes so that response centers may become more effective and lessen their impact on the state. A smart disaster response system, which is a crucial element in ensuring the safety of citizens, is one of the primary aspects of smart cities. Any city's catastrophe response systems must take into account a number of factors.

- The primary component of a disaster response system is comprised of localized communities that receive information from sensors and permit the exchange of this information to get aid.
- Disaster data management enables the study of disaster-related information and maintains data in the event of any distortion through central servers.

Unlike conventional disaster response systems, intelligent systems deal with calamities more effectively by effectively communicating the information supplied by the sensors to the reaction teams via more sophisticated communication methods. The key contribution of the intelligent disaster response system is the exchange of information in real time, which improves the timely reaction to the crisis. A smart disaster response system looks for appropriate items in real time based on the objectives of the communities that comprise the cooperation participants. After collecting data from local catastrophe communities, a centralized disaster management system conducts an exhaustive analysis of the data.

The smart disaster reaction system comprises a local manager, an object application, and a disaster-responsive social network. Initially, a disaster-responsive social network, such as an online social network (OSN), enables members to communicate anytime and anywhere. The second component of the smart disaster response system is the local manager, which is called a super node. This system consists of five components, as in Figure 3.1: the object manager, object data manager, community manager, overlay manager,

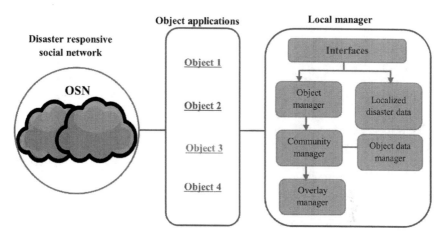

FIGURE 3.1
General scheme of the smart disaster response system architecture.

and localized disaster data processor. The object manager is accountable for managing the interaction of object data with the community manager and the object data manager through the online social network. Real-time administration of the data associated with objects such as locations by the object data manager. The community manager arranges the local community of responsive users who will get object data from the object data manager. Informed by the community manager, the overlay manager creates network configuration files for each member's account in order to facilitate communication between them. Based on big data analytics and cloud computing, the localized disaster data processor controls the catastrophe information of the items and analyses the disaster scenario in real time. The third part of the system is the object application, which includes both an overlay controller and a catastrophe communicator. The overlay controller is the component that is accountable for maintaining the overlay connections between members and the configuration files produced by the overlay manager in the local manager. At the same time, the disaster communicator uses various sharing mechanisms to facilitate communication between members and ensure that everyone has access to relevant information.

Due to the significance of intelligent disaster response systems, their performance must be assessed using criteria that quantify the usefulness of these systems in various circumstances. As with other decision-making difficulties, evaluating smart disaster response systems is one of the decision-making challenges that provide difficulty under unpredictable settings. In order to account for any ambiguity in the assessment process, this research intends to present an integrated framework for evaluating the performance of the smart disaster response system in an uncertain environment. Multi-criteria decision-making (MCDM) is used for the issue of performance assessment based on a set of criteria.

3.3 MCDM Methods for Decision-Making

This part presents a hybrid methodology for assessing smart disaster response systems. For the purpose of this task, we find the integration of the two methods, fuzzy Decision-Making Trial and Evaluation Laboratory (DEMATEL) and fuzzy Evaluation based on Distance from Average Solution (EDAS), which are very well-known approaches to prioritize the main dimensions and their sub-indicators and evaluate specific alternatives for an MCDM problem. Figure 3.2 shows the research approach guiding this study in which the fuzzy DEMATEL method will be used as an initial development level of the analysis, which is then completed with the help of experts to calculate the weights of the main dimensions and their sub-indicators for the pairwise comparison matrix. Next, the fuzzy EDAS method is used to evaluate smart disaster response systems based on selected criteria. We present a brief overview of the methods used in this study, as presented in the following parts.

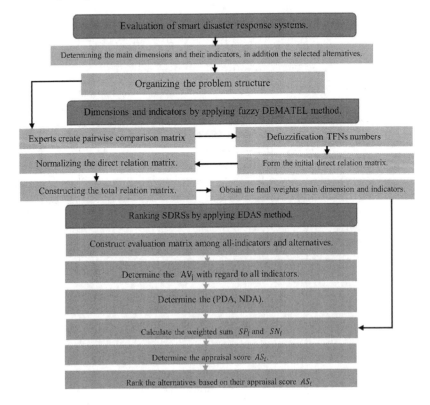

FIGURE 3.2
General scheme of the applied approach.

3.3.1 Fuzzy DEMATEL Method

In 1973, the Battelle Memorial Institute's Geneva Research Centre performed the DEMATEL procedure for the first time (Gabus and Fontela, 1972). DEMATEL is an expanded approach for constructing and evaluating a structural model in order to analyze the influence relationship between complicated criteria. In a hazy environment, however, making judgments based on complicated elements is difficult due to the difficulties in identifying them. The present work used the fuzzy DEMATEL approach for a more precise analysis. The original DEMATEL technique sought integrated solutions for the world's fragmented and adversarial civilizations. The DEMATEL technique has recently gained popularity in Japan due to its capacity to pragmatically depict intricate causal links (Chang, Chang, and Wu, 2011). The DEMATEL approach is specifically based on digraphs, which split involved components into cause-and-effect groups. Digraphs, or directed graphs, are more valuable than undirected graphs because they illustrate the directed interactions between sub-systems. The digraph may reflect a fundamental idea of the contextual relationship between components of a system, where the values indicate the magnitude of the effect (Wan et al., 2021). Therefore, The DEMATEL is able to translate the link between cause-and-effect variables into a system's understandable structural model. The DEMATEL is able to offer the most significant criterion that influences other criteria. The DEMATEL may simultaneously decrease the number of criteria for assessing the efficacy of a factor, allowing businesses to increase the effectiveness of certain factors based on the impact digraph map. The DEMATEL approach transforms the link between cause-and-effect variables into an intelligent system structure model (Nasrollahi et al., 2021).

3.3.2 Fuzzy EDAS Method

In 2015, Ghorabaee et al. introduced the EDAS approach, which is an acronym for the Evaluation based on Distance from Average Solution (Ghorabaee et al., 2015). The method's validity was evaluated by comparing it to various MCDM approaches, including Vise Kriterijumska Optimizacija I Kompromisno Resenje (VIKOR), Technique for Order Preference by Similarity to Ideal Solution (TOPSIS), Simple Additive Weighting (SAW), and Complex Proportional Assessment (COPRAS). According to this test, the EDAS approach is reliable and has shown positive results. This strategy is quite beneficial for comparing criteria. Compared to compromise-based MCDM approaches such as VIKOR and TOPSIS, it is advantageous in this method to compute the distance between ideal and rare solutions in order to pick the optimal choice (Karatop et al., 2021). In this chapter, EDAS was chosen due to its ease of use and reduced computing requirements, two of its most essential characteristics.

3.3.3 The Computational Steps of the Proposed Approach

Step 1: A group of experts is identified to assist the authors and share information on assessing smart disaster response systems. Certain considerations are made in selecting experts according to the problem and its degree of importance. Let $E = \{E_1, E_2, \ldots, E_K\}$ be a set of experts, where E_K denotes the kth expert, $k = 1, 2, \ldots, K$. K is the total number of experts.

Step 2: The problem is organized as a whole so that the main objective of the problem is shown. Also, the most important influential dimensions and sub-indicators are selected. Besides, alternatives that can enter the evaluation process are negotiated.

Step 3: Linguistic terms and corresponding appropriate fuzzy numbers are identified to prioritize key dimensions and sub-indicators, as presented in Table 3.1. Also, linguistic terms and corresponding suitable fuzzy numbers are identified to evaluate the selected alternatives, as exhibited in Table 3.2.

Step 4: Construct a pairwise comparison matrix (D) between the dimensions and itself by each expert as in Eq. (3.1) by using the semantic terms in Table 3.1 and then by using triangular fuzzy numbers (TFNs) as proved in Eq. (3.2).

TABLE 3.1

Semantic Variables for Weighting Key Dimensions and Their Sub-Indicators

Semantic Variables	Abridgments	TFN $\langle l_{ij}, m_{ij}, u_{ij} \rangle$
No effect	$\langle$NOE$\rangle$	$\langle 0.00, 0.00, 0.25 \rangle$
Very low effect	$\langle$VLE$\rangle$	$\langle 0.00, 0.25, 0.50 \rangle$
Low effect	$\langle$LOE$\rangle$	$\langle 0.25, 0.50, 0.75 \rangle$
High effect	$\langle$HIE$\rangle$	$\langle 0.50, 0.75, 1.00 \rangle$
Very high effect	$\langle$VHE$\rangle$	$\langle 0.75, 1.00, 1.00 \rangle$

TABLE 3.2

Semantic Variables for Ranking Alternatives

Semantic Variables	Abridgments	TFN $\langle l_{ij}, m_{ij}, u_{ij} \rangle$
Very poor	$\langle$VEP$\rangle$	$\langle 0.00, 0.00, 0.17 \rangle$
Poor	$\langle$POO$\rangle$	$\langle 0.00, 0.17, 0.33 \rangle$
Medium poor	$\langle$MEP$\rangle$	$\langle 0.17, 0.33, 0.50 \rangle$
Fair	$\langle$FAR$\rangle$	$\langle 0.33, 0.50, 0.67 \rangle$
Medium good	$\langle$MEG$\rangle$	$\langle 0.50, 0.67, 0.83 \rangle$
Good	$\langle$GOO$\rangle$	$\langle 0.67, 0.83, 1.00 \rangle$
Very good	$\langle$VEG$\rangle$	$\langle 0.83, 1.00, 1.00 \rangle$

$$D = \begin{array}{c} \\ D_1 \\ D_2 \\ \vdots \\ D_n \end{array} \begin{array}{cccc} D_1 & D_2 & \dots & D_n \\ \left[\begin{array}{cccc} * & x_{12} & \dots & x_{1i} \\ x_{21} & * & \dots & x_{2i} \\ x_{31} & x_{32} & * & \dots \\ x_{j1} & x_{j2} & x_{j3} & * \end{array} \right] \end{array} \qquad (3.1)$$

where (x_{ij}), $i, j = 1, 2 \dots n$, and x_{ij} is the assessment of the dimensions of the ith element $D_1, D_2, \dots, D_i$ regarding the jth element $D_1, D_2, \dots, D_j$. Also, the key diagonal of the matrix equals 1 such that x_{ij} equals 1.

$$D = \begin{array}{c} \\ D_1 \\ D_2 \\ \vdots \\ D_n \end{array} \begin{array}{cccc} D_1 & D_2 & \dots & D_n \\ \left[\begin{array}{cccc} * & \langle l_{12}, m_{12}, u_{12} \rangle & \dots & \langle l_{1i}, m_{1i}, u_{1i} \rangle \\ \langle l_{21}, m_{21}, u_{21} \rangle & * & \dots & \langle l_{2i}, m_{2i}, u_{2i} \rangle \\ \langle l_{31}, m_{31}, u_{31} \rangle & \langle l_{32}, m_{32}, u_{32} \rangle & * & \dots \\ \langle l_{j1}, m_{j1}, u_{j1} \rangle & \langle l_{j2}, m_{j2}, u_{j2} \rangle & \langle l_{j3}, m_{j3}, u_{j3} \rangle & * \end{array} \right] \end{array}$$

$$(3.2)$$

Let $t_{kij} = \left(t_{kij}^l, t_{kij}^m, t_{kij}^u \right)$ is the initial direct-influence information that D_i has on D_j by ^{Kt}h expert using semantic variables, where t_{kij}^l, t_{kij}^m, t_{kij}^u denote the lower limit, middle limit, and upper limit of the initial direct-influence information, respectively.

Step 5: Aggregate all decision matrices created by all experts into one matrix according to Eq. (3.3).

$$\tilde{T} = t_{1ij} \oplus t_{2ij} \oplus \dots \oplus t_{kij} / K \qquad (3.3)$$

Step 6: Defuzzify the fuzzy combined decision matrix into the crisp combined decision matrix by removing the fuzzy triangular numbers by applying the graded mean integration representation (GMIR) method (Zhao and Guo, 2015) as exhibited in Eq. (3.4). GMIR, which has the benefit of eliminating a zero in the denominator, is employed to create the defuzzification in this work.

$$x_{ij}^{def} = \frac{x_{ij}^l + 4 \times x_{ij}^m + x_{ij}^u}{6} \qquad (3.4)$$

Step 7: Construct the generalized direct relation matrix (G) for all dimensions by applying Eqs. (3.5) and (3.6).

$$q = \frac{1}{Max_{1 \le i \le n} \sum_{j=1}^{n} x_{ij}} \tag{3.5}$$

$$G = q \times D \tag{3.6}$$

where M is the preliminary combined direct relation matrix $n \times n$, and q is a group of dimensions that distinguishes by pairwise comparison to describe the significance of the dimensions.

Step 8: Compute the total relation matrix (T) for all dimensions by applying Eq. (3.7).

$$T = G \times (I - G)^{-1} \tag{3.7}$$

where I is the identity matrix, and the element t_{ij} symbolizes the unintended effects that element i has on j. Thus, T can designate the total relation matrix of each pair of system influences.

Step 9: Establish the influential relation map (IRM); the sum of rows and columns is obtained from the matrix T, expressed as R and C, respectively, in Eqs. (3.8) and (3.9). Then, we can compute the horizontal axis vector R+C, and the vertical axis vector R−C. the IRM will be obtained by computing the ordered pairs (R+C, R−C).

$T = \left[t_{ij} \right]_{n \times n}, i, j = 1, 2, \ldots, n.$

$$R = \left[\sum_{i=1}^{n} t_{ij} \right]_{1 \times n} \tag{3.8}$$

$$C = \left[\sum_{j=1}^{n} t_{ij} \right]_{n \times 1} \tag{3.9}$$

where R and C indicate the total rows and columns of the total-influence matrix, respectively. R and C indicate the total sum of rows and columns of the total-influence matrix i^{th} dimension, respectively.

Step 10: Compute the weights of the main dimensions $D_1, D_2, \ldots, D_n$ based on the R and C that resulting from expert opinions. Accordingly, R+C should be normalized. The value of R+C has been divided by the total of R+C values as exhibited in Eq. (3.10).

$$w = \frac{R + C}{\sum_{i=1}^{n} R + C} \tag{3.10}$$

Step 11: According to the steps for calculating the main dimensions, the weights of the sub-indicators are calculated. Based on the weights of the main dimensions and the weights of the sub-indicators, the final global weights used in the assessment process of smart disaster response systems are calculated.

Step 12: Make a decision matrix (M) among the dimensions identified and the smart disaster response systems designated by the experts as presented in Eqs. (3.11) and (3.12), using semantic terms and TFNs, respectively, as in Table 3.2.

$$
M = \left(y_{ij}\right)_{m \times n} =
\begin{array}{c}
 \\
SDRS_1 \\
SDRS_2 \\
\vdots \\
SDRS_m
\end{array}
\begin{array}{cccc}
D_1 & D_2 & \dots & D_n \\
\left[\begin{array}{cccc}
y_{11} & y_{12} & \dots & y_{1n} \\
y_{21} & y_{22} & \dots & y_{2n} \\
\dots & \dots & \dots & \dots \\
y_{m1} & y_{m2} & \dots & y_{mn}
\end{array}\right]
\end{array}
\tag{3.11}
$$

$$
M = \left(y_{ij}\right)_{m \times n} =
\begin{array}{c}
 \\
SDRS_1 \\
SDRS_2 \\
\vdots \\
SDRS_m
\end{array}
\begin{array}{cccc}
D_1 & D_2 & \dots & D_n \\
\left[\begin{array}{cccc}
\langle l_{11}, m_{11}, u_{11}\rangle & \langle l_{12}, m_{12}, u_{11}\rangle & \dots & l_{1n}, m_{1n}, u_{1n} \\
\langle l_{21}, m_{21}, u_{21}\rangle & \langle l_{22}, m_{22}, u_{22}\rangle & \dots & \langle l_{2n}, m_{2n}, u_{2n}\rangle \\
\dots & \dots & \dots & \dots \\
\langle l_{m1}, m_{m1}, u_{m1}\rangle & \langle l_{m2}, m_{m2}, u_{m2}\rangle & \dots & \langle l_{m2}, m_{m2}, u_{m2}\rangle
\end{array}\right]
\end{array}
$$

$$
\tag{3.12}
$$

where n is the numeral of dimensions, m is the number of the substitutes, and y_{ij} is the performance estimation of the ith substitute $SDRS_1$, $SDRS_2$, ..., $SDRS_n$ concerning the jth dimension $D_1, D_2, ..., D_m$.

Step 13: Aggregate all decision matrices created by all experts among the dimensions identified and the smart disaster response systems designated into one matrix by applying Eq. (3.3).

Step 14: Defuzzify the fuzzy combined decision matrix into the crisp combined decision matrix by removing the TFNs by applying the GMIR method as presented in Eq. (3.4).

Step 15: Compute the AV_j that associated with all sub-indicators according to the definition of the EDAS technique by applying Eq. (3.13).

$$
AV_j = \frac{\sum\limits_{i=1}^{m} y_{ij}}{m} \quad \text{where } m \text{ is the number of substitutes}
\tag{3.13}
$$

Step 16: Compute the positive distance from average (PDA) matrix, which requests to be computed according to the minimum and maximum values of the matrix as exhibited in Eqs. (3.14) and (3.15).

$$PDA_{ij} = \frac{Max\left(0,\left(y_{ij} - AV_j\right)\right)}{AV_j}, \quad \text{for the advantageous dimensions.} \quad (3.14)$$

$$PDA_{ij} = \frac{Max\left(0,\left(AV_j - y_{ij}\right)\right)}{AV_j}, \quad \text{for the non-advantageous dimensions} \quad (3.15)$$

Step 16: Compute the negative distance from average (NDA) matrix, which requests to be computed according to the minimum and maximum values of the matrix as exhibited in Eqs. (3.16) and (3.17).

$$NDA_{ij} = \frac{Max\left(0,\left(AV_j - y_{ij}\right)\right)}{AV_j}, \quad \text{for the advantageous dimensions.} \quad (3.16)$$

$$NDA_{ij} = \frac{Max\left(0,\left(y_{ij} - AV_j\right)\right)}{AV_j}, \quad \text{for the non-advantageous dimensions.} \quad (3.17)$$

Step 17: Compute the weighted sum of PDA (SP_i) by applying Eq. (3.18) and the weighted sum of NDA (SN_i) according to Eq. (3.19).

$$SP_i = \sum_{j=1}^{m} w_j \, PDA_{ij} \quad (3.18)$$

$$SN_i = \sum_{j=1}^{m} w_j \, NDA_{ij} \quad (3.19)$$

Step 18: Compute the standardized values of SP_i and SN_i by applying Eqs. (3.20) and (3.21), respectively.

$$NSP_i = \frac{SP_i}{max_i\left(SP_i\right)} \quad (3.20)$$

$$NSN_i = 1 - \frac{SN_i}{max_i\left(SN_i\right)} \quad (3.21)$$

Step 19: Compute the assessment score AS_i for all substitutes by applying Eq. (3.22). Then, rank the substitutes according to their assessment score AS_i, where the highest value means the best substitute.

$$AS_i = \frac{1}{2}(NSP_i + NSN_i), \quad \text{where } 0 \le AS_i \le 1 \tag{3.22}$$

3.4 An Illustrative Example

The performance evaluation of smart disaster response systems is used to illustrate the suggested paradigm. In the notion of smart cities, human existence has grown more intelligent as a result of vast technological development. One of the concerns of smart cities is a catastrophe response system. It has become vital to incorporate intelligence into disaster response systems to improve citizens' quality of life and achieve more effective disaster response systems. A smart disaster response system is identical to several intelligent systems that offer intelligent services. The performance of intelligent systems must be evaluated from several perspectives in order to evaluate the system's overall functioning and user satisfaction. In this chapter, the performance of the intelligent disaster response system will be assessed based on three dimensions: system usability, results and data management, and user activity. Accordingly, several smart disaster response systems were used in the assessment process, namely, $SDRS_1$, $SDRS_2$, $SDRS_3$, $SDRS_4$, $SDRS_5$, $SDRS_6$, and $SDRS_7$.

3.4.1 Model Implementation

Step 1: Initially, four experts related to smart systems and decision-making were selected to help and collaborate with the authors in completing the questionnaires and data compilation. Communication with experts was conducted several times, including offline through interviews and online via the Internet.

Step 2: The problem is organized in a hierarchical form between the objective, the main dimensions used, their sub-indicators, and the alternatives used, as presented in Figure 3.3.

Step 3: Semantic terms and corresponding TFNs appropriate to express ambiguity in the problem are identified. First, some variables were presented to determine the priorities and weights of the main dimensions and sub-indicators, as presented in Table 3.1. Secondly, some variables were presented to evaluate the smart disaster response systems selected, as exhibited in Table 3.2.

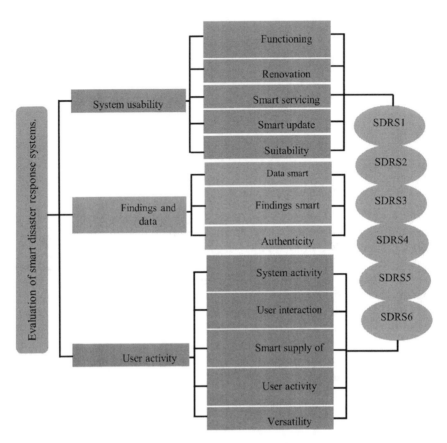

FIGURE 3.3
Hierarchy structure for smart disaster response system evaluation.

Step 4: Each expert constructed a pairwise comparison matrix between the main dimensions and itself according to Eq. (3.1) by using the semantic terms in Table 3.1 as presented in Table 3.3. Also, each expert constructed a pairwise comparison matrix between the main dimensions and itself according to Eq. (3.2) using TFNs in Table 3.1 as presented in Table 3.4.

TABLE 3.3

Evaluation of Main Dimensions Using Semantic Variables by All Experts

Expert$_s$	SUD$_1$	FDD$_2$	UAD$_3$
SUD$_1$	⟨NOE⟩⟨NOE⟩⟨NOE⟩⟨NOE⟩	⟨HIE⟩⟨HIE⟩⟨VLE⟩⟨HIE⟩	⟨VHE⟩⟨HIE⟩⟨VHE⟩⟨LOE⟩
FDD$_2$	⟨LOE⟩⟨VLE⟩⟨LOE⟩⟨LOE⟩	⟨NOE⟩⟨NOE⟩⟨NOE⟩⟨NOE⟩	⟨VLE⟩⟨VLE⟩⟨LOE⟩⟨VLE⟩
UAD$_3$	⟨HIE⟩⟨HIE⟩⟨HIE⟩⟨VHE⟩	⟨LOE⟩⟨LOE⟩⟨LOE⟩⟨LOE⟩	⟨NOE⟩⟨NOE⟩⟨NOE⟩⟨NOE⟩

TABLE 3.4

Evaluation of Main Dimensions Using TFNs by All Experts

Expert$_1$	SUD$_1$	FDD$_2$	UAD$_3$
SUD$_1$	$\langle 0.00, 0.00, 0.25 \rangle$	$\langle 0.50, 0.75, 1.00 \rangle$	$\langle 0.75, 1.00, 1.00 \rangle$
FDD$_2$	$\langle 0.25, 0.50, 0.75 \rangle$	$\langle 0.00, 0.00, 0.25 \rangle$	$\langle 0.00, 0.25, 0.50 \rangle$
UAD$_3$	$\langle 0.50, 0.75, 1.00 \rangle$	$\langle 0.25, 0.50, 0.75 \rangle$	$\langle 0.00, 0.00, 0.25 \rangle$
Expert$_2$	**SUD$_1$**	**FDD$_2$**	**UAD$_3$**
SUD$_1$	$\langle 0.00, 0.00, 0.25 \rangle$	$\langle 0.50, 0.75, 1.00 \rangle$	$\langle 0.50, 0.75, 1.00 \rangle$
FDD$_2$	$\langle 0.00, 0.25, 0.50 \rangle$	$\langle 0.00, 0.00, 0.25 \rangle$	$\langle 0.00, 0.25, 0.50 \rangle$
UAD$_3$	$\langle 0.50, 0.75, 1.00 \rangle$	$\langle 0.25, 0.50, 0.75 \rangle$	$\langle 0.00, 0.00, 0.25 \rangle$
Expert$_3$	**SUD$_1$**	**FDD$_2$**	**UAD$_3$**
SUD$_1$	$\langle 0.00, 0.00, 0.25 \rangle$	$\langle 0.00, 0.25, 0.50 \rangle$	$\langle 0.75, 1.00, 1.00 \rangle$
FDD$_2$	$\langle 0.25, 0.50, 0.75 \rangle$	$\langle 0.00, 0.00, 0.25 \rangle$	$\langle 0.25, 0.50, 0.75 \rangle$
UAD$_3$	$\langle 0.50, 0.75, 1.00 \rangle$	$\langle 0.25, 0.50, 0.75 \rangle$	$\langle 0.00, 0.00, 0.25 \rangle$
Expert$_4$	**SUD$_1$**	**FDD$_2$**	**UAD$_3$**
SUD$_1$	$\langle 0.00, 0.00, 0.25 \rangle$	$\langle 0.50, 0.75, 1.00 \rangle$	$\langle 0.25, 0.50, 0.75 \rangle$
FDD$_2$	$\langle 0.25, 0.50, 0.75 \rangle$	$\langle 0.00, 0.00, 0.25 \rangle$	$\langle 0.00, 0.25, 0.50 \rangle$
UAD$_3$	$\langle 0.75, 1.00, 1.00 \rangle$	$\langle 0.25, 0.50, 0.75 \rangle$	$\langle 0.00, 0.00, 0.25 \rangle$

TABLE 3.5

Aggregated Decision Matrix of All Evaluations to Main Dimensions Using TFNs

Expert$_s$	SUD$_1$	FDD$_2$	UAD$_3$
SUD$_1$	$\langle 0.00, 0.00, 0.25 \rangle$	$\langle 0.38, 0.63, 0.88 \rangle$	$\langle 0.56, 0.81, 0.94 \rangle$
FDD$_2$	$\langle 0.19, 0.44, 0.69 \rangle$	$\langle 0.00, 0.00, 0.25 \rangle$	$\langle 0.06, 0.31, 0.56 \rangle$
UAD$_3$	$\langle 0.56, 0.81, 1.00 \rangle$	$\langle 0.25, 0.50, 0.75 \rangle$	$\langle 0.00, 0.00, 0.25 \rangle$

Step 5: All expert decision matrices created by all experts were aggregated into one matrix by applying Eq. (3.3) as presented in Table 3.5. Then, defuzzify the fuzzy aggregated decision matrix into the crisp combined decision matrix by removing TFNs by applying the GMIR method is applied as shown in Eq. (3.4).

Step 6: The generalized direct relation matrix for main dimensions was developed by applying Eqs. (3.5) and (3.6) as exhibited in Table 3.6.

Step 7: The total relation matrix for main dimensions was computed according to Eq. (3.7), as exhibited in Table 3.7.

Step 8: The IRM of main dimensions was created based on the value of R and C, which was computed according to Eqs. (3.8) and (3.9) and presented in Table 3.7 and Figure 3.4. Also, the final weights of the main dimensions were computed by applying Eq. (3.10) as exhibited in Table 3.7 and Figure 3.5.

TABLE 3.6

Generalized Relation Matrix of Main Dimensions by All Experts

Expert$_s$	SUD$_1$	FDD$_2$	UAD$_3$
SUD$_1$	0.0285	0.4310	0.5405
FDD$_2$	0.2302	0.0285	0.2121
UAD$_3$	0.5473	0.3421	0.0285

TABLE 3.7

Total Relation Matrix of Main Dimensions by All Experts

Expert$_s$	SUD$_1$	FDD$_2$	UAD$_3$	R$_i$	C$_i$	R$_i$ + C$_i$	R$_i$ − C$_i$	Identity	Weight
SUD$_1$	1.3544	1.6311	1.6659	4.6514	3.9221	8.5736	0.7293	Cause	0.367
FDD$_2$	0.9181	0.7510	0.8930	2.5621	3.9177	6.4798	−1.3556	Effect	0.277
UAD$_3$	1.6497	1.5355	1.2823	4.4675	3.8412	8.3087	0.6262	Cause	0.356

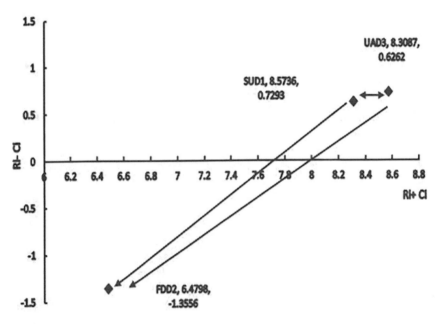

FIGURE 3.4

Causal and effectual illustration of key dimensions by all experts.

Step 9: A pairwise comparison matrix was constructed between the system usability dimension's sub-indicators and itself by each expert according to Eq. (3.1) by using the semantic terms in Table 3.1 as presented in Table 3.8. Also, a pairwise comparison matrix was constructed between

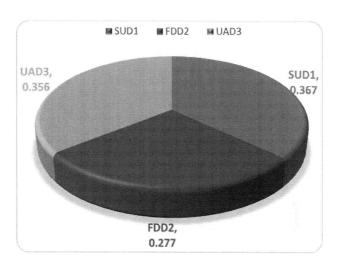

FIGURE 3.5
Final weights of key dimensions computed by fuzzy DEMATEL.

TABLE 3.8

Evaluation of System Usability Dimension's Sub-Indicators Using Semantic Variables by All Experts

Expert₄	FOD₁_₁	RED₁_₂	SSD₁_₃	SUD₁_₄	SBD₁_₅
FOD₁_₁	⟨NOE⟩	⟨HIE⟩	⟨VHE⟩	⟨VHE⟩	⟨LOE⟩
RED₁_₂	⟨HIE⟩	⟨NOE⟩	⟨VLE⟩	⟨LOE⟩	⟨HIE⟩
SSD₁_₃	⟨LOE⟩	⟨VHE⟩	⟨NOE⟩	⟨VHE⟩	VLE
SUD₁_₄	⟨NOE⟩	⟨VLE⟩	⟨HIE⟩	⟨NOE⟩	⟨HIE⟩
SBD₁_₅	⟨HIE⟩	⟨LOE⟩	⟨VHE⟩	⟨LOE⟩	⟨NOE⟩
Expert₂	**FOD₁_₁**	**RED₁_₂**	**SSD₁_₃**	**SUD₁_₄**	**SBD₁_₅**
FOD₁_₁	⟨NOE⟩	⟨HIE⟩	⟨VHE⟩	⟨VHE⟩	⟨LOE⟩
RED₁_₂	⟨HIE⟩	⟨NOE⟩	⟨HIE⟩	⟨LOE⟩	⟨HIE⟩
SSD₁_₃	⟨HIE⟩	⟨VLE⟩	⟨NOE⟩	⟨LOE⟩	⟨HIE⟩
SUD₁_₄	⟨NOE⟩	⟨VLE⟩	⟨HIE⟩	⟨NOE⟩	⟨HIE⟩
SBD₁_₅	⟨HIE⟩	⟨LOE⟩	⟨VHE⟩	⟨VLE⟩	⟨NOE⟩
Expert₃	**FOD₁_₁**	**RED₁_₂**	**SSD₁_₃**	**SUD₁_₄**	**SBD₁_₅**
FOD₁_₁	⟨NOE⟩	⟨HIE⟩	⟨VHE⟩	⟨VHE⟩	LOE
RED₁_₂	⟨HIE⟩	⟨NOE⟩	⟨HIE⟩	⟨VLE⟩	⟨HIE⟩
SSD₁_₃	⟨LOE⟩	⟨HIE⟩	⟨NOE⟩	⟨VHE⟩	⟨HIE⟩
SUD₁_₄	NOE	VLE	⟨HIE⟩	⟨NOE⟩	⟨HIE⟩
SBD₁_₅	⟨HIE⟩	⟨LOE⟩	VHE	⟨LOE⟩	⟨NOE⟩

(Continued)

TABLE 3.8 (*Continued*)

Evaluation of System Usability Dimension's Sub-Indicators Using Semantic Variables by All Experts

Expert$_4$	FOD$_{1\_1}$	RED$_{1\_2}$	SSD$_{1\_3}$	SUD$_{1\_4}$	SBD$_{1\_5}$
FOD$_{1\_1}$	⟨NOE⟩	⟨HIE⟩	⟨VHE⟩	⟨VHE⟩	⟨LOE⟩
RED$_{1\_2}$	⟨HIE⟩	⟨NOE⟩	VLE	⟨LOE⟩	⟨HIE⟩
SSD$_{1\_3}$	⟨LOE⟩	⟨VHE⟩	⟨NOE⟩	⟨VHE⟩	LOE
SUD$_{1\_4}$	⟨LOE⟩	⟨HIE⟩	⟨HIE⟩	⟨NOE⟩	⟨HIE⟩
SBD$_{1\_5}$	⟨HIE⟩	⟨LOE⟩	⟨VHE⟩	⟨VLE⟩	⟨NOE⟩

the system usability dimension's sub-indicators and itself by each expert according to Eq. (3.2) by using TFNs in Table 3.1 as presented in Table 3.9.

Step 10: All decision matrices created by all experts were aggregated into one matrix by applying Eq. (3.3) as presented in Table 3.10. Then, defuzzify the fuzzy aggregated decision matrix into the crisp combined decision matrix by removing TFNs by applying the GMIR method in Eq. (3.4).

Step 11: The generalized direct relation matrix for system usability dimension's sub-indicators was developed by applying Eqs. (3.5) and (3.6), as exhibited in Table 3.11.

Step 12: The total relation matrix for the system usability dimension's sub-indicators was computed according to Eq. (3.7), as exhibited in Table 3.12.

Step 13: The IRM of the system usability dimension's sub-indicators was created based on the value of R and C, which was computed according to Eqs. (3.8) and (3.9) and presented in Table 3.12 and Figure 3.6. Also, the final weights of the system usability dimension's sub-indicators were computed by applying Eq. (3.10) as exhibited in Table 3.12 and Figure 3.7.

Step 14: A pairwise comparison matrix was constructed between the findings and data management dimension's sub-indicators and itself by each expert according to Eq. (3.1) by using the semantic terms in Table 3.1 as presented in Table 3.13. Also, a pairwise comparison matrix was constructed between the findings and data management dimension's sub-indicators and itself by each expert according to Eq. (3.2) by using TFNs in Table 3.1 as presented in Table 3.14.

Step 15: All decision matrices created by all experts were aggregated into one matrix by applying Eq. (3.3) as presented in Table 3.15. Then, defuzzify the fuzzy aggregated decision matrix into the crisp combined decision matrix by removing TFNs by applying the GMIR method in Eq. (3.4).

Step 16: The generalized direct relation matrix for findings and data management dimension's sub-indicators was developed by applying Eqs. (3.5) and (3.6), as exhibited in Table 3.16.

TABLE 3.9

Evaluation of System Usability Dimension's Sub-Indicators Using TFNs by All Experts

Expert$_1$	FOD$_{1\_1}$	RED$_{1\_2}$	SSD$_{1\_3}$	SUD$_{1\_4}$	SBD$_{1\_5}$
FOD$_{1\_1}$	⟨0.00, 0.00, 0.25⟩	⟨0.50, 0.75, 1.00⟩	⟨0.75, 1.00, 1.00⟩	⟨0.75, 1.00, 1.00⟩	⟨0.25, 0.50, 0.75⟩
RED$_{1\_2}$	⟨0.50, 0.75, 1.00⟩	⟨0.00, 0.00, 0.25⟩	⟨0.00, 0.25, 0.50⟩	⟨0.25, 0.50, 0.75⟩	⟨0.50, 0.75, 1.00⟩
SSD$_{1\_3}$	⟨0.25, 0.50, 0.75⟩	⟨0.75, 1.00, 1.00⟩	⟨0.00, 0.00, 0.25⟩	⟨0.75, 1.00, 1.00⟩	⟨0.00, 0.25, 0.50⟩
SUD$_{1\_4}$	⟨0.00, 0.00, 0.25⟩	⟨0.00, 0.25, 0.50⟩	⟨0.50, 0.75, 1.00⟩	⟨0.00, 0.00, 0.25⟩	⟨0.50, 0.75, 1.00⟩
SBD$_{1\_5}$	⟨0.50, 0.75, 1.00⟩	⟨0.25, 0.50, 0.75⟩	⟨0.75, 1.00, 1.00⟩	⟨0.25, 0.50, 0.75⟩	⟨0.00, 0.00, 0.25⟩

Expert$_2$	FOD$_{1\_1}$	RED$_{1\_2}$	SSD$_{1\_3}$	SUD$_{1\_4}$	SBD$_{1\_5}$
FOD$_{1\_1}$	⟨0.00, 0.00, 0.25⟩	⟨0.50, 0.75, 1.00⟩	⟨0.75, 1.00, 1.00⟩	⟨0.75, 1.00, 1.00⟩	⟨0.25, 0.50, 0.75⟩
RED$_{1\_2}$	⟨0.50, 0.75, 1.00⟩	⟨0.00, 0.00, 0.25⟩	⟨0.50, 0.75, 1.00⟩	⟨0.25, 0.50, 0.75⟩	⟨0.50, 0.75, 1.00⟩
SSD$_{1\_3}$	⟨0.50, 0.75, 1.00⟩	⟨0.00, 0.25, 0.50⟩	⟨0.00, 0.00, 0.25⟩	⟨0.25, 0.50, 0.75⟩	⟨0.50, 0.75, 1.00⟩
SUD$_{1\_4}$	⟨0.00, 0.00, 0.25⟩	⟨0.00, 0.25, 0.50⟩	⟨0.50, 0.75, 1.00⟩	⟨0.00, 0.00, 0.25⟩	⟨0.50, 0.75, 1.00⟩
SBD$_{1\_5}$	⟨0.50, 0.75, 1.00⟩	⟨0.25, 0.50, 0.75⟩	⟨0.75, 1.00, 1.00⟩	⟨0.00, 0.25, 0.50⟩	⟨0.00, 0.00, 0.25⟩

Expert$_3$	FOD$_{1\_1}$	RED$_{1\_2}$	SSD$_{1\_3}$	SUD$_{1\_4}$	SBD$_{1\_5}$
FOD$_{1\_1}$	⟨0.00, 0.00, 0.25⟩	⟨0.50, 0.75, 1.00⟩	⟨0.75, 1.00, 1.00⟩	⟨0.75, 1.00, 1.00⟩	⟨0.25, 0.50, 0.75⟩
RED$_{1\_2}$	⟨0.50, 0.75, 1.00⟩	⟨0.00, 0.00, 0.25⟩	⟨0.50, 0.75, 1.00⟩	⟨0.00, 0.25, 0.50⟩	⟨0.50, 0.75, 1.00⟩
SSD$_{1\_3}$	⟨0.25, 0.50, 0.75⟩	⟨0.50, 0.75, 1.00⟩	⟨0.00, 0.00, 0.25⟩	⟨0.75, 1.00, 1.00⟩	⟨0.50, 0.75, 1.00⟩
SUD$_{1\_4}$	⟨0.00, 0.00, 0.25⟩	⟨0.00, 0.25, 0.50⟩	⟨0.50, 0.75, 1.00⟩	⟨0.00, 0.00, 0.25⟩	⟨0.50, 0.75, 1.00⟩
SBD$_{1\_5}$	⟨0.50, 0.75, 1.00⟩	⟨0.25, 0.50, 0.75⟩	⟨0.75, 1.00, 1.00⟩	⟨0.25, 0.50, 0.75⟩	⟨0.00, 0.00, 0.25⟩

Expert$_4$	FOD$_{1\_1}$	RED$_{1\_2}$	SSD$_{1\_3}$	SUD$_{1\_4}$	SBD$_{1\_5}$
FOD$_{1\_1}$	⟨0.00, 0.00, 0.25⟩	⟨0.50, 0.75, 1.00⟩	⟨0.75, 1.00, 1.00⟩	⟨0.75, 1.00, 1.00⟩	⟨0.25, 0.50, 0.75⟩
RED$_{1\_2}$	⟨0.50, 0.75, 1.00⟩	⟨0.00, 0.00, 0.25⟩	⟨0.00, 0.25, 0.50⟩	⟨0.25, 0.50, 0.75⟩	⟨0.50, 0.75, 1.00⟩
SSD$_{1\_3}$	⟨0.25, 0.50, 0.75⟩	⟨0.75, 1.00, 1.00⟩	⟨0.00, 0.00, 0.25⟩	⟨0.75, 1.00, 1.00⟩	⟨0.25, 0.50, 0.75⟩
SUD$_{1\_4}$	⟨0.25, 0.50, 0.75⟩	⟨0.50, 0.75, 1.00⟩	⟨0.50, 0.75, 1.00⟩	⟨0.00, 0.00, 0.25⟩	⟨0.50, 0.75, 1.00⟩
SBD$_{1\_5}$	⟨0.50, 0.75, 1.00⟩	⟨0.25, 0.50, 0.75⟩	⟨0.75, 1.00, 1.00⟩	⟨0.00, 0.25, 0.50⟩	⟨0.00, 0.00, 0.25⟩

TABLE 3.10

Aggregated Decision Matrix of All Evaluations to System Usability Dimension's Sub-Indicators Using TFNs

Expert$_1$	FOD$_{1\_1}$	RED$_{1\_2}$	SSD$_{1\_3}$	SUD$_{1\_4}$	SBD$_{1\_5}$
FOD$_{1\_1}$	⟨0.00, 0.00, 0.25⟩	⟨0.50, 0.75, 1.00⟩	⟨0.75, 1.00, 1.00⟩	⟨0.75, 1.00, 1.00⟩	⟨0.25, 0.50, 0.75⟩
RED$_{1\_2}$	⟨0.50, 0.75, 1.00⟩	⟨0.00, 0.00, 0.25⟩	⟨0.25, 0.50, 0.75⟩	⟨0.19, 0.44, 0.69⟩	⟨0.50, 0.75, 1.00⟩
SSD$_{1\_3}$	⟨0.31, 0.56, 0.81⟩	⟨0.50, 0.75, 0.88⟩	⟨0.00, 0.00, 0.25⟩	⟨0.63, 0.88, 0.94⟩	⟨0.31, 0.56, 0.81⟩
SUD$_{1\_4}$	⟨0.06, 0.13, 0.38⟩	⟨0.13, 0.38, 0.63⟩	⟨0.50, 0.75, 1.00⟩	⟨0.00, 0.00, 0.25⟩	⟨0.50, 0.75, 1.00⟩
SBD$_{1\_5}$	⟨0.50, 0.75, 1.00⟩	⟨0.25, 0.50, 0.75⟩	⟨0.75, 1.00, 1.00⟩	⟨0.13, 0.38, 0.63⟩	⟨0.00, 0.00, 0.25⟩

TABLE 3.11

Generalized Relation Matrix of System Usability Dimension's Sub-Indicators by All Experts

Expert$_1$	FOD$_{1\_1}$	RED$_{1\_2}$	SSD$_{1\_3}$	SUD$_{1\_4}$	SBD$_{1\_5}$
FOD$_{1\_1}$	0.012393	0.223101	0.285570	0.285570	0.193355
RED$_{1\_2}$	0.223101	0.012393	0.193355	0.130886	0.223101
SSD$_{1\_3}$	0.166582	0.217152	0.012393	0.252848	0.166582
SUD$_{1\_4}$	0.047595	0.113038	0.223101	0.012393	0.223101
SBD$_{1\_5}$	0.223101	0.193355	0.285570	0.113038	0.012393

TABLE 3.12

Total Relation Matrix of System Usability Dimension's Sub-Indicators by All Experts

Expert$_s$	FOD$_{1\_1}$	RED$_{1\_2}$	SSD$_{1\_3}$	SUD$_{1\_4}$	SBD$_{1\_5}$	R$_i$	C$_i$	R$_i$+C$_i$	R$_i$ − C$_i$	Identity	Weight
FOD$_{1\_1}$	0.708	0.964	1.205	1.044	0.991	4.912	3.544	8.455	1.368	Cause	0.204
RED$_{1\_2}$	0.780	0.669	0.986	0.800	0.877	4.111	3.940	8.051	0.171	Cause	0.195
SSD$_{1\_3}$	0.729	0.832	0.829	0.885	0.839	4.115	4.939	9.054	−0.825	effect	0.219
SUD$_{1\_4}$	0.519	0.619	0.830	0.541	0.729	3.238	4.094	7.331	−0.856	effect	0.177
SBD$_{1\_5}$	0.809	0.856	1.089	0.825	0.734	4.313	4.171	8.483	0.142	Cause	0.205

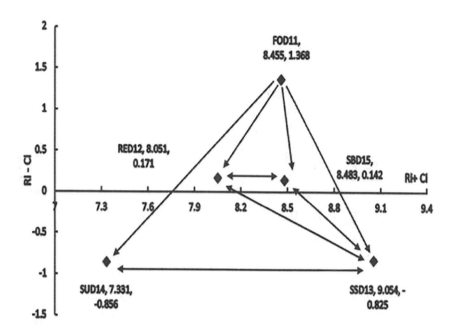

FIGURE 3.6
Causal and effectual illustration of system usability dimension's sub-indicators.

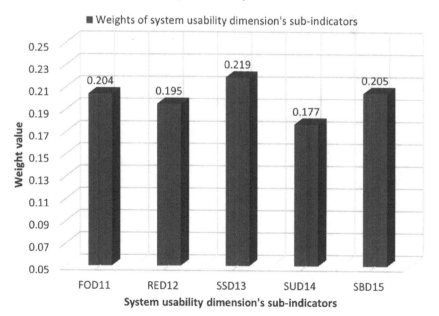

FIGURE 3.7
Final weights of system usability dimension's sub-indicators.

TABLE 3.13

Evaluation of Findings and Data Management Dimension's Sub-Indicators Using Semantic Variables

Expert$_s$	DSD$_{2\_1}$	FSD$_{2\_2}$	AUD$_{2\_3}$
DSD$_{2\_1}$	⟨NOE⟩⟨NOE⟩⟨NOE⟩⟨NOE⟩	⟨LOE⟩⟨VHE⟩⟨VLE⟩⟨HIE⟩	VHEHIEVHELOE
DSD$_{2\_1}$	⟨LOE⟩⟨VLE⟩⟨LOE⟩⟨LOE⟩	⟨NOE⟩⟨NOE⟩⟨NOE⟩⟨NOE⟩	⟨VLE⟩⟨LOE⟩⟨LOE⟩⟨VLE⟩
DSD$_{2\_1}$	⟨HIE⟩⟨HIE⟩⟨LOE⟩⟨VHE⟩	⟨HIE⟩⟨VLE⟩⟨LOE⟩⟨LOE⟩	⟨NOE⟩⟨NOE⟩⟨NOE⟩⟨NOE⟩

TABLE 3.14

Evaluation of Findings and Data Management Dimension's Sub-Indicators Using TFNs

Expert$_1$	DSD$_{2\_1}$	FSD$_{2\_2}$	AUD$_{2\_3}$
DSD$_{2\_1}$	⟨0.00, 0.00, 0.25⟩	⟨0.25, 0.50, 0.75⟩	⟨0.75, 1.00, 1.00⟩
FSD$_{2\_2}$	⟨0.25, 0.50, 0.75⟩	⟨0.00, 0.00, 0.25⟩	⟨0.00, 0.25, 0.50⟩
AUD$_{2\_3}$	⟨0.50, 0.75, 1.00⟩	⟨0.50, 0.75, 1.00⟩	⟨0.00, 0.00, 0.25⟩
Expert$_2$	**DSD$_{2\_1}$**	**FSD$_{2\_2}$**	**AUD$_{2\_3}$**
DSD$_{2\_1}$	⟨0.00, 0.00, 0.25⟩	⟨0.75, 1.00, 1.00⟩	⟨0.50, 0.75, 1.00⟩
FSD$_{2\_2}$	⟨0.00, 0.25, 0.50⟩	⟨0.00, 0.00, 0.25⟩	⟨0.25, 0.50, 0.75⟩
AUD$_{2\_3}$	⟨0.50, 0.75, 1.00⟩	⟨0.00, 0.25, 0.50⟩	⟨0.00, 0.00, 0.25⟩
Expert$_3$	**DSD$_{2\_1}$**	**FSD$_{2\_2}$**	**AUD$_{2\_3}$**
DSD$_{2\_1}$	⟨0.00, 0.00, 0.25⟩	⟨0.00, 0.25, 0.50⟩	⟨0.75, 1.00, 1.00⟩
FSD$_{2\_2}$	⟨0.25, 0.50, 0.75⟩	⟨0.00, 0.00, 0.25⟩	⟨0.25, 0.50, 0.75⟩
AUD$_{2\_3}$	⟨0.25, 0.50, 0.75⟩	⟨0.25, 0.50, 0.75⟩	⟨0.00, 0.00, 0.25⟩
Expert$_4$	**DSD$_{2\_1}$**	**FSD$_{2\_2}$**	**AUD$_{2\_3}$**
DSD$_{2\_1}$	⟨0.00, 0.00, 0.25⟩	⟨0.50, 0.75, 1.00⟩	⟨0.25, 0.50, 0.75⟩
FSD$_{2\_2}$	⟨0.25, 0.50, 0.75⟩	⟨0.00, 0.00, 0.25⟩	⟨0.00, 0.25, 0.50⟩
AUD$_{2\_3}$	⟨0.75, 1.00, 1.00⟩	⟨0.25, 0.50, 0.75⟩	⟨0.00, 0.00, 0.25⟩

TABLE 3.15

Aggregated Decision Matrix of All Evaluations to Findings and Data Management Dimension's Sub-Indicators Using TFNs

Expert$_s$	DSD$_{2\_1}$	FSD$_{2\_2}$	AUD$_{2\_3}$
DSD$_{2\_1}$	⟨0.00, 0.00, 0.25⟩	⟨0.38, 0.63, 0.81⟩	⟨0.56, 0.81, 0.94⟩
FSD$_{2\_2}$	⟨0.13, 0.44, 0.69⟩	⟨0.00, 0.00, 0.25⟩	⟨0.13, 0.38, 0.63⟩
AUD$_{2\_3}$	⟨0.50, 0.75, 0.94⟩	⟨0.25, 0.50, 0.75⟩	⟨0.00, 0.00, 0.25⟩

TABLE 3.16

Generalized Relation Matrix of Findings and Data Management Dimension's Sub-Indicators

Experts	DSD_{2_1}	FSD_{2_2}	AUD_{2_3}
DSD_{2_1}	0.0285	0.4242	0.5405
FSD_{2_2}	0.2942	0.0285	0.2600
AUD_{2_3}	0.5063	0.5131	0.0285

TABLE 3.17

Total Relation Matrix of Findings and Data Management Dimension's Sub-Indicators by All Experts

Experts	DSD_{2_1}	FSD_{2_2}	AUD_{2_3}	R_i	C_i	$R_i + C_i$	$R_i - C_i$	Identity	Weight
DSD_{2_1}	2.0832	2.6229	2.4172	7.1234	6.1169	13.2403	1.0065	Cause	0.347
FSD_{2_2}	1.5881	1.5497	1.5658	4.7037	6.8862	11.5898	−2.1825	Effect	0.303
AUD_{2_3}	2.4455	2.7135	2.1160	7.2751	6.0991	13.3742	1.1760	Cause	0.350

Step 17: The total relation matrix for findings and data management dimension's sub-indicators was computed according to Eq. (3.7), as exhibited in Table 3.17.

Step 18: The IRM of findings and data management dimension's sub-indicators was created based on the value of R and C, which was computed according to Eqs. (3.8) and (3.9) and presented in Table 3.17 and Figure 3.8. Also, the final weights of findings and data management dimension's sub-indicators were computed by applying Eq. (3.10) as exhibited in Table 3.17 and Figure 3.9.

Step 19: A pairwise comparison matrix was constructed between the user activity dimension's sub-indicators and itself by each expert according to Eq. (3.1) by using the semantic terms in Table 3.1 as presented in Table 3.18. Also, a pairwise comparison matrix was constructed between the user activity dimension's sub-indicators and itself by each expert according to Eq. (3.2) by using TFNs in Table 3.1 as presented in Table 3.19.

Step 20: All decision matrices created by all experts were aggregated into one matrix by applying Eq. (3.3) as presented in Table 3.20. Then, defuzzify the fuzzy aggregated decision matrix into the crisp combined decision matrix by removing TFNs by applying the GMIR method in Eq. (3.4).

Step 21: The generalized direct relation matrix for user activity dimension's sub-indicators was developed by applying Eqs. (3.5) and (3.6) as exhibited in Table 3.21.

Step 22: The total relation matrix for user activity dimension's sub-indicators was computed according to Eq. (3.7) as exhibited in Table 3.22.

Step 23: The IRM of user activity dimension's sub-indicators was created based on the value of R and C, which was computed according to

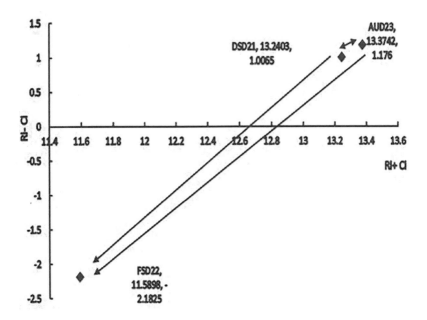

FIGURE 3.8
Causal and effectual illustration of findings and data management dimension's sub-indicators.

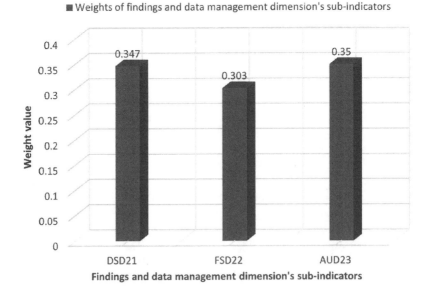

FIGURE 3.9
Final weights of findings and data management dimension's sub-indicators.

TABLE 3.18

Evaluation of User Activity Dimension's Sub-Indicators Using Semantic Variables by All Experts

Expert$_1$	SSD$_{3\_1}$	UID$_{3\_2}$	SRD$_{3\_3}$	UCD$_{3\_4}$	VED$_{3\_5}$
SSD$_{3\_1}$	⟨NOE⟩	⟨HIE⟩	⟨VHE⟩	⟨NOE⟩	⟨LOE⟩
UID$_{3\_2}$	⟨LOE⟩	⟨NOE⟩	⟨VLE⟩	⟨LOE⟩	⟨HIE⟩
SRD$_{3\_3}$	⟨LOE⟩	⟨VLE⟩	⟨NOE⟩	⟨VHE⟩	⟨VLE⟩
UCD$_{3\_4}$	⟨HIE⟩	⟨VLE⟩	⟨LOE⟩	⟨NOE⟩	⟨HIE⟩
VED$_{3\_5}$	⟨HIE⟩	⟨LOE⟩	⟨VHE⟩	⟨LOE⟩	⟨NOE⟩
Expert$_2$	**SSD$_{3\_1}$**	**UID$_{3\_2}$**	**SRD$_{3\_3}$**	**UCD$_{3\_4}$**	**VED$_{3\_5}$**
SSD$_{3\_1}$	⟨NOE⟩	⟨HIE⟩	⟨VHE⟩	⟨VLE⟩	⟨LOE⟩
UID$_{3\_2}$	⟨LOE⟩	⟨NOE⟩	⟨HIE⟩	⟨LOE⟩	⟨HIE⟩
SRD$_{3\_3}$	⟨HIE⟩	⟨VLE⟩	⟨NOE⟩	⟨LOE⟩	⟨HIE⟩
UCD$_{3\_4}$	⟨VLE⟩	⟨VLE⟩	⟨HIE⟩	⟨NOE⟩	⟨HIE⟩
VED$_{3\_5}$	⟨HIE⟩	⟨LOE⟩	⟨VHE⟩	⟨VLE⟩	⟨NOE⟩
Expert$_3$	**SSD$_{3\_1}$**	**UID$_{3\_2}$**	**SRD$_{3\_3}$**	**UCD$_{3\_4}$**	**VED$_{3\_5}$**
SSD$_{3\_1}$	⟨NOE⟩	⟨HIE⟩	⟨VHE⟩	⟨LOE⟩	⟨LOE⟩
UID$_{3\_2}$	⟨VHE⟩	⟨NOE⟩	⟨HIE⟩	⟨VLE⟩	⟨HIE⟩
SRD$_{3\_3}$	⟨LOE⟩	⟨VHE⟩	⟨NOE⟩	⟨VHE⟩	⟨HIE⟩
UCD$_{3\_4}$	⟨VLE⟩	⟨VLE⟩	⟨LOE⟩	⟨NOE⟩	⟨HIE⟩
VED$_{3\_5}$	⟨HIE⟩	⟨LOE⟩	⟨VHE⟩	⟨LOE⟩	⟨NOE⟩
Expert$_4$	**SSD$_{3\_1}$**	**UID$_{3\_2}$**	**SRD$_{3\_3}$**	**UCD$_{3\_4}$**	**VED$_{3\_5}$**
SSD$_{3\_1}$	⟨NOE⟩	⟨HIE⟩	⟨VHE⟩	⟨NOE⟩	⟨LOE⟩
UID$_{3\_2}$	⟨VHE⟩	⟨NOE⟩	⟨VLE⟩	⟨LOE⟩	⟨HIE⟩
SRD$_{3\_3}$	⟨LOE⟩	⟨VLE⟩	⟨NOE⟩	⟨VHE⟩	⟨LOE⟩
UCD$_{3\_4}$	⟨VLE⟩	⟨HIE⟩	⟨LOE⟩	⟨NOE⟩	⟨HIE⟩
VED$_{3\_5}$	⟨HIE⟩	⟨LOE⟩	⟨VHE⟩	⟨VLE⟩	⟨NOE⟩

Eqs. (3.8) and (3.9) and presented in Table 3.22 and Figure 3.10. Also, the final weights of the user activity dimension's sub-indicators were computed by applying Eq. (3.10) as exhibited in Table 3.22 and Figure 3.11.

Step 24: According to the steps for computing the main dimensions, the weights of the sub-indicators are computed. Based on the weights of the main dimensions and the weights of the sub-indicators, the final global weights used in the assessment process of smart disaster response systems are calculated and presented in Table 3.23.

Step 25: All decision matrices among all sub-indicators recognized and the smart disaster response systems designated by the experts were constructed by applying Eqs. (3.11) and (3.12), using semantic terms and TFNs, respectively, as in Table 3.2, and the results are formed in Table 3.24.

TABLE 3.19

Evaluation of User Activity Dimension's Sub-Indicators Using TFNs by All Experts

Expert$_1$	SSD$_{3\_1}$	UID$_{3\_2}$	SRD$_{3\_3}$	UCD$_{3\_4}$	VED$_{3\_5}$
SSD$_{3\_1}$	⟨0.00, 0.00, 0.25⟩	⟨0.50, 0.75, 1.00⟩	⟨0.75, 1.00, 1.00⟩	⟨0.00, 0.00, 0.25⟩	⟨0.25, 0.50, 0.75⟩
UID$_{3\_2}$	⟨0.25, 0.50, 0.75⟩	⟨0.00, 0.00, 0.25⟩	⟨0.00, 0.25, 0.50⟩	⟨0.25, 0.50, 0.75⟩	⟨0.50, 0.75, 1.00⟩
SRD$_{3\_3}$	⟨0.25, 0.50, 0.75⟩	⟨0.00, 0.25, 0.50⟩	⟨0.00, 0.00, 0.25⟩	⟨0.75, 1.00, 1.00⟩	⟨0.00, 0.25, 0.50⟩
UCD$_{3\_4}$	⟨0.50, 0.75, 1.00⟩	⟨0.00, 0.25, 0.50⟩	⟨0.25, 0.50, 0.75⟩	⟨0.00, 0.00, 0.25⟩	⟨0.50, 0.75, 1.00⟩
VED$_{3\_5}$	⟨0.50, 0.75, 1.00⟩	⟨0.25, 0.50, 0.75⟩	⟨0.75, 1.00, 1.00⟩	⟨0.25, 0.50, 0.75⟩	⟨0.00, 0.00, 0.25⟩

Expert$_2$	SSD$_{3\_1}$	UID$_{3\_2}$	SRD$_{3\_3}$	UCD$_{3\_4}$	VED$_{3\_5}$
SSD$_{3\_1}$	⟨0.00, 0.00, 0.25⟩	⟨0.50, 0.75, 1.00⟩	⟨0.75, 1.00, 1.00⟩	⟨0.00, 0.25, 0.50⟩	⟨0.25, 0.50, 0.75⟩
UID$_{3\_2}$	⟨0.25, 0.50, 0.75⟩	⟨0.00, 0.00, 0.25⟩	⟨0.50, 0.75, 1.00⟩	⟨0.25, 0.50, 0.75⟩	⟨0.50, 0.75, 1.00⟩
SRD$_{3\_3}$	⟨0.50, 0.75, 1.00⟩	⟨0.00, 0.25, 0.50⟩	⟨0.00, 0.00, 0.25⟩	⟨0.25, 0.50, 0.75⟩	⟨0.50, 0.75, 1.00⟩
UCD$_{3\_4}$	⟨0.00, 0.25, 0.50⟩	⟨0.00, 0.25, 0.50⟩	⟨0.50, 0.75, 1.00⟩	⟨0.00, 0.00, 0.25⟩	⟨0.50, 0.75, 1.00⟩
VED$_{3\_5}$	⟨0.50, 0.75, 1.00⟩	⟨0.25, 0.50, 0.75⟩	⟨0.75, 1.00, 1.00⟩	⟨0.00, 0.25, 0.50⟩	⟨0.00, 0.00, 0.25⟩

Expert$_3$	SSD$_{3\_1}$	UID$_{3\_2}$	SRD$_{3\_3}$	UCD$_{3\_4}$	VED$_{3\_5}$
SSD$_{3\_1}$	⟨0.00, 0.00, 0.25⟩	⟨0.50, 0.75, 1.00⟩	⟨0.75, 1.00, 1.00⟩	⟨0.75, 1.00, 1.00⟩	⟨0.25, 0.50, 0.75⟩
UID$_{3\_2}$	⟨0.75, 1.00, 1.00⟩	⟨0.00, 0.00, 0.25⟩	⟨0.50, 0.75, 1.00⟩	⟨0.00, 0.25, 0.50⟩	⟨0.50, 0.75, 1.00⟩
SRD$_{3\_3}$	⟨0.25, 0.50, 0.75⟩	⟨0.75, 1.00, 1.00⟩	⟨0.00, 0.00, 0.25⟩	⟨0.75, 1.00, 1.00⟩	⟨0.50, 0.75, 1.00⟩
UCD$_{3\_4}$	⟨0.00, 0.25, 0.50⟩	⟨0.00, 0.25, 0.50⟩	⟨0.25, 0.50, 0.75⟩	⟨0.00, 0.00, 0.25⟩	⟨0.50, 0.75, 1.00⟩
VED$_{3\_5}$	⟨0.50, 0.75, 1.00⟩	⟨0.25, 0.50, 0.75⟩	⟨0.75, 1.00, 1.00⟩	⟨0.25, 0.50, 0.75⟩	⟨0.00, 0.00, 0.25⟩

Expert$_4$	SSD$_{3\_1}$	UID$_{3\_2}$	SRD$_{3\_3}$	UCD$_{3\_4}$	VED$_{3\_5}$
SSD$_{3\_1}$	⟨0.00, 0.00, 0.25⟩	⟨0.50, 0.75, 1.00⟩	⟨0.75, 1.00, 1.00⟩	⟨0.00, 0.00, 0.25⟩	⟨0.25, 0.50, 0.75⟩
UID$_{3\_2}$	⟨0.75, 1.00, 1.00⟩	⟨0.00, 0.00, 0.25⟩	⟨0.00, 0.25, 0.50⟩	⟨0.25, 0.50, 0.75⟩	⟨0.50, 0.75, 1.00⟩
SRD$_{3\_3}$	⟨0.25, 0.50, 0.75⟩	⟨0.00, 0.25, 0.50⟩	⟨0.00, 0.00, 0.25⟩	⟨0.75, 1.00, 1.00⟩	⟨0.25, 0.50, 0.75⟩
UCD$_{3\_4}$	⟨0.00, 0.25, 0.50⟩	⟨0.50, 0.75, 1.00⟩	⟨0.25, 0.50, 0.75⟩	⟨0.00, 0.00, 0.25⟩	⟨0.50, 0.75, 1.00⟩
VED$_{3\_5}$	⟨0.50, 0.75, 1.00⟩	⟨0.25, 0.50, 0.75⟩	⟨0.75, 1.00, 1.00⟩	⟨0.00, 0.25, 0.50⟩	⟨0.00, 0.00, 0.25⟩

TABLE 3.20

Aggregated Decision Matrix of All Evaluations to User Activity Dimension's Sub-Indicators Using TFNs

Expert$_1$	SSD$_{3\_1}$	UID$_{3\_2}$	SRD$_{3\_3}$	UCD$_{3\_4}$	VED$_{3\_5}$
SSD$_{3\_1}$	⟨0.00, 0.00, 0.25⟩	⟨0.50, 0.75, 1.00⟩	⟨0.75, 1.00, 1.00⟩	⟨0.19, 0.31, 0.50⟩	⟨0.25, 0.50, 0.75⟩
UID$_{3\_2}$	⟨0.50, 0.75, 0.88⟩	⟨0.00, 0.00, 0.25⟩	⟨0.25, 0.50, 0.75⟩	⟨0.19, 0.44, 0.69⟩	⟨0.50, 0.75, 1.00⟩
SRD$_{3\_3}$	⟨0.31, 0.56, 0.81⟩	⟨0.19, 0.44, 0.63⟩	⟨0.00, 0.00, 0.25⟩	⟨0.63, 0.88, 0.94⟩	⟨0.31, 0.56, 0.81⟩
UCD$_{3\_4}$	⟨0.13, 0.38, 0.63⟩	⟨0.13, 0.38, 0.63⟩	⟨0.31, 0.56, 0.81⟩	⟨0.00, 0.00, 0.25⟩	⟨0.50, 0.75, 1.00⟩
VED$_{3\_5}$	⟨0.50, 0.75, 1.00⟩	⟨0.25, 0.50, 0.75⟩	⟨0.75, 1.00, 1.00⟩	⟨0.13, 0.38, 0.63⟩	⟨0.00, 0.00, 0.25⟩

TABLE 3.21

Generalized Relation Matrix of User Activity Dimension's Sub-Indicators by All Experts

Expert$_1$	SSD$_{3\_1}$	UID$_{3\_2}$	SRD$_{3\_3}$	UCD$_{3\_4}$	VED$_{3\_5}$
SSD$_{3\_1}$	0.012393	0.223101	0.285570	0.095190	0.193355
UID$_{3\_2}$	0.217152	0.012393	0.193355	0.130886	0.223101
SRD$_{3\_3}$	0.166582	0.127911	0.012393	0.252848	0.166582
UCD$_{3\_4}$	0.113038	0.113038	0.166582	0.012393	0.223101
VED$_{3\_5}$	0.223101	0.193355	0.285570	0.113038	0.012393

TABLE 3.22

Total Relation Matrix of User Activity Dimension's Sub-Indicators by All Experts

Expert$_s$	SSD$_{3\_1}$	UID$_{3\_2}$	SRD$_{3\_3}$	UCD$_{3\_4}$	VED$_{3\_5}$	R$_i$	C$_i$	R$_i$ + C$_i$	R$_i$ − C$_i$	Identity	Weight
SSD$_{3\_1}$	0.528	0.660	0.869	0.539	0.716	3.312	3.030	6.343	0.282	Cause	0.205
UID$_{3\_2}$	0.681	0.472	0.786	0.544	0.721	3.204	2.792	5.996	0.413	Cause	0.194
SRD$_{3\_3}$	0.597	0.534	0.577	0.605	0.640	2.954	3.767	6.721	−0.813	effect	0.217
UCD$_{3\_4}$	0.514	0.480	0.654	0.365	0.628	2.641	2.614	5.255	0.028	Cause	0.170
VED$_{3\_5}$	0.710	0.646	0.881	0.560	0.573	3.370	3.279	6.648	0.091	Cause	0.215

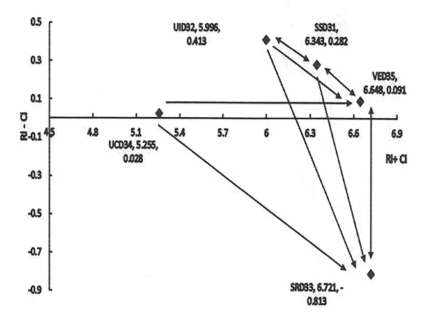

FIGURE 3.10

Causal and effectual illustration of user activity dimension's sub-indicators.

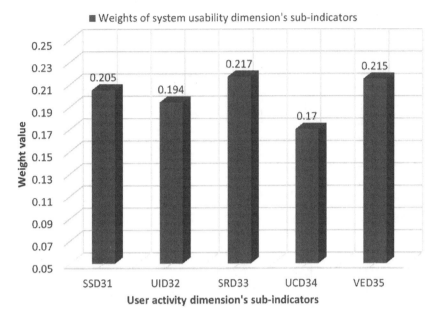

FIGURE 3.11
Final weights of user activity dimension's sub-indicators.

TABLE 3.23

Description and Weight of Main Dimensions and Their Sub-Indicators

Main Dimensions	Weights of Main Dimensions	Sub-Indicators	Description	Local Weight of Sub-Indicators	Global Weight of Sub-Indicators
System usability SUD_1	0.367	Functioning optimization, FOD_{1_1}	Operational optimization and resource utilization	0.204	0.075
		Renovation, RED_{1_2}	Remote monitoring, fault prediction, and prompt maintenance	0.195	0.072
		Smart servicing, SSD_{1_3}	Forecasting dynamic maintenance needs and scheduling predictive maintenance.	0.219	0.080
		Smart update, SUD_{1_4}	Provide intelligent system services, operations, and updates	0.177	0.065

(Continued)

TABLE 3.23 (*Continued*)

Description and Weight of Main Dimensions and Their Sub-Indicators

Main Dimensions	Weights of Main Dimensions	Sub-Indicators	Description	Local Weight of Sub-Indicators	Global Weight of Sub-Indicators
		Suitability, SBD_{1_5}	Adaptability and compatibility with several contexts and conditions	0.205	0.076
Findings and data management FDD_2	0.277	Data smart sharing, DSD_{2_1}	Sharing useful data and information to improve performance	0.347	0.096
		Findings and smart sharing, FSD_{2_2}	Sharing with the consumers the product's outcomes.	0.303	0.084
		Authenticity, AUD_{2_3}	The dependability and precision of prediction findings, as well as the quality of prediction performance under specified situations and time periods	0.350	0.097
User activity UAD_3	0.356	System activity support, SSD_{3_1}	Training users on the operations and activities of the product/system	0.205	0.073
		User interaction analysis, UID_{3_2}	Monitoring and analyzing user activity and recommending the ideal use	0.194	0.069
		Smart supply of activity resource, SRD_{3_3}	Predict the demand for resources, offer information about resources, distribute resources effectively, and intelligently plan resources	0.217	0.077
		User activity environment, UCD_{3_4}	Examine the activity environment, provide informational support to the service, monitor the activity environment, and forecast its changes	0.170	0.060
		Versatility, VED_{3_5}	The usability of the system, the functionality of the service, and the level of user satisfaction	0.215	0.076

TABLE 3.24

Decision Matrix of Six Alternatives According to All Sub-Indicators Using Semantic Terms

Expert₁	FOD₁.₁	RED₁.₂	SSD₁.₃	SUD₁.₄	SBD₁.₅
SDRS₁	⟨VEG⟩⟨VEG⟩⟨VEG⟩⟨VEG⟩	⟨FAR⟩⟨FAR⟩⟨FAR⟩⟨FAR⟩	⟨FAR⟩⟨FAR⟩⟨FAR⟩⟨GOO⟩	⟨GOO⟩⟨GOO⟩⟨GOO⟩⟨GOO⟩	⟨FAR⟩⟨FAR⟩⟨FAR⟩⟨FAR⟩
SDRS₂	⟨POO⟩⟨FAR⟩⟨FAR⟩⟨VEG⟩	⟨VEG⟩⟨VEG⟩⟨VEG⟩⟨VAR⟩	⟨VEG⟩⟨VEG⟩⟨VEG⟩⟨GOO⟩	⟨VEG⟩⟨VEG⟩⟨VEG⟩⟨GOO⟩	⟨VEG⟩⟨VEG⟩⟨VEG⟩⟨VEG⟩
SDRS₃	⟨POO⟩⟨POO⟩⟨POO⟩⟨VEG⟩	⟨POO⟩⟨POO⟩⟨POO⟩⟨FAR⟩	⟨VEG⟩⟨VEG⟩⟨VEG⟩⟨GOO⟩	⟨GOO⟩⟨GOO⟩⟨GOO⟩⟨GOO⟩	⟨GOO⟩⟨VEG⟩⟨VEG⟩⟨VEG⟩
SDRS₄	⟨POO⟩⟨POO⟩⟨POO⟩⟨VEG⟩	⟨GOO⟩⟨GOO⟩⟨GOO⟩⟨FAR⟩	⟨FAR⟩⟨FAR⟩⟨FAR⟩⟨FAR⟩	⟨FAR⟩⟨FAR⟩⟨FAR⟩⟨GOO⟩	⟨GOO⟩⟨GOO⟩⟨GOO⟩⟨GOO⟩
SDRS₅	⟨VEG⟩⟨VEG⟩⟨VEG⟩⟨VEG⟩	⟨GOO⟩⟨GOO⟩⟨GOO⟩⟨FAR⟩	⟨MEP⟩⟨MEP⟩⟨MEP⟩⟨GOO⟩	⟨POO⟩⟨POO⟩⟨POO⟩⟨POO⟩	⟨FAR⟩⟨FAR⟩⟨FAR⟩⟨FAR⟩
SDRS₆	⟨FAR⟩⟨FAR⟩⟨FAR⟩⟨VEG⟩	⟨MEP⟩⟨MEP⟩⟨MEP⟩⟨FAR⟩	⟨FAR⟩⟨FAR⟩⟨FAR⟩⟨GOO⟩	⟨GOO⟩⟨GOO⟩⟨GOO⟩⟨GOO⟩	⟨FAR⟩⟨FAR⟩⟨FAR⟩⟨FAR⟩

Expert₂	DSD₂.₁	FSD₂.₂	AUD₂.₃	SSD₃.₁
SDRS₁	⟨FAR⟩⟨FAR⟩⟨FAR⟩	⟨POO⟩⟨POO⟩⟨POO⟩⟨VEG⟩	⟨FAR⟩⟨FAR⟩⟨FAR⟩⟨FAR⟩	⟨VEG⟩⟨VEG⟩⟨VEG⟩⟨VEG⟩
SDRS₂	⟨VEG⟩⟨VEG⟩⟨VEG⟩	⟨FAR⟩⟨FAR⟩⟨FAR⟩⟨FAR⟩	⟨FAR⟩⟨FAR⟩⟨FAR⟩⟨FAR⟩	⟨VEG⟩⟨VEG⟩⟨VEG⟩⟨VEG⟩
SDRS₃	⟨VEG⟩⟨VEG⟩⟨VEG⟩⟨VEG⟩	⟨GOO⟩⟨GOO⟩⟨GOO⟩⟨GOO⟩	⟨FAR⟩⟨FAR⟩⟨FAR⟩⟨FAR⟩	⟨FAR⟩⟨FAR⟩⟨FAR⟩⟨VEG⟩
SDRS₄	⟨FAR⟩⟨FAR⟩⟨FAR⟩⟨FAR⟩	⟨GOO⟩⟨GOO⟩⟨GOO⟩⟨GOO⟩	⟨MEP⟩⟨MEP⟩⟨MEP⟩⟨FAR⟩	⟨POO⟩⟨POO⟩⟨POO⟩⟨VEG⟩
SDRS₅	⟨MEP⟩⟨MEP⟩⟨MEP⟩⟨MEP⟩	⟨FAR⟩⟨FAR⟩⟨FAR⟩⟨FAR⟩	⟨FAR⟩⟨FAR⟩⟨FAR⟩⟨FAR⟩	⟨FAR⟩⟨FAR⟩⟨FAR⟩⟨VEG⟩
SDRS₆	⟨FAR⟩⟨FAR⟩⟨FAR⟩⟨FAR⟩	⟨FAR⟩⟨FAR⟩⟨FAR⟩⟨FAR⟩	⟨FAR⟩⟨FAR⟩⟨FAR⟩⟨FAR⟩	⟨MEP⟩⟨MEP⟩⟨MEP⟩⟨VEG⟩

Expert₃	UID₃.₂	SRD₃.₃	UCD₃.₄	VED₃.₅
SDRS₁	⟨VEG⟩⟨VEG⟩⟨GOO⟩	⟨FAR⟩⟨FAR⟩⟨FAR⟩⟨FAR⟩	⟨FAR⟩⟨FAR⟩⟨FAR⟩⟨GOO⟩	⟨VEG⟩⟨VEG⟩⟨VEG⟩⟨VEG⟩
SDRS₂	⟨VEG⟩⟨VEG⟩⟨VEG⟩⟨GOO⟩	⟨VEG⟩⟨VEG⟩⟨VEG⟩⟨FAR⟩	⟨POO⟩⟨POO⟩⟨POO⟩⟨POO⟩	⟨POO⟩⟨FAR⟩⟨FAR⟩⟨VEG⟩
SDRS₃	⟨FAR⟩⟨FAR⟩⟨FAR⟩⟨FAR⟩	⟨FAR⟩⟨FAR⟩⟨FAR⟩⟨GOO⟩	⟨GOO⟩⟨GOO⟩⟨GOO⟩⟨GOO⟩	⟨FAR⟩⟨FAR⟩⟨FAR⟩⟨FAR⟩
SDRS₄	⟨VEG⟩⟨VEG⟩⟨VEG⟩⟨GOO⟩	⟨POO⟩⟨POO⟩⟨POO⟩⟨POO⟩	⟨VEG⟩⟨VEG⟩⟨VEG⟩⟨VEG⟩	⟨FAR⟩⟨FAR⟩⟨FAR⟩⟨FAR⟩
SDRS₅	⟨GOO⟩⟨GOO⟩⟨GOO⟩⟨GOO⟩	⟨FAR⟩⟨FAR⟩⟨FAR⟩⟨FAR⟩	⟨FAR⟩⟨FAR⟩⟨FAR⟩⟨VEG⟩	⟨VEG⟩⟨VEG⟩⟨VEG⟩⟨FAR⟩
SDRS₆	⟨VEG⟩⟨VEG⟩⟨VEG⟩⟨GOO⟩	⟨MEP⟩⟨MEP⟩⟨MEP⟩⟨GOO⟩	⟨GOO⟩⟨GOO⟩⟨GOO⟩⟨GOO⟩	⟨MEP⟩⟨MEP⟩⟨MEP⟩⟨FAR⟩

Step 26: All decision matrices created by all experts among the dimensions identified and the smart disaster response systems were aggregated into one matrix by applying Eq. (3.3) as presented in Table 3.25.

Step 27: The fuzzy combined decision matrix was defuzzified into the crisp combined decision matrix by removing the TFNs according to Eq. (3.4), and the results are formed in Table 3.26.

Step 28: The average value AV_j that associated with all sub-indicators according to the definition of the EDAS technique was computed according to Eq. (3.13) as exhibited in Table 3.27.

Step 29: The PDA matrix was computed according to Eqs. (3.14) and (3.15), as exhibited in Table 3.28.

Step 30: The NDA matrix was computed according to Eqs. (3.16) and (3.17), as exhibited in Table 3.29.

Step 31: The weighted sum of PDA (SP_i) was calculated according to Eq. (3.18) as exhibited in Table 3.30, and the weighted sum of NDA (SN_i), according to Eq. (3.19), as exhibited in Table 3.31.

Step 32: The standardized values of SP_i and SN_i were computed according to Eqs. (3.20) and (3.21), as presented in Table 3.32.

Step 33: The assessment score AS_i for all substitutes was computed by applying Eq. (3.22) as presented in Table 2.32 and Figure 3.12. Eventually, rank the substitutes according to their assessment score AS_i.

3.4.2 Discussion

This part discusses the results obtained from applying the methodology used to solve the case study mentioned in the previous section. Initially, the fuzzy DEMATEL method was used to prioritize three main dimensions. According to the results presented in Table 3.23, the system usability dimension has the highest priority with a weight of 0.367, followed by the user activity dimension with a weight of 0.356, while the findings and data management dimension come in the last order with a weight of 0.277.

Then, according to the results of local weights obtained for the sub-indicators of the system usability dimension presented in Table 3.23, they indicate that the smart servicing indicator ranks first in the ranking with a weight of 0.219, followed by the suitability indicator, while the smart update indicator comes in the last rank with a weight of 0.177. Also, according to the results of local weights obtained for the sub-indicators of the findings and data management dimension presented in Table 3.23, they indicate that the authenticity indicator ranks first in the ranking with a weight of 0.350, followed by the data smart sharing indicator, while the findings and smart sharing indicator come in the last rank with a weight of 0.303. Likewise, according to the results of local weights obtained for the sub-indicators of the user activity dimension presented in Table 3.23, they indicate that the smart supply of activity resource indicator ranks

TABLE 3.25

Aggregated Decision Matrix of Six Alternatives According to All Sub-Indicators Using TFNs

Expert$_s$	FOD$_{1,1}$	RED$_{1,2}$	SSD$_{1,3}$	SUD$_{1,4}$	SBD$_{1,5}$	DSD$_{2,1}$	FSD$_{2,2}$
SDRS$_1$	⟨0.83, 1.00, 1.00⟩	⟨0.33, 0.50, 0.67⟩	⟨0.42, 0.58, 0.75⟩	⟨0.67, 0.83, 1.00⟩	⟨0.33, 0.50, 0.67⟩	⟨0.33, 0.50, 0.67⟩	⟨0.21, 0.38, 0.50⟩
SDRS$_2$	⟨0.37, 0.54, 0.67⟩	⟨0.71, 0.88, 0.92⟩	⟨0.79, 0.96, 1.00⟩	⟨0.79, 0.96, 1.00⟩	⟨0.83, 1.00, 1.00⟩	⟨0.83, 1.00, 1.00⟩	⟨0.33, 0.50, 0.67⟩
SDRS$_3$	⟨0.21, 0.38, 0.50⟩	⟨0.08, 0.25, 0.42⟩	⟨0.79, 0.96, 1.00⟩	⟨0.67, 0.83, 1.00⟩	⟨0.79, 0.96, 1.00⟩	⟨0.83, 1.00, 1.00⟩	⟨0.67, 0.83, 1.00⟩
SDRS$_4$	⟨0.21, 0.38, 0.50⟩	⟨0.59, 0.75, 0.92⟩	⟨0.33, 0.50, 0.67⟩	⟨0.42, 0.58, 0.75⟩	⟨0.67, 0.83, 1.00⟩	⟨0.33, 0.50, 0.67⟩	⟨0.67, 0.83, 1.00⟩
SDRS$_5$	⟨0.83, 1.00, 1.00⟩	⟨0.59, 0.75, 0.92⟩	⟨0.30, 0.46, 0.63⟩	⟨0.00, 0.17, 0.33⟩	⟨0.33, 0.50, 0.67⟩	⟨0.17, 0.33, 0.50⟩	⟨0.33, 0.50, 0.67⟩
SDRS$_6$	⟨0.46, 0.63, 0.75⟩	⟨0.21, 0.37, 0.54⟩	⟨0.42, 0.58, 0.75⟩	⟨0.67, 0.83, 1.00⟩	⟨0.33, 0.50, 0.67⟩	⟨0.33, 0.50, 0.67⟩	⟨0.33, 0.50, 0.67⟩

Expert$_s$	AUD$_{2,3}$	SSD$_{3,1}$	SRD$_{3,3}$	UCD$_{3,4}$	VED$_{3,5}$
SDRS$_1$	⟨0.33, 0.50, 0.67⟩	⟨0.83, 1.00, 1.00⟩	⟨0.33, 0.50, 0.67⟩	⟨0.42, 0.58, 0.75⟩	⟨0.83, 1.00, 1.00⟩
SDRS$_2$	⟨0.33, 0.50, 0.67⟩	⟨0.83, 1.00, 1.00⟩	⟨0.71, 0.88, 0.92⟩	⟨0.00, 0.17, 0.33⟩	⟨0.37, 0.54, 0.67⟩
SDRS$_3$	⟨0.33, 0.50, 0.67⟩	⟨0.46, 0.63, 0.75⟩	⟨0.42, 0.58, 0.75⟩	⟨0.67, 0.83, 1.00⟩	⟨0.21, 0.38, 0.50⟩
SDRS$_4$	⟨0.21, 0.37, 0.54⟩	⟨0.21, 0.38, 0.50⟩	⟨0.00, 0.17, 0.33⟩	⟨0.83, 1.00, 1.00⟩	⟨0.33, 0.50, 0.67⟩
SDRS$_5$	⟨0.33, 0.50, 0.67⟩	⟨0.46, 0.63, 0.75⟩	⟨0.33, 0.50, 0.67⟩	⟨0.46, 0.63, 0.75⟩	⟨0.71, 0.88, 0.92⟩
SDRS$_6$	⟨0.33, 0.50, 0.67⟩	⟨0.34, 0.50, 0.63⟩	⟨0.30, 0.46, 0.63⟩	⟨0.67, 0.83, 1.00⟩	⟨0.21, 0.37, 0.54⟩

TABLE 3.26

Defuzzified Decision Matrix of Six Smart Disaster Response Systems According to All Sub-Criteria

Experts_s	$FOD_{1,1}$	$RED_{1,2}$	$SSD_{1,3}$	$SUD_{1,4}$	$SBD_{1,5}$	$DSD_{2,1}$	$FSD_{2,2}$	$AUD_{2,3}$	$SSD_{3,1}$	$UID_{3,2}$	$SRD_{3,3}$	$UCD_{3,4}$	$VED_{3,5}$
$SDRS_1$	0.97	0.50	0.58	0.83	0.50	0.50	0.37	0.50	0.97	0.94	0.50	0.58	0.97
$SDRS_2$	0.53	0.86	0.94	0.94	0.97	0.97	0.50	0.50	0.97	0.94	0.86	0.17	0.53
$SDRS_3$	0.37	0.25	0.94	0.83	0.94	0.97	0.83	0.50	0.62	0.50	0.58	0.83	0.37
$SDRS_4$	0.37	0.75	0.50	0.58	0.83	0.50	0.83	0.37	0.37	0.94	0.17	0.97	0.50
$SDRS_5$	0.97	0.75	0.46	0.17	0.50	0.33	0.50	0.50	0.62	0.83	0.50	0.63	0.86
$SDRS_6$	0.62	0.37	0.58	0.83	0.50	0.50	0.50	0.50	0.50	0.94	0.50	0.83	0.37

TABLE 3.27

Determining of the Average Solution AV_j

Experts_s	$FOD_{1,1}$	$RED_{1,2}$	$SSD_{1,3}$	$SUD_{1,4}$	$SBD_{1,5}$	$DSD_{2,1}$	$FSD_{2,2}$	$AUD_{2,3}$	$SSD_{3,1}$	$UID_{3,2}$	$SRD_{3,3}$	$UCD_{3,4}$	$VED_{3,5}$
$SDRS_1$	0.97	0.50	0.58	0.83	0.50	0.50	0.37	0.50	0.97	0.94	0.50	0.58	0.97
$SDRS_2$	0.53	0.86	0.94	0.94	0.97	0.97	0.50	0.50	0.97	0.94	0.86	0.17	0.53
$SDRS_3$	0.37	0.25	0.94	0.83	0.94	0.97	0.83	0.50	0.62	0.50	0.58	0.83	0.37
$SDRS_4$	0.37	0.75	0.50	0.58	0.83	0.50	0.83	0.37	0.37	0.94	0.17	0.97	0.50
$SDRS_5$	0.97	0.75	0.46	0.17	0.50	0.33	0.50	0.50	0.62	0.83	0.50	0.63	0.86
$SDRS_6$	0.62	0.37	0.58	0.83	0.50	0.50	0.50	0.50	0.50	0.94	0.50	0.83	0.37
AV_j	0.64	0.58	0.67	0.70	0.71	0.63	0.59	0.48	0.68	0.85	0.52	0.67	0.60

TABLE 3.28

Determining of the Positive Distance from Average

Experts$_s$	FOD$_{1,1}$	RED$_{1,2}$	SSD$_{1,3}$	SUD$_{1,4}$	SBD$_{1,5}$	DSD$_{2,1}$	FSD$_{2,2}$	AUD$_{2,3}$	SSD$_{3,1}$	UID$_{3,2}$	SRD$_{3,3}$	UCD$_{3,4}$	VED$_{3,5}$
SDRS$_1$	0.520	0.000	0.000	0.191	0.000	0.000	0.000	0.045	0.437	0.108	0.000	0.000	0.617
SDRS$_2$	0.000	0.483	0.410	0.349	0.373	0.544	0.000	0.045	0.437	0.108	0.659	0.000	0.000
SDRS$_3$	0.000	0.000	0.410	0.191	0.330	0.544	0.411	0.045	0.000	0.000	0.119	0.242	0.000
SDRS$_4$	0.000	0.293	0.000	0.000	0.175	0.000	0.411	0.000	0.000	0.108	0.000	0.451	0.000
SDRS$_5$	0.520	0.293	0.000	0.000	0.000	0.000	0.000	0.045	0.000	0.000	0.000	0.000	0.433
SDRS$_6$	0.000	0.000	0.000	0.191	0.000	0.000	0.000	0.045	0.000	0.108	0.000	0.242	0.000

TABLE 3.29

Determining of the Negative Distance from Average

Experts$_s$	FOD$_{1,1}$	RED$_{1,2}$	SSD$_{1,3}$	SUD$_{1,4}$	SBD$_{1,5}$	DSD$_{2,1}$	FSD$_{2,2}$	AUD$_{2,3}$	SSD$_{3,1}$	UID$_{3,2}$	SRD$_{3,3}$	UCD$_{3,4}$	VED$_{3,5}$
SDRS$_1$	0.000	0.138	0.130	0.000	0.292	0.204	0.371	0.000	0.000	0.000	0.035	0.132	0.000
SDRS$_2$	0.170	0.000	0.000	0.000	0.000	0.000	0.150	0.000	0.000	0.000	0.000	0.746	0.117
SDRS$_3$	0.420	0.569	0.000	0.000	0.000	0.000	0.000	0.000	0.081	0.411	0.000	0.000	0.383
SDRS$_4$	0.420	0.000	0.250	0.167	0.000	0.204	0.000	0.226	0.452	0.000	0.672	0.000	0.167
SDRS$_5$	0.000	0.000	0.310	0.756	0.292	0.475	0.150	0.000	0.081	0.022	0.035	0.057	0.000
SDRS$_6$	0.029	0.362	0.130	0.000	0.292	0.204	0.150	0.000	0.259	0.000	0.035	0.000	0.383

TABLE 3.30

Determining of the Weighted Sum of the Positive Distance from Average

$Experts_s$	$FOD_{1.1}$	$RED_{1.2}$	$SSD_{1.3}$	$SUD_{1.4}$	$SBD_{1.5}$	$DSD_{2.1}$	$FSD_{2.2}$	$AUD_{2.3}$	$SSD_{3.1}$	$UID_{3.2}$	$SRD_{3.3}$	$UCD_{3.4}$	$VED_{3.5}$
$SDRS_1$	0.039	0.000	0.000	0.012	0.000	0.000	0.000	0.004	0.032	0.007	0.000	0.000	0.047
$SDRS_2$	0.000	0.035	0.033	0.023	0.028	0.052	0.000	0.004	0.032	0.007	0.051	0.000	0.000
$SDRS_3$	0.000	0.000	0.033	0.012	0.025	0.052	0.035	0.004	0.000	0.000	0.009	0.015	0.000
$SDRS_4$	0.000	0.021	0.000	0.000	0.013	0.000	0.035	0.000	0.000	0.007	0.000	0.027	0.000
$SDRS_5$	0.039	0.021	0.000	0.000	0.000	0.000	0.000	0.004	0.000	0.000	0.000	0.000	0.033
$SDRS_6$	0.000	0.000	0.000	0.012	0.000	0.000	0.000	0.004	0.000	0.007	0.000	0.015	0.000

TABLE 3.31

Determining of the Weighted Sum of the Negative Distance from Average

$Experts_s$	$FOD_{1.1}$	$RED_{1.2}$	$SSD_{1.3}$	$SUD_{1.4}$	$SBD_{1.5}$	$DSD_{2.1}$	$FSD_{2.2}$	$AUD_{2.3}$	$SSD_{3.1}$	$UID_{3.2}$	$SRD_{3.3}$	$UCD_{3.4}$	$VED_{3.5}$
$SDRS_1$	0.000	0.010	0.010	0.000	0.022	0.020	0.031	0.000	0.000	0.000	0.003	0.008	0.000
$SDRS_2$	0.013	0.000	0.000	0.000	0.000	0.000	0.013	0.000	0.000	0.000	0.000	0.045	0.009
$SDRS_3$	0.032	0.041	0.000	0.000	0.000	0.000	0.000	0.000	0.006	0.028	0.000	0.000	0.029
$SDRS_4$	0.032	0.000	0.020	0.011	0.000	0.020	0.000	0.022	0.033	0.000	0.052	0.000	0.013
$SDRS_5$	0.000	0.000	0.025	0.049	0.022	0.046	0.013	0.000	0.006	0.001	0.003	0.003	0.000
$SDRS_6$	0.002	0.026	0.010	0.000	0.022	0.020	0.013	0.000	0.019	0.000	0.003	0.000	0.029

TABLE 3.32

Ranking of Six Smart Disaster Response Systems by Applying the EDAS Method

Alternatives	SP_i	SN_i	NSP_i	NSN_i	AS_i	Rank (AS)
$SDRS_1$	0.1420	0.1040	0.5354	0.4836	0.5095	3
$SDRS_2$	0.2653	0.0789	1.0000	0.6080	0.8040	1
$SDRS_3$	0.1851	0.1359	0.6978	0.3251	0.5114	2
$SDRS_4$	0.1034	0.2014	0.3898	0.0000	0.1949	6
$SDRS_5$	0.0974	0.1680	0.3671	0.1660	0.2666	4
$SDRS_6$	0.0388	0.1439	0.1463	0.2857	0.2160	5

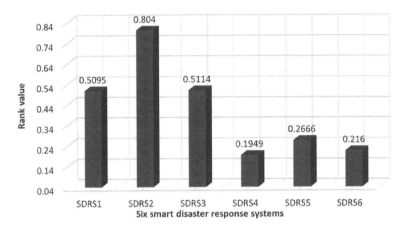

FIGURE 3.12

Final ranking of six smart disaster response systems.

first in the ranking with a weight of 0.217, followed by the versatility indicator, while the user activity environment indicator comes in the last rank with a weight of 0.170.

In the last part of the discussion of the results of applying the proposed approach, it is found that six SDRSs were evaluated using the fuzzy EDAS method. The results in Table 3.32 indicate that $SDRS_2$ has the highest rank with a weight of 0.8040, followed by $SDRS_3$ with a weight of 0.5114, while $SDRS_4$ occupies the last rank with a weight of 0.1949.

3.5 Summary

- This chapter provides a comprehensive description of disaster response systems.
- This chapter reviews the importance and needs of assessing disaster response systems.

- This chapter presents the most important criteria used in evaluating a city's disaster response system after a comprehensive analysis of a number of research articles.
- This chapter suggests two very recent MCDM techniques, fuzzy DEMATEL and fuzzy EDAS assess disaster response systems for a city.
- This chapter presents a real case study evaluating a number of smart disaster response systems around the world.

3.6 Exercises

a. How do you define the "smart disaster response system"? Why is an evaluation of a smart and sustainable disaster response system important?

b. What are the differences between DEMATEL and EDAS methods? Discuss their relative advantages while making a decision.

c. Discuss the features of smart disaster response systems in terms of the characteristics and formation of a smart city.

d. What are the key steps to embedding fuzzy linguistics in an MCDM framework?

e. Discuss the differences between fuzzy DEMATEL and fuzzy EDAS methods.

f. Why MCDM approach is required to assess a sustainable smart disaster response system?

References

Chang, Betty, Chih-Wei Chang, and Chih-Hung Wu. 2011. "Fuzzy DEMATEL Method for Developing Supplier Selection Criteria." *Expert Systems with Applications* 38(3): 1850–58. doi: 10.1016/j.eswa.2010.07.114.

Gabus Andre, Emilio Fontela. 1972. World problems, an invitation to further thought within the framework of DEMATEL. Battelle Geneva Research Centre.

Karatop, Buket, Buşra Taşkan, Elanur Adar, and Cemalettin Kubat. 2021. "Decision Analysis Related to the Renewable Energy Investments in Turkey Based on a Fuzzy AHP-EDAS-Fuzzy FMEA Approach." *Computers & Industrial Engineering* 151: 106958. doi: 10.1016/j.cie.2020.106958.

Keshavarz Ghorabaee, Mehdi, Edmundas Kazimieras Zavadskas, Laya Olfat, and Zenonas Turskis. 2015. "Multi-Criteria Inventory Classification Using a New Method of Evaluation Based on Distance from Average Solution (EDAS)." *Informatica* 26: 435–51.

Nasrollahi, Mahdi, Mohammad Reza Fathi, Seyed Mohammad Sobhani, Abolfazl Khosravi, and Asgar Noorbakhsh. 2021. "Modeling Resilient Supplier Selection Criteria in Desalination Supply Chain Based on Fuzzy DEMATEL and ISM." *International Journal of Management Science and Engineering Management* 16(4): 264–78. doi: 10.1080/17509653.2021.1965502.

Wan, Zheng, Anwei Nie, Jihong Chen, Jiawei Ge, Chen Zhang, and Qiang Zhang. 2021. "Key Barriers to the Commercial Use of the Northern Sea Route: View from China with a Fuzzy DEMATEL Approach." *Ocean & Coastal Management* 208: 105630. doi: 10.1016/j.ocecoaman.2021.105630.

Zhao, Huiru, and Sen Guo. 2015. "External Benefit Evaluation of Renewable Energy Power in China for Sustainability." *Sustainability*. doi: 10.3390/su7054783.

4

A Facilitating Paradigm for Analyzing the Adaptation of Internet of Things Obstacles (IoTBs) to Waste Management in Smart Cities

4.1 Introduction

The smart city is touted as a potential solution to the problems caused by urbanization in developing countries. In the last two decades, the relevance of smart cities has increased, and their progressive techniques are seen as an essential prerequisite for emerging countries. Numerous studies have attempted to describe the notion of a smart city, with the majority conceptualizing it as a multi-dimensional system designed to create sustainable communities. Smart cities need the combination of ICT and Internet technologies to change their design in diverse forms such as sophisticated infrastructure, transportation, environment, healthcare, and government to create a sustainable ecosystem. A smart city is the confluence of ICT technologies, sustainability, and technical, social, and economic performance metrics. The key stakeholders are government, service providers, policymakers, people, and developers. The Internet of Things (IoT) is the most significant technical breakthrough driving smart city projects worldwide. IoT-enabled technologies serve as a catalyst for the development of metropolitan communities to improve infrastructure, waste management, transportation, and the quality of human life. IoT technology should supply upgraded services and revamp current procedures in smart cities. A network, scalability, heterogeneity, coverage, and end-user interaction form the basis of the architecture of an IoT-enabled smart city.

The United Nations projects that by 2050, about two-thirds of the world's population will be urbanized (Mishra et al., 2022). Therefore, infrastructure and other far-reaching services will be required to meet the needs of an urbanized population. Suppose a city's population expands at a pace of 3–5 percent per year. In that case, the quantity of garbage

DOI: 10.1201/9781003357681-4

created will double every decade, creating a dire scenario for smart cities and a significant financial burden for collection, disposal, and recycling. Prior research has shown that waste management is a significant problem for urban populations and that developing a sustainable environment is required to mitigate the danger to urban life.

Both developed and developing countries use Internet technologies to promote sustainable growth and economic development. Despite the presence of several elements, the development of smart cities is an increasing part of economic growth and a means of meeting the requirements of the people. Developed countries have access to modern technology, enough resources, and a stable framework for developing smart cities; moreover, existing smart cities help and advise them in taking action. However, the situation in emerging nations is quite another. Due to financial, technological, and economic restrictions, underdeveloped nations struggle to undertake smart city development initiatives. Developing nations aspire to build smart cities to improve the living conditions of their citizens and communities. The working conditions of developing nations differ from those of developed nations; thus, it is necessary to build a structural framework that will assist developing nations in initiating and implementing IoT-enabled ecosystems in smart cities.

Smart cities are required to apply IoT principles since it connects items and interacts intelligently with people in response to the tough environment. Effective trash management in smart cities is one of the most important IoT-based services that grows in importance every day. Previously, waste management used technology and models such as Geographical Information System (GIS), better routing and scheduling, and other techniques to optimize garbage collection, storage, and disposal procedures. These technologies are devoid of innovation, which IoT technology may remedy. Prior studies did not view stakeholders as an important element of IoT-enabled waste management techniques (policymakers, smart city planners, municipal administration, etc.) but rather as separate entities.

An IoT-enabled smart city is a viable option to meet the demands of urbanization; it has the ability to convert societies into smart communities by improving public services such as transportation, water management, smart buildings, healthcare, and education. The adoption of IoT technology faces various obstacles, including scalability, security concerns, heterogeneity, architecture, and governance, among others. Few studies have been undertaken on IoT practices and implementation in the context of waste management; most of these studies concentrate on designing and optimizing IoT technology for trash-collecting techniques. In addition to trash collection, it is necessary to investigate the elements that impact waste management in smart cities. This chapter intends to establish a knowledge of and analyze the level or severity of IoT hurdles impacting smart city waste management so that stakeholders may take proactive measures to install IoT-enabled technologies in a smooth manner.

This chapter is an effort to comprehend the IoT adoption situation of smart cities in underdeveloped nations and the different implementation issues that may be experienced. The building of an IoT network, with solid backing from services and technology, needs an integrated waste management control strategy for smart cities. Aside from the technological obstacles, a clear, standardized strategy for implementing IoT and an appropriate direction for smart city activities have not yet been offered. This chapter seeks to identify the key IoT obstacles (IoTBs) and their strengths as they pertain to trash management in smart cities. A multi-criteria decision-making (MCDM) technique was applied to accomplish these goals. The IoTBs are investigated using current literature and validated by specialists. Fuzzy DEMATEL examines the interaction between obstacles to demonstrate the intensity/strength of IoTBs impacting one another and managing waste management methods in smart cities.

4.2 IoTBs and Waste Management in Smart Cities

Previous research has highlighted impediments to IoT adoption in various industries (Sharma et al., 2020). To meet the needs of smart cities in emerging nations, it is vital to investigate IoTBs, which impact smart city waste management. The obstacles that prevent the adoption of the Internet of Things have been divided into three main groups, as shown in Figure 4.1.

- **Security and privacy problems (IoTB$_1$)**
  It is comprehensible that systems may encounter several threats, such as cross-site scripting or side channels, that lead to vulnerabilities. Additionally, security risks and data loss may increase as a result of multi-tenancy. The fundamental challenge is achieving interoperability among networked devices and providing them with the best services via adaptive behavior while ensuring the security and privacy of end-users and their personal data (Papadakis et al., 2021). The IoT systems use network technologies such as RFID, NFC, and protocols such as ZigBee, Z-wave, and many more, which may lead to compatibility across communication standards. In this sense, data privacy and security have a detrimental impact on the waste management capabilities of IoT in smart cities since it may disclose the municipal corporations' access to individual home data.
- **Absence of regulatory norms, policies, and guidelines (IoTB$_2$)**
  A lack of regulatory norms and policies will lead to insecure standards and faulty guidance in performing actions. A legal framework needs to be robust to support IoT implementation.

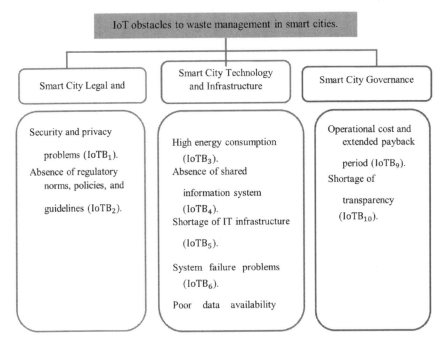

FIGURE 4.1
Common IoT barriers to waste management in smart cities.

Researchers have shown that a proper legal framework contributes positively to waste management in smart cities, while the absence of regulations is harmful to the system.

- **High energy consumption ($IoTB_3$)**

  Power consumption of Internet-of-Things devices is a major problem. For IoT deployment, RFID-equipped yet battery-less devices will be favored. With the rising demand for IoT devices, it is anticipated that the energy costs of value chains will continue to rise.

- **Absence of shared information system ($IoTB_4$)**

  These obstacles restrict the provision of end-to-end waste management visibility in smart cities. Prior research on IoT-enabled infrastructure has primarily focused on smart bins and sensors, but it is necessary to configure an integrated platform of information systems such as DSS, PLM, and geospatial technology among devices, applications, and service providers for real-time data and information exchange.

- **Shortage of IT infrastructure ($IoTB_5$)**

  Smart cities' information technology (IT) infrastructure must be constructed to meet their needs. The updated technology cannot be implemented without the appropriate architecture first being in place (Elahi et al., 2019).

- **System failure problems (IoTB$_6$)**

  Data may be corrupted by causes outside an individual's control, such as a server breakdown or failure. Data integrity refers to the protection of both data and the system. The data is regularly updated and is always accessible in its original format by end-users.

- **Poor data availability (IoTB$_7$)**

  The instant accessibility of data ensures that people have immediate access to information. The IoT-enabled system aims to offer consumers data whenever they want it. Insufficient data availability may impede the flow of information.

- **Shortage of technical knowledge between planners (IoTB$_8$)**

  It is possible that the authorities and policymakers lack the organizational capacities and professional skills necessary, which will affect the waste management system.

- **Operational cost and extended payback period (IoTB$_9$)**

  Due to the high cost of specialists, smart devices, installation, maintenance, and training for imparting information to workers, costs are the primary issue of IoT stakeholders.

- **Shortage of transparency (IoTB$_{10}$)**

  In an IoT-enabled system, responsibility for facilities to be supplied might be both ambiguous and transparent. The technology of smart cities increases the possibility of social isolation for residents.

4.3 Data Collection and Methodology

This part presents the fuzzy DEMATEL method for analyzing IoT obstacles to waste management in smart cities, prioritization, and weighting. Figure 4.2 illustrates the research approach guiding the study in which the fuzzy DEMATEL method will be used as an initial development level of the analysis, which is then completed with the help of experts to calculate the weights of the IoT obstacles to waste management in smart cities. Then, we present a brief overview of the method used in the study as follows.

4.3.1 Fuzzy DEMATEL Technique

The DEMATEL analysis is an all-encompassing approach that may be used to investigate the components of complex systems. In the early

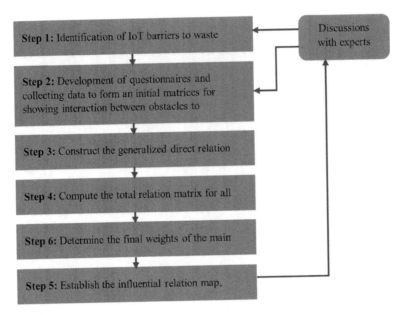

FIGURE 4.2
General scheme of the applied method.

1970s, two researchers working at a significant laboratory in the United States named Gabus and Fontela were the ones who first offered the idea (Hasheminezhad, Hadadi, and Shirmohammadi, 2021). The DEMATEL analysis is based on graph theory and matrix theory, which enables complicated issues to be analyzed and solved via the use of visualization techniques (Li and Xu, 2021). This methodology begins by constructing the initial direct-relation matrix by utilizing the logical relations that exist between the components of the system. Next, it determines the degrees of effect that each component has on the other components, and finally, it establishes the centrality and causality of the components. A readily digestible structural model of the system may be derived from a DEMATEL analysis, which maps the link between the identified elements in a straightforward manner. The link between the many different components may be broken down into the groupings of causes and effects, and an understandable visual representation of this can be obtained from a causal diagram. In addition, DEMATEL is a technique that is both extremely suited and effective for determining the interdependence of a number of different components in a complex system (Hosseini, Paydar, and Hajiaghaei-Keshteli, 2021). The study's findings may assist enhance management and decision-making issues present in process industries, and it can also help prioritize the aspects that have been found.

Analyzing the causes of accidents in complex systems using the DEMATEL technique, which distinguishes the components' characteristics,

TABLE 4.1

Linguistic Variables for Weighting IoT Barriers to Waste Management in Smart Cities

Linguistic Variables	Abridgments	TFN $\langle l_{ij}, m_{ij}, u_{ij} \rangle$
No influence	$\langle$NFL$\rangle$	$\langle 0.00, 0.00, 0.25 \rangle$
Very low influence	$\langle$VLF$\rangle$	$\langle 0.00, 0.25, 0.50 \rangle$
Low influence	$\langle$LFL$\rangle$	$\langle 0.25, 0.50, 0.75 \rangle$
High influence	$\langle$HFL$\rangle$	$\langle 0.50, 0.75, 1.00 \rangle$
Very high influence	$\langle$VHL$\rangle$	$\langle 0.75, 1.00, 1.00 \rangle$

has several distinct benefits. These advantages include the following: The system factors are separated into those that influence the system and those that are affected by the system using this technique. Because effect factors have such a huge and all-encompassing impact on other variables, their significance may be inferred from this by putting numbers on the connections that exist between the elements. After the experts have identified the direct-relation matrix, a DEMATEL analysis is performed so that the degrees of influence that each element has on the other factors may be determined.

4.3.2 The Implementation Steps of the Fuzzy DEMATEL Technique

Step 1: A group of experts is identified to assist the authors and share information on analyzing IoT barriers to waste management in smart cities. Let $Ex = \{Ex_1, Ex_2, ..., Ex_K\}$ be a set of experts, where Ex_K denotes the Kth expert, $k = 1, 2, ..., K$. K is the total number of experts.

Step 2: The problem is studied from all sides and determined for its main purpose. In addition, the barriers used in the evaluation process as criteria are studied.

Step 3: Linguistic variables and corresponding appropriate triangular fuzzy numbers (TFNs) are determined to prioritize IoT barriers to waste management in smart cities, as exhibited in Table 4.1.

Step 4: Build a pairwise comparison matrix (B) among the barriers and themselves by each expert as in Eq. (4.1) by using the linguistic variables in Table 4.1 and then by using TFNs as proved in Eq. (4.2).

$$B = \begin{array}{c} \\ B_1 \\ B_2 \\ \vdots \\ B_n \end{array} \begin{array}{cccc} B_1 & B_2 & \cdots & B_n \\ \left[\begin{array}{cccc} * & x_{12} & \cdots & x_{1i} \\ x_{21} & * & \cdots & x_{2i} \\ x_{31} & x_{32} & * & \cdots \\ x_{j1} & x_{j2} & x_{j3} & * \end{array} \right] \end{array} \quad (4.1)$$

where (x_{ij}), $i, j = 1, 2, \ldots, n$, and x_{ij} is the valuation of the barriers to the ith element B_1, B_2, ..., B_i regarding the jth element B_1, B_2, ..., B_j. Also, the key diagonal of the matrix equals 1 such that x_{ij} equal 1.

$$
B =
\begin{array}{c}
\\
B_1 \\
B_2 \\
\vdots \\
B_n
\end{array}
\begin{array}{cccc}
B_1 & B_2 & \cdots & B_n \\
\left[
\begin{array}{cccc}
* & \langle l_{12}, m_{12}, u_{12} \rangle & \cdots & \langle l_{1i}, m_{1i}, u_{1i} \rangle \\
\langle u_{21}, m_{21}, l_{21} \rangle & * & \cdots & \langle l_{2i}, m_{2i}, u_{2i} \rangle \\
\langle u_{21}, m_{21}, l_{21} \rangle & \langle u_{32}, m_{32}, l_{32} \rangle & * & \cdots \\
\langle u_{j1}, m_{j1}, l_{j1} \rangle & \langle u_{j2}, m_{j2}, l_{j2} \rangle & \langle u_{j3}, m_{j3}, l_{j3} \rangle & *
\end{array}
\right]
\end{array}
$$

(4.2)

Let $f_{kij} = \left(f_{kij}^l, f_{kij}^m, f_{kij}^u \right)$ is the initial direct-effect information that B_i has on B_j by K^{th} expert by applying linguistic variables, where $f_{kij}^l, f_{kij}^m, f_{kij}^u$ refer to the lower limit, middle limit, and upper limit of the initial direct-effect information, respectively.

Step 5: Collect all decision matrices created by all experts into a single matrix according to Eq. (4.3).

$$\tilde{F}_{ij} = f_{1ij} \oplus f_{2ij} \oplus \ldots \oplus f_{kij} / K$$

(4.3)

Step 6: Construct the generalized direct-relation matrix for all IoT barriers to waste management in smart cities $\tilde{U}$ by standardizing $\tilde{F}$ by applying Eq. (4.4).

$$\tilde{U}_{ij} = \tilde{F}_{ij} / r = \left(f_{ij}^l / r, f_{ij}^m / r, f_{ij}^u / r \right) = \left(U_{ij}^l, U_{ij}^m, U_{ij}^u \right)$$

(4.4)

where $\tilde{U}_{ij}$ is the standardized direct-effect information that B_i has on B_j, where $U_{ij}^l, U_{ij}^m, U_{ij}^u$ refer to the lower limit, median limit, and upper limit of the normalized direct-effect matrix, correspondingly. r is $\text{Max}_{1 \leq i \leq n} \sum_{j=1}^{n} U_{ij}^u$, and Max_i indicates the máximum of ith IoT barrier.

Step 7: Compute the total-relation matrix $\tilde{T}$ for all IoT barriers by applying Eq. (4.5).

$$\tilde{T} = \lim_{k \to \infty} \left(\tilde{U}^1 \oplus \tilde{U}^2 \oplus \cdots \oplus \tilde{U}^K \right) = \tilde{U} \times \left(1 - \tilde{U} \right)^{-1}$$

(4.5)

where $\tilde{T}_{ij} = \left(T_{ij}^l, T_{ij}^m, T_{ij}^u \right)$, and $\tilde{T}_{ij}$ is the total-effect information that B_i has on B_j, where $\left(T_{ij}^l, T_{ij}^m, T_{ij}^u \right)$ refer to the lower limit, median limit, and upper limit of the total-effect matrix, correspondingly. Here, $T_{ij}^l = U_{ij}^l \times \left(1 - U_{ij}^l \right)^{-1}, U_{ij}^m \times \left(1 - U_{ij}^m \right)^{-1}$, and $U_{ij}^u \times \left(1 - U_{ij}^u \right)^{-1}$.

Step 8: Construct the influential relation map (IRM) by computing the sum of rows and columns from the matrix $\tilde{T}$, stated as vector $\tilde{R}$ and $\tilde{C}$, respectively, in Eqs. (4.6) and (4.7). The IRM will be calculated by computing the ordered pairs $(\tilde{R}+\tilde{C}, \tilde{R}-\tilde{C})$.

$$\tilde{R} = \left(\tilde{R}_i\right)_{1\times n} = \left[\sum_{j=1}^{n}\tilde{T}_{ij}\right]_{1\times n} \tag{4.6}$$

$$\tilde{C} = \left(\tilde{C}_i\right)_{1\times n} = \left[\sum_{j=1}^{n}\tilde{T}_{ij}\right]_{1\times n} \tag{4.7}$$

where $\tilde{R}$ and $\tilde{C}$ indicate the total of rows and columns of the total-effect matrix, respectively. $\tilde{R}_i$ and $\tilde{C}_i$ indicate the total of rows and columns of ith barrier, respectively.

Step 9: Defuzzify the $(\tilde{R}+\tilde{C}, \tilde{R}-\tilde{C})$ to the crisp value $\left(\left(\tilde{R}+\tilde{C}\right)^{\text{def}}, \left(\tilde{R}-\tilde{C}\right)^{\text{def}}\right)$ by removing the triangular fuzzy numbers by applying the graded mean integration representation (GMIR) method (Zhao and Guo 2015) as exhibited in Eq. (4.8).

$$x_{ij}^{\text{def}} = \frac{x_{ij}^{l} + 4\times x_{ij}^{m} + x_{ij}^{u}}{6} \tag{4.8}$$

Step 10: Compute the threshold value (α) by adding the average of all the numbers presented in the total-effect matrix and dividing by the number of items present in the matrix as presented in Eq. (4.9).

$$\alpha = \frac{\sum_{i=1}^{n}\sum_{j=1}^{n}T_{ij}}{n^2} \tag{4.9}$$

where n^2 means the whole number of elements in the total-effect matrix.

Step 11: Compute the weights of ith IoT barriers to waste management in smart cities w_i by applying Eq. (4.10).

$$w_i = \frac{\left[\left(\left(\tilde{R}+\tilde{C}\right)^{\text{def}}\right)^2 + \left(\left(\tilde{R}-\tilde{C}\right)^{\text{def}}\right)^2\right]^{\frac{1}{2}}}{\sum_{i=1}^{n}\left[\left(\left(\tilde{R}+\tilde{C}\right)^{\text{def}}\right)^2 + \left(\left(\tilde{R}-\tilde{C}\right)^{\text{def}}\right)^2\right]^{\frac{1}{2}}} \tag{4.10}$$

4.4 Model Implementation

In this chapter, semi-structured interviews were conducted with industry professionals, extensive evaluations were conducted of the development plans for smart cities, and waste management reports and databases were analyzed. The goal of the chapter is to establish a holistic model. A qualitative research technique is used in this chapter because its primary purpose is to construct a study framework of IoT adoption obstacles to waste management in smart cities using the expertise and experience of industry professionals, as well as the findings of prior studies.

Step 1: In this chapter, we applied the fuzzy DEMATEL method to analyze IoT barriers to waste management in smart cities. The implementation of the fuzzy DEMATEL method in this chapter differs from the previous chapter. In this chapter, all the steps of the fuzzy DEMATEL method without defuzzification are applied from the beginning, unlike in the previous chapter.

Step 2: We formed a panel of four domain experts and requested their assistance in evaluating the IoT adoption obstacles to waste management in smart cities. Two specialists from the IT area, one from the smart cities' development project and one from waste management, comprise the three experts. Two scientists verified the stated obstacles to adoption. The majority of their time is spent creating the smart cities' project and constructing infrastructure.

Step 3: Linguistic variables and corresponding appropriate TFNs have been created to prioritize IoT barriers to waste management in smart cities, as presented in Table 4.1.

Step 4: A pairwise comparison matrix among the barriers and itself by all experts was created according to Eq. (4.1) by using the linguistic variable as presented in Table 4.2 and then by using TFNs according to Eq. (4.2) as presented in Table 4.3.

TABLE 4.2

Assessment of IoT Barriers to Waste Management in Smart Cities Using Linguistic Variables by All Experts

$Expert_1$	$IoTB_1$	$IoTB_2$	$IoTB_3$	$IoTB_4$	$IoTB_5$	$IoTB_6$	$IoTB_7$	$IoTB_8$	$IoTB_9$	$IoTB_{10}$
$IoTB_1$	⟨NFL⟩	⟨HFL⟩	⟨VLF⟩	⟨HFL⟩	⟨LFL⟩	⟨VLF⟩	⟨HFL⟩	⟨VHL⟩	⟨LFL⟩	⟨LFL⟩
$IoTB_2$	⟨LFL⟩	⟨NFL⟩	⟨HFL⟩	⟨VLF⟩	⟨NFL⟩	⟨VLF⟩	⟨LFL⟩	⟨LFL⟩	⟨VLF⟩	⟨LFL⟩
$IoTB_3$	VHL	⟨LFL⟩	⟨NFL⟩	⟨LFL⟩	⟨VLF⟩	⟨LFL⟩	⟨HFL⟩	⟨HFL⟩	⟨LFL⟩	⟨HFL⟩
$IoTB_4$	⟨NFL⟩	⟨HFL⟩	⟨LFL⟩	⟨NFL⟩	⟨NFL⟩	⟨VLF⟩	⟨NFL⟩	⟨LFL⟩	⟨HFL⟩	⟨LFL⟩
$IoTB_5$	⟨VLF⟩	⟨VLF⟩	⟨HFL⟩	⟨VLF⟩	⟨NFL⟩	⟨LFL⟩	⟨VLF⟩	⟨LFL⟩	⟨NFL⟩	⟨VLF⟩
$IoTB_6$	⟨VLF⟩	⟨LFL⟩	⟨LFL⟩	⟨LFL⟩	⟨HFL⟩	⟨NFL⟩	⟨NFL⟩	⟨HFL⟩	⟨VLF⟩	⟨LFL⟩
$IoTB_7$	⟨NFL⟩	VHL	⟨VLF⟩	⟨LFL⟩	⟨VHL⟩	⟨NFL⟩	⟨NFL⟩	⟨LFL⟩	⟨NFL⟩	⟨LFL⟩
$IoTB_8$	⟨LFL⟩	⟨HFL⟩	⟨LFL⟩	⟨VHL⟩	⟨HFL⟩	⟨VLF⟩	⟨VLF⟩	⟨NFL⟩	⟨HFL⟩	⟨HFL⟩

(Continued)

TABLE 4.2 (*Continued*)

Assessment of IoT Barriers to Waste Management in Smart Cities Using Linguistic Variables by All Experts

Expert₁	IoTB₁	IoTB₂	IoTB₃	IoTB₄	IoTB₅	IoTB₆	IoTB₇	IoTB₈	IoTB₉	IoTB₁₀
IoTB₉	⟨LFL⟩	⟨NFL⟩	⟨LFL⟩	⟨VHL⟩	⟨NFL⟩	⟨NFL⟩	⟨LFL⟩	⟨VLF⟩	⟨NFL⟩	⟨LFL⟩
IoTB₁₀	⟨LFL⟩	⟨LFL⟩	⟨NFL⟩	VHL	⟨HFL⟩	⟨HFL⟩	⟨HFL⟩	⟨LFL⟩	⟨HFL⟩	⟨NFL⟩

Expert₂	IoTB₁	IoTB₂	IoTB₃	IoTB₄	IoTB₅	IoTB₆	IoTB₇	IoTB₈	IoTB₉	IoTB₁₀
IoTB₁	⟨NFL⟩	⟨HFL⟩	⟨VLF⟩	⟨HFL⟩	⟨LFL⟩	⟨VLF⟩	⟨HFL⟩	⟨VHL⟩	⟨LFL⟩	⟨LFL⟩
IoTB₂	⟨LFL⟩	⟨NFL⟩	⟨HFL⟩	⟨VLF⟩	⟨NFL⟩	⟨VLF⟩	⟨LFL⟩	⟨LFL⟩	⟨VLF⟩	⟨HFL⟩
IoTB₃	VHL	⟨LFL⟩	⟨NFL⟩	⟨LFL⟩	⟨VLF⟩	⟨LFL⟩	⟨HFL⟩	⟨HFL⟩	⟨LFL⟩	⟨HFL⟩
IoTB₄	⟨NFL⟩	⟨HFL⟩	⟨LFL⟩	NFL	⟨NFL⟩	⟨VLF⟩	⟨HFL⟩	⟨LFL⟩	⟨HFL⟩	⟨LFL⟩
IoTB₅	⟨VLF⟩	⟨VLF⟩	⟨HFL⟩	⟨HFL⟩	⟨NFL⟩	⟨LFL⟩	⟨VLF⟩	⟨LFL⟩	⟨NFL⟩	⟨VLF⟩
IoTB₆	⟨VLF⟩	⟨LFL⟩	⟨LFL⟩	⟨LFL⟩	⟨HFL⟩	⟨NFL⟩	⟨HFL⟩	⟨HFL⟩	⟨VLF⟩	⟨LFL⟩
IoTB₇	⟨NFL⟩	⟨VHL⟩	⟨VLF⟩	⟨LFL⟩	⟨VHL⟩	⟨NFL⟩	⟨NFL⟩	⟨LFL⟩	⟨NFL⟩	⟨LFL⟩
IoTB₈	⟨HFL⟩	⟨HFL⟩	⟨LFL⟩	⟨VHL⟩	⟨HFL⟩	⟨VLF⟩	⟨VLF⟩	⟨NFL⟩	⟨HFL⟩	⟨HFL⟩
IoTB₉	⟨LFL⟩	⟨NFL⟩	⟨LFL⟩	⟨VHL⟩	⟨NFL⟩	⟨NFL⟩	⟨LFL⟩	⟨VLF⟩	⟨NFL⟩	⟨LFL⟩
IoTB₁₀	⟨LFL⟩	⟨LFL⟩	⟨NFL⟩	⟨VHL⟩	⟨HFL⟩	⟨HFL⟩	⟨HFL⟩	⟨LFL⟩	⟨HFL⟩	⟨NFL⟩

Expert₃	IoTB₁	IoTB₂	IoTB₃	IoTB₄	IoTB₅	IoTB₆	IoTB₇	IoTB₈	IoTB₉	IoTB₁₀
IoTB₁	⟨NFL⟩	⟨HFL⟩	⟨VLF⟩	⟨HFL⟩	⟨LFL⟩	⟨VLF⟩	⟨HFL⟩	⟨VHL⟩	⟨LFL⟩	⟨LFL⟩
IoTB₂	⟨VLF⟩	⟨NFL⟩	⟨HFL⟩	⟨VLF⟩	⟨NFL⟩	⟨VLF⟩	⟨HFL⟩	⟨LFL⟩	⟨VLF⟩	⟨LFL⟩
IoTB₃	⟨VHL⟩	⟨LFL⟩	⟨NFL⟩	⟨LFL⟩	⟨VLF⟩	⟨LFL⟩	⟨HFL⟩	⟨HFL⟩	⟨LFL⟩	⟨HFL⟩
IoTB₄	⟨NFL⟩	⟨HFL⟩	⟨LFL⟩	⟨NFL⟩	⟨NFL⟩	⟨VLF⟩	⟨NFL⟩	⟨LFL⟩	⟨HFL⟩	⟨LFL⟩
IoTB₅	⟨VLF⟩	⟨VLF⟩	⟨HFL⟩	⟨VLF⟩	⟨NFL⟩	⟨LFL⟩	⟨VLF⟩	⟨LFL⟩	⟨NFL⟩	⟨VLF⟩
IoTB₆	⟨VLF⟩	⟨LFL⟩	⟨LFL⟩	⟨LFL⟩	⟨HFL⟩	⟨NFL⟩	⟨NFL⟩	⟨HFL⟩	⟨VLF⟩	⟨LFL⟩
IoTB₇	⟨NFL⟩	⟨VHL⟩	⟨VLF⟩	⟨LFL⟩	⟨VHL⟩	⟨NFL⟩	⟨NFL⟩	⟨LFL⟩	⟨NFL⟩	⟨LFL⟩
IoTB₈	⟨LFL⟩	⟨HFL⟩	⟨HFL⟩	⟨VHL⟩	⟨HFL⟩	⟨VLF⟩	⟨VLF⟩	⟨NFL⟩	⟨HFL⟩	⟨HFL⟩
IoTB₉	⟨HFL⟩	⟨NFL⟩	⟨LFL⟩	⟨VHL⟩	⟨NFL⟩	⟨NFL⟩	⟨LFL⟩	⟨VLF⟩	⟨NFL⟩	⟨LFL⟩
IoTB₁₀	⟨LFL⟩	⟨LFL⟩	⟨NFL⟩	⟨VHL⟩	⟨HFL⟩	⟨HFL⟩	⟨HFL⟩	⟨LFL⟩	⟨HFL⟩	⟨NFL⟩

Expert₄	IoTB₁	IoTB₂	IoTB₃	IoTB₄	IoTB₅	IoTB₆	IoTB₇	IoTB₈	IoTB₉	IoTB₁₀
IoTB₁	⟨NFL⟩	⟨HFL⟩	⟨VLF⟩	⟨HFL⟩	⟨LFL⟩	⟨VLF⟩	⟨HFL⟩	⟨VHL⟩	⟨LFL⟩	⟨LFL⟩
IoTB₂	⟨VLF⟩	⟨NFL⟩	⟨HFL⟩	⟨VLF⟩	⟨NFL⟩	⟨HFL⟩	⟨LFL⟩	⟨LFL⟩	⟨VLF⟩	⟨VLF⟩
IoTB₃	⟨VHL⟩	⟨LFL⟩	⟨NFL⟩	⟨LFL⟩	⟨VLF⟩	⟨LFL⟩	⟨HFL⟩	⟨HFL⟩	⟨LFL⟩	⟨HFL⟩
IoTB₄	⟨NFL⟩	⟨HFL⟩	⟨LFL⟩	⟨NFL⟩	⟨NFL⟩	⟨VLF⟩	⟨NFL⟩	⟨LFL⟩	⟨HFL⟩	⟨LFL⟩
IoTB₅	⟨VLF⟩	⟨VLF⟩	⟨HFL⟩	⟨VLF⟩	⟨NFL⟩	⟨LFL⟩	⟨VLF⟩	⟨HFL⟩	⟨NFL⟩	⟨VLF⟩
IoTB₆	⟨VLF⟩	⟨VLF⟩	⟨LFL⟩	⟨LFL⟩	⟨HFL⟩	⟨NFL⟩	⟨NFL⟩	⟨HFL⟩	⟨VLF⟩	⟨VLF⟩
IoTB₇	⟨NFL⟩	⟨VHL⟩	⟨VLF⟩	⟨VLF⟩	⟨VHL⟩	⟨NFL⟩	⟨NFL⟩	⟨LFL⟩	⟨NFL⟩	⟨LFL⟩
IoTB₈	⟨LFL⟩	⟨HFL⟩	⟨LFL⟩	⟨VHL⟩	⟨HFL⟩	⟨VLF⟩	⟨VLF⟩	⟨NFL⟩	⟨HFL⟩	⟨HFL⟩
IoTB₉	⟨LFL⟩	⟨NFL⟩	⟨LFL⟩	⟨VHL⟩	⟨NFL⟩	⟨NFL⟩	⟨LFL⟩	⟨VLF⟩	⟨NFL⟩	⟨LFL⟩
IoTB₁₀	⟨LFL⟩	⟨LFL⟩	⟨NFL⟩	⟨VHL⟩	⟨HFL⟩	⟨HFL⟩	⟨HFL⟩.	⟨LFL⟩	⟨HFL⟩	NFL

TABLE 4.3

Valuation of IoT Barriers to Waste Management in Smart Cities Using TFNs by All Experts

Expert₁	IoTB₁	IoTB₂	IoTB₃	IoTB₄	IoTB₅
IoTB₁	⟨0.00, 0.00, 0.25⟩	⟨0.50, 0.75, 1.00⟩	⟨0.00, 0.25, 0.50⟩	⟨0.50, 0.75, 1.00⟩	⟨0.25, 0.50, 0.75⟩
IoTB₂	⟨0.25, 0.50, 0.75⟩	⟨0.00, 0.00, 0.25⟩	⟨0.50, 0.75, 1.00⟩	⟨0.00, 0.25, 0.50⟩	⟨0.00, 0.00, 0.25⟩
IoTB₃	⟨0.75, 1.00, 1.00⟩	⟨0.25, 0.50, 0.75⟩	⟨0.00, 0.00, 0.25⟩	⟨0.25, 0.50, 0.75⟩	⟨0.00, 0.25, 0.50⟩
IoTB₄	⟨0.00, 0.00, 0.25⟩	⟨0.50, 0.75, 1.00⟩	⟨0.25, 0.50, 0.75⟩	⟨0.00, 0.00, 0.25⟩	⟨0.00, 0.00, 0.25⟩
IoTB₅	⟨0.00, 0.25, 0.50⟩	⟨0.00, 0.25, 0.50⟩	⟨0.50, 0.75, 1.00⟩	⟨0.00, 0.25, 0.50⟩	⟨0.00, 0.00, 0.25⟩
IoTB₆	⟨0.00, 0.25, 0.50⟩	⟨0.25, 0.50, 0.75⟩	⟨0.25, 0.50, 0.75⟩	⟨0.25, 0.50, 0.75⟩	⟨0.50, 0.75, 1.00⟩
IoTB₇	⟨0.00, 0.00, 0.25⟩	⟨0.75, 1.00, 1.00⟩	⟨0.00, 0.25, 0.50⟩	⟨0.25, 0.50, 0.75⟩	⟨0.75, 1.00, 1.00⟩
IoTB₈	⟨0.25, 0.50, 0.75⟩	⟨0.50, 0.75, 1.00⟩	⟨0.25, 0.50, 0.75⟩	⟨0.75, 1.00, 1.00⟩	⟨0.50, 0.75, 1.00⟩
IoTB₉	⟨0.25, 0.50, 0.75⟩	⟨0.00, 0.00, 0.25⟩	⟨0.25, 0.50, 0.75⟩	⟨0.75, 1.00, 1.00⟩	⟨0.00, 0.00, 0.25⟩
IoTB₁₀	⟨0.25, 0.50, 0.75⟩	⟨0.25, 0.50, 0.75⟩	⟨0.00, 0.00, 0.25⟩	⟨0.75, 1.00, 1.00⟩	⟨0.50, 0.75, 1.00⟩

Expert₁	IoTB₆	IoTB₇	IoTB₈	IoTB₉	IoTB₁₀
IoTB₁	⟨0.00, 0.25, 0.50⟩	⟨0.50, 0.75, 1.00⟩	⟨0.75, 1.00, 1.00⟩	⟨0.25, 0.50, 0.75⟩	⟨0.25, 0.50, 0.75⟩
IoTB₂	⟨0.00, 0.25, 0.50⟩	⟨0.25, 0.50, 0.75⟩	⟨0.25, 0.50, 0.75⟩	⟨0.00, 0.25, 0.50⟩	⟨0.25, 0.50, 0.75⟩
IoTB₃	⟨0.25, 0.50, 0.75⟩	⟨0.50, 0.75, 1.00⟩	⟨0.50, 0.75, 1.00⟩	⟨0.25, 0.50, 0.75⟩	⟨0.50, 0.75, 1.00⟩
IoTB₄	⟨0.00, 0.25, 0.50⟩	⟨0.00, 0.00, 0.25⟩	⟨0.25, 0.50, 0.75⟩	⟨0.50, 0.75, 1.00⟩	⟨0.25, 0.50, 0.75⟩
IoTB₅	⟨0.25, 0.50, 0.75⟩	⟨0.00, 0.25, 0.50⟩	⟨0.25, 0.50, 0.75⟩	⟨0.00, 0.00, 0.25⟩	⟨0.00, 0.25, 0.50⟩
IoTB₆	⟨0.00, 0.00, 0.25⟩	⟨0.00, 0.00, 0.25⟩	⟨0.50, 0.75, 1.00⟩	⟨0.00, 0.25, 0.50⟩	⟨0.25, 0.50, 0.75⟩
IoTB₇	⟨0.00, 0.00, 0.25⟩	⟨0.00, 0.00, 0.25⟩	⟨0.25, 0.50, 0.75⟩	⟨0.00, 0.00, 0.25⟩	⟨0.25, 0.50, 0.75⟩
IoTB₈	⟨0.00, 0.25, 0.50⟩	⟨0.00, 0.25, 0.50⟩	⟨0.00, 0.00, 0.25⟩	⟨0.50, 0.75, 1.00⟩	⟨0.50, 0.75, 1.00⟩
IoTB₉	⟨0.00, 0.00, 0.25⟩	⟨0.25, 0.50, 0.75⟩	⟨0.00, 0.25, 0.50⟩	⟨0.00, 0.00, 0.25⟩	⟨0.25, 0.50, 0.75⟩
IoTB₁₀	⟨0.50, 0.75, 1.00⟩	⟨0.50, 0.75, 1.00⟩	⟨0.25, 0.50, 0.75⟩	⟨0.50, 0.75, 1.00⟩	⟨0.00, 0.00, 0.25⟩

Expert₂	IoTB₁	IoTB₂	IoTB₃	IoTB₄	IoTB₅
IoTB₁	⟨0.00, 0.00, 0.25⟩	⟨0.50, 0.75, 1.00⟩	⟨0.00, 0.25, 0.50⟩	⟨0.50, 0.75, 1.00⟩	⟨0.25, 0.50, 0.75⟩
IoTB₂	⟨0.25, 0.50, 0.75⟩	⟨0.00, 0.00, 0.25⟩	⟨0.50, 0.75, 1.00⟩	⟨0.00, 0.25, 0.50⟩	⟨0.00, 0.00, 0.25⟩
IoTB₃	⟨0.75, 1.00, 1.00⟩	⟨0.25, 0.50, 0.75⟩	⟨0.00, 0.00, 0.25⟩	⟨0.25, 0.50, 0.75⟩	⟨0.00, 0.25, 0.50⟩
IoTB₄	⟨0.00, 0.00, 0.25⟩	⟨0.50, 0.75, 1.00⟩	⟨0.25, 0.50, 0.75⟩	⟨0.00, 0.00, 0.25⟩	⟨0.00, 0.00, 0.25⟩
IoTB₅	⟨0.00, 0.25, 0.50⟩	⟨0.00, 0.25, 0.50⟩	⟨0.50, 0.75, 1.00⟩	⟨0.50, 0.75, 1.00⟩	⟨0.00, 0.00, 0.25⟩
IoTB₆	⟨0.00, 0.25, 0.50⟩	⟨0.25, 0.50, 0.75⟩	⟨0.25, 0.50, 0.75⟩	⟨0.25, 0.50, 0.75⟩	⟨0.50, 0.75, 1.00⟩
IoTB₇	⟨0.00, 0.00, 0.25⟩	⟨0.75, 1.00, 1.00⟩	⟨0.00, 0.25, 0.50⟩	⟨0.25, 0.50, 0.75⟩	⟨0.75, 1.00, 1.00⟩
IoTB₈	⟨0.50, 0.75, 1.00⟩	⟨0.50, 0.75, 1.00⟩	⟨0.25, 0.50, 0.75⟩	⟨0.75, 1.00, 1.00⟩	⟨0.50, 0.75, 1.00⟩
IoTB₉	⟨0.25, 0.50, 0.75⟩	⟨0.00, 0.00, 0.25⟩	⟨0.25, 0.50, 0.75⟩	⟨0.75, 1.00, 1.00⟩	⟨0.00, 0.00, 0.25⟩
IoTB₁₀	⟨0.25, 0.50, 0.75⟩	⟨0.25, 0.50, 0.75⟩	⟨0.00, 0.00, 0.25⟩	⟨0.75, 1.00, 1.00⟩	⟨0.50, 0.75, 1.00⟩

(Continued)

TABLE 4.3 (*Continued*)

Valuation of IoT Barriers to Waste Management in Smart Cities Using TFNs by All Experts

Expert$_2$	IoTB$_6$	IoTB$_7$	IoTB$_8$	IoTB$_9$	IoTB$_{10}$
IoTB$_1$	⟨0.00, 0.25, 0.50⟩	⟨0.50, 0.75, 1.00⟩	⟨0.75, 1.00, 1.00⟩	⟨0.25, 0.50, 0.75⟩	⟨0.25, 0.50, 0.75⟩
IoTB$_2$	⟨0.00, 0.25, 0.50⟩	⟨0.25, 0.50, 0.75⟩	⟨0.25, 0.50, 0.75⟩	⟨0.00, 0.25, 0.50⟩	⟨0.50, 0.75, 1.00⟩
IoTB$_3$	⟨0.25, 0.50, 0.75⟩	⟨0.50, 0.75, 1.00⟩	⟨0.50, 0.75, 1.00⟩	⟨0.25, 0.50, 0.75⟩	⟨0.50, 0.75, 1.00⟩
IoTB$_4$	⟨0.00, 0.25, 0.50⟩	⟨0.50, 0.75, 1.00⟩	⟨0.25, 0.50, 0.75⟩	⟨0.50, 0.75, 1.00⟩	⟨0.25, 0.50, 0.75⟩
IoTB$_5$	⟨0.25, 0.50, 0.75⟩	⟨0.00, 0.25, 0.50⟩	⟨0.25, 0.50, 0.75⟩	⟨0.00, 0.00, 0.25⟩	⟨0.00, 0.25, 0.50⟩
IoTB$_6$	⟨0.00, 0.00, 0.25⟩	⟨0.50, 0.75, 1.00⟩	⟨0.50, 0.75, 1.00⟩	⟨0.00, 0.25, 0.50⟩	⟨0.25, 0.50, 0.75⟩
IoTB$_7$	⟨0.00, 0.00, 0.25⟩	⟨0.00, 0.00, 0.25⟩	⟨0.25, 0.50, 0.75⟩	⟨0.00, 0.00, 0.25⟩	⟨0.25, 0.50, 0.75⟩
IoTB$_8$	⟨0.00, 0.25, 0.50⟩	⟨0.00, 0.25, 0.50⟩	⟨0.00, 0.00, 0.25⟩	⟨0.50, 0.75, 1.00⟩	⟨0.50, 0.75, 1.00⟩
IoTB$_9$	⟨0.00, 0.00, 0.25⟩	⟨0.25, 0.50, 0.75⟩	⟨0.00, 0.25, 0.50⟩	⟨0.00, 0.00, 0.25⟩	⟨0.25, 0.50, 0.75⟩
IoTB$_{10}$	⟨0.50, 0.75, 1.00⟩	⟨0.50, 0.75, 1.00⟩	⟨0.25, 0.50, 0.75⟩	⟨0.50, 0.75, 1.00⟩	⟨0.00, 0.00, 0.25⟩

Expert$_3$	IoTB$_1$	IoTB$_2$	IoTB$_3$	IoTB$_4$	IoTB$_5$
IoTB$_1$	⟨0.00, 0.00, 0.25⟩	⟨0.50, 0.75, 1.00⟩	⟨0.00, 0.25, 0.50⟩	⟨0.50, 0.75, 1.00⟩	⟨0.25, 0.50, 0.75⟩
IoTB$_2$	⟨0.00, 0.25, 0.50⟩	⟨0.00, 0.00, 0.25⟩	⟨0.50, 0.75, 1.00⟩	⟨0.00, 0.25, 0.50⟩	⟨0.00, 0.00, 0.25⟩
IoTB$_3$	⟨0.75, 1.00, 1.00⟩	⟨0.25, 0.50, 0.75⟩	⟨0.00, 0.00, 0.25⟩	⟨0.25, 0.50, 0.75⟩	⟨0.00, 0.25, 0.50⟩
IoTB$_4$	⟨0.00, 0.00, 0.25⟩	⟨0.50, 0.75, 1.00⟩	⟨0.25, 0.50, 0.75⟩	⟨0.00, 0.00, 0.25⟩	⟨0.00, 0.00, 0.25⟩
IoTB$_5$	⟨0.00, 0.25, 0.50⟩	⟨0.00, 0.25, 0.50⟩	⟨0.50, 0.75, 1.00⟩	⟨0.00, 0.25, 0.50⟩	⟨0.00, 0.00, 0.25⟩
IoTB$_6$	⟨0.00, 0.25, 0.50⟩	⟨0.25, 0.50, 0.75⟩	⟨0.25, 0.50, 0.75⟩	⟨0.25, 0.50, 0.75⟩	⟨0.50, 0.75, 1.00⟩
IoTB$_7$	⟨0.00, 0.00, 0.25⟩	⟨0.75, 1.00, 1.00⟩	⟨0.00, 0.25, 0.50⟩	⟨0.25, 0.50, 0.75⟩	⟨0.75, 1.00, 1.00⟩
IoTB$_8$	⟨0.25, 0.50, 0.75⟩	⟨0.50, 0.75, 1.00⟩	⟨0.50, 0.75, 1.00⟩	⟨0.75, 1.00, 1.00⟩	⟨0.50, 0.75, 1.00⟩
IoTB$_9$	⟨0.50, 0.75, 1.00⟩	⟨0.00, 0.00, 0.25⟩	⟨0.25, 0.50, 0.75⟩	⟨0.75, 1.00, 1.00⟩	⟨0.00, 0.00, 0.25⟩
IoTB$_{10}$	⟨0.25, 0.50, 0.75⟩	⟨0.25, 0.50, 0.75⟩	⟨0.00, 0.00, 0.25⟩	⟨0.75, 1.00, 1.00⟩	⟨0.50, 0.75, 1.00⟩

Expert$_3$	IoTB$_6$	IoTB$_7$	IoTB$_8$	IoTB$_9$	IoTB$_{10}$
IoTB$_1$	⟨0.00, 0.25, 0.50⟩	⟨0.50, 0.75, 1.00⟩	⟨0.75, 1.00, 1.00⟩	⟨0.25, 0.50, 0.75⟩	⟨0.25, 0.50, 0.75⟩
IoTB$_2$	⟨0.00, 0.25, 0.50⟩	⟨0.50, 0.75, 1.00⟩	⟨0.25, 0.50, 0.75⟩	⟨0.00, 0.25, 0.50⟩	⟨0.25, 0.50, 0.75⟩
IoTB$_3$	⟨0.25, 0.50, 0.75⟩	⟨0.50, 0.75, 1.00⟩	⟨0.50, 0.75, 1.00⟩	⟨0.25, 0.50, 0.75⟩	⟨0.50, 0.75, 1.00⟩
IoTB$_4$	⟨0.00, 0.25, 0.50⟩	⟨0.00, 0.00, 0.25⟩	⟨0.25, 0.50, 0.75⟩	⟨0.50, 0.75, 1.00⟩	⟨0.25, 0.50, 0.75⟩
IoTB$_5$	⟨0.25, 0.50, 0.75⟩	⟨0.00, 0.25, 0.50⟩	⟨0.25, 0.50, 0.75⟩	⟨0.00, 0.00, 0.25⟩	⟨0.00, 0.25, 0.50⟩
IoTB$_6$	⟨0.00, 0.00, 0.25⟩	⟨0.00, 0.00, 0.25⟩	⟨0.50, 0.75, 1.00⟩	⟨0.00, 0.25, 0.50⟩	⟨0.25, 0.50, 0.75⟩
IoTB$_7$	⟨0.00, 0.00, 0.25⟩	⟨0.00, 0.00, 0.25⟩	⟨0.25, 0.50, 0.75⟩	⟨0.00, 0.00, 0.25⟩	⟨0.25, 0.50, 0.75⟩
IoTB$_8$	⟨0.00, 0.25, 0.50⟩	⟨0.00, 0.25, 0.50⟩	⟨0.00, 0.00, 0.25⟩	⟨0.50, 0.75, 1.00⟩	⟨0.50, 0.75, 1.00⟩
IoTB$_9$	⟨0.00, 0.00, 0.25⟩	⟨0.25, 0.50, 0.75⟩	⟨0.00, 0.25, 0.50⟩	⟨0.00, 0.00, 0.25⟩	⟨0.25, 0.50, 0.75⟩
IoTB$_{10}$	⟨0.50, 0.75, 1.00⟩	⟨0.50, 0.75, 1.00⟩	⟨0.25, 0.50, 0.75⟩	⟨0.50, 0.75, 1.00⟩	⟨0.00, 0.00, 0.25⟩

(Continued)

TABLE 4.3 (*Continued*)

Valuation of IoT Barriers to Waste Management in Smart Cities Using TFNs by All Experts

Expert₄	IoTB₁	IoTB₂	IoTB₃	IoTB₄	IoTB₅
IoTB₁	⟨0.00, 0.00, 0.25⟩	⟨0.50, 0.75, 1.00⟩	⟨0.00, 0.25, 0.50⟩	⟨0.50, 0.75, 1.00⟩	⟨0.25, 0.50, 0.75⟩
IoTB₂	⟨0.00, 0.25, 0.50⟩	⟨0.00, 0.00, 0.25⟩	⟨0.50, 0.75, 1.00⟩	⟨0.00, 0.25, 0.50⟩	⟨0.00, 0.00, 0.25⟩
IoTB₃	⟨0.75, 1.00, 1.00⟩	⟨0.25, 0.50, 0.75⟩	⟨0.00, 0.00, 0.25⟩	⟨0.25, 0.50, 0.75⟩	⟨0.00, 0.25, 0.50⟩
IoTB₄	⟨0.00, 0.00, 0.25⟩	⟨0.50, 0.75, 1.00⟩	⟨0.25, 0.50, 0.75⟩	⟨0.00, 0.00, 0.25⟩	⟨0.00, 0.00, 0.25⟩
IoTB₅	⟨0.00, 0.25, 0.50⟩	⟨0.00, 0.25, 0.50⟩	⟨0.50, 0.75, 1.00⟩	⟨0.00, 0.25, 0.50⟩	⟨0.00, 0.00, 0.25⟩
IoTB₆	⟨0.00, 0.25, 0.50⟩	⟨0.00, 0.25, 0.50⟩	⟨0.25, 0.50, 0.75⟩	⟨0.25, 0.50, 0.75⟩	⟨0.50, 0.75, 1.00⟩
IoTB₇	⟨0.00, 0.00, 0.25⟩	⟨0.75, 1.00, 1.00⟩	⟨0.00, 0.25, 0.50⟩	⟨0.00, 0.25, 0.50⟩	⟨0.75, 1.00, 1.00⟩
IoTB₈	⟨0.25, 0.50, 0.75⟩	⟨0.50, 0.75, 1.00⟩	⟨0.25, 0.50, 0.75⟩	⟨0.75, 1.00, 1.00⟩	⟨0.50, 0.75, 1.00⟩
IoTB₉	⟨0.25, 0.50, 0.75⟩	⟨0.00, 0.00, 0.25⟩	⟨0.25, 0.50, 0.75⟩	⟨0.75, 1.00, 1.00⟩	⟨0.00, 0.00, 0.25⟩
IoTB₁₀	⟨0.25, 0.50, 0.75⟩	⟨0.25, 0.50, 0.75⟩	⟨0.00, 0.00, 0.25⟩	⟨0.75, 1.00, 1.00⟩	⟨0.50, 0.75, 1.00⟩

Expert₄	IoTB₆	IoTB₇	IoTB₈	IoTB₉	IoTB₁₀
IoTB₁	⟨0.00, 0.25, 0.50⟩	⟨0.50, 0.75, 1.00⟩	⟨0.75, 1.00, 1.00⟩	⟨0.25, 0.50, 0.75⟩	⟨0.25, 0.50, 0.75⟩
IoTB₂	⟨0.50, 0.75, 1.00⟩	⟨0.25, 0.50, 0.75⟩	⟨0.25, 0.50, 0.75⟩	⟨0.00, 0.25, 0.50⟩	⟨0.00, 0.25, 0.50⟩
IoTB₃	⟨0.25, 0.50, 0.75⟩	⟨0.50, 0.75, 1.00⟩	⟨0.50, 0.75, 1.00⟩	⟨0.25, 0.50, 0.75⟩	⟨0.50, 0.75, 1.00⟩
IoTB₄	⟨0.00, 0.25, 0.50⟩	⟨0.00, 0.00, 0.25⟩	⟨0.25, 0.50, 0.75⟩	⟨0.50, 0.75, 1.00⟩	⟨0.25, 0.50, 0.75⟩
IoTB₅	⟨0.25, 0.50, 0.75⟩	⟨0.00, 0.25, 0.50⟩	⟨0.50, 0.75, 1.00⟩	⟨0.00, 0.00, 0.25⟩	⟨0.00, 0.25, 0.50⟩
IoTB₆	⟨0.00, 0.00, 0.25⟩	⟨0.00, 0.00, 0.25⟩	⟨0.50, 0.75, 1.00⟩	⟨0.00, 0.25, 0.50⟩	⟨0.00, 0.25, 0.50⟩
IoTB₇	⟨0.00, 0.00, 0.25⟩	⟨0.00, 0.00, 0.25⟩	⟨0.25, 0.50, 0.75⟩	⟨0.00, 0.00, 0.25⟩	⟨0.25, 0.50, 0.75⟩
IoTB₈	⟨0.00, 0.25, 0.50⟩	⟨0.00, 0.25, 0.50⟩	⟨0.00, 0.00, 0.25⟩	⟨0.50, 0.75, 1.00⟩	⟨0.50, 0.75, 1.00⟩
IoTB₉	⟨0.00, 0.00, 0.25⟩	⟨0.25, 0.50, 0.75⟩	⟨0.00, 0.25, 0.50⟩	⟨0.00, 0.00, 0.25⟩	⟨0.25, 0.50, 0.75⟩
IoTB₁₀	⟨0.50, 0.75, 1.00⟩	⟨0.50, 0.75, 1.00⟩	⟨0.25, 0.50, 0.75⟩	⟨0.50, 0.75, 1.00⟩	⟨0.00, 0.00, 0.25⟩

Step 5: All decision matrices created by all experts were aggregated into a single matrix according to Eq. (4.3), as presented in Table 4.4.

Step 6: The generalized direct-relation matrix for all IoT barriers to waste management in smart cities was constructed for the lower, median, and upper limits according to Eq. (4.4), as presented in Table 4.5.

Step 7: The total-relation matrix for all IoT barriers to waste management in smart cities was computed for the lower limit, median limit, and upper limit according to Eq. (4.5), and the results are formed in Table 4.6.

Step 8: The IRM was constructed by computing the sum of rows and columns $\tilde{R}$ and $\tilde{C}$, according to Eqs. (4.6) and (4.7), respectively, as presented in Table 4.7.

TABLE 4.4

Aggregation Valuations of IoT Barriers to Waste Management in Smart Cities Using TFNs by All Experts

Expert$_1$	IoTB$_1$	IoTB$_2$	IoTB$_3$	IoTB$_4$	IoTB$_5$
IoTB$_1$	⟨0.00, 0.00, 0.25⟩	⟨0.50, 0.75, 1.00⟩	⟨0.00, 0.25, 0.50⟩	⟨0.50, 0.75, 1.00⟩	⟨0.25, 0.50, 0.75⟩
IoTB$_2$	⟨0.13, 0.38, 0.63⟩	⟨0.00, 0.00, 0.25⟩	⟨0.50, 0.75, 1.00⟩	⟨0.00, 0.25, 0.50⟩	⟨0.00, 0.00, 0.25⟩
IoTB$_3$	⟨0.75, 1.00, 1.00⟩	⟨0.25, 0.50, 0.75⟩	⟨0.00, 0.00, 0.25⟩	⟨0.25, 0.50, 0.75⟩	⟨0.00, 0.25, 0.50⟩
IoTB$_4$	⟨0.00, 0.00, 0.25⟩	⟨0.50, 0.75, 1.00⟩	⟨0.25, 0.50, 0.75⟩	⟨0.00, 0.00, 0.25⟩	⟨0.00, 0.00, 0.25⟩
IoTB$_5$	⟨0.00, 0.25, 0.50⟩	⟨0.00, 0.25, 0.50⟩	⟨0.50, 0.75, 1.00⟩	⟨0.00, 0.25, 0.50⟩	⟨0.00, 0.00, 0.25⟩
IoTB$_6$	⟨0.00, 0.25, 0.50⟩	⟨0.13, 0.44, 0.69⟩	⟨0.25, 0.50, 0.75⟩	⟨0.25, 0.50, 0.75⟩	⟨0.50, 0.75, 1.00⟩
IoTB$_7$	⟨0.00, 0.00, 0.25⟩	⟨0.75, 1.00, 1.00⟩	⟨0.00, 0.25, 0.50⟩	⟨0.13, 0.44, 0.69⟩	⟨0.75, 1.00, 1.00⟩
IoTB$_8$	⟨0.31, 0.56, 0.81⟩	⟨0.50, 0.75, 1.00⟩	⟨0.31, 0.56, 0.81⟩	⟨0.75, 1.00, 1.00⟩	⟨0.50, 0.75, 1.00⟩
IoTB$_9$	⟨0.25, 0.50, 0.75⟩	⟨0.00, 0.00, 0.25⟩	⟨0.25, 0.50, 0.75⟩	⟨0.75, 1.00, 1.00⟩	⟨0.00, 0.00, 0.25⟩
IoTB$_{10}$	⟨0.25, 0.50, 0.75⟩	⟨0.25, 0.50, 0.75⟩	⟨0.00, 0.00, 0.25⟩	⟨0.75, 1.00, 1.00⟩	⟨0.50, 0.75, 1.00⟩

Expert$_1$	IoTB$_6$	IoTB$_7$	IoTB$_8$	IoTB$_9$	IoTB$_{10}$
IoTB$_1$	⟨0.00, 0.25, 0.50⟩	⟨0.50, 0.75, 1.00⟩	⟨0.75, 1.00, 1.00⟩	⟨0.25, 0.50, 0.75⟩	⟨0.25, 0.50, 0.75⟩
IoTB$_2$	⟨0.13, 0.38, 0.63⟩	⟨0.25, 0.50, 0.75⟩	⟨0.25, 0.50, 0.75⟩	⟨0.00, 0.25, 0.50⟩	⟨0.25, 0.50, 0.75⟩
IoTB$_3$	⟨0.25, 0.50, 0.75⟩	⟨0.50, 0.75, 1.00⟩	⟨0.50, 0.75, 1.00⟩	⟨0.25, 0.50, 0.75⟩	⟨0.50, 0.75, 1.00⟩
IoTB$_4$	⟨0.00, 0.25, 0.50⟩	⟨0.13, 0.19, 0.63⟩	⟨0.25, 0.50, 0.75⟩	⟨0.50, 0.75, 1.00⟩	⟨0.25, 0.50, 0.75⟩
IoTB$_5$	⟨0.25, 0.50, 0.75⟩	⟨0.00, 0.25, 0.50⟩	⟨0.31, 0.56, 0.81⟩	⟨0.00, 0.25, 0.50⟩	⟨0.00, 0.25, 0.50⟩
IoTB$_6$	⟨0.00, 0.25, 0.50⟩	⟨0.00, 0.00, 0.25⟩	⟨0.50, 0.75, 1.00⟩	⟨0.00, 0.25, 0.50⟩	⟨0.25, 0.43, 0.69⟩
IoTB$_7$	⟨0.00, 0.00, 0.25⟩	⟨0.13, 0.19, 0.44⟩	⟨0.25, 0.50, 0.75⟩	⟨0.00, 0.00, 0.25⟩	⟨0.25, 0.50, 0.75⟩
IoTB$_8$	⟨0.00, 0.25, 0.50⟩	⟨0.00, 0.25, 0.50⟩	⟨0.00, 0.00, 0.25⟩	⟨0.50, 0.75, 1.00⟩	⟨0.50, 0.75, 1.00⟩
IoTB$_9$	⟨0.00, 0.00, 0.25⟩	⟨0.25, 0.50, 0.75⟩	⟨0.00, 0.25, 0.50⟩	⟨0.00, 0.00, 0.25⟩	⟨0.25, 0.50, 0.75⟩
IoTB$_{10}$	⟨0.50, 0.75, 1.00⟩	⟨0.50, 0.75, 1.00⟩	⟨0.25, 0.50, 0.75⟩	⟨0.50, 0.75, 1.00⟩	⟨0.00, 0.00, 0.25⟩

Step 9: The $(\tilde{R} + \tilde{C}, \tilde{R} - \tilde{C})$ was defuzzified by applying the GMIR method according to Eq. (4.8) as presented in Table 4.7.

Step 10: The weights of IoT barriers to waste management in smart cities were computed according to Eq. (4.10), as shown in Table 4.7 and Figure 4.3.

Step 11: The total-relation matrix for all IoT barriers to waste management in smart cities was defuzzified for the lower limit, median limit, and upper limit according to Eq. (4.8), and then, the α was computed by adding the average of all the numbers presented in the total-effect matrix and dividing by the number of items present in the matrix according to Eq. (4.9) as presented in Table 4.8 and as shown in Figure 4.4.

TABLE 4.5

Generalized Relation Matrix of IoT Barriers to Waste Management in Smart Cities by All Experts

Expert$_s$	IoTB$_1$	IoTB$_2$	IoTB$_3$	IoTB$_4$	IoTB$_5$	IoTB$_6$	IoTB$_7$	IoTB$_8$	IoTB$_9$	IoTB$_{10}$
Lower Element Matrix										
IoTB$_1$	0.000	0.143	0.000	0.143	0.071	0.000	0.143	0.214	0.071	0.071
IoTB$_2$	0.037	0.000	0.143	0.000	0.000	0.037	0.071	0.071	0.000	0.071
IoTB$_3$	0.214	0.071	0.000	0.071	0.000	0.071	0.143	0.143	0.071	0.143
IoTB$_4$	0.000	0.143	0.071	0.000	0.000	0.000	0.037	0.071	0.143	0.071
IoTB$_5$	0.000	0.000	0.143	0.000	0.000	0.071	0.000	0.089	0.000	0.000
IoTB$_6$	0.000	0.037	0.071	0.071	0.143	0.000	0.000	0.143	0.000	0.071
IoTB$_7$	0.000	0.214	0.000	0.037	0.214	0.000	0.037	0.071	0.000	0.071
IoTB$_8$	0.089	0.143	0.089	0.214	0.143	0.000	0.000	0.000	0.143	0.143
IoTB$_9$	0.071	0.000	0.071	0.214	0.000	0.000	0.071	0.000	0.000	0.071
IoTB$_{10}$	0.071	0.071	0.000	0.214	0.143	0.143	0.143	0.071	0.143	0.000
Median Element Matrix										
IoTB$_1$	0.000	0.133	0.044	0.133	0.089	0.044	0.133	0.178	0.089	0.089
IoTB$_2$	0.068	0.000	0.133	0.044	0.000	0.068	0.089	0.089	0.044	0.089
IoTB$_3$	0.178	0.089	0.000	0.089	0.044	0.089	0.133	0.133	0.089	0.133
IoTB$_4$	0.000	0.133	0.089	0.000	0.000	0.044	0.034	0.089	0.133	0.089
IoTB$_5$	0.044	0.062	0.133	0.044	0.000	0.089	0.044	0.100	0.000	0.044
IoTB$_6$	0.044	0.078	0.089	0.089	0.133	0.000	0.000	0.133	0.044	0.077
IoTB$_7$	0.000	0.178	0.044	0.078	0.178	0.000	0.034	0.089	0.000	0.089
IoTB$_8$	0.100	0.133	0.100	0.178	0.133	0.044	0.044	0.000	0.133	0.133
IoTB$_9$	0.089	0.000	0.089	0.178	0.000	0.000	0.089	0.044	0.000	0.089
IoTB$_{10}$	0.089	0.089	0.000	0.178	0.133	0.133	0.133	0.089	0.133	0.000
Upper Element Matrix										
IoTB$_1$	0.032	0.127	0.064	0.127	0.095	0.064	0.127	0.127	0.095	0.095
IoTB$_2$	0.080	0.032	0.127	0.064	0.032	0.080	0.095	0.095	0.064	0.095
IoTB$_3$	0.127	0.095	0.032	0.095	0.064	0.095	0.127	0.127	0.095	0.127
IoTB$_4$	0.032	0.127	0.095	0.032	0.032	0.064	0.080	0.095	0.127	0.095
IoTB$_5$	0.064	0.064	0.127	0.064	0.032	0.095	0.064	0.103	0.032	0.064
IoTB$_6$	0.064	0.088	0.095	0.095	0.127	0.032	0.032	0.127	0.064	0.088
IoTB$_7$	0.032	0.127	0.064	0.088	0.127	0.032	0.056	0.095	0.032	0.095
IoTB$_8$	0.103	0.127	0.103	0.127	0.127	0.064	0.064	0.032	0.127	0.127
IoTB$_9$	0.095	0.032	0.095	0.127	0.032	0.032	0.095	0.064	0.032	0.095
IoTB$_{10}$	0.095	0.095	0.032	0.127	0.127	0.127	0.127	0.095	0.127	0.032

TABLE 4.6

Total-Relation Matrix of IoT Barriers to Waste Management in Smart Cities by All Experts

Expert$_s$	Lower Element Matrix									
	IoTB$_1$	IoTB$_2$	IoTB$_3$	IoTB$_4$	IoTB$_5$	IoTB$_6$	IoTB$_7$	IoTB$_8$	IoTB$_9$	IoTB$_{10}$
IoTB$_1$	0.120	0.365	0.172	0.379	0.246	0.080	0.289	0.390	0.239	0.257
IoTB$_2$	0.129	0.140	0.222	0.153	0.117	0.094	0.178	0.202	0.103	0.189
IoTB$_3$	0.342	0.344	0.173	0.372	0.225	0.163	0.337	0.385	0.267	0.353
IoTB$_4$	0.095	0.269	0.175	0.170	0.102	0.057	0.152	0.190	0.241	0.194
IoTB$_5$	0.075	0.093	0.204	0.111	0.076	0.108	0.072	0.183	0.075	0.094
IoTB$_6$	0.092	0.172	0.185	0.230	0.246	0.065	0.100	0.270	0.119	0.192
IoTB$_7$	0.079	0.334	0.135	0.172	0.315	0.071	0.136	0.205	0.095	0.183
IoTB$_8$	0.226	0.361	0.266	0.468	0.294	0.101	0.191	0.223	0.324	0.332
IoTB$_9$	0.144	0.153	0.156	0.348	0.101	0.050	0.179	0.131	0.116	0.183
IoTB$_{10}$	0.182	0.299	0.182	0.445	0.317	0.217	0.292	0.283	0.300	0.190

Expert$_s$	Median Element Matrix									
	IoTB$_1$	IoTB$_2$	IoTB$_3$	IoTB$_4$	IoTB$_5$	IoTB$_6$	IoTB$_7$	IoTB$_8$	IoTB$_9$	IoTB$_{10}$
IoTB$_1$	0.242	0.487	0.339	0.520	0.357	0.252	0.413	0.515	0.367	0.419
IoTB$_2$	0.250	0.268	0.329	0.338	0.211	0.220	0.304	0.350	0.254	0.332
IoTB$_3$	0.424	0.479	0.309	0.520	0.350	0.309	0.444	0.515	0.392	0.484
IoTB$_4$	0.179	0.358	0.281	0.278	0.180	0.186	0.237	0.321	0.320	0.314
IoTB$_5$	0.214	0.299	0.316	0.303	0.186	0.227	0.236	0.336	0.191	0.268
IoTB$_6$	0.239	0.346	0.313	0.388	0.329	0.170	0.225	0.400	0.266	0.329
IoTB$_7$	0.181	0.426	0.266	0.350	0.361	0.167	0.244	0.343	0.202	0.324
IoTB$_8$	0.352	0.495	0.401	0.580	0.396	0.270	0.356	0.380	0.426	0.473
IoTB$_9$	0.240	0.249	0.265	0.426	0.180	0.139	0.281	0.280	0.197	0.304
IoTB$_{10}$	0.312	0.440	0.300	0.551	0.392	0.326	0.403	0.438	0.398	0.328

Expert$_s$	Upper Element Matrix									
	IoTB$_1$	IoTB$_2$	IoTB$_3$	IoTB$_4$	IoTB$_5$	IoTB$_6$	IoTB$_7$	IoTB$_8$	IoTB$_9$	IoTB$_{10}$
IoTB$_1$	0.472	0.680	0.571	0.690	0.571	0.482	0.650	0.693	0.584	0.648
IoTB$_2$	0.450	0.499	0.540	0.541	0.437	0.429	0.536	0.572	0.475	0.558
IoTB$_3$	0.585	0.680	0.561	0.694	0.571	0.532	0.678	0.724	0.610	0.705
IoTB$_4$	0.404	0.581	0.512	0.507	0.428	0.410	0.519	0.566	0.531	0.555
IoTB$_5$	0.408	0.497	0.514	0.504	0.407	0.420	0.471	0.546	0.415	0.495
IoTB$_6$	0.451	0.570	0.537	0.589	0.539	0.402	0.492	0.622	0.494	0.570
IoTB$_7$	0.382	0.563	0.467	0.532	0.501	0.369	0.472	0.546	0.421	0.531
IoTB$_8$	0.565	0.704	0.632	0.720	0.620	0.507	0.621	0.635	0.639	0.704
IoTB$_9$	0.426	0.461	0.471	0.556	0.397	0.351	0.498	0.498	0.410	0.515
IoTB$_{10}$	0.536	0.657	0.551	0.699	0.608	0.544	0.653	0.674	0.616	0.594

TABLE 4.7

Final Results of R_i and C_i by All Experts

Expert$_s$	R^l	R^m	R^U	C^l	C^m	C^U	R_i	C_i	$R_i + C_i$	$R_i - C_i$	Identity	Weight
IoTB$_1$	2.536	3.911	6.041	1.484	2.631	4.679	4.037	2.781	6.818	1.255	Cause	0.100
IoTB$_2$	1.526	2.856	5.038	2.532	3.848	5.892	2.998	3.970	6.968	−0.971	Effect	0.102
IoTB$_3$	2.960	4.226	6.341	1.869	3.120	5.356	4.368	3.284	7.652	1.084	Cause	0.112
IoTB$_4$	1.646	2.655	5.012	2.849	4.253	6.031	2.879	4.315	7.195	−1.436	Effect	0.105
IoTB$_5$	1.092	2.575	4.677	2.038	2.941	5.079	2.678	3.147	5.825	−0.468	Effect	0.085
IoTB$_6$	1.670	3.004	5.267	1.005	2.267	4.447	3.159	2.420	5.579	0.739	Cause	0.082
IoTB$_7$	1.724	2.863	4.785	1.927	3.143	5.590	2.993	3.348	6.342	−0.355	Effect	0.093
IoTB$_8$	2.786	4.129	6.347	2.460	3.877	6.075	4.275	4.008	8.283	0.268	Cause	0.121
IoTB$_9$	1.562	2.559	4.581	1.879	3.013	5.196	2.730	3.188	5.917	−0.458	Effect	0.087
IoTB$_{10}$	2.706	3.889	6.132	2.167	3.573	5.875	4.065	3.723	7.788	0.343	Cause	0.114

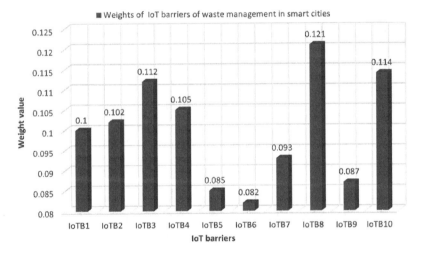

FIGURE 4.3

Final evaluation of IoT barriers to waste management in smart cities.

4.4.1 Results and Discussion

This part discusses the results obtained from applying the fuzzy DEMATEL method used to solve the case study mentioned in the previous section. Initially, the fuzzy DEMATEL method was used to analyze IoT barriers to waste management in smart cities.

According to the results presented in Table 4.7, the shortage of technical knowledge between planners' barrier is the highest obstacle with a weight of 0.367, followed by the shortage of transparency criterion with a weight of 0.356, while the system failure problems' barrier comes in the last order with a weight of 0.277.

TABLE 4.8

Final Results of the Threshold Value $(\alpha) = 0.342$

Experts	IoTB$_1$	IoTB$_2$	IoTB$_3$	IoTB$_4$	IoTB$_5$	IoTB$_6$	IoTB$_7$	IoTB$_8$	IoTB$_9$	IoTB$_{10}$
IoTB$_1$	0.260	0.499	0.350	0.525	0.374	0.262	0.432	0.524	0.382	0.430
IoTB$_2$	0.263	0.286	0.347	0.341	0.233	0.234	0.321	0.362	0.266	0.346
IoTB$_3$	0.437	0.490	0.328	0.524	0.366	0.322	0.465	0.528	0.407	0.499
IoTB$_4$	0.202	0.380	0.302	0.298	0.209	0.202	0.270	0.340	0.342	0.334
IoTB$_5$	0.223	0.298	0.330	0.304	0.204	0.240	0.248	0.345	0.209	0.277
IoTB$_6$	0.250	0.355	0.329	0.395	0.350	0.191	0.249	0.415	0.279	0.347
IoTB$_7$	0.197	0.433	0.278	0.350	0.376	0.184	0.264	0.354	0.221	0.335
IoTB$_8$	0.366	0.508	0.417	0.585	0.416	0.281	0.373	0.396	0.444	0.488
IoTB$_9$	0.255	0.268	0.281	0.435	0.203	0.159	0.300	0.291	0.219	0.319
IoTB$_{10}$	0.328	0.453	0.322	0.558	0.416	0.344	0.426	0.452	0.418	0.349

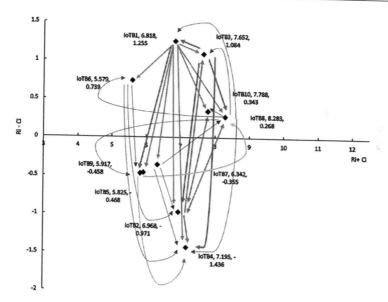

FIGURE 4.4

Cause-and-effect diagram of IoT barriers to waste management in smart cities.

Also, based on Table 4.8, a cause-and-effect diagram was charted among IoT barriers to waste management in smart cities, as in Figure 4.4. In this regard, Figure 4.4 shows that IoTB$_8$ is the highest value in IoT barriers to waste management in smart cities of the strength of impact given and dispatched (8.283 in sum (R+C)), followed by IoTB$_{10}$ and IoTB$_4$.

To sum, IoTB$_8$ is the most significant impact on IoT barriers to waste management in smart cities. Also, the values of R−C for IoTB$_2$, IoTB$_4$, IoTB$_5$, IoTB$_7$, and IoTB$_9$ are negative; it interprets that these barriers are affected by other barriers.

4.5 Summary

- This chapter provides a comprehensive description of waste management in smart cities.
- This chapter highlights a few obstacles to adopting the Internet of Things (IoT) in smart waste management
- This chapter reviews the importance and needs of assessing obstacles to adopting the Internet of Things (IoT) in smart waste management.
- This chapter presents the most important criteria for evaluating obstacles to adopting the Internet of Things (IoT) in smart waste management after a comprehensive analysis of several research articles.
- This chapter suggests a fuzzy DEMATEL technique to assess obstacles to adopting the Internet of Things (IoT) in smart waste management for a city.
- This chapter presents a real case study while evaluating obstacles to adopting the Internet of Things (IoT) in smart waste management.

4.6 Exercises

a. How do you define "smart waste management"? Why is an evaluation of a smart and sustainable waste management system important?

b. What are the differences between smart waste management and smart disaster response system? Discuss their relative advantages while making a decision.

c. Why is the adoption of IoT in waste management considered an obstacle? Why assessing those obstacles is important?

d. Discuss the features of smart waste management in terms of the characteristics and formation of a smart city.

e. Why is the MCDM approach required to assess obstacles to adopting the Internet of Things (IoT) in smart waste management?

References

Elahi, Haroon, Guojun Wang, Tao Peng, and Jianer Chen. 2019. "On Transparency and Accountability of Smart Assistants in Smart Cities." *Applied Sciences*. doi: 10.3390/app9245344.

Hasheminezhad, Araz, Farhad Hadadi, and Hamid Shirmohammadi. 2021. "Investigation and Prioritisation of Risk Factors in the Collision of Two Passenger Trains Based on Fuzzy COPRAS and Fuzzy DEMATEL Methods." *Soft Computing* 25(6): 4677–97. doi: 10.1007/s00500-020-05478-3.

Hosseini, Seyyed Mehdi, Mohammad Mahdi Paydar, and Mostafa Hajiaghaei-Keshteli. 2021. "Recovery Solutions for Ecotourism Centers during the Covid-19 Pandemic: Utilising Fuzzy DEMATEL and Fuzzy VIKOR Methods." *Expert Systems with Applications* 185: 115594. doi: 10.1016/j.eswa.2021.115594.

Li, Jishuo, and Kaili Xu. 2021. "A Combined Fuzzy DEMATEL and Cloud Model Approach for Risk Assessment in Process Industries to Improve System Reliability." *Quality and Reliability Engineering International* 37(5): 2110–33. doi: 10.1002/qre.2848.

Mishra, Arunodaya Roy, Pratibha Rani, Abhijit Saha, Ibrahim M Hezam, Dragan Pamucar, Minja Marinovi, and Kiran Pandey. 2022. "Assessing the Adaptation of Internet of Things (IoT) Barriers for Smart Cities Waste Management Using Fermatean Fuzzy Combined Compromise Solution Approach." *IEEE Access* 10: 37109–30. doi: 10.1109/ACCESS.2022.3164096.

Papadakis, Nikos, Nikos Koukoulas, Ioannis Christakis, Ilias Stavrakas, and Dionisis Kandris. 2021. "An IoT-Based Participatory Antitheft System for Public Safety Enhancement in Smart Cities." *Smart Cities*. doi: 10.3390/smartcities4020047.

Sharma, Manu, Sudhanshu Joshi, Devika Kannan, Kannan Govindan, Rohit Singh, and Harsh Chandra Purohit. 2020. "Internet of Things (IoT) Adoption Barriers of Smart Cities' Waste Management: An Indian Context." *Journal of Cleaner Production* 270: 122047. doi: 10.1016/j.jclepro.2020.122047.

Zhao, Huiru, and Sen Guo. 2015. "External Benefit Evaluation of Renewable Energy Power in China for Sustainability." *Sustainability*. doi: 10.3390/su7054783.

5

A Fusion Approach for Cloud Service Performance Assessment and Selection from Smart Data

5.1 Introduction

Cloud computing is a new way of allocating computer resources through the Internet. This computing paradigm delivers significant advantages to enterprises by relieving them of low-level activities associated with IT infrastructure setup and allowing them to start with limited resources and scale up as needed, freeing up time for innovation and the production of commercial value. The advent of distributed computing sparked a boom in the development of cloud computing, which has continued to thrive. Cloud computing is a new paradigm in Internet-based computing that is adaptable and transforms how computing, storage, and service solutions are implemented. Cloud computing has made it possible to provide three primary service models: Infrastructure as a Service (IaaS), Software as a Service (SaaS), and Platform as a Service (PaaS). These models have been developed to cater to each customer's specific requirements. Cloud computing is often broken down into three categories: public, private, and hybrid clouds. The deployment methodologies determine these categories.

In today's world, moving apps, data, and/or infrastructure to the cloud is a process that is almost certain to be difficult. The use of cloud computing is hampered by a number of barriers that prohibit it from delivering all of its promised benefits. These challenges are due to the fact that existing applications, data, and/or infrastructure have certain requirements and settings that the cloud provider must meet. Those challenges may be broken down into three categories. Each system in an organization has its own configuration performance and elements that impact workload parameters. This is true from the standpoint of an organization. Additionally, each cloud service provider provides its services with a variety of characteristics such as performance, affordability, and security

DOI: 10.1201/9781003357681-5

options to choose from. Because of this, it may be difficult for businesses to choose the cloud service provider that offers the features and capabilities that are the most suitable for their needs.

In its most basic form, cloud computing is the provision of virtual services across a network. These services may then be used by users anywhere in the world on a pay-per-usage basis, with the amount of payment being determined by the customers' desired quality of service (QoS). Because of the cloud's inherent flexibility and agility, top software companies such as Microsoft, Amazon, and Google now have the chance to move their present operations onto the cloud and expand their customer base as a result. It should come as no surprise that clients have various choices when it comes to selecting the finest cloud service providers to meet their QoS requirements, given the vast number of cloud service providers from whom they may choose. Because of the enormous progress made in cloud computing and the growing number of people using it, it is necessary to develop cloud service selection approaches that are both efficient and accurate on a worldwide scale. This is because raising the level of confidence between customers and service providers requires both parties to make an appropriate choice of a cloud service provider that meets their requirements. In this context, the key performance indicators (KPIs) for assessing cloud services are provided by the service measurement index (SMI), which is produced by the Cloud Service Measurement Initiative Consortium (CSMIC).

Choosing a cloud service is an example of multi-criteria decision-making (MCDM), a process in which several aspects of QoS play an important part in the decision-making process. As a result, a more effective MCDM strategy could be necessary to cope with client demands and rank cloud services according to their capabilities. In this chapter, we provide a systematic assessment approach for picking an ideal cloud service from a range of multiple comparable options, with the selection being made based on the QoS requirements associated with cloud services. Using this framework, customers can evaluate several cloud service providers according to their preferred choice and several other factors.

5.2 Mathematical Preliminary

5.2.1 Inceptions

Intuitionistic fuzzy sets (IFSs), Pythagorean fuzzy sets (PFSs), and q-rung orthopair fuzzy sets (q-ROFSs) are all terms that are discussed in this part, along with the associated ideas, techniques, and essential definitions.

5.2.1.1 Intuitionistic Fuzzy Sets (IFSs)

IFSs were first established by Atanassov in 1986 as an extension of fuzzy set theory. IFSs are separated from one another by the grade of membership and the grade of non-membership, the sum of which must be 1 or less than 1. This is addressed in detail in Explanation 5.1, which can be found in Atanassov (1999) and Alkan and Kahraman (2021).

Explanation 5.1: Let be Y a constant set. An IFS $\tilde{e}$ in Y is an object having the formula specified by:

$$\tilde{e} = \left\{ \left(\maltese, \mathcal{U}_{\tilde{e}}(\maltese), \vartheta_{\tilde{e}}(\maltese) \right) \mid \maltese \in \maltese \right\} \tag{5.1}$$

where the function $\mathcal{U}_{\tilde{e}} \colon Y \to [0, 1]$ designates the degree of membership of a component to the sets $\tilde{e}$, and $\vartheta_{\tilde{e}} \colon Y \to [0, 1]$ designates the degree of non-membership of a component to the sets $\tilde{e}$, with the condition that:

$$0 \le \mathcal{U}_{\tilde{e}}(\maltese) + \vartheta_{\tilde{e}}(\maltese) \le 1, \text{ for } \forall \ \maltese \in \maltese \tag{5.2}$$

The degree of uncertainty is computed as follows:

$$\pi_{\tilde{e}}(\maltese) = 1 - \mathcal{U}_{\tilde{e}}(\maltese) - \vartheta_{\tilde{e}}(\maltese) \tag{5.3}$$

Explanation 5.2. Let $\tilde{A} = \left(\mathcal{U}_{\tilde{A}}, \vartheta_{\tilde{A}} \right)$ and $\tilde{B} = \left(\mathcal{U}_{\tilde{B}}, \vartheta_{\tilde{B}} \right)$ be two intuitionistic fuzzy numbers (IFNs); then, the addition and multiplication procedures on these two IFNs are as follows:

$$\tilde{A} \oplus \tilde{B} = \left(\mathcal{U}_{\tilde{A}} + \mathcal{U}_{\tilde{B}} - \mathcal{U}_{\tilde{A}} \mathcal{U}_{\tilde{B}}, \vartheta_{\tilde{A}} \vartheta_{\tilde{B}} \right) \tag{5.4}$$

$$\tilde{A} \otimes \tilde{B} = \left(\mathcal{U}_{\tilde{A}} \mathcal{U}_{\tilde{B}}, \vartheta_{\tilde{A}} + \vartheta_{\tilde{B}} - \vartheta_{\tilde{A}} \vartheta_{\tilde{B}} \right) \tag{5.5}$$

5.2.1.2 Pythagorean Fuzzy Sets (PFSs)

In order to extend the capabilities of the IFSs, Yager created PFSs (Yager, 2013). It has two different membership degrees, which are referred to as membership and non-membership, respectively. In PFSs, the sum of the membership grade and the non-membership grade is considered; in IFSs, only the membership grade is considered. There is a possibility of having more than one membership grade and non-membership grade in PFSs. PFSs are clarified as specified in Explanation 5.3.

Explanation 5.3: Let be Y a constant set. A PFS $\tilde{P}$ in Y is an object having the formula assumed by:

$$\tilde{P} = \left\{ \left(\maltese, \mathcal{U}_{\tilde{P}}(\maltese), \vartheta_{\tilde{P}}(\maltese) \right) \mid \maltese \in \maltese \right\} \tag{5.6}$$

where the function $\mathcal{U}_{\tilde{P}} : \Psi \rightarrow [0, 1]$ designates the degree of membership of a component $\Psi \in \Psi$ to the sets $\tilde{P}$, and $\vartheta_{\tilde{P}} : \Psi \rightarrow [0, 1]$ designates the degree of non-membership of a component $\Psi \in \Psi$ to the sets $\tilde{P}$, with the condition that:

$$0 \leq \left(\mathcal{U}_{\tilde{P}}(\Psi)\right)^2 + \left(\vartheta_{\tilde{P}}(\Psi)\right)^2 \leq 1, \text{ for } \forall \ \Psi \in \Psi \tag{5.7}$$

The degree of vagueness is calculated as follows:

$$\pi_{\tilde{P}}(\Psi) = \sqrt{1 - \mathcal{U}_{\tilde{P}}(\Psi)^2 - \vartheta_{\tilde{P}}(\Psi)^2} \tag{5.8}$$

Explanation 5.4: Let $\tilde{P}_1 = \mathcal{U}_{\tilde{P}_1}, \vartheta_{\tilde{P}_1}$ and $\tilde{P}_2 = \mathcal{U}_{\tilde{P}_2}, \vartheta_{\tilde{P}_2}$ be two Pythagorean fuzzy numbers (PFNs); then, the addition and multiplication procedures on these two PFNs are as follows:

$$\tilde{P}_1 \oplus \tilde{P}_2 = \left(\sqrt{\mathcal{U}_{\tilde{P}_1}^2 + \mathcal{U}_{\tilde{P}_2}^2 - \mathcal{U}_{\tilde{P}_1}^2 \mathcal{U}_{\tilde{P}_2}^2}, \vartheta_{\tilde{P}_1} \vartheta_{\tilde{P}_2}\right) \tag{5.9}$$

$$\tilde{P}_1 \otimes \tilde{P}_2 = \left(\mathcal{U}_{\tilde{P}_1}, \mathcal{U}_{\tilde{P}_2}, \sqrt{\vartheta_{\tilde{P}_1}^2 + \vartheta_{\tilde{P}_2}^2 - \vartheta_{\tilde{P}_1}^2 \vartheta_{\tilde{P}_2}^2}\right) \tag{5.10}$$

5.2.1.3 q-Rung Orthopair Fuzzy Sets (q-ROFSs)

In 2018, Yager gave presentations on q-ROFSs, in which grades of membership and non-membership were given. When using q-ROFS, the sum of the qth powers of both the membership and non-membership grades must not be more than 1 (Yager, 2017). It is easy to see in Figure 5.1 that q-ROFSs have a membership degree extent that is much higher than that of IFSs and PFSs. q-ROFSs are clarified as specified in Explanation 5.5.

Explanation 5.5: A q-ROFS $\breve{Q}$ in a finite universe of discourse $\Psi = \Psi_1, \Psi_2, \ldots, \Psi_n$ is cleared by Yager as follows (Yager, 2017):

$$Q = \left\{\left(\Psi, \mathcal{U}_Q(\Psi), \vartheta_Q(\Psi)\right) | \Psi \in \Psi\right\} \tag{5.11}$$

where the function $\mathcal{U}_{\breve{Q}} : \Psi \rightarrow [0, 1]$ describes the degree of membership of a component $\Psi \in \Psi$ to the sets $\tilde{Q}$, and $\vartheta_{\breve{Q}} : \Psi \rightarrow [0, 1]$ describes the degree of non-membership of a component $\Psi \in \Psi$ to the sets $\tilde{Q}$, with the state that:

$$0 \leq \mathcal{U}_{\breve{Q}}(\Psi) + \vartheta_{\breve{Q}}(\Psi) \leq 1, \text{ for } \forall \ \Psi \in \Psi \tag{5.12}$$

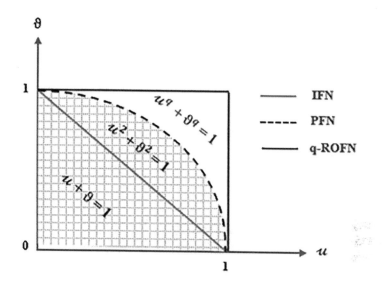

FIGURE 5.1
Comparison of the geometric space of different fuzzy memberships.

The degree of vagueness is calculated as follows:

$$\pi_{\breve{Q}}(\yen) = \sqrt[q]{1 - \mathcal{U}_{\breve{Q}}(\yen)^q - \vartheta_{\breve{Q}}(\yen)^q} \qquad (5.13)$$

Explanation 5.6: Let $\breve{Q} = \left(\mu_{\breve{Q}}, \vartheta_{\breve{Q}}\right)$, $\breve{Q}_1 = \left(\mu_{\breve{Q}_1}, \vartheta_{\breve{Q}_1}\right)$, and $\breve{Q}_2 = \left(\mu_{\breve{Q}_2}, \vartheta_{\breve{Q}_2}\right)$ be three q-ROFNs; then, their processes can be described as follows (Yager, 2017):

$$\breve{Q}_1 \cap \breve{Q}_2 = \left(\min\left\{\mu_{\breve{Q}_1}, \mu_{\breve{Q}_2}\right\}, \max\left\{\vartheta_{\breve{Q}_2}, \vartheta_{\breve{Q}_2}\right\}\right) \qquad (5.14)$$

$$\breve{Q}_1 \cup \breve{Q}_2 = \left(\max\left\{\mathcal{U}_{\breve{Q}_1}, \mathcal{U}_{\breve{Q}_2}\right\}, \min\left\{\vartheta_{\breve{Q}_1}, \vartheta_{\breve{Q}_2}\right\}\right) \qquad (5.15)$$

$$\breve{Q}_1 \oplus \breve{Q}_2 = \left(\left(\mathcal{U}_{\breve{Q}_1}^q + \mathcal{U}_{\breve{Q}_2}^q - \mathcal{U}_{\breve{Q}_1}^q \mathcal{U}_{\breve{Q}_2}^q\right)^{\frac{1}{q}}, \vartheta_{\breve{Q}_1} \vartheta_{\breve{Q}_2}\right) \qquad (5.16)$$

$$\breve{Q}_1 \otimes \breve{Q}_2 = \left(\mathcal{U}_{\breve{Q}_1} \mathcal{U}_{\breve{Q}_2} \left(\vartheta_{\breve{Q}_1}^q + \vartheta_{\breve{Q}_2}^q - \vartheta_{\breve{Q}_1}^q \vartheta_{\breve{Q}_2}^q\right)^{\frac{1}{q}}\right) \qquad (5.17)$$

$$\lambda \breve{Q} = \left(\left(1 - \left(1 - \mathcal{U}_{\breve{Q}}^q\right)^\lambda\right)^{\frac{1}{q}}, \vartheta_{\breve{Q}}^\lambda\right), \ \lambda > 0 \qquad (5.18)$$

$$\breve{Q}^{\lambda} = \left(\mathcal{U}_{\breve{Q}}^{\lambda}, \left(1 - \left(1 - \vartheta_{\breve{Q}}^{q} \right)^{\lambda} \right)^{\frac{1}{q}} \right), \lambda > 0 \tag{5.19}$$

Explanation 5.7: Let $\breve{Q} = \left(\mathcal{U}_{\breve{Q}}, \vartheta_{\breve{Q}} \right)$ be a q-ROFN; then, the score function $S\left(\breve{Q} \right)$ of $\breve{Q}$ can be stated by Wang et al. (2019), and accuracy function $A\left(\breve{Q} \right)$ of $\breve{Q}$ can be stated by Liu and Wang (2018) as in Eqs. (5.20) and (5.21), respectively.

$$S\left(\breve{Q} \right) = \frac{1}{2} \left(1 + \mathcal{U}_{\breve{Q}}^{q} - \vartheta_{\breve{Q}}^{q} \right) \tag{5.20}$$

$$A\left(\breve{Q} \right) = \mathcal{U}_{\breve{Q}}^{q} + \vartheta_{\breve{Q}}^{q} \tag{5.21}$$

Explanation 5.8: Let $\breve{Q}_i = \left(\mathcal{U}_{\breve{Q}_i}, \vartheta_{\breve{Q}_i} \right)$ (i=1, 2, …, n) be set of q-ROFNs and $\omega = \left(\omega_1, \omega_2, \ldots, \omega_n \right)^{T}$ be weight vector of $\breve{Q}_i$ with $\sum_{i=1}^{n} \omega_i = 1$ and $\omega_i \in [0,1]$. q-Rung orthopair fuzzy weighted average (q-ROFWA) and q-rung orthopair fuzzy weighted geometric (q-ROFWG) operators can be expressed by Liu and Wang (2018) as presented in Eqs. (5.22) and (5.23), respectively.

$$q\text{-}ROFWA\left(\breve{Q}_1, \breve{Q}_2, \ldots, \breve{Q}_n \right) = \left(\left(1 - \prod_{i=1}^{n} \left(1 - \mathcal{U}_{\breve{Q}_i}^{q} \right)^{\omega_i} \right)^{\frac{1}{q}}, \prod_{i=1}^{n} \vartheta_{\breve{Q}_i}^{\omega_i} \right) \tag{5.22}$$

$$q\text{-}ROFWA\left(\breve{Q}_1, \breve{Q}_2, \ldots, \breve{Q}_n \right) = \left(\prod_{i=1}^{n} \mathcal{U}_{\breve{Q}_i}^{\omega_i}, \left(1 - \prod_{i=1}^{n} \left(1 - \vartheta_{\breve{Q}_i}^{q} \right)^{\omega_i} \right)^{\frac{1}{q}} \right) \tag{5.23}$$

Explanation 5.9: Darko and Liang (2020) established an operator called the weighted q-rung orthopair fuzzy Hamacher average (Wq-ROFHA) as presented in Eqs. (5.24) and (5.25). Let $\breve{Q}_i = \left(\mathcal{U}_{\breve{Q}_i}, \vartheta_{\breve{Q}_i} \right)$ (i=1, 2, …, n) be set of q-ROFNs and $\omega = \left(\omega_1, \omega_2, \ldots, \omega_n \right)^{T}$ be weight vector of $\breve{Q}_i$ with $\sum_{i=1}^{n} \omega_i = 1$ and $\omega_i \in [0,1]$.

$$q\text{-}ROFWA\left(\breve{Q}_1, \breve{Q}_2, \ldots, \breve{Q}_n \right) = \omega_1 \left(\breve{Q}_1 \right) \oplus \omega_2 \left(\breve{Q}_2 \right) \oplus \cdots \oplus \omega_n \left(\breve{Q}_n \right)$$
$$= \oplus_{i=1}^{n} \omega_i \left(\breve{Q}_i \right) \tag{5.24}$$

$$q\text{-}ROFWA\left(\breve{Q}_1,\breve{Q}_2,\ldots,\breve{Q}_n\right)$$

$$=\sqrt[q]{\frac{\prod_{i=1}^{n}\left(1+(\gamma-1)\left(\mu_{\breve{Q}_i}\right)^q\right)^{\omega_i}-\prod_{i=1}^{n}\left(1-\left(\mathcal{U}_{\breve{Q}_i}\right)^q\right)^{\omega_i}}{\prod_{i=1}^{n}\left(1+(\gamma-1)\left(\mu_{\breve{Q}_i}\right)^q\right)^{\omega_i}+(\gamma-1)\prod_{i=1}^{n}\left(1-\left(\mu_{\breve{Q}_i}\right)^q\right)^{\omega_i}}},$$

$$\frac{\sqrt[q]{\gamma}\prod_{i=1}^{n}\left(\vartheta_{\breve{Q}_i}\right)^{\omega_i}}{\sqrt[q]{\prod_{i=1}^{n}\left(1+(\gamma-1)\left(1-\left(\vartheta_{\breve{Q}_i}\right)^q\right)\right)^{\omega_i}+(\gamma-1)\prod_{i=1}^{n}\left(\vartheta_{\breve{Q}_i}\right)^{q\omega_i}}} \quad (5.25)$$

where $\gamma>0$, $q\geq0$.

Explanation 5.10: Darko and Liang (2020) developed an operator called the weighted q-rung orthopair fuzzy Hamacher geometric mean (Wq-ROFHGM) as presented in Eqs. (5.26) and (5.27). Let $\breve{Q}_i=\left(\mathcal{U}_{\breve{Q}_i},\vartheta_{\breve{Q}_i}\right)$ (i=1, 2... n) be set of q-ROFNs and $\omega=(\omega_1,\omega_2,\ldots,\omega_n)^T$ be weight vector of $\breve{Q}_i$ with $\sum_{i=1}^{n}\omega_i=1$ and $\omega_i\in[0,1]$.

$$q\text{-}ROFHGM\left(\breve{Q}_1,\breve{Q}_2,\ldots,\breve{Q}_n\right)=\omega_1\left(\breve{Q}_1\right)\oplus\omega_2\left(\breve{Q}_2\right)\oplus\cdots\oplus\omega_n\left(\breve{Q}_n\right)$$

$$=\oplus_{i=1}^{n}\omega_i\left(\breve{Q}_i\right) \quad (5.26)$$

$$q\text{-}ROFHGM\left(\breve{Q}_1,\breve{Q}_2,\ldots,\breve{Q}_n\right)=$$

$$\frac{\sqrt[q]{\gamma}\prod_{i=1}^{n}\left(\mathcal{U}_{\breve{Q}_i}\right)^{\omega_i}}{\sqrt[q]{\prod_{i=1}^{n}\left(1+(\gamma-1)\left(1-\left(\mathcal{U}_{\breve{Q}_i}\right)^q\right)\right)^{\omega_i}+(\gamma-1)\prod_{i=1}^{n}\left(\mathcal{U}_{\breve{Q}_i}\right)^{q\omega_i}}},$$

$$\sqrt[q]{\frac{\prod_{i=1}^{n}\left(1+(\gamma-1)\left(\vartheta_{\breve{Q}_i}\right)^q\right)^{\omega_i}-\prod_{i=1}^{n}\left(1-\left(\vartheta_{\breve{Q}_i}\right)^q\right)^{\omega_i}}{\prod_{i=1}^{n}\left(1+(\gamma-1)\left(\vartheta_{\breve{Q}_i}\right)^q\right)^{\omega_i}+(\gamma-1)\prod_{i=1}^{n}\left(1-\left(\vartheta_{\breve{Q}_i}\right)^q\right)^{\omega_i}}} \quad (5.27)$$

where $\gamma>0$, $q\geq0$.

5.3 Model

This section presents the steps of a hybrid MCDM approach for evaluating multiple cloud service providers (CSPs). The approach consists of two MCDM approaches: the entropy and the combined compromised solution (CoCoSo). The applied approach was carried out under the q-ROFS environment and using q-rung orthopair fuzzy numbers (q-ROFNs). Figure 5.2 shows the steps of the approach used in evaluating several CSPs. The approach is divided into three parts: data aggregation, determination of criteria weights using the entropy technique, and arranging the used alternatives according to their importance using the CoCoSo technique. In this regard, we provide a brief overview of the methods used in applying the case study for this chapter. This section is divided into several parts as follows.

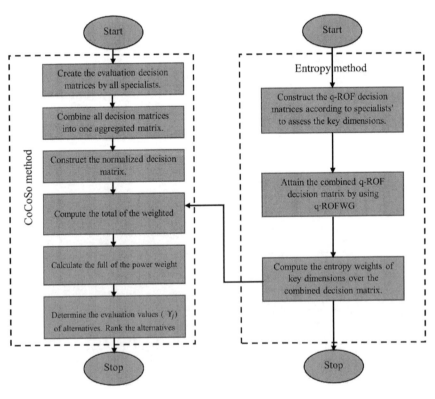

FIGURE 5.2
Diagrammatic representation of the applied approach for choosing cloud services.

5.3.1 Entropy Method

Shannon and Weaver came up with the idea for the entropy weight technique in 1947, which is a weighing approach that evaluates the value dispersion that occurs during decision-making (Chodha et al., 2022). The entropy weight approach is used to determine the objective weights of the criteria and characteristics. Probability theory is used whenever uncertain information has to be computed (entropy) (Vaid et al., 2022). It evaluates the significance of each answer parameter independently, without taking into account the preferences of the individual making the decision. A higher weight index value is considered to have a greater value than a lower weight index value from the standpoint of the entropy weight measuring system. This method begins with determining the objectives (decision matrix), followed by determining the normalized decision matrix, the probability of the criteria or attribute occurring, the entropy value of the criteria or attribute, the degrees of divergence produced by each response, and finally, the entropy weight.

5.3.2 CoCoSo Method

In the CoCoSo technique, options are ranked according to compromise methods derived from the Weighted Sum Model (WSM) and Weighted Product Model (WPM) (Deveci, Pamucar, and Gokasar, 2021). As a result of a compromise, the final criteria function on which the ranking of alternatives is based was determined. It demonstrates that a combination of compromise tactics delivers objective outcomes when the ratings of options in the initial choice matrix have consistent values. However, when extreme values arrive at the location of the most important criterion in the initial choice matrix, the values of the WSM and WPM functions undergo drastic modifications (Torkayesh et al., 2021). This results in a disproportionate rise in the value function of the criteria for the evaluated option. Extreme values in the first choice matrix may develop for a variety of causes, including, but not limited to, disproportional disparities between the examined options, measurement mistakes, and biased specialist judgments (deliberate or accidental). Another drawback of WSM and WPM aggregation is that they disregard the interrelationships and reciprocal impact between the criteria.

5.3.3 Computational Steps of the Applied Approach

The computational steps of the approach used in the problem presented in this chapter are presented as follows:

Step 1: The target case is carefully studied from all directions, and the most important key dimensions that affect the evaluation of cloud service providers are identified. Then, some specialists are negotiated to help the authors compile the data needed to solve the problem. Accordingly, some criteria have been set on the basis of which specialists are selected (SP$_s$), such as the scientific degree and the number of years of experience. Also, the most appropriate ways to communicate with experts are identified.

Step 2: The most important main dimensions affecting the selection of cloud service providers are determined based on expert surveys and previous studies. $D_j = \{D_1, D_2, \ldots, D_n\}$, with $j=1, 2, \ldots, n$. Let $\omega = (\omega_1, \omega_2, \ldots, \omega_n)$ be the vector set applied for identifying the dimension weights, where $\omega_j > 0$ and $\sum_{j=1}^{n} \omega_j = 1$.

Step 3: The most important available alternatives that can be used in the evaluation process are determined, in addition to preparing a final list of these alternatives according to the opinions of specialists. The group $CSP_i = \{CSP_1, CSP_2, \ldots, CSP_m\}$, having $i=1, 2, \ldots, m$ substitutes, is assessed by n decision dimensions of group $D_j = \{D_1, D_2, \ldots, D_n\}$, with $j=1, 2, \ldots, n$.

Step 4: After studying the main dimensions of the case study and identifying the most important aspects affecting the problem, all the parties used are organized in the form of a hierarchical structure.

Step 5: According to the evaluation process conducted by the specialists, this requires the presence of linguistic terms that help them in carrying out the various evaluations, whether to determine the weights of the main dimensions or to arrange the selected alternatives as in Tables 5.1 and 5.2.

Step 6: Form the judgment matrices rendering to specialists' preferences (SP$_s$) to assess the dimensions of each specialist by utilizing linguistic terms as presented in Table 5.1, and then by utilizing q-ROFNs as exhibited in Table 5.3.

TABLE 5.1

Linguistic Terms and Their Equivalent q-ROFNs for Evaluating Factors

Linguistic Terms	Abridgments	q-ROFNs	
		u	ϑ
Exceedingly low	EXL	0.11	0.99
Very low	VEL	0.22	0.88
Low	LOW	0.33	0.77
Medium low	MLO	0.44	0.66
Medium	MED	0.55	0.55
Medium well	MEW	0.66	0.44
Well	WEL	0.77	0.33
Very well	VRL	0.88	0.22
Exceedingly well	EWL	0.99	0.11

TABLE 5.2

Linguistic Terms and Their Equivalent q-ROFNs for Rating Substitutes

		q-ROFNs	
Linguistic Terms	**Abridgments**	u	ϑ
Exceedingly little	EDL	0.11	0.99
Very little	VRL	0.22	0.88
Little	LTT	0.33	0.77
Intermediate little	TNL	0.44	0.66
Intermediate	INE	0.55	0.55
Intermediate great	ING	0.66	0.44
Great	GRE	0.77	0.33
Very great	VEG	0.88	0.22
Exceedingly great	EGT	0.99	0.11

TABLE 5.3

Evaluation Matrix for Criteria Based on q-ROFN with Respect to Experts

	Specialists			
Dimensions	**SP$_1$**	**SP$_2$**	**SP$_3$**	**SP$_4$**
D$_1$	$\left[u_{1SP_1}, \vartheta_{1SP_1} \right]$	$\left[u_{1SP_2}, \vartheta_{1SP_2} \right]$	$\left[u_{1SP_3}, \vartheta_{1SP_3} \right]$	$\left[u_{1SP_4}, \vartheta_{1SP_4} \right]$
D$_2$	$\left[u_{2SP_1}, \vartheta_{2Ex_1} \right]$	$\left[u_{2SP_2}, \vartheta_{2SP_2} \right]$	$\left[u_{2SP_3}, \vartheta_{2SP_3} \right]$	$\left[u_{2SP_4}, \vartheta_{2SP_4} \right]$
$\vdots$	$\vdots$	$\vdots$	$\vdots$	$\vdots$
D$_n$	$\left[u_{nSP_1}, \vartheta_{nSP_1} \right]$	$\left[u_{nSP_2}, \vartheta_{nSP_2} \right]$	$\left[u_{nSP_3}, \vartheta_{nSP_3} \right]$	$\left[u_{nSP_4}, \vartheta_{nSP_4} \right]$

Step 7: Combine the assessments on dimensions and weights. The distinct specialist assessments were aggregated by applying q-ROFWG presented in Eq. (5.23). At this point, $\left(\omega_j \right)_{1 \times n}$ introduces q-ROF weight of jth dimension.

Step 8: Calculate the entropy values of all q-ROFN of the collected specialists' assessments by applying Eqs. (5.28) and (5.29).

$$\mathbb{k}\mathbb{E}_{q,ij}(y) = \frac{1}{\sqrt{2}} \left(\left(\left(\mathcal{U}(y) \right)^q \right)^2 + \left(\left(\vartheta(y) \right)^q \right)^2 + \left(\left(\mathcal{U}(y) \right)^q + \left(\vartheta(y) \right)^q \right)^2 \right)^{0.5} \quad (5.28)$$

$$\mathbb{E}\mathbb{N}_{q,ij}(y) = 1 - \mathbb{k}\mathbb{E}_{q,ij}(y)$$

$$= 1 - \left(\left(\left(\mathcal{U}(y) \right)^q \right)^2 + \left(\left(\vartheta(y) \right)^q \right)^2 + \left(\left(\mathcal{U}(y) \right)^q + \left(\vartheta(y) \right)^q \right)^2 \right)^{0.5} \quad (5.29)$$

Step 9: Compute the key dimension weights based on the entropy values according to Eq. (5.30).

$$\omega_j = \frac{1 - \xi_j}{\sum_{j=1}^{n} \left(1 - \xi_j\right)}; j = 1, 2, \ldots, n. \quad (5.30)$$

where $\xi_j = \dfrac{\sum_{i=1}^{m} EN_{q,ij}}{\sum_{i=1}^{m} \sum_{j=1}^{n} EN_{q,ij}}$ indicates the q-ROF entropy value.

Step 10: Generate the assessment judgment matrix by each specialist separately (SP$_s$) between the determined key dimensions and the available alternatives to assess the cloud service providers by utilizing the linguistic terms as presented in Table 5.2, then by applying the q-ROFNs in Table 5.2 as exhibited in Table 5.4.

Step 11: Aggregate the assessment judgment matrix by each specialist separately (SP$_s$) between the determined key dimensions and the available alternatives to assess the cloud service providers into one matrix by applying q-ROFWG as exhibited in Eq. (5.23) as presented in Table 5.5.

TABLE 5.4

Judgment Assessment Matrix for Substitutes in Terms of Dimensions Based on q-ROFN

Dimensions	Substitutes			
	CSP$_1$	CSP$_2$	...	CSP$_m$
D$_1$	$[u_{11SP}, \vartheta_{11SP}]$	$[u_{12SP}, \vartheta_{12SP}]$	...	$[u_{1mSP}, \vartheta_{1mSP}]$
D$_2$	$[u_{21SP}, \vartheta_{21SP}]$	$[u_{22SP}, \vartheta_{22SP}]$	...	$[u_{2mSP}, \vartheta_{2mSP}]$
⋮	⋮	⋮	⋱	⋮
D$_n$	$[u_{n1SP}, \vartheta_{n1SP}]$	$[u_{n2SP}, \vartheta_{n2SP}]$	...	$[u_{nmSP}, \vartheta_{nmSP}]$

TABLE 5.5

Aggregated Assessment Matrix for Alternatives in Terms of Dimensions Based on q-ROFN

Dimensions	Alternatives			
	CSP$_1$	CSP$_2$	...	CSP$_m$
D$_1$	$[u_{11}, \vartheta_{11}]$	$[u_{12}, \vartheta_{12}]$	...	$[u_{1m}, \vartheta_{1m}]$
D$_2$	$[u_{21}, \vartheta_{21}]$	$[u_{22}, \vartheta_{22}]$	...	$[u_{2m}, \vartheta_{2m}]$
⋮	⋮	⋮	⋱	⋮
D$_n$	$[u_{n1}, \vartheta_{n1}]$	$[u_{n2}, \vartheta_{n2}]$	...	$[u_{nm}, \vartheta_{nm}]$

Step 12: Calculate the standardized combined q-ROF assessment judgment matrix (S̆) by using Eq. (5.31).

$$\breve{S} = \left(\breve{s}_{ij} \right)_{m \times n} = \left[\breve{\mathcal{U}}_{ij}, \breve{\vartheta}_{ij} \right] = \begin{cases} \left(\breve{\mathcal{U}}_{ij}, \breve{\vartheta}_{ij} \right) & \text{if } i \in B \\ \left(\breve{\vartheta}_{ij}, \breve{\mathcal{U}}_{ij} \right) & \text{if } i \in \mathrm{\c{C}} \end{cases} \tag{5.31}$$

where B indicates the group of advantage dimensions, and Ç denotes the group of cost dimensions.

Step 13: Compute the overall weighted comparability compromises (α) for all cloud service providers by utilizing the Wq-ROFHA factor as exhibited in Eq. (5.24) and Eq. (5.25).

Step 14: Compute the complete power weight (β) of comparability compromises for all cloud service providers by utilizing the Wq-ROFHGM factor as exhibited in Eqs. (5.26) and (5.27).

Step 15: Compute the score values for all cloud service providers (alternatives) by utilizing the values of Wq-ROFHA and Wq-ROFHGM factors for each alternative by utilizing Eq. (5.20).

Step 16: Compute the proportionate weight of the cloud service providers (alternatives) with the help of Eqs. (5.32), (5.33), and (5.34).

$$\gamma_{ja} = \frac{\alpha_j + \beta_j}{\sum_{j=1}^{n} \left(\alpha_j + \beta_j \right)} \tag{5.32}$$

$$\gamma_{jb} = \frac{\alpha_j}{\min\left(\alpha_j \right)} + \frac{\beta_j}{\min\left(\beta_j \right)} \tag{5.33}$$

$$\gamma_{jc} = \frac{\varphi \alpha_j + (1 - \varphi) \beta_j}{\varphi \max\left(\alpha_j \right) + (1 - \varphi) \max\left(\beta_j \right)}, \quad 0 \leq \varphi \leq 1, \tag{5.34}$$

where γ_{ja} indicates the WSM and WPM scores. Then, γ_{jb} refers to the total comparative scores of WSM and WPM. Also, γ_{jc} indicates the established decisions of WSM and WPM scores.

Step 17: Compute the assessment values (γ_j) of all cloud service providers (alternatives) by utilizing Eq. (5.35). Then, rate the selected alternatives according to the most potential score of the assessment values (γ_j).

$$\gamma_j = \sqrt[3]{\gamma_{ja} \gamma_{jb} \gamma_{jc}} + \frac{\gamma_{ja} + \gamma_{jb} + \gamma_{jc}}{3} \tag{5.35}$$

5.4 Model Implementation

The applied approach being conducted is tested with a real-world issue about the selection of cloud services, which exhibits both its efficiency and accuracy. The primary objective of this chapter is to identify the cloud service that is superior to the others that are now accessible in terms of a number of different qualities and then choose that service as the most appropriate option. A genuine dataset that is used in the article (Jatoth, Gangadharan, and Fiore, 2017) has been used by our team. Running benchmark programs on a number of dynamically launched virtual machines (VMs) for a predetermined amount of time is what the Cloud Harmony dataset is used for in order to offer a performance assessment of various cloud services. In addition, the values of CPU, memory, disk performance, and I/O consistency of big cloud services based on various virtual cores are measured by this dataset. While collecting the data, we failed to consider the logically inconsistent data, which are defined as the data that are outside of the range or have very high values.

Step 1: The problem was studied from all directions, and the main objective was determined, which is to evaluate some cloud service providers and the main dimensions affecting the selection of the best cloud service provider. In addition, four specialists were identified to collaborate with the authors, and four weights were assigned to determine each specialist's impact: 0.2, 0.3, 0.3, and 0.2. In addition, the parameter was selected subjectively to represent the experts' opinions on optimism and pessimism. In this instance, $q=5$ further illustrates the vagueness.

Step 2: Five main dimensions have been identified that affect the selection of the best cloud service providers according to the opinions of experts and previous studies, which are CPU utilization, disk I/O consistency, disk utilization, memory utilization, and cost, and their abbreviations are $CUTD_1$, $DIOD_2$, $SKUD_3$, $MEMD_4$, and $COSD_5$, respectively.

Step 3: A final list of cloud service providers has been determined that will be evaluated according to the case study and according to the applicable study, namely, Azure, Soft Layer, Amazon, HP, Century Link, Google, Rackspace, Joynet, Linode, GoGrid, and City Cloud, and their abbreviations are CSP_1, CSP_2, CSP_3, CSP_4, CSP_5, CSP_6, CSP_7, CSP_8, CSP_9, and CSP_{10}, respectively.

Step 4: A hierarchical structure of the problem is drawn to show the main objective of the problem, the dimensions that affect the problem, and the alternatives used as presented in Figure 5.3.

Step 5: Linguistic terms and equivalent q-ROFNs are selected to prioritize the dimensions used as in Table 5.1. Also, some linguistic terminology and equivalent q-ROFNs have been defined to evaluate selected CSPs, as exhibited in Table 5.2.

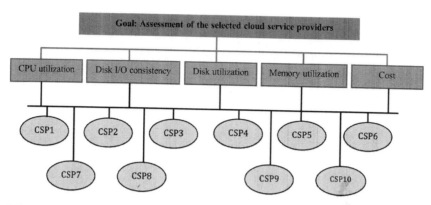

FIGURE 5.3
Hierarchy for cloud service choosing.

Step 6: The judgment matrices rendering specialists' preferences were formed to assess the dimensions of each specialist by utilizing linguistic terms as presented in Table 5.6.

Step 7: The distinct specialist assessments were combined by applying q-ROFWG according to Eq. (5.23) as presented in Table 5.6.

Step 8: The entropy values of all q-ROFNs of the collected specialists' assessments were computed according to Eqs. (5.28) and (5.29), as presented in Table 5.6.

Step 9: The key dimension weights based on the entropy values were computed according to Eq. (5.30) as presented in Table 5.6 and Figure 5.4.

Step 10: The assessment judgment matrix by each specialist separately (SP_s) between the determined key dimensions and the available alternatives to assess the CSPs was generated by utilizing the linguistic terms as presented in Table 5.7, then by applying the q-ROFNs in Table 5.2 as exhibited in Table 5.8.

Step 11: The assessment judgment matrix by each specialist separately (SP_s) between the determined key dimensions and the available alternatives to assess the CSPs was aggregated into one matrix by applying q-ROFWG as exhibited in Eq. (5.23), and the results are formed in Table 5.9.

Step 12: The standardized combined q-ROF assessment judgment matrix $(\tilde{S})$ was calculated by applying Eq. (5.31) as presented in Table 5.10.

Step 13: The overall weighted comparability compromises (α) for all CSPs were computed by utilizing the Wq-ROFHA factor according to Eqs. (5.24) and (5.25) as presented in Table 5.11.

Step 14: The complete power weight (β) of comparability compromises for all cloud service providers was computed by utilizing the Wq-ROFHGM factor according to Eqs. (5.26) and (5.27) as presented in Table 5.11.

TABLE 5.6

Linguistic Terms of Key Factors by each Specialist and Combined Key Factor Weights

Key Factors	SP_1	SP_2	SP_3	SP_4	Combined Outcomes	$fE_{q,ji}(y)$	$fN_{q,ji}(y)$	ξ_j	ω_j
$CUTD_1$	WEL	VRL	EWL	VRL	[0.887, 0.253]	0.549576	0.450424	0.139094	0.215
$DIOD_2$	MED	MEW	MEW	WEL	[0.656, 0.461]	0.133121	0.866879	0.267698	0.183
$SKUD_3$	WEL	VRL	VRL	VRL	[0.856, 0.260]	0.460183	0.539817	0.166699	0.208
$MEMD_4$	MEW	LOW	VRL	MLO	[0.538, 0.651]	0.144820	0.855180	0.264085	0.184
$COSD_5$	MED	WEL	WEL	EXL	[0.488, 0.856]	0.474032	0.525968	0.162422	0.209

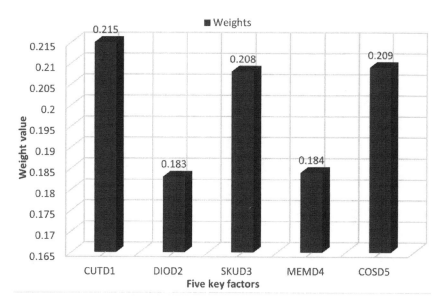

FIGURE 5.4
Final weights of key factors that are used for weighting cloud service providers.

Step 15: The score values for all CSPs were computed by utilizing the values of Wq-ROFHA and Wq-ROFHGM factors for each alternative by utilizing Eq. (5.20) as presented in Table 5.12.

Step 16: The proportionate weight of the CSPs was computed with the help of Eqs. (5.32), (5.33), and (5.34) as presented in Table 5.13.

Step 17: The assessment values (γ_j) of all CSPs were computed according to Eq. (5.35) as presented in Table 5.13 and Figure 5.5. The selected CSPs were ranked according to the most potential score of the assessment values (γ_j).

5.5 Results and Discussion

This part discusses the results obtained from applying the entropy-CoCoSo approach using q-ROFNs. Initially, the entropy method was used to prioritize the dimensions used. According to the evaluation results of the dimensions, the CPU utilization dimension has the highest evaluation with a weight of 0.215, followed by the cost dimension with a weight of 0.209, while the disk I/O consistency dimension has the lowest evaluation and priority with a weight of 0.183.

TABLE 5.7

Assessments of CSPs in Terms of Key Factors Using Linguistic Terms

CSP$_s$	SP$_s$	CUTD$_1$	DIOD$_2$	SKUD$_3$	MEMD$_4$	COSD$_5$
CSP$_1$	SP$_1$	VEG	VEG	VEG	VEG	ING
	SP$_2$	VEG	VEG	VEG	GRE	VEG
	SP$_3$	GRE	GRE	GRE	GRE	GRE
	SP$_4$	GRE	GRE	GRE	VEG	EGT
CSP$_2$	SP$_1$	GRE	LTT	EDL	VEG	LTT
	SP$_2$	VEG	LTT	EDL	GRE	GRE
	SP$_3$	GRE	LTT	EDL	GRE	TNL
	SP$_4$	GRE	LTT	EDL	EGT	VEG
CSP$_3$	SP$_1$	GRE	VEG	VEG	VEG	GRE
	SP$_2$	VEG	VEG	VEG	GRE	EGT
	SP$_3$	GRE	GRE	GRE	GRE	VEG
	SP$_4$	GRE	GRE	GRE	VEG	EGT
CSP$_4$	SP$_1$	VEG	VEG	VEG	VEG	LTT
	SP$_2$	VEG	VEG	VEG	GRE	GRE
	SP$_3$	GRE	GRE	GRE	GRE	TNL
	SP$_4$	GRE	GRE	GRE	EGT	VEG
CSP$_5$	SP$_1$	GRE	VEG	VRL	VEG	GRE
	SP$_2$	VEG	VEG	GRE	GRE	EGT
	SP$_3$	GRE	GRE	TNL	GRE	VEG
	SP$_4$	GRE	GRE	VRL	VEG	EGT
CSP$_6$	SP$_1$	GRE	VEG	VEG	VEG	GRE
	SP$_2$	VEG	VEG	VEG	GRE	EGT
	SP$_3$	GRE	GRE	GRE	GRE	VEG
	SP$_4$	GRE	GRE	GRE	VEG	EGT
CSP$_7$	SP$_1$	ING	GRE	GRE	GRE	VRL
	SP$_2$	GRE	GRE	VEG	VEG	TNL
	SP$_3$	GRE	GRE	VEG	VEG	INE
	SP$_4$	GRE	GRE	EGT	VEG	GRE
CSP$_8$	SP$_1$	TNL	GRE	VEG	VEG	VRL
	SP$_2$	ING	VEG	VEG	VEG	TNL
	SP$_3$	INE	GRE	VEG	VEG	INE
	SP$_4$	INE	GRE	EGT	VEG	GRE
CSP$_9$	SP$_1$	INE	GRE	VEG	TNL	VRL
	SP$_2$	VEG	VEG	VEG	TNL	TNL
	SP$_3$	ING	GRE	VEG	TNL	INE
	SP$_4$	GRE	GRE	VEG	TNL	GRE
CSP$_{10}$	SP$_1$	TNL	GRE	GRE	INE	VRL
	SP$_2$	ING	VEG	GRE	INE	TNL
	SP$_3$	INE	GRE	GRE	INE	INE
	SP$_4$	INE	GRE	GRE	INE	GRE

TABLE 5.8

Assessments of CSPs in Terms of Key Factors Using q-ROFNs

CSP_s	SP_s	$CUTD_1$	$DIOD_2$	$SKUD_3$	$MEMD_4$	$COSD_5$
CSP_1	SP_1	[0.88, 0.22]	[0.88, 0.22]	[0.88, 0.22]	[0.88, 0.22]	[0.66, 0.44]
	SP_2	[0.88, 0.22]	[0.88, 0.22]	[0.88, 0.22]	[0.77, 0.33]	[0.88, 0.22]
	SP_3	[0.77, 0.33]	[0.77, 0.33]	[0.77, 0.33]	[0.77, 0.33]	[0.77, 0.33]
	SP_4	[0.77, 0.33]	[0.77, 0.33]	[0.77, 0.33]	[0.88, 0.22]	[0.99, 0.11]
CSP_2	SP_1	[0.77, 0.33]	[0.33, 0.77]	[0.11, 0.99]	[0.88, 0.22]	[0.33, 0.77]
	SP_2	[0.88, 0.22]	[0.33, 0.77]	[0.11, 0.99]	[0.77, 0.33]	[0.77, 0.33]
	SP_3	[0.77, 0.33]	[0.33, 0.77]	[0.11, 0.99]	[0.77, 0.33]	[0.44, 0.66]
	SP_4	[0.77, 0.33]	[0.33, 0.77]	[0.11, 0.99]	[0.99, 0.11]	[0.88, 0.22]
CSP_3	SP_1	[0.77, 0.33]	[0.88, 0.22]	[0.88, 0.22]	[0.88, 0.22]	[0.77, 0.33]
	SP_2	[0.88, 0.22]	[0.88, 0.22]	[0.88, 0.22]	[0.77, 0.33]	[0.99, 0.11]
	SP_3	[0.77, 0.33]	[0.77, 0.33]	[0.77, 0.33]	[0.77, 0.33]	[0.88, 0.22]
	SP_4	[0.77, 0.33]	[0.77, 0.33]	[0.77, 0.33]	[0.88, 0.22]	[0.99, 0.11]
CSP_4	SP_1	[0.88, 0.22]	[0.88, 0.22]	[0.88, 0.22]	[0.88, 0.22]	[0.33, 0.77]
	SP_2	[0.88, 0.22]	[0.88, 0.22]	[0.88, 0.22]	[0.77, 0.33]	[0.77, 0.33]
	SP_3	[0.77, 0.33]	[0.77, 0.33]	[0.77, 0.33]	[0.77, 0.33]	[0.44, 0.66]
	SP_4	[0.77, 0.33]	[0.77, 0.33]	[0.77, 0.33]	[0.99, 0.11]	[0.88, 0.22]
CSP_5	SP_1	[0.77, 0.33]	[0.88, 0.22]	[0.22, 0.88]	[0.88, 0.22]	[0.77, 0.33]
	SP_2	[0.88, 0.22]	[0.88, 0.22]	[0.77, 0.33]	[0.77, 0.33]	[0.99, 0.11]
	SP_3	[0.77, 0.33]	[0.77, 0.33]	[0.44, 0.66]	[0.77, 0.33]	[0.88, 0.22]
	SP_4	[0.77, 0.33]	[0.77, 0.33]	[0.22, 0.88]	[0.88, 0.22]	[0.99, 0.11]
CSP_6	SP_1	[0.77, 0.33]	[0.88, 0.22]	[0.88, 0.22]	[0.88, 0.22]	[0.77, 0.33]
	SP_2	[0.88, 0.22]	[0.88, 0.22]	[0.88, 0.22]	[0.77, 0.33]	[0.99, 0.11]
	SP_3	[0.77, 0.33]	[0.77, 0.33]	[0.77, 0.33]	[0.77, 0.33]	[0.88, 0.22]
	SP_4	[0.77, 0.33]	[0.77, 0.33]	[0.77, 0.33]	[0.88, 0.22]	[0.99, 0.11]
CSP_7	SP_1	[0.66, 0.44]	[0.77, 0.33]	[0.77, 0.33]	[0.77, 0.33]	[0.22, 0.88]
	SP_2	[0.77, 0.33]	[0.77, 0.33]	[0.88, 0.22]	[0.88, 0.22]	[0.44, 0.66]
	SP_3	[0.77, 0.33]	[0.77, 0.33]	[0.88, 0.22]	[0.88, 0.22]	[0.55, 0.55]
	SP_4	[0.77, 0.33]	[0.77, 0.33]	[0.99, 0.11]	[0.88, 0.22]	[0.77, 0.33]
CSP_8	SP_1	[0.44, 0.66]	[0.77, 0.33]	[0.88, 0.22]	[0.88, 0.22]	[0.22, 0.88]
	SP_2	[0.66, 0.44]	[0.88, 0.22]	[0.88, 0.22]	[0.88, 0.22]	[0.44, 0.66]
	SP_3	[0.55, 0.55]	[0.77, 0.33]	[0.88, 0.22]	[0.88, 0.22]	[0.55, 0.55]
	SP_4	[0.55, 0.55]	[0.77, 0.33]	[0.99, 0.11]	[0.88, 0.22]	[0.77, 0.33]
CSP_9	SP_1	[0.55, 0.55]	[0.77, 0.33]	[0.88, 0.22]	[0.44, 0.66]	[0.22, 0.88]
	SP_2	[0.88, 0.22]	[0.88, 0.22]	[0.88, 0.22]	[0.44, 0.66]	[0.44, 0.66]
	SP_3	[0.66, 0.44]	[0.77, 0.33]	[0.88, 0.22]	[0.44, 0.66]	[0.55, 0.55]
	SP_4	[0.77, 0.33]	[0.77, 0.33]	[0.88, 0.22]	[0.44, 0.66]	[0.77, 0.33]
CSP_{10}	SP_1	[0.44, 0.66]	[0.77, 0.33]	[0.77, 0.33]	[0.55, 0.55]	[0.22, 0.88]
	SP_2	[0.66, 0.44]	[0.88, 0.22]	[0.77, 0.33]	[0.55, 0.55]	[0.44, 0.66]
	SP_3	[0.55, 0.55]	[0.77, 0.33]	[0.77, 0.33]	[0.55, 0.55]	[0.55, 0.55]
	SP_4	[0.55, 0.55]	[0.77, 0.33]	[0.77, 0.33]	[0.55, 0.55]	[0.77, 0.33]

TABLE 5.9

Combined Assessment Matrix of CSPs

CSP_s	$CUTD_1$	$DIOD_2$	$SKUD_3$	$MEMD_4$	$COSD_5$
CSP_1	[0.823, 0.295]	[0.823, 0.295]	[0.823, 0.295]	[0.823, 0.295]	[0.817, 0.342]
CSP_2	[0.801, 0.318]	[0.330, 0.770]	[0.110, 0.990]	[0.832, 0.301]	[0.564, 0.630]
CSP_3	[0.801, 0.318]	[0.823, 0.295]	[0.823, 0.295]	[0.832, 0.301]	[0.909, 0.248]
CSP_4	[0.823, 0.295]	[0.823, 0.295]	[0.823, 0.295]	[0.832, 0.301]	[0.817, 0.342]
CSP_5	[0.801, 0.318]	[0.823, 0.295]	[0.394, 0.780]	[0.812, 0.303]	[0.909, 0.284]
CSP_6	[0.801, 0.318]	[0.823, 0.295]	[0.823, 0.295]	[0.812, 0.303]	[0.909, 0.284]
CSP_7	[0.747, 0.365]	[0.770, 0.330]	[0.877, 0.259]	[0.857, 0.260]	[0.458, 0.713]
CSP_8	[0.555, 0.562]	[0.801, 0.311]	[0.901, 0.211]	[0.880, 0.220]	[0.458, 0.715]
CSP_9	[0.715, 0.438]	[0.801, 0.311]	[0.880, 0.220]	[0.440, 0.660]	[0.458, 0.714]
CSP_{10}	[0.555, 0.562]	[0.801, 0.311]	[0.770, 0.330]	[0.550, 0.550]	[0.458, 0.714]

TABLE 5.10

Normalized Assessment Matrix of CSPs

CSP_s	$CUTD_1$	$DIOD_2$	$SKUD_3$	$MEMD_4$	$COSD_5$
CSP_1	[0.823, 0.295]	[0.823, 0.295]	[0.823, 0.295]	[0.823, 0.295]	[0.817, 0.342]
CSP_2	[0.801, 0.318]	[0.330, 0.770]	[0.110, 0.990]	[0.832, 0.301]	[0.564, 0.630]
CSP_3	[0.801, 0.318]	[0.823, 0.295]	[0.823, 0.295]	[0.832, 0.301]	[0.909, 0.248]
CSP_4	[0.823, 0.295]	[0.823, 0.295]	[0.823, 0.295]	[0.832, 0.301]	[0.817, 0.342]
CSP_5	[0.801, 0.318]	[0.823, 0.295]	[0.394, 0.780]	[0.812, 0.303]	[0.909, 0.284]
CSP_6	[0.801, 0.318]	[0.823, 0.295]	[0.823, 0.295]	[0.812, 0.303]	[0.909, 0.284]
CSP_7	[0.747, 0.365]	[0.770, 0.330]	[0.877, 0.259]	[0.857, 0.260]	[0.458, 0.713]
CSP_8	[0.555, 0.562]	[0.801, 0.311]	[0.901, 0.211]	[0.880, 0.220]	[0.458, 0.715]
CSP_9	[0.715, 0.438]	[0.801, 0.311]	[0.880, 0.220]	[0.440, 0.660]	[0.458, 0.714]
CSP_{10}	[0.555, 0.562]	[0.801, 0.311]	[0.770, 0.330]	[0.550, 0.550]	[0.458, 0.714]

TABLE 5.11

α_j and β_j Values of CSPs

CSP_s	Wq-ROFHA Factor		Wq-ROFHGM Factor	
	α	β	α	β
CSP_1	0.822	0.305	0.164	0.307
CSP_2	0.706	0.541	0.084	0.873
CSP_3	0.846	0.291	0.167	0.295
CSP_4	0.823	0.306	0.165	0.308
CSP_5	0.818	0.366	0.143	0.588
CSP_6	0.843	0.299	0.167	0.300
CSP_7	0.796	0.361	0.144	0.536
CSP_8	0.806	0.364	0.137	0.559
CSP_9	0.755	0.426	0.127	0.586
CSP_{10}	0.686	0.473	0.122	0.577

TABLE 5.12

Score Values of CSPs for α_j and β_j

CSP$_s$	α_j	β_j
CSP$_1$	0.7585	0.4285
CSP$_2$	0.5823	0.1056
CSP$_3$	0.7777	0.4364
CSP$_4$	0.7588	0.4282
CSP$_5$	0.7260	0.2775
CSP$_6$	0.7718	0.4334
CSP$_7$	0.7176	0.3040
CSP$_8$	0.7207	0.2890
CSP$_9$	0.6644	0.2705
CSP$_{10}$	0.6063	0.2724

TABLE 5.13

Comparative Prominence and the Concluding Rating of the CSPs

CSP$_s$	γ_{ja}	γ_{jb}	γ_{jc}	γ_j	Rank
CSP$_1$	0.149	5.3596	0.9777	2.9952	3
CSP$_2$	0.0666	2.0000	0.5666	1.3003	10
CSP$_3$	0.1175	5.4669	1.0000	3.0577	1
CSP$_4$	0.1149	5.3571	0.9777	2.9942	4
CSP$_5$	0.0972	3.8746	0.8266	2.2771	7
CSP$_6$	0.1167	5.4284	0.9927	3.0359	2
CSP$_7$	0.0989	4.1111	0.8415	2.3833	5
CSP$_8$	0.0977	3.9736	0.8317	2.3205	6
CSP$_9$	0.0905	3.7019	0.7700	2.1574	8
CSP$_{10}$	0.0851	3.6204	0.7238	2.0828	9

Secondly, the CoCoSo method was used to rank the ten cloud service providers used in the study. According to the results in Table 5.13 and Figure 5.5, it is found that Amazon provider occupies the first rank with a weight of 3.0577, followed by Google provider with a weight of 3.0359, while Soft Layer provider occupies the last rank with a weight of 1.3003.

5.6 Summary

- This chapter provides a comprehensive description of cloud computing and its relevant merits.

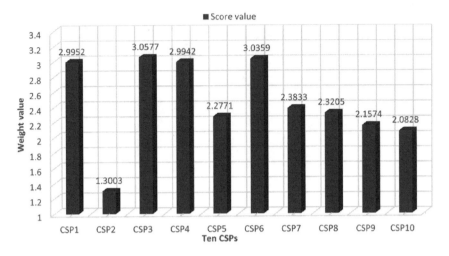

FIGURE 5.5
Final ranking of the available CSPs.

- This chapter reviews the importance and needs of assessing cloud service performance and smart data selection for cloud computing.
- This chapter presents the most important criteria used in evaluating cloud service performance and smart data selection for cloud computing after a comprehensive analysis of a number of research articles.
- This chapter suggests the steps of a hybrid MCDM approach for evaluating multiple cloud service providers (CSPs). The hybrid approach consists of two advanced MCDM techniques: entropy and the combined compromised solution (CoCoSo).
- This chapter presents a real case study while evaluating cloud service performance and smart data selection for cloud computing.

5.7 Exercises

a. How do you define "cloud computing"? Why is an evaluation of multiple cloud service providers important for cloud computing?

b. What are the differences between entropy and the CoCoSo approaches? Discuss their relative advantages while making a decision.

c. Why is the adoption of IoT in cloud computing considered an obstacle? Why assessing those obstacles is important?

d. Discuss the features of cloud service providers for cloud computing in terms of the characteristics and formation of a smart city.

e. Why is MCDM approach required to assess cloud service performance and smart data selection for cloud computing?

References

Alkan, Nurşah, and Cengiz Kahraman. 2021. "Evaluation of Government Strategies against COVID-19 Pandemic Using q-Rung Orthopair Fuzzy TOPSIS Method." *Applied Soft Computing* 110: 107653. doi: 10.1016/j.asoc.2021.107653.

Atanassov, Krassimir T. 1999. "Intuitionistic fuzzy sets." In: *Intuitionistic Fuzzy Sets*, pp. 1–137. Physica, Heidelberg.

Chodha, Varun, Rohit Dubey, Raman Kumar, Sehijpal Singh, and Swapandeep Kaur. 2022. "Selection of Industrial Arc Welding Robot with TOPSIS and Entropy MCDM Techniques." *Materials Today: Proceedings* 50: 709–15. doi: 10.1016/j.matpr.2021.04.487.

Darko, Adjei Peter, and Decui Liang. 2020. "Some Q-Rung Orthopair Fuzzy Hamacher Aggregation Operators and Their Application to Multiple Attribute Group Decision Making with Modified EDAS Method." *Engineering Applications of Artificial Intelligence* 87: 103259. doi: 10.1016/j.engappai.2019.103259.

Deveci, Muhammet, Dragan Pamucar, and Ilgin Gokasar. 2021. "Fuzzy Power Heronian Function Based CoCoSo Method for the Advantage Prioritization of Autonomous Vehicles in Real-Time Traffic Management." *Sustainable Cities and Society* 69: 102846. doi: 10.1016/j.scs.2021.102846.

Jatoth, Chandrashekar, Gagan Roy Gangadharan, and Ugo Fiore. 2017. "Evaluating the Efficiency of Cloud Services Using Modified Data Envelopment Analysis and Modified Super-Efficiency Data Envelopment Analysis." *Soft Computing* 21(23): 7221–34. doi: 10.1007/s00500-016-2267-y.

Liu, Peide, and Peng Wang. 2018. "Some Q-Rung Orthopair Fuzzy Aggregation Operators and Their Applications to Multiple-Attribute Decision Making." *International Journal of Intelligent Systems* 33(2): 259–80. doi: 10.1002/int.21927.

Torkayesh, Ali Ebadi, Dragan Pamucar, Fatih Ecer, and Prasenjit Chatterjee. 2021. "An Integrated BWM-LBWA-CoCoSo Framework for Evaluation of Healthcare Sectors in Eastern Europe." *Socio-Economic Planning Sciences* 78: 101052. doi: 10.1016/j.seps.2021.101052.

Vaid, Sanjay Kumar, Gopal Vaid, Swapandeep Kaur, Raman Kumar, and Manpreet Singh Sidhu. 2022. "Application of Multi-Criteria Decision-Making Theory with VIKOR-WASPAS-Entropy Methods: A Case Study of Silent Genset." *Materials Today: Proceedings* 50: 2416–23. doi: 10.1016/j.matpr.2021.10.259.

Wang, Jie, Guiwu Wei, Jianping Lu, Fuad E Alsaadi, Tasawar Hayat, Cun Wei, and Yi Zhang. 2019. "Some Q-Rung Orthopair Fuzzy Hamy Mean Operators in Multiple Attribute Decision-Making and Their Application to Enterprise Resource Planning Systems Selection." *International Journal of Intelligent Systems* 34(10): 2429–58. doi: 10.1002/int.22155.

Yager, Ronald R. 2013. "Pythagorean Fuzzy Subsets." *In 2013 Joint IFSA World Congress and NAFIPS Annual Meeting (IFSA/NAFIPS)*, pp. 57–61. doi: 10.1109/IFSA-NAFIPS.2013.6608375.

Yager, Ronald R. 2017. "Generalized Orthopair Fuzzy Sets." *IEEE Transactions on Fuzzy Systems* 25(5): 1222–30. doi: 10.1109/TFUZZ.2016.2604005.

6

An Evaluation Approach for Prioritizing Performance of Sustainability Indicators for Smart Campuses

6.1 Introduction

The quality of life for city residents is the primary focus of initiatives about smart cities. In order to accomplish this goal, the focus has been on a number of different domains, including the economic, operational, social, environmental, health, administrative, and governmental aspects, always adhering to the principles of providing citizens with effective and practical service. Despite this, the development process for smart cities is notoriously difficult due to the vast number of projects that fall under this category. Numerous imponderables come up, which usually results in the abandonment of ongoing projects or, at most, leads to a more modest reinterpretation of these initiatives. Very frequently, all that is left of the smart city is its name or the idea that was behind its inception. A university of medium size with a single campus is a sufficiently complex environment to be highly reflective of a city of medium size. It also strive to attain the same quality of life for their community as anticipated in a smart city.

We conceived of the smart university as a model for universities that improves the quality of life by making intensive, global, efficient, and sustainable use of information technology to deliver services for the benefit of the entire university community. This idea was based on the factors that were discussed above. We are in a position to affirm that a university campus is an appropriate mock-up for a smart city initiative. A university campus is a representative, and in addition to serving as an example, guide, and case study with which to develop viable projects in our cities, the partial results would be useful in and of themselves to effectively and efficiently improve the quality of life of a large number of citizens. This is because the results of the smart city initiative would be based on the lessons learned from the university campus. It is possible that the planning

DOI: 10.1201/9781003357681-6

and execution of a smart university might have a beneficial effect on the campus of any institution. On the other hand, this presents a substantial obstacle; consequently, such initiatives sometimes fail to materialize. In order to successfully coordinate a smart university project, the entire endeavor must first be broken down into a series of smaller, more manageable projects. These projects may be spread out over several fiscal years, led by various teams, and incorporate various technological applications. Even when projects are completed successfully, the end result is often a dispersion of services that cannot connect with one another or generate new value-added services; eventually, a wide variety of technologies and services are reproduced and maintained.

The high degree of dependency on non-renewable resources inside university campuses as a consequence of the absence of sustainable practices has led to certain institutions having a large carbon footprint. For instance, the majority of the nation's public colleges get their source of electrical energy from oil. The vast majority of educational establishments at the university level are now participating in a variety of challenging activities. Some institutions consist of a number of campuses spread out throughout a state or other geopolitical territory in various places geographically. On the contrary, many of them have expanded beyond the scope of the initial master plan that was supposed to guide the phase plan of their campus expansion. Some of the difficulties that have been producing discussions and disputes within the previous several decades include the need for land, housing, and essential infrastructure between the campuses of higher education institutions and the adjacent community. The success that may be achieved in resolving these issues is directly proportional to the level of willingness shown by the heads of institutions and the community leaders, as well as the deployment of creative, smart spatial strategies. It is clear from the research that cities that can implement new technology and an innovative solution driven by smart technology will be able to overcome their issues. On the contrary, those who cannot do so face a greater number of challenges while making little progress.

Unless higher education institutions embrace the smart campus sustainability model and evaluation procedures, most campuses will use a greater proportion of local oil, and other serious difficulties will intensify in the near future. The obstacles posed by limited data access for the evaluation process will also be addressed. The indicators will be based on environmental dimensions that may be obtained geographically and incorporated into the software for smart spatial techniques. Higher education institutions have an urgent need to move toward adopting and establishing a smart framework employing spatial software for campus sustainability. Furthermore, the relevance and significance of building a smart spatial-based framework to analyze the appropriateness and sustainability performance of higher education institution campuses are derived from the worldwide adage "think globally, act locally." A further rationale is a country-specific approach that offers a complete information repository for government and higher education institution managers. This chapter addresses this research vacuum by evaluating the relative relevance of spatial-based indicators that fit with the stakeholders' degree of awareness and the nature of the local context in every given nation. This relative significance will assist the development of a method for smart university campuses to embrace the local environment in order to achieve a smart city objectively.

6.2 Methodology

In this part, the MCDM-blended approach is presented to prioritize the performance of sustainability indicators and to assess the sustainability performance of smart campuses (SCs). The applied approach was carried out under q-rung orthopair fuzzy set (q-ROFS) environment and using q-rung orthopair fuzzy numbers (q-ROFNs). The approach used consists of two methods q-ROFS entropy and the q-ROFS Technique for Order of Preference by Similarity to Ideal Solution (q-ROFS TOPSIS). Figure 6.1 shows the steps of the approach used to evaluate several SCs. In this regard, we provide a brief overview of the methods used in applying this chapter's case study. This section is divided into several parts as follows.

6.2.1 Entropy Method

The Shannon entropy, which was first created by Shannon, serves as the foundation for the entropy weight approach (Shannon 1948). Entropy is a measurement of the information disorder degree of a particular system and has the potential to fully use the information that is included in the original material. Although it overly relies on objective data, which cannot accurately reflect experts' knowledge and practical experience, entropy weight can indicate useful information provided by the index (Xu et al. 2018). As a result, the results can sometimes be inconsistent with reality and individual comprehension. The Shannon entropy is a notion that has been developed in terms of probability theory and is presented as a measure of uncertainty in information (Delgado and Romero 2016). It is an excellent and easy option for our goal since the idea of entropy is well adapted to assessing the relative intensities of contrast criteria to reflect the average intrinsic information supplied for decision-making.

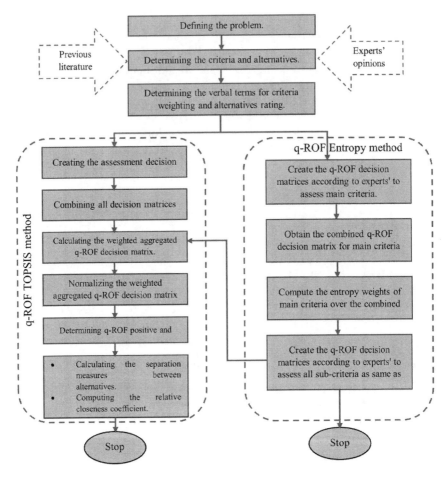

FIGURE 6.1
Illustrative representation of the used approach for evaluating smart campuses.

6.2.2 TOPSIS Method

In 1981, Yoon and Hwang created what is now known as the TOPSIS approach (Yoon and Hwang 1985). Alternatives are evaluated with the use of parameters by the procedure. The fundamental reasoning behind this approach is to find the positive and negative solutions that are most effective overall. The alternative that is the farthest away from the optimum positive solution is the one that is considered to be the best alternative. An ideal alternative is the closest to the optimal negative solution. TOPSIS assigns weights to choose options according to how close they are to both a positive ideal solution (PIS) and a negative ideal solution (NIS) simultaneously. The PIS prioritizes criteria of the "the more, the better" kind while giving less weight to those of the "the less, the better" variety, while the

NIS prioritizes criteria of the "the more, the better" variety while giving less weight to those of "the less, the better" variety. The distance to the PIS is cut down to a minimum, while the distance to the NIS is increased to its greatest possible level. The approach is one of the most extensively used ranking systems since it validates a large number of appropriate qualities (Bouslah et al. 2022). As a result, it has been widely used for actual choice issues in a variety of situations due to its widespread usefulness.

6.2.3 Computational Steps of the Approach Used

This part presents detailed steps to solve the problem of identifying sustainability indicators for smart campuses and providing steps for arranging some smart campuses.

Step 1: The problem is studied in some detail in order to reach the points of importance and weakness and to identify the most important main aspects that affect the identification of sustainability indicators for the smart campus and the assessment of the smart campus. In this regard, some experts have agreed to help the authors compile data to solve the problem. Accordingly, some rules have been established for selecting experts, such as academic degrees and years of experience. Also, it was agreed on ways to communicate with experts, whether online or offline.

Step 2: The most significant main criteria and sub-criteria affecting the selection of smart campuses are determined based on expert surveys and previous studies. $C_j = \{C_1, C_2, ..., C_n\}$, with j=1, 2...n. Let $w = (w_1, w_2, ..., w_n)$ be the vector set used for recognizing the criteria weights, where $w_j > 0$ and $\sum_{j=1}^{n} w_j = 1$.

Step 3: The most significant available alternatives that can be used in the assessment process are determined, in addition to preparing a final list of these alternatives according to experts' opinions. The group $SC_i = \{SC_1, SC_2, ..., SC_m\}$, having i=1, 2,..., m alternatives, is measured by n decision measurements of group $C_j = \{C_1, C_2, ..., C_n\}$, with j=1, 2, ..., n.

Step 4: According to the study of the problem, its dimensions are organized in a hierarchical form between the main objective, sub-criteria, and the selected alternatives.

Step 5: Linguistic variables that help experts evaluate the main criteria and sub-criteria are identified as presented in Table 6.1. Also, linguistic terms that help in evaluating alternatives are identified, as shown in Table 6.2.

Step 6: Create the judgment matrices rendering to experts' preferences (E_s) to measure the main criteria by each expert by using verbal terms as presented in Table 6.1, and then by using q-ROFNs as presented in Table 6.3.

TABLE 6.1

Verbal Terms and Their Equivalent q-ROFNs
for Assessing Criteria

		q-ROFNs	
Verbal Terms	**Definitions**	u	ϑ
Extremely low	EXT	0.11	0.99
Very low	VLO	0.22	0.88
low	LOW	0.33	0.77
Moderate low	MOL	0.44	0.66
Moderate	MOD	0.55	0.55
Moderate well	MOW	0.66	0.44
Well	WLL	0.77	0.33
Very well	VEW	0.88	0.22
Extremely well	EWL	0.99	0.11

TABLE 6.2

Verbal Terms and Their Equivalent q-ROFNs
for Classification Alternatives

		q-ROFNs	
Verbal Terms	**Definitions**	u	ϑ
Extremely little	EXL	0.11	0.99
Very little	VEL	0.22	0.88
Little	LEL	0.33	0.77
Medium little	MEL	0.44	0.66
Medium	MED	0.55	0.55
Medium great	MEG	0.66	0.44
Great	GRE	0.77	0.33
Very great	VRG	0.88	0.22
Extremely great	ETG	0.99	0.11

TABLE 6.3

Evaluation Matrix for Criteria Is Based on q-ROFN with Respect
to Experts

	Experts			
Criteria	E_1	E_2	E_3	E_4
C_1	$\left[u_{1E_1}, \vartheta_{1E_1} \right]$	$\left[u_{1E_2}, \vartheta_{1E_2} \right]$	$\left[u_{1E_3}, \vartheta_{1E_3} \right]$	$\left[u_{1E_4}, \vartheta_{1E_4} \right]$
C_2	$\left[u_{2E_1}, \vartheta_{2E_1} \right]$	$\left[u_{2E_2}, \vartheta_{2E_2} \right]$	$\left[u_{2E_3}, \vartheta_{2E_3} \right]$	$\left[u_{2E_4}, \vartheta_{2E_4} \right]$
$\vdots$	$\vdots$	$\vdots$	$\vdots$	$\vdots$
C_n	$\left[u_{nE_1}, \vartheta_{nE_1} \right]$	$\left[u_{nE_2}, \vartheta_{nE_2} \right]$	$\left[u_{nE_3}, \vartheta_{nE_3} \right]$	$\left[u_{nE_4}, \vartheta_{nE_4} \right]$

Step 7: Aggregate the valuations on criterion weights. The distinct expert valuations were combined by applying q-ROFWG presented in Eq. (6.1). At this point, $(w_j)_{1 \times n}$ introduces q-ROF weight of jth criterion. It can refer to the connotation of Eq. (6.1) in the previous chapter (Chapter 5).

$$\text{q-ROFWG}\left(\breve{Q}_1, \breve{Q}_2, \ldots, \breve{Q}_n\right) = \left(\prod_{i=1}^{n} \mathcal{U}_{\breve{Q}_i}{}^{w_i}, \left(1 - \prod_{i=1}^{n}\left(1 - \vartheta_{\breve{Q}_i}{}^q\right)^{w_i}\right)^{\frac{1}{q}}\right) \quad (6.1)$$

Step 8: Compute the entropy values of all q-ROFN of the collected experts' assessments by applying Eqs. (6.2) and (6.3).

$$k\mathbb{E}_{q,ij}(x) = \frac{1}{\sqrt{2}}\left(\left(\left(\mathcal{U}(x)\right)^q\right)^2 + \left(\left(\vartheta(x)\right)^q\right)^2 + \left(\left(\mathcal{U}(x)\right)^q + \left(\vartheta(x)\right)^q\right)^2\right)^{0.5} \quad (6.2)$$

$$\mathbb{EN}_{q,ij}(x) = -k\mathbb{E}_{q,ij}(x) = 1 - \left(\left(\left(\mathcal{U}(x)\right)^q\right)^2 + \left(\left(\vartheta(x)\right)^q\right)^2 + \left(\left(\mathcal{U}(x)\right)^q + \left(\vartheta(x)\right)^q\right)^2\right)^{0.5}$$
$$(6.3)$$

Step 9: Compute the main criterion weights based on the entropy values according to Eq. (6.4).

$$w_j = \frac{1 - \xi_j}{\sum_{j=1}^{n}\left(1 - \xi_j\right)} \; ; \; j = 1, 2 \ldots n. \quad (6.4)$$

where $\xi_j = \dfrac{\sum_{i=1}^{m} \mathbb{EN}_{q, ij}}{\sum_{i=1}^{m}\sum_{j=1}^{n} \mathbb{EN}_{q, ij}}$ refers to the q-ROF entropy value.

Step 10: In this regard, the weights of the sub-criteria are calculated in the same steps as the weights of the main criteria. Based on the weights of the main criteria, the global weights of the sub-criteria are calculated.

Step 11: Construct the assessment decision matrix by each expert separately (E_s) between the determined sub-criteria and the available alternatives to assess the smart campuses by utilizing the verbal terms as presented in Table 6.2, then by applying the q-ROFNs in Table 6.2 as exhibited in Table 6.4.

Step 12: Aggregate the assessment decision matrix by each expert separately (E_s) between the determined sub-criteria and the available alternatives to assess the smart campuses into one matrix by applying the q-ROFWG as exhibited in Eq. (6.1) as exhibited in Table 6.5.

TABLE 6.4

Judgment Assessment Matrix for Alternatives in Terms of
All Sub-Criteria Based on q-ROFN

Sub-Criteria	Alternatives			
	SC_1	SC_2	...	SC_m
C_1	$\left[\mathcal{U}_{11E}, \vartheta_{11E} \right]$	$\left[\mathcal{U}_{12E}, \vartheta_{12E} \right]$	...	$\left[\mathcal{U}_{1mE}, \vartheta_{1mE} \right]$
C_2	$\left[\mathcal{U}_{21E}, \vartheta_{21E} \right]$	$\left[\mathcal{U}_{22E}, \vartheta_{22E} \right]$	...	$\left[\mathcal{U}_{2mE}, \vartheta_{2mE} \right]$
$\vdots$	$\vdots$	$\vdots$	$\ddots$	$\vdots$
C_n	$\left[\mathcal{U}_{n1E}, \vartheta_{n1E} \right]$	$\left[\mathcal{U}_{n2E}, \vartheta_{n2E} \right]$	...	$\left[\mathcal{U}_{nmE}, \vartheta_{nmE} \right]$

TABLE 6.5

Aggregated Assessment Matrix for Alternatives in
Terms of Sub-Criteria Based on q-ROFN

Sub-Criteria	Alternatives			
	SC_1	SC_2	...	SC_m
C_1	$\left[\mathcal{U}_{11}, \vartheta_{11} \right]$	$\left[\mathcal{U}_{12}, \vartheta_{12} \right]$	...	$\left[\mathcal{U}_{1m}, \vartheta_{1m} \right]$
C_2	$\left[\mathcal{U}_{21}, \vartheta_{21} \right]$	$\left[\mathcal{U}_{22}, \vartheta_{22} \right]$	...	$\left[\mathcal{U}_{2m}, \vartheta_{2m} \right]$
$\vdots$	$\vdots$	$\vdots$	$\ddots$	$\vdots$
C_n	$\left[\mathcal{U}_{n1}, \vartheta_{n1} \right]$	$\left[\mathcal{U}_{n2}, \vartheta_{n2} \right]$	...	$\left[\mathcal{U}_{nm}, \vartheta_{nm} \right]$

TABLE 6.6

Weighted Aggregated Assessment Matrix

Sub-Criteria	Alternatives			
	SC_1	SC_2	...	SC_m
C_1	$\left[\mathcal{U}_{11}, \vartheta_{11} \right]$	$\left[\mathcal{U}_{12}, \vartheta_{12} \right]$	...	$\left[\mathcal{U}_{1m}, \vartheta_{1m} \right]$
C_2	$\left[\mathcal{U}_{21}, \vartheta_{21} \right]$	$\left[\mathcal{U}_{22}, \vartheta_{22} \right]$	...	$\left[\mathcal{U}_{2m}, \vartheta_{2m} \right]$
$\vdots$	$\vdots$	$\vdots$	$\ddots$	$\vdots$
C_n	$\left[\mathcal{U}_{n1}, \vartheta_{n1} \right]$	$\left[\mathcal{U}_{n2}, \vartheta_{n2} \right]$	...	$\left[\mathcal{U}_{nm}, \vartheta_{nm} \right]$

Step 13: Compute the weighted aggregated q-ROF assessment judgment matrix ($\breve{R}$). The weighted aggregated q-ROF decision matrix ($\breve{R}$) is obtained by multiplying the weights w_j with the aggregated q-ROF decision matrix as presented in Table 6.6.

Step 14: Calculate the normalized combined q-ROF assessment judgment matrix ($\breve{A}$) by using Eq. (6.5).

$$\tilde{A}=\left(\tilde{a}_{ij}\right)_{m\times n}=\left[\breve{U}_{ij},\breve{\vartheta}_{ij}\right]=\begin{cases}\left(\breve{U}_{ij},\breve{\vartheta}_{ij}\right) & \text{if } i\in B\\\left(\breve{\vartheta}_{ij},\breve{U}_{ij}\right) & \text{if } i\in\varsigma\end{cases} \tag{6.5}$$

where n indicates the group of benefit criteria, and ς denotes the group of cost criteria.

Step 15: Identify q-ROF PIS and q-ROF NIS given in Eqs. (6.6) and (6.7) based on the normalized decision matrix.

$$\tilde{A}_{ij}^{*}=\left\{\left\langle C_{1},\left(U_{1}^{*},\vartheta_{1}^{*}\right),C_{2},\left(U_{2}^{*},\vartheta_{2}^{*}\right)\right\rangle,...,\left\langle C_{n},\left(U_{n}^{*},\vartheta_{n}^{*}\right)\right\rangle\right\} \tag{6.6}$$

$$\tilde{A}_{ij}^{-}=\left\{\left\langle C_{1},\left(U_{1}^{-},\vartheta_{1}^{-}\right),C_{2},\left(U_{2}^{-},\vartheta_{2}^{-}\right)\right\rangle,...,\left\langle C_{n},\left(U_{n}^{-},\vartheta_{n}^{-}\right)\right\rangle\right\} \tag{6.7}$$

Step 16: Compute the separation measures by obtaining the distances for each substitute according to $\tilde{A}^{*}$ and $\tilde{A}^{-}$ by applying Eqs. (6.8) and (6.9), respectively.

$$d\left(A_{i},A^{*}\right)=\left(\frac{1}{2n}\sum_{j=1}^{n}\left(\left|U_{ij}^{q}-\left(U_{j}^{*}\right)^{q}\right|^{2}+\left|\vartheta_{ij}^{q}-\left(\vartheta_{j}^{*}\right)^{q}\right|^{2}\right)\right)^{1/2} \tag{6.8}$$

$$d\left(A_{i},A^{-}\right)=\left(\frac{1}{2n}\sum_{j=1}^{n}\left(\left|U_{ij}^{q}-\left(U_{j}^{-}\right)^{q}\right|^{2}+\left|\vartheta_{ij}^{q}-\left(\vartheta_{j}^{-}\right)^{q}\right|^{2}\right)\right)^{1/2} \tag{6.9}$$

Step 17: Compute the relative closeness coefficient (CC_i) of substitutes by applying Eq. (6.10). Then, rank the alternatives in descending order of the values of CC_i.

$$CC_{i}=\frac{d\left(A_{i},A^{-}\right)}{d\left(A_{i},A^{-}\right)+d\left(A_{i},A^{-}\right)} \tag{6.10}$$

6.3 Case Study

Universities play a pivotal role in fostering a culture of sustainability in society by establishing themselves as examples and incubators for sustainable development. Consequently, evaluating institutions' sustainability integration is essential to their contribution to sustainable development. This study conducted an evaluation of some public sector universities in one of the Arab countries on the basis of the sustainability criteria that were identified in the previous section. Thus, six smart campuses have been identified to be evaluated according to the approach used in this chapter, which is as follows: SC_1, SC_2, SC_3, SC_4, SC_5, and SC_6.

Step 1: The problem was studied, and the main objective of it was determined, which is to determine the sustainability indicators for the smart campus and to evaluate the smart campuses. In this regard, four experts were selected according to the criteria set for selecting the participating experts. The weight value of each expert was determined as follows: 0.25, 0.25, 0.25, and 0.25. Also, the experts were contacted through live interviews and online meetings. In addition, the parameter was selected subjectively to represent the experts' opinions on optimism and pessimism. In this instance, q=5 is used to further illustrate the vagueness.

Step 2: The main criteria that affect the selection of smart campuses have been identified, which are the environment criterion, government criterion, mobility criterion, and economy criterion. Also, sub-criteria have been defined, which are pollution air and water criterion, natural resource management criterion, environmental protection instruments criterion, smart building criterion, energy efficiency criterion, transparency criterion, taxation criterion, service efficiency criterion, IT tools criterion, connectivity and local transport criterion, regional connectivity criterion, industry diversification criterion, eco-efficient tourism criterion, green clusters criterion, support for the green economy criterion, and tax incentives and aid criterion.

Step 3: Six alternatives that were identified to be used in the evaluation process are SC_1, SC_2, SC_3, SC_4, SC_5, and SC_6.

Step 4: The dimensions of the problem are organized in a hierarchical form between the main objective, main criteria, and sub-criteria, in addition to the selected alternatives, as presented in Figure 6.2.

Step 5: A set of verbal terms has been identified for use by experts in prioritizing the main criteria and their sub-criteria, as shown in Table 6.1. Also, a set of verbal terms were identified for use by experts in evaluating alternatives, as shown in Table 6.2.

Step 6: The judgment matrices rendering to experts' preferences (E_s) to measure the main criteria by each expert by using verbal terms as presented in Table 6.1 were created according to Table 6.3 as presented in Table 6.7.

Step 7: The distinct expert valuations were aggregated by applying q-ROFWG presented in Eq. (6.1) as presented in Table 6.7.

Step 8: The entropy values of all q-ROFN of the collected experts' assessments were computed by applying Eqs. (6.2) and (6.3).

Step 9: The main criteria weights based on the entropy values were calculated according to Eq. (6.4) as presented in Table 6.7 and Figure 6.3.

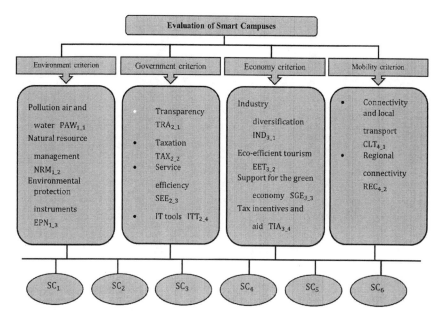

FIGURE 6.2
Hierarchical form of the problem.

TABLE 6.7

Verbal Terms of Main Criteria by Each Expert and Aggregated Main Criteria Weights

Main Criteria	E_1	E_2	E_3	E_4	Aggregated Results	$ƙE_{q,ij}(y)$	$ƀN_{q,ij}(y)$	ξ_j	ω_j
ENV$_1$	WLL	VEW	VEW	EWL	[0.877, 0.262]	0.51807	0.48193	0.20804	0.264
GOV$_2$	MOL	EWL	EWL	WLL	[0.759, 0.508]	0.27059	0.72941	0.31487	0.228
ECO$_3$	LOW	EXT	MOD	WLL	[0.310, 0.902]	0.60001	0.39999	0.17266	0.276
MOB$_4$	MOD	WLL	EWL	VEW	[0.779, 0.425]	0.29476	0.70524	0.30443	0.232

Step 10: The judgment matrices rendering to experts' preferences (E_s) to measure the environment criterion's sub-criteria by each expert by using verbal terms as presented in Table 6.1 were created according to Table 6.3 as presented in Table 6.8.

Step 11: The distinct expert valuations of the environment criterion's sub-criteria were aggregated by applying q-ROFWG presented in Eq. (6.1) as presented in Table 6.8.

Step 12: The entropy values of all q-ROFN of the collected experts' assessments of the environment criterion's sub-criteria were computed by applying Eqs. (6.2) and (6.3).

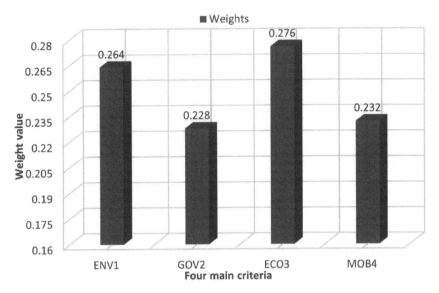

FIGURE 6.3
Final weights of main criteria that are used for weighting smart campuses.

TABLE 6.8

Verbal Terms of Environment Criterion's Sub-Criteria by Each Expert and Aggregated Weights

Environment Criterion's Sub-Criteria	E_1	E_2	E_3	E_4	Aggregated Results	$kE_{q,ij}(y)$	$EN_{q,ij}(y)$	ξ_j	ω_j
PAW_{1_1}	WLL	VEW	VEW	VEW	[0.851, 0.267]	0.44729	0.55271	0.19859	0.200
NRM_{1_2}	VLO	MOL	MOD	MOW	[0.433, 0.733]	0.21985	0.78015	0.28031	0.180
EPN_{1_3}	WLL	MOL	EXT	VLO	[0.301, 0.910]	0.62439	0.37561	0.13496	0.216
SMB_{1_4}	VLO	MOL	MOW	VEW	[0.487, 0.726]	0.21670	0.78330	0.28144	0.180
ENE_{1_5}	EWL	EWL	VEW	VEW	[0.933, 0.193]	0.70856	0.29144	0.10471	0.224

Step 13: The environment criterion's sub-criterion weights based on the entropy values were calculated according to Eq. (6.4) as presented in Table 6.8 and Figure 6.4.

Step 14: The judgment matrices rendering to experts' preferences (E_s) to measure the government criterion's sub-criteria by each expert by using verbal terms as presented in Table 6.1 were created according to Table 6.3 as presented in Table 6.9.

Step 15: The distinct expert valuations of the government criterion's sub-criteria were aggregated by applying q-ROFWG presented in Eq. (6.1) as presented in Table 6.9.

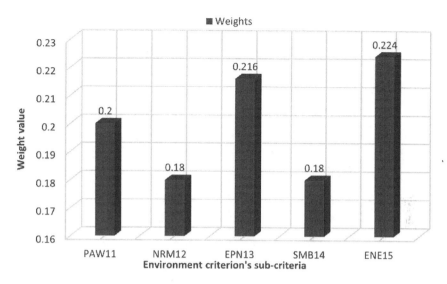

FIGURE 6.4

Final weights of environment criterion's sub-criteria.

TABLE 6.9

Verbal Terms of Government Criterion's Sub-Criteria by Each Expert and Aggregated Weights

Government Criterion's Sub-Criteria	E_1	E_2	E_3	E_4	Aggregated Results	$\hbar E_{q,ij}(y)$	$\hbar N_{q,ij}(y)$	ξ_j	ω_j
TRA_{2_1}	VLO	MOD	VEW	EWL	[0.570, 0.711]	0.21808	0.78192	0.34656	0.218
TAX_{2_2}	MOL	EWL	LOW	WLL	[0.577, 0.640]	0.14967	0.85033	0.37688	0.208
SEE_{2_3}	MOL	EXT	MOD	WLL	[0.378, 0.888]	0.55516	0.44484	0.19716	0.268
ITT_{2_4}	EWL	EWL	EWL	VEW	[0.961, 0.170]	0.82087	0.17913	0.07940	0.307

Step 16: The entropy values of all q-ROFN of the collected experts' assessments of the government criterion's sub-criteria were computed by applying Eqs. (6.2) and (6.3).

Step 17: The government criterion's sub-criterion weights based on the entropy values were calculated according to Eq. (6.4) as presented in Table 6.9 and Figure 6.5.

Step 18: The judgment matrices rendering to experts' preferences (E_s) to measure the economy criterion's sub-criteria by each expert by using verbal terms as presented in Table 6.1 were created according to Table 6.3 as presented in Table 6.10.

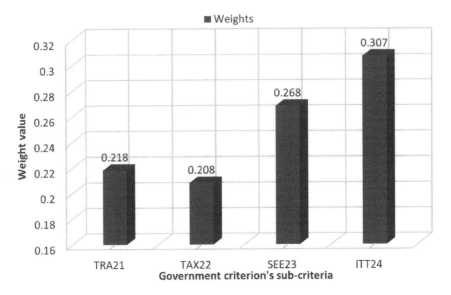

FIGURE 6.5

Final weights of government criterion's sub-criteria.

TABLE 6.10

Verbal Terms of Economy Criterion's Sub-Criteria by Each Expert and Aggregated Weights

Economy Criterion's Sub-Criteria	E_1	E_2	E_3	E_4	Aggregated Results	$\hbar E_{q,ij}(y)$	$E N_{q,ij}(y)$	ξ_j	ω_j
IND_{3_1}	VLO	MOD	MOL	MOW	[0.433, 0.733]	0.21985	0.78015	0.26462	0.245
EET_{3_2}	MOL	EWL	MOW	WLL	[0.686, 0.520]	0.17389	0.82611	0.28021	0.240
SGE_{3_3}	MOL	VLO	MOD	WLL	[0.450, 0.731]	0.21915	0.78085	0.26486	0.245
TIA_{3_4}	WLL	WLL	EWL	VEW	[0.848, 0.291]	0.43895	0.56105	0.19031	0.270

Step 19: The distinct expert valuations of the economy criterion's sub-criteria were aggregated by applying q-ROFWG presented in Eq. (6.1) as presented in Table 6.10.

Step 20: The entropy values of all q-ROFN of the collected experts' assessments of the economy criterion's sub-criteria were computed by applying Eqs. (6.2) and (6.3).

Step 21: The economy criterion's sub-criterion weights based on the entropy values were calculated according to Eq. (6.4) as presented in Table 6.10 and Figure 6.6.

Step 22: The judgment matrices rendering to experts' preferences (E_s) to measure the mobility criterion's sub-criteria by each expert by using verbal

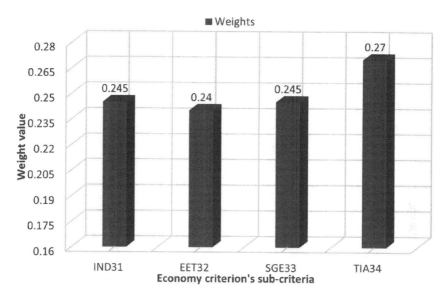

FIGURE 6.6

Final weights of economy criterion's sub-criteria.

TABLE 6.11

Verbal Terms of Mobility Criterion's Sub-Criteria by Each Expert and Aggregated Weights

Mobility Criterion's Sub-Criteria	E_1	E_2	E_3	E_4	Aggregated Results	$ƙE_{q,ij}(y)$	$ƙN_{q,ij}(y)$	$ξ_j$	$ω_j$
CLT_{4_1}	VEW	MOD	WLL	MOW	[0.704, 0.448]	0.18289	0.81711	0.48998	0.510
REC_{4_2}	MOL	MOD	EWL	WLL	[0.655, 0.541]	0.14948	0.85052	0.51002	0.490

terms as presented in Table 6.1 were created according to Table 6.3 as presented in Table 6.11.

Step 23: The distinct expert valuations of the mobility criterion's sub-criteria were aggregated by applying q-ROFWG presented in Eq. (6.1) as presented in Table 6.11.

Step 24: The entropy values of all q-ROFN of the collected experts' assessments of the mobility criterion's sub-criteria were computed by applying Eqs. (6.2) and (6.3).

Step 25: The mobility criterion's sub-criterion weights based on the entropy values were calculated according to Eq. (6.4) as presented in Table 6.11 and Figure 6.7.

Step 26: After calculating the final weights for the main criteria and calculating the local weights for the sub-criteria, the final global weights for

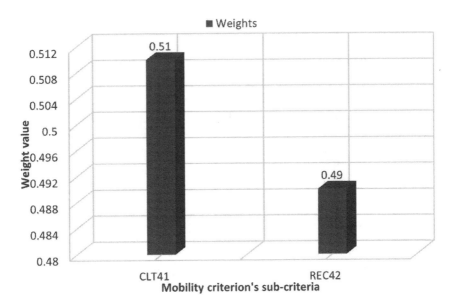

FIGURE 6.7
Final weights of mobility criterion's sub-criteria.

TABLE 6.12

Weights of Main Criteria and Their Sub-Criteria

Main Criteria	Weights of Main Criteria	Sub-Criteria	Local Weight of Sub-Criteria	Global Weight of Sub-Criteria
Environment ENV_1	0.264	Pollution of air and water, PAW_{1_1}	0.200	0.054
		Natural resource management, NRM_{1_2}	0.180	0.048
		Environmental protection instruments, EPN_{1_3}	0.216	0.057
		Smart building, SMB_{1_4}	0.180	0.048
		Energy efficiency, ENE_{1_5}	0.224	0.059
Government GOV_2	0.228	Transparency, TRA_{2_1}	0.218	0.049
		Taxation, TAX_{2_2}	0.208	0.047
		Service efficiency, SEE_{2_3}	0.268	0.061
		IT tools, ITT_{2_4}	0.307	0.069
Economy ECO_3	0.276	Industry diversification, IND_{3_1}	0.245	0.068
		Eco-efficient tourism, EET_{3_2}	0.240	0.066
		Support for the green economy, SGE_{3_3}	0.245	0.068
		Tax incentives and aid, TIA_{3_4}	0.270	0.075
Mobility MOB_3	0.232	Connectivity and local transport, CLT_{4_1}	0.510	0.118
		Regional connectivity, REC_{4_2}	0.490	0.113

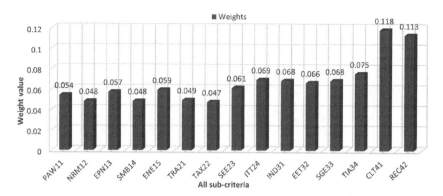

FIGURE 6.8
Final global weights of all sub-criteria.

the sub-criteria are calculated, which are used in evaluating alternatives as in Table 6.12 and Figure 6.8.

Step 27: The assessment decision matrix by each expert separately (E_s) between the determined sub-criteria and the available alternatives was created to assess the smart campuses by utilizing the verbal terms as presented in Table 6.2, then by applying the q-ROFNs in Table 6.2 according to Table 6.4 as presented in Table 6.13.

Step 28: The assessment decision matrix by each expert separately (E_s) between the determined sub-criteria and the available alternatives was aggregated to assess the smart campuses into one matrix by applying q-ROFWG as exhibited in Eq. (6.1) according to Table 6.5 as exhibited in Table 6.14.

Step 29: The weighted aggregated q-ROF assessment judgment matrix ($\check{R}$) was computed. The weighted aggregated q-ROF decision matrix ($\check{R}$) is obtained by multiplying the weights w_j with the aggregated q-ROF decision matrix according to Table 6.6.

Step 30: The normalized combined q-ROF assessment judgment matrix ($\check{A}$) was calculated by using Eq. (6.5) as presented in Table 6.15.

Step 31: q-ROF PIS and q-ROF NIS were determined according to Eqs. (6.6) and (6.7) based on the normalized decision matrix as exhibited in Table 6.16.

Step 32: The separation measures were computed by obtaining the distances for each alternative according to Eqs. (6.8) and (6.9) as presented in Table 6.17.

Step 33: The relative closeness coefficient (CC_i) of alternatives was computed according to Eq. (6.10) as presented in Table 6.18 and Figure 6.9. The six smart campuses were ranked in descending order of the values of CC_i as in Figure 6.9.

TABLE 6.13

Decision Matrices of Six Alternatives according to All Sub-Criteria Using Verbal Terms

Experts	PAW$_{1\_1}$	NRM$_{1\_2}$	EPN$_{1\_3}$	SMB$_{1\_4}$	ENE$_{1\_5}$
SC$_1$	⟨VEL⟩⟨VEL⟩⟨VEL⟩	⟨GRE⟩⟨GRE⟩⟨GRE⟩	⟨GRE⟩⟨GRE⟩⟨VRG⟩	⟨VRG⟩⟨VRG⟩⟨VRG⟩	⟨GRE⟩⟨GRE⟩⟨GRE⟩
SC$_2$	⟨MEL⟩⟨GRE⟩⟨VEL⟩	⟨VEL⟩⟨VEL⟩⟨GRE⟩	⟨VEL⟩⟨VEL⟩⟨VRG⟩	⟨VEL⟩⟨VEL⟩⟨VRG⟩	⟨VEL⟩⟨VEL⟩⟨VEL⟩
SC$_3$	⟨MEL⟩⟨MEL⟩⟨LEL⟩	⟨MEL⟩⟨MEL⟩⟨GRE⟩	⟨LEL⟩⟨VEL⟩⟨VRG⟩	⟨VRG⟩⟨VRG⟩⟨VRG⟩	⟨VRG⟩⟨VEL⟩⟨VEL⟩
SC$_4$	⟨MEL⟩⟨MEL⟩⟨VEL⟩	⟨VRG⟩⟨VRG⟩⟨GRE⟩	⟨GRE⟩⟨GRE⟩⟨GRE⟩	⟨GRE⟩⟨GRE⟩⟨VRG⟩	⟨VRG⟩⟨VRG⟩⟨VRG⟩
SC$_5$	⟨VEL⟩⟨VEL⟩⟨VEL⟩	⟨VRG⟩⟨VRG⟩⟨GRE⟩	⟨MED⟩⟨MED⟩⟨VRG⟩	⟨MEL⟩⟨MEL⟩⟨MEL⟩	⟨GRE⟩⟨GRE⟩⟨GRE⟩
SC$_6$	⟨VRG⟩⟨VRG⟩⟨VRG⟩	⟨MEL⟩⟨MEL⟩⟨VEL⟩	⟨LEL⟩⟨MED⟩⟨GRE⟩	⟨MEL⟩⟨MEL⟩⟨MEL⟩	⟨VRG⟩⟨VRG⟩⟨VRG⟩

Experts	TRA$_{2\_1}$	TAX$_{2\_2}$	SEE$_{2\_3}$	ITT$_{2\_4}$	IND$_{3\_1}$
SC$_1$	⟨GRE⟩⟨GRE⟩⟨GRE⟩	⟨GRE⟩⟨GRE⟩⟨GRE⟩	⟨MEL⟩⟨MEL⟩⟨VEL⟩	⟨GRE⟩⟨GRE⟩⟨GRE⟩	⟨VEL⟩⟨VEL⟩⟨VEL⟩
SC$_2$	⟨GRE⟩⟨GRE⟩⟨GRE⟩	⟨GRE⟩⟨GRE⟩⟨GRE⟩	⟨GRE⟩⟨GRE⟩⟨GRE⟩	⟨GRE⟩⟨GRE⟩⟨GRE⟩	⟨VEL⟩⟨VEL⟩⟨VEL⟩
SC$_3$	⟨MED⟩⟨MED⟩⟨MED⟩	⟨VRG⟩⟨VRG⟩⟨VRG⟩	⟨VRG⟩⟨VRG⟩⟨VRG⟩	⟨GRE⟩⟨GRE⟩⟨GRE⟩	⟨GRE⟩⟨GRE⟩⟨VEL⟩
SC$_4$	⟨GRE⟩⟨GRE⟩⟨GRE⟩	⟨GRE⟩⟨GRE⟩⟨GRE⟩	⟨VRG⟩⟨VRG⟩⟨VRG⟩	⟨MED⟩⟨MED⟩⟨GRE⟩	⟨MEL⟩⟨MEL⟩⟨VEL⟩
SC$_5$	⟨GRE⟩⟨GRE⟩⟨GRE⟩	⟨LEL⟩⟨MED⟩⟨GRE⟩	⟨GRE⟩⟨GRE⟩⟨GRE⟩	⟨GRE⟩⟨GRE⟩⟨GRE⟩	⟨GRE⟩⟨GRE⟩⟨LEL⟩
SC$_6$	⟨MED⟩⟨MED⟩⟨MED⟩	⟨MED⟩⟨MED⟩⟨MED⟩	⟨GRE⟩⟨GRE⟩⟨GRE⟩	⟨GRE⟩⟨GRE⟩⟨GRE⟩	⟨MED⟩⟨MED⟩⟨VEL⟩

Experts	EET$_{3\_2}$	SGE$_{3\_3}$	TIA$_{3\_4}$	CLT$_{4\_1}$	REC$_{4\_2}$
SC$_1$	⟨LEL⟩⟨VEL⟩⟨VRG⟩	⟨GRE⟩⟨GRE⟩⟨VRG⟩	⟨GRE⟩⟨GRE⟩⟨GRE⟩	⟨GRE⟩⟨GRE⟩⟨GRE⟩	⟨VEL⟩⟨VEL⟩⟨VEL⟩
SC$_2$	⟨VEL⟩⟨VEL⟩⟨VRG⟩	⟨VEL⟩⟨VEL⟩⟨VRG⟩	⟨LEL⟩⟨VEL⟩⟨GRE⟩	⟨MEL⟩⟨MEL⟩⟨MEL⟩	⟨MEL⟩⟨MEL⟩⟨VEL⟩
SC$_3$	⟨GRE⟩⟨GRE⟩⟨GRE⟩	⟨GRE⟩⟨GRE⟩⟨GRE⟩	⟨GRE⟩⟨GRE⟩⟨VRG⟩	⟨VRG⟩⟨VRG⟩⟨VRG⟩	⟨MEL⟩⟨MEL⟩⟨VEL⟩
SC$_4$	⟨VEL⟩⟨VEL⟩⟨VRG⟩	⟨LEL⟩⟨VEL⟩⟨VRG⟩	⟨MEL⟩⟨MEL⟩⟨MEL⟩	⟨VEL⟩⟨VEL⟩⟨VEL⟩	⟨GRE⟩⟨GRE⟩⟨GRE⟩
SC$_5$	⟨VRG⟩⟨VRG⟩⟨VRG⟩	⟨VEL⟩⟨VEL⟩⟨VRG⟩	⟨GRE⟩⟨GRE⟩⟨GRE⟩	⟨GRE⟩⟨GRE⟩⟨VEL⟩	⟨VEL⟩⟨VEL⟩⟨GRE⟩
SC$_6$	⟨VEL⟩⟨VEL⟩⟨VRG⟩	⟨VEL⟩⟨VEL⟩⟨VRG⟩	⟨MED⟩⟨MED⟩⟨VRG⟩	⟨VRG⟩⟨VRG⟩⟨VRG⟩	⟨MED⟩⟨MED⟩⟨GRE⟩

TABLE 6.14

Combined Assessment Matrix of Smart Campuses

Expert$_s$	PAW$_{1\_1}$	NRM$_{1\_2}$	EPN$_{1\_3}$	SMB$_{1\_4}$	ENE$_{1\_5}$
SC$_1$	[0.220, 0.880]	[0.770, 0.330]	[0.796, 0.314]	[0.880, 0.220]	[0.770, 0.330]
SC$_2$	[0.489, 0.725]	[0.301, 0.845]	[0.311, 0.845]	[0.311, 0.845]	[0.220, 0.880]
SC$_3$	[0.409, 0.697]	[0.506, 0.626]	[0.344, 0.817]	[0.880, 0.220]	[0.311, 0.845]
SC$_4$	[0.370, 0.758]	[0.851, 0.267]	[0.770, 0.330]	[0.796, 0.314]	[0.880, 0.220]
SC$_5$	[0.220, 0.880]	[0.851, 0.267]	[0.619, 0.520]	[0.440, 0.660]	[0.770, 0.330]
SC$_6$	[0.880, 0.220]	[0.370, 0.758]	[0.527, 0.631]	[0.440, 0.660]	[0.880, 0.220]
Expert$_s$	TRA$_{2\_1}$	TAX$_{2\_2}$	SEE$_{2\_3}$	ITT$_{2\_4}$	IND$_{3\_1}$
SC$_1$	[0.770, 0.330]	[0.770, 0.330]	[0.370, 0.758]	[0.770, 0.330]	[0.220, 0.880]
SC$_2$	[0.770, 0.330]	[0.770, 0.330]	[0.770, 0.330]	[0.770, 0.330]	[0.220, 0.880]
SC$_3$	[0.550, 0.550]	[0.880, 0.220]	[0.880, 0.220]	[0.770, 0.330]	[0.563, 0.704]
SC$_4$	[0.770, 0.330]	[0.770, 0.330]	[0.880, 0.220]	[0.598, 0.522]	[0.370, 0.758]
SC$_5$	[0.770, 0.330]	[0.527, 0.631]	[0.770, 0.330]	[0.770, 0.330]	[0.623, 0.601]
SC$_6$	[0.550, 0.550]	[0.550, 0.550]	[0.770, 0.330]	[0.770, 0.330]	[0.437, 0.727]
Expert$_s$	EET$_{3\_2}$	SGE$_{3\_3}$	TIA$_{3\_4}$	CLT$_{4\_1}$	REC$_{4\_2}$
SC$_1$	[0.355, 0.817]	[0.796, 0.314]	[0.770, 0.330]	[0.796, 0.314]	[0.220, 0.880]
SC$_2$	[0.320, 0.845]	[0.311, 0.845]	[0.344, 0.817]	[0.440, 0.660]	[0.489, 0.725]
SC$_3$	[0.770, 0.330]	[0.770, 0.330]	[0.796, 0.314]	[0.880, 0.220]	[0.370, 0.758]
SC$_4$	[0.311, 0.845]	[0.344, 0.817]	[0.440, 0.660]	[0.220, 0.880]	[0.770, 0.330]
SC$_5$	[0.880, 0.220]	[0.311, 0.845]	[0.770, 0.330]	[0.563, 0.704]	[0.301, 0.845]
SC$_6$	[0.961, 0.170]	[0.311, 0.845]	[0.550, 0.550]	[0.880, 0.220]	[0.598, 0.522]

TABLE 6.15

Normalized Aggregated Decision Matrix

Expert$_s$	PAW$_{1\_1}$	NRM$_{1\_2}$	EPN$_{1\_3}$	SMB$_{1\_4}$	ENE$_{1\_5}$
SC$_1$	[0.220, 0.880]	[0.770, 0.330]	[0.796, 0.314]	[0.880, 0.220]	[0.770, 0.330]
SC$_2$	[0.489, 0.725]	[0.301, 0.845]	[0.311, 0.845]	[0.311, 0.845]	[0.220, 0.880]
SC$_3$	[0.409, 0.697]	[0.506, 0.626]	[0.344, 0.817]	[0.880, 0.220]	[0.311, 0.845]
SC$_4$	[0.370, 0.758]	[0.851, 0.267]	[0.770, 0.330]	[0.796, 0.314]	[0.880, 0.220]
SC$_5$	[0.220, 0.880]	[0.851, 0.267]	[0.619, 0.520]	[0.440, 0.660]	[0.770, 0.330]
SC$_6$	[0.880, 0.220]	[0.370, 0.758]	[0.527, 0.631]	[0.440, 0.660]	[0.880, 0.220]
Expert$_s$	TRA$_{2\_1}$	TAX$_{2\_2}$	SEE$_{2\_3}$	ITT$_{2\_4}$	IND$_{3\_1}$
SC$_1$	[0.770, 0.330]	[0.770, 0.330]	[0.370, 0.758]	[0.770, 0.330]	[0.220, 0.880]
SC$_2$	[0.770, 0.330]	[0.770, 0.330]	[0.770, 0.330]	[0.770, 0.330]	[0.220, 0.880]
SC$_3$	[0.550, 0.550]	[0.880, 0.220]	[0.880, 0.220]	[0.770, 0.330]	[0.563, 0.704]
SC$_4$	[0.770, 0.330]	[0.770, 0.330]	[0.880, 0.220]	[0.598, 0.522]	[0.370, 0.758]
SC$_5$	[0.770, 0.330]	[0.527, 0.631]	[0.770, 0.330]	[0.770, 0.330]	[0.623, 0.601]
SC$_6$	[0.550, 0.550]	[0.550, 0.550]	[0.770, 0.330]	[0.770, 0.330]	[0.437, 0.727]

(Continued)

TABLE 6.15 (*Continued*)

Normalized Aggregated Decision Matrix

Expert$_s$	EET$_{3\_2}$	SGE$_{3\_3}$	TIA$_{3\_4}$	CLT$_{4\_1}$	REC$_{4\_2}$
SC$_1$	[0.355, 0.817]	[0.796, 0.314]	[0.770, 0.330]	[0.796, 0.314]	[0.220, 0.880]
SC$_2$	[0.320, 0.845]	[0.311, 0.845]	[0.344, 0.817]	[0.440, 0.660]	[0.489, 0.725]
SC$_3$	[0.770, 0.330]	[0.770, 0.330]	[0.796, 0.314]	[0.880, 0.220]	[0.370, 0.758]
SC$_4$	[0.311, 0.845]	[0.344, 0.817]	[0.440, 0.660]	[0.220, 0.880]	[0.770, 0.330]
SC$_5$	[0.880, 0.220]	[0.311, 0.845]	[0.770, 0.330]	[0.563, 0.704]	[0.301, 0.845]
SC$_6$	[0.961, 0.170]	[0.311, 0.845]	[0.550, 0.550]	[0.880, 0.220]	[0.598, 0.522]

TABLE 6.16

Positive and Negative Ideal Solutions

Criteria	q-ROF Positive Ideal Solution	q-ROF Negative Ideal Solution
PAW$_{1\_1}$	[0.880, 0.220]	[0.220, 0.880]
NRM$_{1\_2}$	[0.851, 0.267]	[0.301, 0.845]
EPN$_{1\_3}$	[0.796, 0.314]	[0.311, 0.845]
SMB$_{1\_4}$	[0.880, 0.220]	[0.311, 0.845]
ENE$_{1\_5}$	[0.880, 0.220]	[0.220, 0.880]
TRA$_{2\_1}$	[0.770, 0.330]	[0.550, 0.550]
TAX$_{2\_2}$	[0.880, 0.220]	[0.527, 0.631]
SEE$_{2\_3}$	[0.880, 0.220]	[0.370, 0.758]
ITT$_{2\_4}$	[0.770, 0.330]	[0.598, 0.522]
IND$_{3\_1}$	[0.623, 0.601]	[0.220, 0.880]
EET$_{3\_2}$	[0.961, 0.170]	[0.311, 0.845]
SGE$_{3\_3}$	[0.796, 0.314]	[0.311, 0.845]
TIA$_{3\_4}$	[0.796, 0.314]	[0.344, 0.817]
CLT$_{4\_1}$	[0.880, 0.220]	[0.220, 0.880]
REC$_{4\_2}$	[0.770, 0.330]	[0.220, 0.880]

TABLE 6.17

Separation Measures of the Substitutes

	SC$_1$	SC$_2$	SC$_3$	SC$_4$	SC$_5$	SC$_6$
d (A$_i$, A*)	0.25775	0.43433	0.42385	0.60108	0.53302	0.41208
d (A$_i$, A$^-$)	0.60706	0.42532	0.43156	0.23670	0.38077	0.48673

TABLE 6.18

Closeness Coefficient and Rates of the Substitutes

	SC_1	SC_2	SC_3	SC_4	SC_5	SC_6
CC_i	0.70195	0.49475	0.50466	0.28253	0.41669	0.54153
Rank	1	4	3	6	5	2

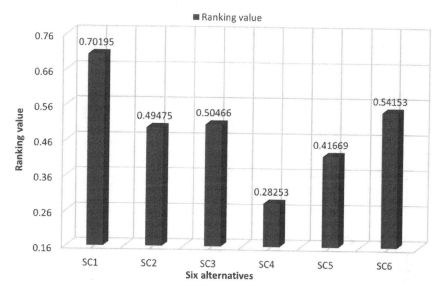

FIGURE 6.9
Final ranking of smart campuses.

6.4 Results and Discussion

This part discusses the results obtained using the approach used to solve the smart campuses' assessment problem. Initially, the weights of the main criteria are calculated using the q-ROF entropy method. According to the results obtained regarding the main criteria, it is found that the economy criterion ranks first with a weight of 0.276, followed by the environment criterion with a weight of 0.264, while the government criterion ranks last with a weight of 0.228 as presented in Table 6.12. In this regard, according to the results of the weighting of the environment criterion's sub-criteria, it is found that the energy efficiency criterion ranks first with a weight of 0.224, followed by the environmental protection instruments criterion with a weight of 0.216, while the natural resource management criterion and smart building criterion rank last with a weight of 0.180 as presented in Table 6.12. Also, according to the results of the weighting of the government criterion's sub-criteria, it is found that the IT tools criterion ranks first with a weight of 0.307, followed by the service efficiency criterion with a weight of 0.268. In contrast, the taxation criterion ranks last with a weight of 0.208 as exhibited in Table 6.12. Then, according to the results of the weighting of the economy criterion's sub-criteria, it is found that the tax incentives and aid criterion ranks first with a weight of 0.270, followed by the industry diversification criterion and support for the green economy criterion with a weight of 0.245, while the eco-efficient tourism criterion ranks last with a weight of 0.240 as exhibited in Table 6.12. In the end, according to the results of the weighting of the mobility criterion's sub-criteria, it is found that the connectivity and local transport criterion ranks first with a weight of 0.510, while the regional connectivity criterion ranks last with a weight of 0.490 as exhibited in Table 6.12.

Secondly, the q-ROF TOPSIS method was used to arrange the alternatives used in the case study for this chapter, as mentioned in the previous section. According to the obtained results, it is found that SC_1 occupies the first rank, followed by SC_6, while SC_4 occupies the last rank, as shown in Table 6.18 and Figure 6.9.

6.5 Summary

- This chapter provides a comprehensive description of smart campuses and their relevant merits.
- This chapter reviews the importance and needs of assessing sustainability performance indicators for smart campuses.
- This chapter presents the most important criteria for evaluating smart campuses after a comprehensive analysis of several research articles.
- This chapter suggests the steps of a hybrid MCDM approach for evaluating sustainability indicators for smart campuses. The applied approach was carried out under q-rung orthopair fuzzy set (q-ROFS) environment and using q-rung orthopair fuzzy numbers (q-ROFNs).
- The hybrid approach consists of two methods q-ROFS entropy and the q-ROFS Technique for Order of Preference by Similarity to Ideal Solution (q-ROFS TOPSIS).
- This chapter presents a real case study while evaluating sustainability indicators for smart campuses.

6.6 Exercises

a. How do you define "smart campuses"? Why is an evaluation of smart campuses regarding sustainability performance indicators important?

b. What are the differences between entropy and the TOPSIS approaches? Discuss their relative advantages while making a decision.

c. Why are the challenges in deciding sustainability performance indicators for smart campuses?

d. Discuss the features of smart campuses in terms of the characteristics and formation of a sustainable and smart campus.

e. Why is the MCDM approach required to assess sustainability criteria for smart campuses?

References

Bouslah, Kais, Vicente Liern, Jamal Ouenniche, and Blanca Pérez-Gladish. 2022. "Ranking Firms Based on Their Financial and Diversity Performance Using Multiple-Stage Unweighted TOPSIS." *International Transactions in Operational Research.* https://doi.org/https://doi.org/10.1111/itor.13143.

Delgado, Alexi, and Inmaculada Romero. 2016. "Environmental Conflict Analysis Using an Integrated Grey Clustering and Entropy-Weight Method: A Case Study of a Mining Project in Peru." *Environmental Modelling & Software* 77: 108–21. https://doi.org/https://doi.org/10.1016/j.envsoft.2015.12.011.

Shannon, Claude Elwood. 1948. "A Mathematical Theory of Communication." *The Bell System Technical Journal* 27 (3): 379–423. https://doi.org/10.1002/j.1538-7305.1948.tb01338.x.

Xu, Hongshi, Chao Ma, Jijian Lian, Kui Xu, and Evance Chaima. 2018. "Urban Flooding Risk Assessment Based on an Integrated K-Means Cluster Algorithm and Improved Entropy Weight Method in the Region of Haikou, China." *Journal of Hydrology* 563: 975–86. https://doi.org/https://doi.org/10.1016/j.jhydrol.2018.06.060.

Yoon, Kwangsun, and Ching-Lai Hwang. 1985. "Manufacturing Plant Location Analysis by Multiple Attribute Decision Making: Part I—Single-Plant Strategy." *International Journal of Production Research* 23 (2): 345–59. https://doi.org/10.1080/00207548508904712.

7

Sustainable Supplier Selection for Smart Supply Chain

7.1 Introduction

The demand that has emerged in recent years from consumers for high levels of service delivered on time in conjunction with high levels of quality presents difficulties that were not there in the past. Companies are looking to form strategic partnerships within their supply chain to increase their chances of success in this industry. The process of analyzing and choosing suppliers in order to achieve the strategic objectives of the organization plays a vital role in this context. Before 1980, supplier selection was mostly driven by price considerations. Nevertheless, in recent years, in addition to economic reasons, environmental and social concerns have been required to be concurrently evaluated for the selection of suppliers. Environmental criteria are being included because of the rising concern over contamination of the environment on a worldwide scale. One other reason to include environmental factors in the limitations is that it will reduce the number of accessible resources.

Additionally, over the last several years, due to the globalization of the market, the level of competition in many different sectors has dramatically grown, leading to unstable demand. There is also the problem that access to various providers is not the same throughout different periods. Furthermore, depending on the conditions, only a small number of possible suppliers would be able to satisfy the demand from producers. In order to thrive and expand in such an environment, manufacturers need to have an all-encompassing strategy. Small- and medium-sized businesses employ more than 60% of the workforce, and they are the primary source of job possibilities for society as a whole. Small- and medium-sized businesses account for more than 99% of all businesses worldwide. Both establishing a sustainable supply chain and maintaining the sustainable growth of small- and medium-sized businesses are vital guarantees for the stabilization of the national economy.

Due to the fact that they often have insufficient resources, small- and medium-sized businesses are very reliant on the supplemental resources provided by outside sources. Both the effectiveness of the procurement process and the quality of the product are determined by the performance of the supplier. Small- and medium-sized businesses have benefited greatly from careful attention paid to the selection of their suppliers, which has resulted in increased market competitiveness and continued sustainable growth. Nevertheless, much of the research on sustainable supplier selection has been conducted with big companies. The negotiating leverage and risk mitigation capabilities of small- and medium-sized businesses are distinct from those of big companies. This is because scale, money, and market limits all play a role. Large companies may have reliable manufacturing capacities and provide goods of a high standard. Still, they use economies of scale to drive up the extra expenses incurred by the transaction process for small- and medium-sized businesses. In addition, small- and medium-sized businesses with fewer resources should emphasize the process of monitoring their suppliers when choosing providers.

The recent development and implementation of advanced smart technologies, such as the Internet-of-Things (IoT), big data analytics (BDA), and artificial intelligence (AI) techniques, have made it possible for all components in a supply chain to be perceptible, diagnosable, interpretable, predictable, controllable, and optimizable, which has accelerated the transformation of the traditional supply chain into a smart supply chain. The use of cutting-edge smart technology results in the creation of a supply chain that is not only designed to be quick and responsive but also individualized to be adaptable. It provides enhanced economic, environmental, and social sustainability by using smart technology as a critical facilitator for improving sustainable supply chain management practices. The use of smart technologies accomplishes this.

The phrase "sustainable supply chain management techniques" refers to a collection of tactical activities that may assist a corporation in achieving more sustainability in the economic, environmental, and social aspects of sustainability. These kinds of activities center on the process of implementing sustainable supply chain management, which significantly impacts the level of sustainability performance a firm achieves. It is generally agreed upon that one of the most important aspects of sustainable supply chain management strategies is identifying sustainable vendors. This is due to the fact that the activities of suppliers are essential to assisting downstream businesses in achieving a collaborative and sustained competitive advantage. This is because the activities of suppliers give original inputs to organizational supply chains. In addition, the selection of a supplier may be thought of as a process of multi-criteria decision-making (MCDM), which is comprised of two stages: the calculation of the weights of the criteria and the ranking of the suppliers.

7.2 Mathematical Preliminary

This part discusses fundamental aspects of intuitionistic fuzzy sets (IFSs), such as their operations and concepts, in further detail. Atanassov (1999) has developed IFSs, which are an extension of conventional fuzzy sets. IFSs defined by degrees of membership and non-membership enable decision-makers to voice their viewpoints with more flexibility. As stated in Explanation 7.1, the total of the membership and non-membership degrees of elements in an IFS is equal to or less than one. IFSs have been effectively applied to real-world issues in a variety of sectors owing to their characteristics.

Explanation 7.1: Let X be a non-empty set. An IFS $\tilde{I}$ in X is an object having the formula specified by:

$$\tilde{I} = \left\{ \left(x, \mathcal{U}_{\tilde{I}}(x), \vartheta_{\tilde{I}}(x) \right) \mid x \in X \right\} \tag{7.1}$$

where the function $\mathcal{U}_{\tilde{I}} : X \to [0, 1]$ designates the degree of membership of a component to the sets $\tilde{I}$, and $\vartheta_{\tilde{I}} : X \to [0, 1]$ designates the degree of non-membership of a component to the sets $\tilde{I}$, with the condition that:

$$0 \le \mathcal{U}_{\tilde{I}}(x) + \vartheta_{\tilde{I}}(x) \le 1, \text{ for } \forall x \in X \tag{7.2}$$

The degree of uncertainty is computed as follows:

$$\pi_{\tilde{I}}(x) = 1 - \mathcal{U}_{\tilde{I}}(x) - \vartheta_{\tilde{I}}(x) \tag{7.3}$$

Explanation 7.2: Let $\tilde{A} = \left(\mathcal{U}_{\tilde{A}}, \vartheta_{\tilde{A}} \right)$ and $\tilde{B} = \left(\mathcal{U}_{\tilde{B}}, \vartheta_{\tilde{B}} \right)$ be two intuitionistic fuzzy numbers (IFNs); then, some operations of two IFNs are defined as follows.

$$\tilde{A} \oplus \tilde{B} = \left(\mathcal{U}_{\tilde{A}} + \mathcal{U}_{\tilde{B}} - \mathcal{U}_{\tilde{A}} \mathcal{U}_{\tilde{B}}, \vartheta_{\tilde{A}} \vartheta_{\tilde{B}} \right) \tag{7.4}$$

$$\tilde{A} \otimes \tilde{B} = \left(\mathcal{U}_{\tilde{A}} \mathcal{U}_{\tilde{B}}, \vartheta_{\tilde{A}} + \vartheta_{\tilde{B}} - \vartheta_{\tilde{A}} \vartheta_{\tilde{B}} \right) \tag{7.5}$$

$$\lambda \tilde{A} = \left(\left(1 - \left(1 - \mathcal{U}_{\tilde{A}} \right)^{\lambda} \right), \mathcal{U}_{\tilde{A}}^{\lambda} \right), \lambda > 0 \tag{7.6}$$

$$\tilde{A}^{\lambda} = \left(\mathcal{U}_{\tilde{A}}^{\lambda}, \left(1 - \left(1 - \vartheta_{\tilde{A}} \right)^{\lambda} \right) \right), \lambda > 0 \tag{7.7}$$

Explanation 7.3: The subtraction $\ominus$ and division $\oslash$ operations for two IFNs $\tilde{A}$ and $\tilde{B}$ are well defined as assumed in Eqs. (7.8) and (7.9) (Du, 2021).

$$\tilde{A} \ominus \tilde{B} = \begin{cases} \left\langle 0, \dfrac{\vartheta_{\tilde{A}}}{\vartheta_{\tilde{B}}} \right\rangle, & \text{if } \mathcal{U}_{\tilde{A}} \le \mathcal{U}_{\tilde{B}}, \vartheta_{\tilde{A}} \le \vartheta_{\tilde{B}} \\[2mm] \left\langle \dfrac{\mathcal{U}_{\tilde{A}} - \mathcal{U}_{\tilde{B}}}{1 - \mathcal{U}_{\tilde{B}}}, \dfrac{\vartheta_{\tilde{A}}}{\vartheta_{\tilde{B}}} \right\rangle, & \text{if } 0 \le \dfrac{\vartheta_{\tilde{A}}}{\vartheta_{\tilde{B}}} \le \dfrac{1 - \mathcal{U}_{\tilde{A}}}{1 - \mathcal{U}_{\tilde{B}}} < 1 \\[2mm] \left\langle \dfrac{\mathcal{U}_{\tilde{A}} - \mathcal{U}_{\tilde{B}}}{1 - \mathcal{U}_{\tilde{B}}}, \dfrac{1 - \mathcal{U}_{\tilde{A}}}{1 - \mathcal{U}_{\tilde{B}}} \right\rangle, & \text{if } \mathcal{U}_{\tilde{A}} \ge \mathcal{U}_{\tilde{B}}, \dfrac{1 - \mathcal{U}_{\tilde{A}}}{1 - \mathcal{U}_{\tilde{B}}} < \dfrac{\vartheta_{\tilde{A}}}{\vartheta_{\tilde{B}}} \\[2mm] \langle 0, 1 \rangle, & \text{if } \mathcal{U}_{\tilde{A}} \le \mathcal{U}_{\tilde{B}}, \vartheta_{\tilde{A}} > \vartheta_{\tilde{B}} \end{cases} \tag{7.8}$$

$$\tilde{A} \oslash \tilde{B} = \begin{cases} \left\langle \dfrac{\mathcal{U}_{\tilde{A}}}{\mathcal{U}_{\tilde{B}}}, 0 \right\rangle, & \text{if } \mathcal{U}_{\tilde{A}} \le \mathcal{U}_{\tilde{B}}, \vartheta_{\tilde{A}} \le \vartheta_{\tilde{B}} \\[2mm] \left\langle \dfrac{\mathcal{U}_{\tilde{A}}}{\mathcal{U}_{\tilde{B}}}, \dfrac{\vartheta_{\tilde{A}} - \vartheta_{\tilde{B}}}{1 - \vartheta_{\tilde{B}}} \right\rangle, & \text{if } 0 \le \dfrac{\mathcal{U}_{\tilde{A}}}{\mathcal{U}_{\tilde{B}}} \le \dfrac{1 - \vartheta_{\tilde{A}}}{1 - \vartheta_{\tilde{B}}} < 1 \\[2mm] \left\langle \dfrac{1 - \vartheta_{\tilde{A}}}{1 - \vartheta_{\tilde{B}}}, \dfrac{\vartheta_{\tilde{A}} - \vartheta_{\tilde{B}}}{1 - \vartheta_{\tilde{B}}} \right\rangle, & \text{if } \dfrac{1 - \vartheta_{\tilde{A}}}{1 - \vartheta_{\tilde{B}}} < \dfrac{\mathcal{U}_{\tilde{A}}}{\mathcal{U}_{\tilde{B}}}, \vartheta_{\tilde{A}} \ge \vartheta_{\tilde{B}}, \\[2mm] \langle 1, 0 \rangle, & \text{if } \mathcal{U}_{\tilde{A}} > \mathcal{U}_{\tilde{B}}, \vartheta_{\tilde{A}} \le \vartheta_{\tilde{B}} \end{cases} \tag{7.9}$$

Explanation 7.4: Let $\tilde{I} = \left(\mathcal{U}_{\tilde{I}}, \vartheta_{\tilde{I}} \right)$ be an IFN; then, the score function $S(\tilde{I})$ and accuracy function $H(\tilde{I})$ of $\tilde{I}$ can be defined as in Eqs. (7.10) and (7.11) (Chen and Tan, 1994).

$$S(\tilde{I}) = \mathcal{U}_{\tilde{I}} - \vartheta_{\tilde{I}} \tag{7.10}$$

$$H(\tilde{I}) = \mathcal{U}_{\tilde{I}} + \vartheta_{\tilde{I}} \tag{7.11}$$

Explanation 7.5: Let $\tilde{A} = \left(\mathcal{U}_{\tilde{A}}, \vartheta_{\tilde{A}} \right)$ be an IFN; then, the defuzzification function $\mathfrak{I}(\tilde{A})$ of this number is established as in Eq. (7.12).

$$\mathfrak{I}(\tilde{A}) = \mathcal{U}_{\tilde{A}} + \left(\frac{\mathcal{U}_{\tilde{A}} \vartheta_{\tilde{A}} e^{(1 - \mathcal{U}_{\tilde{A}} - \vartheta_{\tilde{A}})}}{2} \right)^2, \text{ where } \mathfrak{I}(\tilde{A}) \in [0, 1]. \tag{7.12}$$

Explanation 7.6. Let $\breve{A}_i = \left(\mathcal{U}_{\breve{A}_i}, \vartheta_{\breve{A}_i} \right)$ (i=1, 2, ..., n) be set of IFNs, and $w = (w_1, w_2, ..., w_n)^T$ be weight vector of $\breve{A}_i$ with $\sum_{i=1}^{n} w_i$; then, an intuitionistic fuzzy weighted average (IFWA) operator is established as in Eq. (7.13):

$$\text{IFWA}\left(\breve{A}_1, \breve{A}_2, ..., \breve{A}_n \right) = \left(\left(1 - \prod_{i=1}^{n} \left(1 - u_{\breve{A}_i} \right)^{w_i} \right), \prod_{i=1}^{n} \vartheta_{\breve{A}_i}^{w_i} \right) \tag{7.13}$$

Explanation 7.7. Let $\breve{A}_i = \left(\mathcal{U}_{\breve{A}_i}, \vartheta_{\breve{A}_i} \right)$ (i=1, 2, ..., n) be set of IFNs, and $w = (w_1, w_2, ..., w_n)^T$ be weight vector of $\breve{A}_i$ with $\sum_{i=1}^{n} w_i$; then, an intuitionistic fuzzy weighted geometric (IFWG) operator is established as in Eq. (7.14) (Xu and Yager, 2006):

$$\text{IFWG}\left(\breve{A}_1, \breve{A}_2, ..., \breve{A}_n \right) = \left(\prod_{i=1}^{n} \mathcal{U}_{\breve{A}_i}^{w_i}, \left(1 - \prod_{i=1}^{n} \left(1 - \vartheta_{\breve{A}_i} \right)^{w_i} \right) \right) \tag{7.14}$$

7.3 Methodology

In this part, the model used to solve the problem of selecting the best sustainable resource is presented. The model used consists of two multi-criteria decision-making (MCDM) methods, the CRiteria Importance through Intercriteria Correlation (CRITIC) method, and the Combinative Distance-based ASsessment (CODAS) method. The model used is conducted under the IFS environment and using IFNS. Initially, the CRITIC method prioritizes criteria and determines their weights. Then, the CODAS method ranks and selects the best available alternatives. Figure 7.1 shows the steps of the approach used to evaluate several sustainable suppliers. In this regard, we provide a brief overview of the methods used in applying this chapter's case study. This section is divided into several parts as follows.

7.3.1 CRITIC Method

CRITIC is a correlation-based approach that uses analytical testing to retrieve information underlying the decision criteria. It is well known that Diakoulaki, Mavrotas, and Papayannakis (1995) first introduced CRITIC to acquire objective weights in MCDM issues. It captures all preference

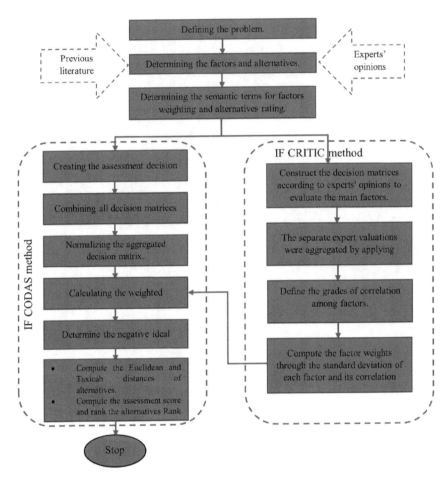

FIGURE 7.1
Overall framework of the problem.

data provided in the assessment criteria based on the evaluation matrix analysis. In other words, the objective weight is determined by measuring the information intrinsic to each evaluative criterion. In addition to the standard deviation of criteria, the process of generating objective weight also considers the connection between criteria and other criteria (Peng, Zhang, and Luo, 2020).

7.3.2 CODAS Method

The CODAS approach was developed to measure an alternative's general performances by using the Hamming distance and the Euclidean distance from the anti-ideal point (Keshavarz Ghorabaee et al., 2016). It is a cutting-edge and very effective method for resolving issues that are connected to MCDM. In this method, the Euclidean distance is considered to be the most significant criterion in the assessment procedures. In its most basic version, CODAS computes the assessment ratings of alternatives by combining the taxicab distance and the Euclidean distance. This is done in order to provide the most accurate results possible. On the basis of the anti-ideal point, the Euclidean distance (the main measure) and the taxicab distance (the secondary measure) are computed in order to evaluate which option is the most appropriate (Bolturk and Kahraman, 2018). In this context, the alternative that involves a higher distance is the one that is recommended.

7.3.3 Computation Steps

In this part, the detailed steps for studying the problem of evaluating and selecting sustainable suppliers (SS_i) presented in this chapter are presented.

Step 1: The problem is studied from all sides to identify the points of importance that affect the identification of the main factors and their sub-factors that affect the identification of sustainable suppliers. Some experts are contacted to share with the authors the aggregating of information on the problem. In this regard, the experts are selected according to some criteria such as academic degrees and number of years of experience. Also, it is agreed on the method of communication, whether online or through interviews.

Step 2: Determine the substitutes, related factors, and their sub-factors to build the framework of the application. The set $SS_i = \{SS_1, SS_2, \ldots, SS_m\}$ having i=1, 2, ..., m alternatives is measured by n decision factors of $F_j = \{F_1, F_2, \ldots, F_n\}$, with j=1, 2, ..., n. Let $w = (w_1, w_2, \ldots, w_n)$ be the vector set utilized for determining the factor and their sub-factors weights, $w_j > 0$ and $\sum_{j=1}^{n} w_j = 1$. Experts are introduced with $E_1, E_2, \ldots, E_k$, who are experts in their fields to make judgments.

Step 3: According to the study of the problem, its dimensions are organized in a hierarchical form between the objective, main factors, sub-factors, and the selected sustainable suppliers.

Step 4: Semantic terms that help experts assess the main factors and sub-factors are recognized in Table 7.1. Also, semantic terms that help in evaluating alternatives are recognized, as presented in Table 7.2.

Step 5: Construct the decision matrices according to experts' opinions (E_k) to evaluate the main factors by each expert by using semantic terms established in Table 7.1, and then by using IFNs as presented in Table 7.3.

Step 6: Aggregate the valuations on criteria weights. The separate expert valuations were aggregated by applying IFWG presented in Eq. (7.14) as

TABLE 7.1

Semantic Terms and Their Equivalent IFNs for Assessing Factors

Semantic Terms	Abbreviations	IFNs	
		u	ϑ
Absolutely low	ABL	0.10	0.85
Very low	VLO	0.20	0.75
Low	LOW	0.30	0.65
Medium low	MEL	0.40	0.55
Approximately	APP	0.50	0.45
Medium high	MEH	0.60	0.35
High	HIG	0.70	0.25
Very high	VEH	0.80	0.15
Absolutely high	ABH	0.90	0.05

TABLE 7.2

Semantic Terms and Their Equivalent IFNs for Ranking Alternatives

Semantic Terms	Abbreviations	IFNs	
		u	ϑ
Absolutely low value	ABV	0.10	0.85
Very low value	VLV	0.20	0.75
Low value	LOV	0.30	0.65
Medium low value	MLV	0.40	0.55
Approximate value	APV	0.50	0.45
Medium high value	MHV	0.60	0.35
High value	HIV	0.70	0.25
Very high value	VEV	0.80	0.15
Absolutely high value	AHV	0.90	0.05

TABLE 7.3

Decision Matrix Based on IFNs According to Expert E_k

Factors	Alternatives			
	SS_1	SS_2	$\cdots$	SS_M
F_1	$\left[u_{11_k}^f, \vartheta_{11_k}^f\right]$	$\left[u_{12_k}^f, \vartheta_{12_k}^f\right]$	$\cdots$	$\left[u_{1m_k}^f, \vartheta_{1m_k}^f\right]$
F_2	$\left[u_{21_k}^f, \vartheta_{21_k}^f\right]$	$\left[u_{22_k}^f, \vartheta_{22_k}^f\right]$	$\cdots$	$\left[u_{2m_k}^f, \vartheta_{2m_k}^f\right]$
$\vdots$	$\vdots$	$\vdots$	$\ddots$	$\vdots$
F_n	$\left[u_{n1_k}^f, \vartheta_{n1_k}^f\right]$	$\left[u_{32_k}^f, \vartheta_{32_k}^f\right]$	$\cdots$	$\left[u_{nm_k}^f, \vartheta_{nm_k}^f\right]$

TABLE 7.4

Aggregated Decision Matrix Based on IFNs

	Alternatives			
Factors	SS_1	SS_2	...	SS_m
F_1	$\left[\mathcal{U}_{11}^f, \vartheta_{11}^f\right]$	$\left[\mathcal{U}_{12}^f, \vartheta_{12}^f\right]$	...	$\left[\mathcal{U}_{1m}^f, \vartheta_{1m}^f\right]$
F_2	$\left[\mathcal{U}_{21}^f, \vartheta_{21}^f\right]$	$\left[\mathcal{U}_{22}^f, \vartheta_{22}^f\right]$	...	$\left[\mathcal{U}_{2m}^f, \vartheta_{2m}^f\right]$
$\vdots$	$\vdots$	$\vdots$	$\ddots$	$\vdots$
F_n	$\left[\mathcal{U}_{n1}^f, \vartheta_{n1}^f\right]$	$\left[\mathcal{U}_{32}^f, \vartheta_{32}^f\right]$	...	$\left[\mathcal{U}_{nm}^f, \vartheta_{nm}^f\right]$

exhibited in Table 7.4. At this point, $\left(w_j\right)_{1\times n}$ introduces IFNs weight of jth factors

Step 7: Define the grades of correlation among factors. For this, the judgment matrix is primarily defuzzified by applying Eqs. (7.15) and (7.16) by considering the factor type, which can be profit and non-profit. Then, the standard deviation for each factor is calculated by utilizing Eq. (7.17), and the correlation relationship of each factor with other factors is determined by applying Eq. (7.18).

$$\phi_{ij} = \frac{1 - \dfrac{\mathcal{U}_{ij}\times\mathcal{U}_- + \vartheta_{ij}\times\vartheta_- + \pi_{ij}\times\pi_-}{\mathcal{U}_{ij}^2 \vee \mathcal{U}_-^2 + \vartheta_{ij}^2 \vee \vartheta_-^2 + \pi_{ij}^2 \vee \pi_-^2}}{1 - \dfrac{\mathcal{U}_-\times\mathcal{U}_+ + \vartheta_-\times\vartheta_+ + \pi_-\times\pi_+}{\mathcal{U}_-^2 \vee \mathcal{U}_+^2 + \vartheta_-^2 \vee \vartheta_+^2 + \pi_-^2 \vee \pi_+^2}}, \quad (7.15)$$

$i = 1,2,\ldots,m; \; j = 1,2,\ldots,n$, for positive attributes.

$$\phi_{ij} = \frac{1 - \dfrac{\mathcal{U}_{ij}\times\mathcal{U}_+ + \vartheta_{ij}\times\vartheta_+ + \pi_{ij}\times\pi_+}{\mathcal{U}_{ij}^2 \vee \mathcal{U}_+^2 + \vartheta_{ij}^2 \vee \vartheta_+^2 + \pi_{ij}^2 \vee \pi_+^2}}{1 - \dfrac{\mathcal{U}_-\times\mathcal{U}_+ + \vartheta_-\times\vartheta_+ + \pi_-\times\pi_+}{\mathcal{U}_-^2 \vee \mathcal{U}_+^2 + \vartheta_-^2 \vee \vartheta_+^2 + \pi_-^2 \vee \pi_+^2}}, \quad (7.16)$$

$i = 1,2,\ldots,m; \; j = 1,2,\ldots,n$, for negative attributes.

$$\sigma_j = \sqrt{\frac{\sum_{i=1}^m \left(\phi_{ij} - \bar{\phi}_j\right)^2}{m}}, j = 1,2,\ldots,n. \quad (7.17)$$

$$r_{ik} = \frac{\sum_{i=1}^m \left(\phi_{ij} - \bar{\phi}_j\right)\left(\phi_{ik} - \bar{\phi}_k\right)}{\sqrt{\sum_{i=1}^m \left(\phi_{ij} - \bar{\phi}_j\right)^2 \sum_{i=1}^m \left(\phi_{ik} - \bar{\phi}_k\right)^2}}, j = 1,2,\ldots,n; \; k = 1,2,\ldots,n. \quad (7.18)$$

where $\mathcal{U}_-$, $\mathcal{U}_+$, ϑ_-, and ϑ_+ are the lowest and highest grades of membership and non-membership, respectively.

Step 8: Compute the factor weights through the standard deviation of each factor and its correlation among other factors by applying Eq. (7.19). Then, the objective weights of factors were standardized, and the weight of each factor is computed by applying Eq. (7.20).

$$F_j = \sigma_j \sum_{k=1}^{n} (1 - r_{jk}), j = 1, 2, \ldots, n. \tag{7.19}$$

$$w_j = \frac{F_j}{\sum_{j=1}^{n} F_j} \tag{7.20}$$

Step 9: In this regard, the weights of the sub-factors are computed in the same steps as the weights of the main factors. Based on the weights of the main factors, the global weights of the sub-factors are computed.

Step 10: Create the valuation decision matrix by each expert distinctly (E_k) among the determined sub-factors and the selected alternatives to assess the sustainable suppliers by utilizing the semantic terms as exhibited in Table 7.2, then by applying the IFNs in Table 7.2 as exhibited in Table 7.5.

Step 11: Aggregate the assessment decision matrix by each expert distinctly (E_k) among the defined sub-factors and the available alternatives to assess the sustainable suppliers into one matrix by applying IFWG as exhibited in Eq. (7.14) as exhibited in Table 7.6.

Step 12: Defuzzification of the fuzzy aggregated decision matrix into the crisp combined decision matrix by removing the IFNs by applying Eq. (7.12) as presented in Table 7.7.

Step 13: Compute the normalized decision matrix according to Eq. (7.21).

TABLE 7.5

Decision Matrix for Alternatives in Terms of All Sub-Factors Based on IFNs

Factors	Alternatives			
	SS_1	SS_2	$\ldots$	SS_m
F_1	$\left[\mathcal{U}_{11_k}^f, \vartheta_{11_k}^f\right]$	$\left[\mathcal{U}_{12_k}^f, \vartheta_{12_k}^f\right]$	$\ldots$	$\left[\mathcal{U}_{1m_k}^f, \vartheta_{1m_k}^f\right]$
F_2	$\left[\mathcal{U}_{21_k}^f, \vartheta_{21_k}^f\right]$	$\left[\mathcal{U}_{22_k}^f, \vartheta_{22_k}^f\right]$	$\ldots$	$\left[\mathcal{U}_{2m_k}^f, \vartheta_{2m_k}^f\right]$
$\vdots$	$\vdots$	$\vdots$	$\ddots$	$\vdots$
F_n	$\left[\mathcal{U}_{n1_k}^f, \vartheta_{n1_k}^f\right]$	$\left[\mathcal{U}_{32_k}^f, \vartheta_{32_k}^f\right]$	$\ldots$	$\left[\mathcal{U}_{nm_k}^f, \vartheta_{nm_k}^f\right]$

TABLE 7.6

Aggregated Decision Matrix for Alternatives in Terms of Sub-Factors Based on IFNs

Factors	Alternatives			
	SS_1	SS_2	...	SS_m
F_1	$\left[\mathcal{U}_{11}^f, \vartheta_{11}^f \right]$	$\left[\mathcal{U}_{12}^f, \vartheta_{12}^f \right]$	...	$\left[\mathcal{U}_{1m}^f, \vartheta_{1m}^f \right]$
F_2	$\left[\mathcal{U}_{21}^f, \vartheta_{21}^f \right]$	$\left[\mathcal{U}_{22}^f, \vartheta_{22}^f \right]$	...	$\left[\mathcal{U}_{2m}^f, \vartheta_{2m}^f \right]$
$\vdots$	$\vdots$	$\vdots$	$\ddots$	$\vdots$
F_n	$\left[\mathcal{U}_{n1}^f, \vartheta_{n1}^f \right]$	$\left[\mathcal{U}_{32}^f, \vartheta_{32}^f \right]$	...	$\left[\mathcal{U}_{nm}^f, \vartheta_{nm}^f \right]$

TABLE 7.7

Defuzzified Decision Matrix for Alternatives in Terms of Sub-Factors

Factors	Alternatives			
	SS_1	SS_2	...	SS_m
F_1	$x_{11} = \left[\mathcal{U}_{11}^f, \vartheta_{11}^f \right]$	$x_{12} = \left[\mathcal{U}_{12}^f, \vartheta_{12}^f \right]$	...	$x_{1m} = \left[\mathcal{U}_{1m}^f, \vartheta_{1n}^f \right]$
F_2	$x_{21} = \left[\mathcal{U}_{21}^f, \vartheta_{21}^f \right]$	$x_{22} = \left[\mathcal{U}_{22}^f, \vartheta_{22}^f \right]$	...	$x_{2m} = \left[\mathcal{U}_{2m}^f, \vartheta_{2m}^f \right]$
$\vdots$	$\vdots$	$\vdots$	$\ddots$	$\vdots$
F_n	$x_{n1} = \left[\mathcal{U}_{n1}^f, \vartheta_{n1}^f \right]$	$x_{32} = \left[\mathcal{U}_{32}^f, \vartheta_{32}^f \right]$	...	$x_{nm} = \left[\mathcal{U}_{nm}^f, \vartheta_{nm}^f \right]$

$$\mathcal{N}_{ij} = \begin{cases} \dfrac{X_{ij}}{\max\limits_i X_{ij}} & \text{if } j \in N_b \\[2ex] \dfrac{\min\limits_i X_{ij}}{X_{ij}} & \text{if } j \in N_c \end{cases} \tag{7.21}$$

where N_b characterizes advantage, and N_c characterizes non-advantage factors.

Step 14: Calculate the weighted normalized decision matrix according to Eq. (7.22).

$$\mathcal{R}_{ij} = w_j \times \mathcal{N}_{ij} \tag{7.22}$$

Step 15: Determine the negative ideal solution points by applying Eq. (7.23).

$$\mathcal{N}S = \left[\mathcal{N}S_j \right]_{1 \times m}$$

$$\mathcal{N}S_j = \min_i \mathcal{R}_{ij} \tag{7.23}$$

Step 16: Compute the Euclidean and taxicab distances of alternatives from the negative ideal solution according to Eqs. (7.24) and (7.25).

$$E_i = \sqrt{\sum_{j=1}^{m} \left(\mathcal{R}_{ij} - \mathcal{N}S_j \right)^2} \tag{7.24}$$

$$T_i = \sum_{j=1}^{m} \left| \mathcal{R}_{ij} - \mathcal{N}S_j \right| \tag{7.25}$$

Step 17: Create the comparative valuation matrix by applying Eq. (7.26).

$$\mathcal{R}a = \left[h_{ik} \right]_{n \times n}$$

$$h_{ik} = (E_i - E_k) + \left(\psi (E_i - E_k) \times (T_i - T_k) \right) \tag{7.26}$$

Step 18: Compute the assessment score and rank the alternatives by applying the Eq. (7.27). Then, rank the alternatives in descending order of the values of H_i.

$$H_i = \sum_{k=1}^{n} h_{ik} \tag{7.27}$$

7.4 Model Implementation

In this part, we present a case study of the problem of selecting sustainable suppliers for a company and the steps for applying the approach.

7.4.1 Case Study

We used our strategy for selecting suppliers and distributing orders while dealing with the Composite Products Company. The composite materials have a wide variety of applications, including but not limited to those in the aerospace sector, the maintenance of transition lines, and thermal insulation. Within this industry, the company's activities include providing advisory services, creating production projects, and putting those designs into action. Price and quality are considered when deciding which vendors to work with in this particular business. Considering several sustainability factors, the management of this organization plans to improve how the company evaluates its suppliers and distributes orders to those suppliers. To accomplish this goal, this organization's managers and specialists identified the products' suppliers and selected appropriate criteria based on the list of global sustainability standards.

7.4.2 Steps to Apply the Used Model

Step 1: The problem has been studied from all dimensions, and the main objective of the problem has been determined to determine the best sustainable supplier, in addition to determining the most important factors affecting the selection of the best sustainable supplier. Also, three experts agreed to participate in data collection and filling out questionnaires, and the impact weight of each expert was determined as 0.3, 0.4, and 0.3.

Step 2: A set of alternatives has been identified to be used in the evaluation process as follows: SS_1, SS_2, SS_3, SS_4, SS_5, and SS_6. Accordingly, the main factors affecting the selection of sustainable suppliers have been identified: economic, environmental, and social. The sub-factors that influence the solution of the problem have also been identified, namely, cost decreasing by smart technologies factor, product quality enhancement based on big data analytics factor, smart delivery to customer factor, improvement of supply flexibility factor, green design in a digital way factor, green purchasing based on a digital platform factor, green and smart manufacturing factor, green and smart logistics factor, smart working environment factor, employee's improvement in a smart atmosphere factor, and social activities for encouraging smart technologies factor.

Step 3: The dimensions of the problem are organized in a hierarchical form between the objective, the main factors, the sub-factors, and the selected sustainable suppliers, as charted in Figure 7.2.

Step 4: A set of semantic terms are developed to assist experts in assessing and prioritizing the main factors and their sub-factors, as presented in Table 7.1. Also, a set of semantic terms are presented to assist experts in evaluating the sustainable suppliers selected in the case study, as exhibited in Table 7.2.

Step 5: The decision matrices according to experts' opinions (E_3) were constructed to evaluate the main factors by each expert by using semantic terms established in Table 7.1 as presented in Table 7.8, and then by using IFNs according to Table 7.3 as presented in Table 7.9.

Step 6: The distinct expert valuations of main factors were aggregated by applying IFWG presented in Eq. (7.14) according to Table 7.4 as presented in Table 7.10.

Step 7: The standard deviation for main factors was calculated by using Eq. (7.17) as presented in Table 7.11. The correlation relationship of each

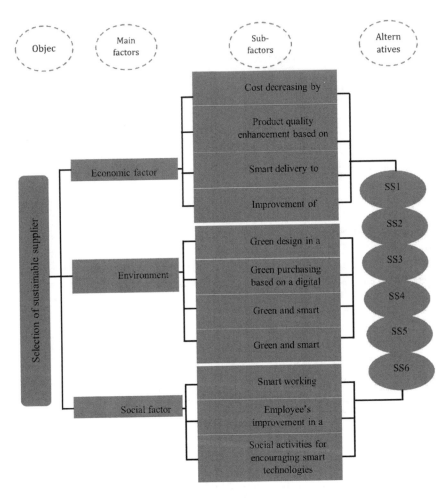

FIGURE 7.2
Hierarchical structure for the problem dimensions.

TABLE 7.8

Decision Matrix Based on Main Factors for Each Expert Using Semantic Terms

Main Factors	Expert₁			Expert₂			Expert₃		
	EOF_1	ENF_2	SCF_3	EOF_1	ENF_2	SCF_3	EOF_1	ENF_2	SCF_3
SS_1	. APP	VEH	MEH	ABH	MEL	HIG	VEH	VEH	MEL
SS_2	MEH	HIG	APP	ABH	HIG	APP	ABH	MEH	APP
SS_3	ABH	VEH	MEL	MEH	APP	MEL	ABH	ABH	MEH
SS_4	ABH	MEL	MEH	ABH	MEL	APP	APP	HIG	MEH
SS_5	MEL	MEL	MEH	MEL	HIG	MEH	MEL	APP	APP
SS_6	VEH	HIG	MEL	VEH	HIG	MEH	ABH	HIG	VEH

TABLE 7.9

Decision matrix based on main factors for each expert using IFNs.

	Expert$_1$			Expert$_2$			Expert$_3$		
	EOF$_1$	ENF$_2$	SCF$_3$	EOF$_1$	ENF$_2$	SCF$_3$	EOF$_1$	ENF$_2$	SCF$_3$
SS$_1$	[0.90, 0.05]	[0.80, 0.15]	[0.60, 0.35]	[0.90, 0.05]	[0.40, 0.55]	[0.70, 0.25]	[0.80, 0.15]	[0.80, 0.15]	[0.40, 0.55]
SS$_2$	[0.60, 0.35]	[0.70, 0.25]	[0.50, 0.45]	[0.90, 0.05]	[0.70, 0.25]	[0.50, 0.45]	[0.90, 0.05]	[0.60, 0.35]	[0.50, 0.45]
SS$_3$	[0.90, 0.05]	[0.80, 0.15]	[0.40, 0.55]	[0.60, 0.35]	[0.50, 0.45]	[0.40, 0.55]	[0.90, 0.05]	[0.90, 0.05]	[0.60, 0.35]
SS$_4$	[0.90, 0.05]	[0.40, 0.55]	[0.60, 0.35]	[0.90, 0.05]	[0.40, 0.55]	[0.50, 0.45]	[0.50, 0.45]	[0.70, 0.25]	[0.60, 0.35]
SS$_5$	[0.40, 0.55]	[0.40, 0.55]	[0.60, 0.35]	[0.40, 0.55]	[0.70, 0.25]	[0.60, 0.35]	[0.40, 0.55]	[0.50, 0.45]	[0.50, 0.45]
SS$_6$	[0.80, 0.15]	[0.70, 0.25]	[0.40, 0.55]	[0.80, 0.15]	[0.70, 0.25]	[0.60, 0.35]	[0.90, 0.05]	[0.70, 0.25]	[0.80, 0.15]

TABLE 7.10

Aggregated Decision Matrix Based on Main Factors by All Experts Using IFNs

Main Factors	EOF$_1$	ENF$_2$	SCF$_3$
SS$_1$	[0.87, 0.08]	[0.61, 0.34]	[0.57, 0.38]
SS$_2$	[0.80, 0.15]	[0.67, 0.28]	[0.50, 0.45]
SS$_3$	[0.77, 0.18]	[0.69, 0.26]	[0.45, 0.50]
SS$_4$	[0.75, 0.19]	[0.47, 0.48]	[0.56, 0.39]
SS$_5$	[0.40, 0.55]	[0.53, 0.41]	[0.57, 0.38]
SS$_6$	[0.83, 0.12]	[0.70, 0.25]	[0.58, 0.37]

TABLE 7.11

Normalized Decision Matrix Based on Main Factors by All Experts

Main Factors	EOF$_1$	ENF$_2$	SCF$_3$
SS$_1$	1.00000	0.59197	0.89096
SS$_2$	0.84864	0.86304	0.38273
SS$_3$	0.78238	0.94225	0.00000
SS$_4$	0.75982	0.00000	0.83490
SS$_5$	0.00000	0.27753	0.91455
SS$_6$	0.91556	1.00000	1.00000
Standard deviation	0.36250	0.40235	0.39399

TABLE 7.12

Correlation Coefficient of the Relationship among the Main Factors

Main Factors	EOF$_1$	ENF$_2$	SCF$_3$	Weights
EOF$_1$	1.0000	0.4657	−0.1706	0.253
ENF$_2$	0.4657	1.0000	−0.4447	0.326
SCF$_3$	−0.1706	−0.4447	1.0000	0.421

factor with other factors was determined by applying Eq. (7.18), as exhibited in Table 7.12.

Step 8: The main factors' weights were calculated through the standard deviation of each factor and its correlation among other factors by applying Eq. (7.19). Then, the objective weights of the main factors were standardized, and the weight of each factor was computed by applying Eq. (7.20) as presented in Table 7.12 and charted in Figure 7.3.

Step 9: The decision matrices according to experts' opinions (E_3) were constructed to evaluate the economic factor's sub-factors by each expert by using semantic terms established in Table 7.1 as presented in Table 7.13, and then by using IFNs according to Table 7.3 as presented in Table 7.14

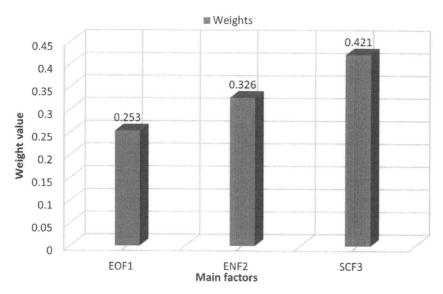

FIGURE 7.3
Final weights of main factors.

Step 10: The distinct expert valuations of economic factor's sub-factors were aggregated by applying IFWG presented in Eq. (7.14) according to Table 7.4 as presented in Table 7.15.

Step 11: The standard deviation for the economic factor's sub-factors was calculated by utilizing Eq. (7.17) as presented in Table 7.16, and the correlation relationship of each factor with other factors was determined by applying Eq. (7.18) as exhibited in Table 7.17.

Step 12: The economic factor's sub-factors weights were calculated through the standard deviation of each factor and its correlation among other factors by applying Eq. (7.19). Then, objective weights of the economic factor's sub-factors were standardized, and the weight of each factor is computed by applying Eq. (7.20) as presented in Table 7.17 and charted in Figure 7.4.

Step 13: The decision matrices according to experts' opinions (E_3) were constructed to evaluate the environmental factor's sub-factors by each expert by using semantic terms established in Table 7.1 as presented in Table 7.18, and then by using IFNs according to Table 7.3 as presented in Table 7.19.

Step 14: The distinct expert valuations of environmental factor's sub-factors were aggregated by applying IFWG presented in Eq. (7.14) according to Table 7.4 as presented in Table 7.20.

Step 15: The standard deviation for the environmental factor's sub-factors was calculated by utilizing Eq. (7.17) as presented in Table 7.21,

TABLE 7.13

Decision Matrix Based on Economic Factor's Sub-Factors for Each Expert

EOF₁	Expert₁				Expert₂				Expert₃			
	CDS_{1_1}	PEB_{1_2}	SDC_{1_3}	ISF_{1_4}	CDS_{1_1}	PEB_{1_2}	SDC_{1_3}	ISF_{1_4}	CDS_{1_1}	PEB_{1_2}	SDC_{1_3}	ISF_{1_4}
SS_1	APP	VLO	MEH	APP	ABH	HIG	HIG	VEH	VEH	APP	MEL	MEH
SS_2	MEH	LOW	APP	VEH	ABH	LOW	APP	MEL	ABH	HIG	APP	LOW
SS_3	ABH	HIG	MEL	APP	MEH	VEH	MEL	HIG	ABH	ABH	MEH	VEH
SS_4	ABH	MEL	MEH	VLO	ABH	MEL	APP	ABH	APP	HIG	MEH	VLO
SS_5	MEL	MEL	MEH	MEH	MEL	HIG	MEH	MEH	MEL	APP	APP	ABH
SS_6	VEH	HIG	MEL	ABH	VEH	HIG	MEH	MEL	ABH	HIG	VEH	HIG

TABLE 7.14

Decision Matrix Based on Economic Factor's Sub-Factors for Each Expert Using IFNs

EOF_1	$Expert_1$				$Expert_2$	
	$CDS_{1.1}$	$PEB_{1.2}$	$SDC_{1.3}$	$ISF_{1.4}$	$CDS_{1.1}$	$PEB_{1.2}$
SS_1	[0.90, 0.05]	[0.20, 0.75]	[0.60, 0.35]	[0.50, 0.45]	[0.90, 0.05]	[0.70, 0.25]
SS_2	[0.60, 0.35]	[0.30, 0.65]	[0.50, 0.45]	[0.80, 0.15]	[0.90, 0.05]	[0.30, 0.65]
SS_3	[0.90, 0.05]	[0.70, 0.25]	[0.40, 0.55]	[0.50, 0.45]	[0.60, 0.35]	[0.80, 0.15]
SS_4	[0.90, 0.05]	[0.40, 0.55]	[0.60, 0.35]	[0.20, 0.75]	[0.90, 0.05]	[0.40, 0.55]
SS_5	[0.40, 0.55]	[0.40, 0.55]	[0.60, 0.35]	[0.60, 0.35]	[0.40, 0.55]	[0.70, 0.25]
SS_6	[0.80, 0.15]	[0.70, 0.25]	[0.40, 0.55]	[0.90, 0.05]	[0.80, 0.15]	[0.70, 0.25]

EOF_1	$Expert_2$		$Expert_3$			
	$SDC_{1.3}$	$ISF_{1.4}$	$CDS_{1.1}$	$PEB_{1.2}$	$SDC_{1.3}$	$ISF_{1.4}$
SS_1	[0.70, 0.25]	[0.80, 0.15]	[0.80, 0.15]	[0.50, 0.45]	[0.40, 0.55]	[0.60, 0.35]
SS_2	[0.50, 0.45]	[0.40, 0.55]	[0.90, 0.05]	[0.70, 0.25]	[0.50, 0.45]	[0.30, 0.65]
SS_3	[0.40, 0.55]	[0.70, 0.25]	[0.90, 0.05]	[0.90, 0.05]	[0.60, 0.35]	[0.80, 0.15]
SS_4	[0.50, 0.45]	[0.90, 0.05]	[0.50, 0.45]	[0.70, 0.25]	[0.60, 0.35]	[0.20, 0.75]
SS_5	[0.60, 0.35]	[0.60, 0.35]	[0.40, 0.55]	[0.50, 0.45]	[0.50, 0.45]	[0.90, 0.05]
SS_6	[0.60, 0.35]	[0.40, 0.55]	[0.90, 0.05]	[0.70, 0.25]	[0.80, 0.15]	[0.70, 0.25]

TABLE 7.15

Aggregated Decision Matrix Based on Economic Factor's Sub-Factors by All
Experts Using IFNs

EOF$_1$	CDS$_{1\_1}$	PEB$_{1\_2}$	SDC$_{1\_3}$	ISF$_{1\_4}$
SS$_1$	[0.48, 0.46]	[0.76, 0.19]	[0.49, 0.46]	[0.64, 0.31]
SS$_2$	[0.51, 0.43]	[0.48, 0.47]	[0.57, 0.38]	[0.45, 0.49]
SS$_3$	[0.81, 0.14]	[0.83, 0.12]	[0.62, 0.32]	[0.66, 0.29]
SS$_4$	[0.75, 0.19]	[0.47, 0.48]	[0.56, 0.39]	[0.37, 0.57]
SS$_5$	[0.40, 0.55]	[0.53, 0.41]	[0.57, 0.38]	[0.68, 0.27]
SS$_6$	[0.83, 0.12]	[0.70, 0.25]	[0.58, 0.37]	[0.60, 0.34]

TABLE 7.16

Normalized Decision Matrix Based on Economic Factor's Sub-Factors by All
Experts

EOF$_1$	CDS$_{1\_1}$	PEB$_{1\_2}$	SDC$_{1\_3}$	ISF$_{1\_4}$
SS$_1$	0.18245	0.80448	0.00000	0.87495
SS$_2$	0.27226	0.00886	0.60073	0.28502
SS$_3$	0.96590	1.00000	1.00000	0.94122
SS$_4$	0.82989	0.00000	0.49224	0.00000
SS$_5$	0.00000	0.17834	0.57061	1.00000
SS$_6$	1.00000	0.64259	0.65468	0.76871
Standard deviation	0.44003	0.43254	0.32318	0.40683

TABLE 7.17

Correlation Coefficient of the Relationship among the Economic Factor's
Sub-Factors

EOF$_1$	CDS$_{1\_1}$	PEB$_{1\_2}$	SDC$_{1\_3}$	ISF$_{1\_4}$	Weights
CDS$_{1\_1}$	1.0000	0.3474	0.5555	−0.2027	0.287
PEB$_{1\_2}$	0.3474	1.0000	0.1015	0.7057	0.226
SDC$_{1\_3}$	0.5555	0.1015	1.0000	0.0701	0.208
ISF$_{1\_4}$	−0.2027	0.7057	0.0701	1.0000	0.280

and the correlation relationship of each factor with other factors was
determined by applying Eq. (7.18) as exhibited in Table 7.22.

Step 16: The environmental factor's sub-factors' weights were calculated through the standard deviation of each factor and its correlation
among other factors by applying Eq. (7.19). Then, objective weights of the
environmental factor's sub-factors were standardized, and the weight of

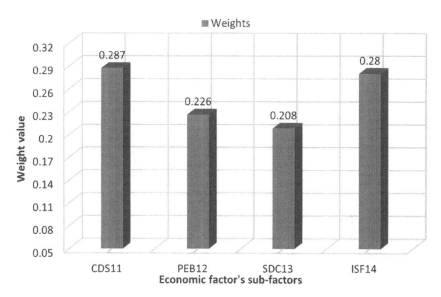

FIGURE 7.4
Final weights of economic factor's sub-factors.

each factor is computed by applying Eq. (7.20) as presented in Table 7.22 and charted in Figure 7.5.

Step 17: The decision matrices according to experts' opinions (E_3) were constructed to evaluate the social factor's sub-factors by each expert by using semantic terms established in Table 7.1 as presented in Table 7.23, and then by using IFNs according to Table 7.3 as presented in Table 7.24.

Step 18: The distinct expert valuations of social factor's sub-factors were aggregated by applying IFWG presented in Eq. (7.14) according to Table 7.4 as presented in Table 7.25.

Step 19: The standard deviation for social factor's sub-factors was calculated by utilizing Eq. (7.17) as presented in Table 7.26, and the correlation relationship of each factor with other factors was determined by applying Eq. (7.18) as exhibited in Table 7.27.

Step 20: The social factor's sub-factors weights were calculated through the standard deviation of each factor and its correlation among other factors by applying Eq. (7.19). Then, objective weights of the social factor's sub-factors were standardized, and the weight of each factor was computed by applying Eq. (7.20) as presented in Table 7.27 and charted in Figure 7.6.

Step 21: The global weights of the sub-factors were calculated by multiplying the weights of the main factors by the local weights of the sub-factors as presented in Table 7.28 and charted in Figure 7.7.

TABLE 7.18

Decision Matrix Based on Environmental Factor's Sub-Factors for each Expert

ENF$_2$	Expert$_1$				Expert$_2$				Expert$_3$			
	GDD$_{2.1}$	GPP$_{2.2}$	GSM$_{2.3}$	GSL$_{2.4}$	GDD$_{2.1}$	GPP$_{2.2}$	GSM$_{2.3}$	GSL$_{2.4}$	GDD$_{2.1}$	GPP$_{2.2}$	GSM$_{2.3}$	GSM$_{2.4}$
SS$_1$	APP	VEH	MEH	APP	ABH	HIG	HIG	VEH	VEH	APP	MEL	MEH
SS$_2$	MEH	VEH	APP	VEH	ABH	VEH	APP	MEL	ABH	HIG	APP	LOW
SS$_3$	ABH	HIG	MEL	APP	MEH	VEH	MEL	HIG	ABH	ABH	ABH	VEH
SS$_4$	ABH	MEL	ABH	VLO	ABH	MEL	APP	ABH	APP	HIG	ABH	VLO
SS$_5$	MEL	VEH	ABH	MEH	MEL	HIG	ABH	MEH	MEL	VEH	APP	ABH
SS$_6$	VEH	HIG	MEL	ABH	VEH	HIG	MEH	MEL	ABH	HIG	VEH	HIG

TABLE 7.19

Decision Matrix Based on Environmental Factor's Sub-Factors for each Expert Using IFNs

ENF_2	$Expert_1$				$Expert_2$	
	$GDD_{2.1}$	$GPP_{2.2}$	$GSM_{2.3}$	$GSL_{2.4}$	$GDD_{2.1}$	$GPP_{2.2}$
SS_1	[0.90, 0.05]	[0.80, 0.15]	[0.60, 0.35]	[0.50, 0.45]	[0.90, 0.05]	[0.70, 0.25]
SS_2	[0.60, 0.35]	[0.80, 0.15]	[0.50, 0.45]	[0.80, 0.15]	[0.90, 0.05]	[0.80, 0.15]
SS_3	[0.90, 0.05]	[0.70, 0.25]	[0.40, 0.55]	[0.50, 0.45]	[0.60, 0.35]	[0.80, 0.15]
SS_4	[0.90, 0.05]	[0.40, 0.55]	[0.90, 0.05]	[0.20, 0.75]	[0.90, 0.05]	[0.40, 0.55]
SS_5	[0.40, 0.55]	[0.80, 0.15]	[0.90, 0.05]	[0.60, 0.35]	[0.40, 0.55]	[0.70, 0.25]
SS_6	[0.80, 0.15]	[0.70, 0.25]	[0.40, 0.55]	[0.90, 0.05]	[0.80, 0.15]	[0.70, 0.25]

ENF_2	$Expert_2$		$Expert_3$			
	$GSM_{2.3}$	$GSL_{2.4}$	$GDD_{2.1}$	$GPP_{2.2}$	$GSM_{2.3}$	$GSL_{2.4}$
SS_1	[0.70, 0.25]	[0.80, 0.15]	[0.80, 0.15]	[0.50, 0.45]	[0.40, 0.55]	[0.60, 0.35]
SS_2	[0.50, 0.45]	[0.40, 0.55]	[0.90, 0.05]	[0.70, 0.25]	[0.50, 0.45]	[0.30, 0.65]
SS_3	[0.40, 0.55]	[0.70, 0.25]	[0.90, 0.05]	[0.90, 0.05]	[0.90, 0.05]	[0.80, 0.15]
SS_4	[0.50, 0.45]	[0.90, 0.05]	[0.50, 0.45]	[0.70, 0.25]	[0.90, 0.05]	[0.20, 0.75]
SS_5	[0.90, 0.05]	[0.60, 0.35]	[0.40, 0.55]	[0.80, 0.15]	[0.50, 0.45]	[0.90, 0.05]
SS_6	[0.60, 0.35]	[0.40, 0.55]	[0.90, 0.05]	[0.70, 0.25]	[0.80, 0.15]	[0.70, 0.25]

TABLE 7.20

Aggregated Decision Matrix Based on Environmental Factor's Sub-Factors by All Experts Using IFNs

ENF_2	GDD_{2_1}	GPP_{2_2}	GSM_{2_3}	GSL_{2_4}
SS_1	[0.48, 0.46]	[0.76, 0.19]	[0.49, 0.46]	[0.64, 0.31]
SS_2	[0.51, 0.43]	[0.73, 0.22]	[0.57, 0.38]	[0.45, 0.49]
SS_3	[0.81, 0.14]	[0.80, 0.15]	[0.71, 0.24]	[0.66, 0.29]
SS_4	[0.75, 0.19]	[0.47, 0.48]	[0.71, 0.24]	[0.37, 0.57]
SS_5	[0.40, 0.55]	[0.69, 0.25]	[0.75, 0.19]	[0.68, 0.27]
SS_6	[0.83, 0.12]	[0.70, 0.25]	[0.58, 0.37]	[0.60, 0.34]

TABLE 7.21

Normalized Decision Matrix Based on Environmental Factor's Sub-Factors by All Experts

ENF_2	GDD_{2_1}	GPP_{2_2}	GSM_{2_3}	GSL_{2_4}
SS_1	0.18245	0.88462	0.00000	0.87495
SS_2	0.27226	0.80979	0.30497	0.28502
SS_3	0.96590	1.00000	0.81488	0.94122
SS_4	0.82989	0.00000	0.83710	0.00000
SS_5	0.00000	0.69050	1.00000	1.00000
SS_6	1.00000	0.70660	0.33236	0.76871
Standard deviation	0.44003	0.35336	0.39115	0.40683

TABLE 7.22

Correlation Coefficient of the Relationship among the Environmental Factor's Sub-Factors

ENF_2	GDD_{2_1}	GPP_{2_2}	GSM_{2_3}	GSL_{2_4}	Weights
GDD_{2_1}	1.0000	−0.2086	0.1339	−0.2027	0.306
GPP_{2_2}	−0.2086	1.0000	−0.3702	0.7523	0.212
GSM_{2_3}	0.1339	−0.3702	1.0000	−0.0153	0.270
GSL_{2_4}	−0.2027	0.7523	−0.0153	1.0000	0.213

Step 22: The valuation decision matrices by experts distinctly (E_3) among the determined sub-factors and the selected sustainable suppliers were created by utilizing the semantic terms as exhibited in Table 7.2, according to Table 7.5 as presented in Table 7.29.

Step 23: The assessment decision matrix by each expert distinctly (E_k) among the defined sub-factors and the selected sustainable suppliers was aggregated into one matrix by applying IFWG as exhibited in Eq. (7.14) according to Table 7.6 as presented in Table 7.30. Then, the aggregated

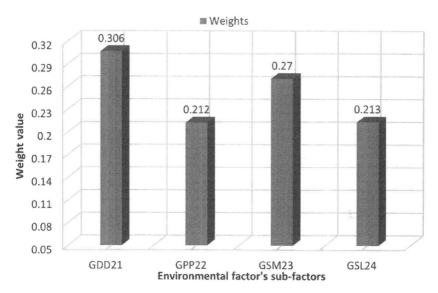

FIGURE 7.5
Final weights of environmental factor's sub-factors.

TABLE 7.23

Decision Matrix Based on Social Factor's Sub-Factors for each Expert Using Semantic Terms

SCF_3	Expert$_1$			Expert$_2$			Expert$_3$		
	SOE_{3_1}	EIS_{3_2}	SAE_{3_3}	SOE_{3_1}	EIS_{3_2}	SAE_{3_3}	SOE_{3_1}	EIS_{3_2}	SAE_{3_3}
SS_1	APP	VEH	MEH	ABH	MEL	HIG	VEH	VEH	HIG
SS_2	MEH	HIG	APP	ABH	HIG	APP	ABH	MEH	APP
SS_3	ABH	VEH	MEL	MEH	APP	MEL	ABH	ABH	HIG
SS_4	ABH	MEL	VLO	ABH	MEL	APP	APP	HIG	MEH
SS_5	MEL	MEL	VLO	MEL	HIG	MEL	MEL	APP	APP
SS_6	VEH	HIG	MEL	VEH	HIG	MEH	ABH	HIG	VEH

decision matrix was defuzzified by applying Eq. (7.12) according to Table 7.7.

Step 24: The normalized decision matrix was calculated according to Eq. (7.21) as presented in Table 7.31.

Step 25: The weighted normalized decision matrix was computed according to Eq. (7.22) as presented in Table 7.32. Then, the negative ideal solution was determined according to Eq. (7.23), as presented in Table 7.32.

Step 26: The Euclidean and taxicab distances were computed according to Eqs. (7.24) and (7.25), as presented in Table 7.33.

TABLE 7.24

Decision Matrix Based on Social Factor's Sub-Factors for Each Expert Using IFNs

SCF$_3$	Expert$_1$			Expert$_2$			Expert$_3$		
	SOE$_{3\_1}$	EIS$_{3\_2}$	SAE$_{3\_3}$	SOE$_{3\_1}$	EIS$_{3\_2}$	SAE$_{3\_3}$	SOE$_{3\_1}$	EIS$_{3\_2}$	SAE$_{3\_3}$
SS$_1$	[0.90, 0.05]	[0.80, 0.15]	[0.60, 0.35]	[0.90, 0.05]	[0.40, 0.55]	[0.70, 0.25]	[0.80, 0.15]	[0.80, 0.15]	[0.70, 0.25]
SS$_2$	[0.60, 0.35]	[0.70, 0.25]	[0.50, 0.45]	[0.90, 0.05]	[0.70, 0.25]	[0.50, 0.45]	[0.90, 0.05]	[0.60, 0.35]	[0.50, 0.45]
SS$_3$	[0.90, 0.05]	[0.80, 0.15]	[0.40, 0.55]	[0.60, 0.35]	[0.50, 0.45]	[0.40, 0.55]	[0.90, 0.05]	[0.90, 0.05]	[0.70, 0.25]
SS$_4$	[0.90, 0.05]	[0.40, 0.55]	[0.20, 0.75]	[0.90, 0.05]	[0.40, 0.55]	[0.50, 0.45]	[0.50, 0.45]	[0.70, 0.25]	[0.60, 0.35]
SS$_5$	[0.40, 0.55]	[0.40, 0.55]	[0.20, 0.75]	[0.40, 0.55]	[0.70, 0.25]	[0.40, 0.55]	[0.40, 0.55]	[0.50, 0.45]	[0.50, 0.45]
SS$_6$	[0.80, 0.15]	[0.70, 0.25]	[0.40, 0.55]	[0.80, 0.15]	[0.70, 0.25]	[0.60, 0.35]	[0.90, 0.05]	[0.70, 0.25]	[0.80, 0.15]

TABLE 7.25

Aggregated Decision Matrix Based on Social Factor's Sub-Factors by All Experts Using IFNs

SCF$_3$	SOE$_{3\_1}$	EIS$_{3\_2}$	SAE$_{3\_3}$
SS$_1$	[0.87, 0.08]	[0.61, 0.34]	[0.67, 0.28]
SS$_2$	[0.80, 0.15]	[0.67, 0.28]	[0.50, 0.45]
SS$_3$	[0.77, 0.18]	[0.69, 0.26]	[0.47, 0.48]
SS$_4$	[0.75, 0.19]	[0.47, 0.48]	[0.40, 0.54]
SS$_5$	[0.40, 0.55]	[0.53, 0.41]	[0.35, 0.60]
SS$_6$	[0.83, 0.12]	[0.70, 0.25]	[0.58, 0.37]

TABLE 7.26

Normalized Decision Matrix Based on Social Factor's Sub-Factors by All Experts

SCF$_3$	SOE$_{3\_1}$	EIS$_{3\_2}$	SAE$_{3\_3}$
SS$_1$	1.00000	0.59197	1.00000
SS$_2$	0.84864	0.86304	0.48490
SS$_3$	0.78238	0.94225	0.40066
SS$_4$	0.75982	0.00000	0.17260
SS$_5$	0.00000	0.27753	0.00000
SS$_6$	0.91556	1.00000	0.72918
Standard deviation	0.36250	0.40235	0.36394

TABLE 7.27

Correlation Coefficient of the Relationship among the Social Factor's Sub-Factors

SCF$_3$	SOE$_{3\_1}$	EIS$_{3\_2}$	SAE$_{3\_3}$	Weights
SOE$_{3\_1}$	1.0000	0.4657	0.7931	0.300
EIS$_{3\_2}$	0.4657	1.0000	0.5600	0.437
SAE$_{3\_3}$	0.7931	0.5600	1.0000	0.263

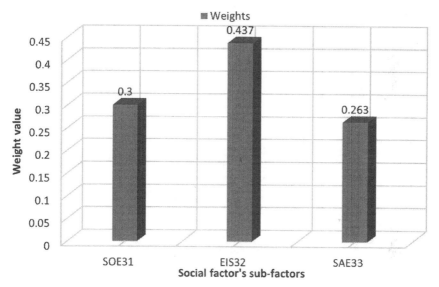

FIGURE 7.6
Final weights of social factor's sub-factors.

Step 27: The relative evaluation matrix was computed according to Eq. (7.26) as presented in Table 7.34. In this regard, the assessment score was computed according to Eq. (7.27) as presented in Table 7.34. Then, the sustainable suppliers are ranked in descending order of the values of H_i, and results are charted in Figure 7.8.

7.5 Results and Discussion

This part explains and analyses the results obtained from applying the model used to solve the problem of selecting sustainable suppliers. The model used consists of two MCDM methods, the IF CRITIC method and

TABLE 7.28

Weights of Main Factors and Their Sub-Factors

Main Factors	Weights of Main Factors	Sub-Factors	Local Weight of Sub-Factors	Global Weight of Sub-Factors
Economic EOF_1	0.253	Cost decreasing by smart technologies, CDS_{1_1}	0.287	0.073
		Product quality enhancement based on big data analytics, PEP_{1_2}	0.226	0.057
		Smart delivery to the customer, SDC_{1_3}	0.208	0.053
		Improvement of supply flexibility, ISF_{1_4}	0.280	0.071
Environmental ENF_2	0.326	Green design in a digital way, GDD_{2_1}	0.306	0.101
		Green purchasing based on a digital platform, GPP_{2_2}	0.212	0.069
		Green and smart manufacturing, GSM_{2_3}	0.270	0.088
		Green and smart logistics, GSL_{2_4}	0.213	0.069
Social SCF_3	0.421	Smart working environment, SOE_{3_1}	0.300	0.126
		Employee's improvement in a smart atmosphere, EIS_{3_2}	0.437	0.183
		Social activities for encouraging smart technologies, SAE_{3_3}	0.263	0.110

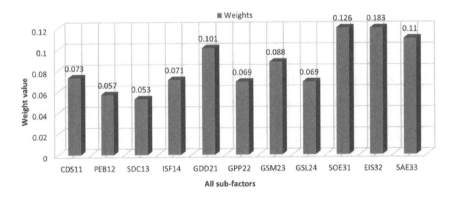

FIGURE 7.7
Final global weights of all sub-factors.

TABLE 7.29

Decision Matrices of Six Sustainable Suppliers According to All Sub-Factors Using Semantic Terms

Expert$_s$	CDS$_{1\_1}$	PEB$_{1\_2}$	SDC$_{1\_3}$	ISF$_{1\_4}$	GDD$_{2\_1}$	GPP$_{2\_2}$
SS$_1$	APP, ABH, VEH	VLO, HIG, APP	MEH, HIG, MEL	APP, VEH, MEH	APP, ABH, VEH	VEH, HIG, APP
SS$_2$	MEH, ABH, ABH	LOW, LOW, HIG	APP, APP, APP	VEH, MEL, LOW	MEH, ABH, ABH	VEH, VEH, HIG
SS$_3$	ABH, MEH, ABH	HIG, VEH, ABH	MEL, MEL, MEH	APP, HIG, VEH	ABH, MEH, ABH	HIG, VEH, ABH
SS$_4$	ABH, ABH, APP	MEL, MEL, HIG	MEH, APP, MEH	VLO, ABH, VLO	ABH, ABH, APP	MEL, MEL, HIG
SS$_5$	MEL, MEL, MEL	MEL, HIG, APP	MEH, MEH, APP	MEH, MEH, ABH	MEL, MEL, MEL	VEH, HIG, VEH
SS$_6$	VEH, VEH, ABH	HIG, HIG, HIG	MEL, MEH, VEH	ABH, MEL, HIG	VEH, VEH, ABH	HIG, HIG, HIG

Expert$_s$	GSM$_{2\_3}$	GSL$_{2\_4}$	SOE$_{3\_1}$	EIS$_{3\_2}$	SAE$_{3\_3}$
SC$_1$	MEH, HIG, MEL	APP, VEH, MEH	APP, ABH, VEH	VEH, MEL, VEH	MEH, HIG, HIG
SC$_2$	APP, APP, APP	VEH, MEL, LOW	MEH, ABH, ABH	HIG, HIG, MEH	APP, APP, APP
SC$_3$	MEL, MEL, ABH	APP, HIG, VEH	ABH, MEH, ABH	VEH, APP, ABH	MEL, MEL, HIG
SC$_4$	ABH, APP, ABH	VLO, ABH, VLO	ABH, ABH, APP	MEL, MEL, HIG	VLO, APP, MEH
SC$_5$	ABH, ABH, APP	MEH, MEH, ABH	MEL, MEL, MEL	MEL, HIG, APP	VLO, MEL, APP
SC$_6$	MEL, MEH, VEH	ABH, MEL, HIG	VEH, VEH, ABH	HIG, HIG, HIG	MEL, MEH, VEH

TABLE 7.30

Aggregated Decision Matrix of Six Sustainable Suppliers According to All Sub-Factors

Expert$_s$	CDS_{1_1}	PEB_{1_2}	SDC_{1_3}	ISF_{1_4}	GDD_{2_1}	GPP_{2_2}
SS$_1$	[0.48, 0.46]	[0.76, 0.19]	[0.49, 0.46]	[0.64, 0.31]	[0.48, 0.46]	[0.76, 0.19]
SS$_2$	[0.51, 0.43]	[0.48, 0.47]	[0.57, 0.38]	[0.45, 0.49]	[0.51, 0.43]	[0.73, 0.22]
SS$_3$	[0.81, 0.14]	[0.83, 0.12]	[0.62, 0.32]	[0.66, 0.29]	[0.81, 0.14]	[0.80, 0.15]
SS$_4$	[0.75, 0.19]	[0.47, 0.48]	[0.56, 0.39]	[0.37, 0.57]	[0.75, 0.19]	[0.47, 0.48]
SS$_5$	[0.40, 0.55]	[0.53, 0.41]	[0.57, 0.38]	[0.68, 0.27]	[0.40, 0.55]	[0.69, 0.25]
SS$_6$	[0.83, 0.12]	[0.70, 0.25]	[0.58, 0.37]	[0.60, 0.34]	[0.83, 0.12]	[0.70, 0.25]

Expert$_s$	GSM_{2_3}	GSL_{2_4}	SOE_{3_1}	EIS_{3_2}	SAE_{3_3}
SC$_1$	[0.49, 0.46]	[0.64, 0.31]	[0.87, 0.08]	[0.61, 0.34]	[0.67, 0.28]
SC$_2$	[0.57, 0.38]	[0.45, 0.49]	[0.80, 0.15]	[0.67, 0.28]	[0.50, 0.45]
SC$_3$	[0.71, 0.24]	[0.66, 0.29]	[0.77, 0.18]	[0.69, 0.26]	[0.47, 0.48]
SC$_4$	[0.71, 0.24]	[0.37, 0.57]	[0.75, 0.19]	[0.47, 0.48]	[0.40, 0.54]
SC$_5$	[0.75, 0.19]	[0.68, 0.27]	[0.40, 0.55]	[0.53, 0.41]	[0.35, 0.60]
SC$_6$	[0.58, 0.37]	[0.60, 0.34]	[0.83, 0.12]	[0.70, 0.25]	[0.58, 0.37]

the IF CODAS method. In this regard, the model has been applied in two parts. The first part relates to the evaluation of the main factors and their sub-factors. The second part relates to an evaluation of the six sustainable suppliers selected in the case study.

According to the results in Table 7.12, it is clear that the social factor ranks first with a weight of 0.421, followed by the environment factor with a weight of 0.326, while the economic factor comes in the last rank with a weight of 0.253.

According to the results of the economic factor's sub-factors in Table 7.28, it is clear that the cost decreasing by smart technologies factor ranks first with a weight of 0.287, followed by the improvement of supply flexibility factor with a weight of 0.280, while the smart delivery to customer factor comes in the last rank with a weight of 0.208.

According to the results of the environmental factor's sub-factors in Table 7.28, it is clear that the green design in a digital way factor ranks first with a weight of 0.306, followed by the green and smart manufacturing factor with a weight of 0.270, while the green purchasing based on a digital platform factor comes in the last rank with a weight of 0.212.

According to the results of the social factor's sub-factors in Table 7.28, it is clear that the employee's improvement in a smart atmosphere factor ranks first with a weight of 0.437, followed by the smart working environment factor with a weight of 0.300, while the social activities for encouraging smart technologies factor comes in the last rank with a weight of 0.263.

TABLE 7.31

Normalized Decision Matrix of Six Sustainable Suppliers According to All Sub-Factors

Experts	$CDS_{1,1}$	$PEB_{1,2}$	$SDC_{1,3}$	$ISF_{1,4}$	$GDD_{2,1}$	$GPP_{2,2}$	$GSM_{2,3}$	$GSL_{2,4}$	$SOE_{3,1}$	$EIS_{3,2}$	$SAE_{3,3}$
SS_1	0.5889	0.9190	0.7985	0.9436	0.5889	0.9548	0.6679	0.9436	1.0000	0.8725	1.0000
SS_2	0.6340	0.5895	0.9195	0.6778	0.6340	0.9256	0.7692	0.6778	0.9205	0.9572	0.7579
SS_3	0.9829	1.0000	1.0000	0.9735	0.9829	1.0000	0.9385	0.9735	0.8858	0.9820	0.7183
SS_4	0.9145	0.5858	0.8977	0.5494	0.9145	0.6087	0.9459	0.5494	0.8739	0.6876	0.6112
SS_5	0.4971	0.6597	0.9135	1.0000	0.4971	0.8789	1.0000	1.0000	0.4751	0.7743	0.5300
SS_6	1.0000	0.8520	0.9304	0.8958	1.0000	0.8852	0.7783	0.8958	0.9557	1.0000	0.8727

TABLE 7.32

Weighted Normalized Decision Matrix of Six Sustainable Suppliers According to All Sub-Factors

Experts	$CDS_{1,1}$	$PEB_{1,2}$	$SDC_{1,3}$	$ISF_{1,4}$	$GDD_{2,1}$	$GPP_{2,2}$	$GSM_{2,3}$	$GSL_{2,4}$	$SOE_{3,1}$	$EIS_{3,2}$	$SAE_{3,3}$
SS_1	0.0430	0.0524	0.0423	0.0670	0.0595	0.0659	0.0588	0.0651	0.1260	0.1597	0.1100
SS_2	0.0463	0.0336	0.0487	0.0481	0.0640	0.0639	0.0677	0.0468	0.1160	0.1752	0.0834
SS_3	0.0717	0.0570	0.0530	0.0691	0.0993	0.0690	0.0826	0.0672	0.1116	0.1797	0.0790
SS_4	0.0668	0.0334	0.0476	0.0390	0.0924	0.0420	0.0832	0.0379	0.1101	0.1258	0.0672
SS_5	0.0363	0.0376	0.0484	0.0710	0.0502	0.0606	0.0880	0.0690	0.0599	0.1417	0.0583
SS_6	0.0730	0.0486	0.0493	0.0636	0.1010	0.0611	0.0685	0.0618	0.1204	0.1830	0.0960
Negative ideal	0.0363	0.0334	0.0423	0.0390	0.0502	0.0420	0.0588	0.0379	0.0599	0.1258	0.0583

TABLE 7.33

Euclidean and Taxicab Distances

Expert$_s$	E$_i$	T$_i$
SS$_1$	0.10382	0.26572
SS$_2$	0.08523	0.20974
SS$_3$	0.11577	0.35533
SS$_4$	0.07705	0.16152
SS$_5$	0.05915	0.13713
SS$_6$	0.11915	0.34237

TABLE 7.34

Relative Assessment Matrix and Final Ranking of the Selected Sustainable Suppliers

Expert$_s$	SS$_1$	SS$_2$	SS$_3$	SS$_4$	SS$_5$	SS$_6$	H$_i$	Rank
SS$_1$	0.0000	0.0188	−0.0117	0.0273	0.0458	−0.0151	0.0651	3
SS$_2$	−0.0184	0.0000	−0.0297	0.0083	0.0265	−0.0330	−0.0463	4
SS$_3$	0.0122	0.0314	0.0000	0.0402	0.0591	−0.0034	0.1395	2
SS$_4$	−0.0262	−0.0081	−0.0372	0.0000	0.0180	−0.0406	−0.0941	5
SS$_5$	−0.0435	−0.0257	−0.0542	−0.0178	0.0000	−0.0575	−0.1987	6
SS$_6$	0.0156	0.0348	0.0034	0.0436	0.0625	0.0000	0.1599	1

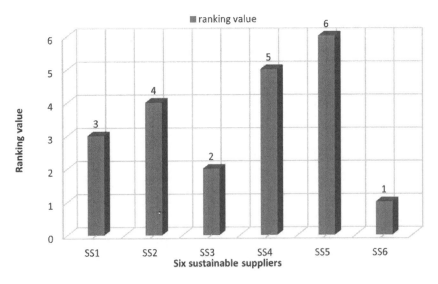

FIGURE 7.8
Final ranking of the selected sustainable suppliers.

Secondly, sustainable suppliers are ranked using the IF CODAS method. According to the results in Table 7.34, it is clear that SS_6 ranks first, followed by SS_3, while SS_5 comes in last.

7.6 Summary

- This chapter comprehensively describes smart supply chain and their relevant merits.
- This chapter reviews the importance and needs of assessing sustainable suppliers for a smart supply chain network.
- This chapter presents the most important criteria for evaluating sustainable suppliers for a smart supply chain after a comprehensive analysis of several research articles.
- This chapter suggests the steps of a hybrid MCDM approach for evaluating sustainable suppliers for smart supply chains.
- The hybrid MCDM approach consists of CRiteria Importance through Intercriteria Correlation (CRITIC) and the Combinative Distance-based ASsessment (CODAS) methods.
- This chapter presents a real case study while evaluating suppliers.

7.7 Exercises

a. How do you define "smart supply chain"? Why is an evaluation of sustainable suppliers important for smart supply chain?

b. What are the differences between CRiteria Importance through Intercriteria Correlation (CRITIC) and the Combinative Distance-based ASsessment (CODAS) methods? Discuss their relative advantages while making a decision.

c. Why are the challenges in deciding on sustainable suppliers for smart supply chain networks?

d. Discuss the features of sustainable suppliers in terms of the characteristics and formation of a sustainable and smart supply chain.

e. Why is the MCDM approach required to assess sustainability criteria for suppliers in a smart supply chain framework?

References

Atanassov, Krassimir T. 1999. "Intuitionistic fuzzy sets." In: *Intuitionistic Fuzzy Sets*, pp. 1–137. Physica, Heidelberg.

Bolturk, Eda, and Cengiz Kahraman. 2018. "Interval-Valued Intuitionistic Fuzzy CODAS Method and Its Application to Wave Energy Facility Location Selection Problem." *Journal of Intelligent & Fuzzy Systems* 35: 4865–77. doi: 10.3233/JIFS-18979.

Chen, Shyi-Ming, and Jiann-Mean Tan. 1994. "Handling Multicriteria Fuzzy Decision-Making Problems Based on Vague Set Theory." *Fuzzy Sets and Systems* 67(2): 163–72. doi: 10.1016/0165-0114(94)90084-1.

Diakoulaki, Danae, Georges Mavrotas, and Lefteris Papayannakis. 1995. "Determining Objective Weights in Multiple Criteria Problems: The Critic Method." *Computers & Operations Research* 22(7): 763–70. doi: 10.1016/0305-0548(94)00059-H.

Du, Wen Sheng. 2021. "Subtraction and Division Operations on Intuitionistic Fuzzy Sets Derived from the Hamming Distance." *Information Sciences* 571: 206–24. doi: 10.1016/j.ins.2021.04.068.

Keshavarz Ghorabaee, Mehdi, Edmundas Kazimieras Zavadskas, Zenonas Turskis, and Jurgita Antucheviciene. 2016. "A New Combinative Distance-Based Assessment (CODAS) Method for Multi-Criteria Decision-Making." *Economic Computation and Economic Cybernetics Studies and Research* 50(3): 25–44.

Peng, Xindong, Xiang Zhang, and Zhigang Luo. 2020. "Pythagorean Fuzzy MCDM Method Based on CoCoSo and CRITIC with Score Function for 5G Industry Evaluation." *Artificial Intelligence Review* 53(5): 3813–47. doi: 10.1007/s10462-019-09780-x.

Xu, Zeshui, and Ronald R Yager. 2006. "Some Geometric Aggregation Operators Based on Intuitionistic Fuzzy Sets." *International Journal of General Systems* 35(4): 417–33. doi: 10.1080/03081070600574353.

8

Analyzing and Evaluating Smart Card Systems for Public Transportation

8.1 Introduction

The choice regarding the expansion of public transportation is a difficult one, as it will have short-term and long-term major repercussions in terms of both the economy and the environment. The people in charge of making decisions need to consider a number of physical and intangible variables and investigate a number of potential enhancements. The demand for public transportation is growing worldwide, making it more essential than ever to have a standardized and interconnected public transit network. Public transportation is gaining more and more users as a result of a rise in population, an increase in the price of gasoline, an increase in the number of carbon emissions produced, and global warming. In recent years, an increasing number of countries have adopted a contactless smart card system as a mode of payment in public transportation services. These countries have done so on a large scale by integrating smart card systems across the country or on a small- to medium-scale capacity by integrating smart card systems in specific cities. In particular, the relevance of contactless payment systems increased during the pandemic because of their capacity to eliminate the need for direct contact with money and keypads, reducing the likelihood of contracting the COVID-19 virus. Traditional paper tickets and magnetic cards are being phased out in favor of smart card systems, which are electronic devices that may store data and be used to process it as necessary. These systems are portable and durable. These systems need an automated fare collection and administration system in all of the public transportation hubs and provide consistent service throughout the city. Standards for Industry 4.0 also encourage economies to use already available technology, such as the Internet of Things (IoT). IoT enables numerous domains of innovation, and these innovations provide many chances for integrating smart cards into public transit networks. In many countries, the use of a contactless travel smart card has

DOI: 10.1201/9781003357681-8

become more prevalent, encompassing practically all forms of transportation and creating an integrated public transit system. These smart cards are also referred to as city cards.

Fare-collecting automated systems provide customers and operators with a convenient and dependable service. The provision of a public transportation system that is both efficient and effective is a critical component to the achievement of success and the maintenance of sustainability in urban transport. Taking advantage of public transportation is important because it helps reduce traffic congestion during rush hours, shortens the total time spent during journeys, and improves the passenger experience. As a result, public transport authorities are encouraged to invest in technologies that improve the service quality of public transportation. As a result, transportation authorities that are working toward comparable objectives are attempting to include smart card systems into the fare collection procedures of public transit. Integrating these systems improves service quality by reducing the amount of time spent on at least the processes of payment, ticketing, and boarding. This indirectly prevents excess carbon emissions caused by transportation vehicles that are idling while waiting for payment processes.

In order to construct an efficient nationwide integrated transportation system, intelligent systems such as those that use smart cards, for example, must be put in place. A complete purpose of an intelligent transport system is to enhance the operations of transportation systems, which will support the goals of improving efficiency and production in all areas. This improvement will be made possible by using an intelligent transport system. It is the goal of an integrated transportation system to achieve seamless cooperation between the various modes of transportation and create a clear and transparent system, with standardized fees and operating conditions for all kinds of transportation. Customers will benefit from an environment that is both secure and quick to pay, thanks to an efficient fare payment and administration system, which will also increase public transportation usage. As a consequence of greater customer satisfaction and time savings during payment and transit operations, adopting smart systems helps improve the utilization rate of public transportation systems. This improvement is brought about by an increase in the usage rate of public transportation systems.

Nevertheless, the introduction of an integrated fare system has been met with several challenges. In certain nations, formal public transportation services might sometimes be unreliable, inconvenient, or even dangerous. As a result, many passengers are more inclined to utilize alternative modes of transportation provided by private companies. During the planning phase of the transition project, many elements of smart card systems, including all of their benefits and drawbacks for each kind of transportation, should be considered to ensure that the system is adopted in the most effective manner possible. Because of the nature of this kind of transition, it brings about contradictory goals. Because of this, the current problem area is suitable for the application of multi-criteria decision-making (MCDM) methods since a dependable and rational decision support system is required to support authorities through the valuation of differences between the planned system and the existing one. It is essential to have access to a decision model in its own right for decision-makers to have a clear understanding of the enhancements that may be accomplished by switching to a smart system. As a consequence of this, the objective of this chapter is to provide an MCDM framework that is both efficient and accurate in order to assess and compare the performance of various fare systems.

8.2 Methodology

In this section, a methodology is presented to solve the problem of analyzing and evaluating smart card systems for public transportation. Also, the methodology is presented under an intuitionistic fuzzy environment. The methodology used consists of two MCDM methods, namely, the intuitionistic fuzzy CRiteria Importance through Intercriteria Correlation (IF-CRITIC) method and the intuitionistic fuzzy Preference Ranking Organization Method for Enrichment Evaluation II (IF-PROMETHEE II) method. The methodology used is performed under an intuitionistic fuzzy environment and using intuitionistic fuzzy numbers (IFNs). The methodology is divided into three stages. The first stage expresses the collection of data and the identification of final alternatives and evaluation criteria. The second stage is the stage of determining the priorities and weights of the criteria used in evaluating the selected alternatives using the IF-CRITIC method. The third stage is the stage of ranking the available alternatives according to their criteria using the IF-PROMETHEE II method. Figure 8.1 shows the steps of the methodology used to analyze and evaluate smart card systems for public transportation. Also, we provide a brief overview of the methods used in the methodology used. This section is divided into several parts as follows.

8.2.1 PROMETHEE Method

The PROMETHEE approach of MCDM is one that is well known and widely used. Brans was the one who first devised this methodology, and Vincke and Brans went on to refine it further (Brans and Vincke 1985). When compared to other multi-criteria techniques, the PROMETHEE ranking strategy is quite straightforward (Brans, Vincke, and Mareschal 1986). PROMETHEE is an outranking approach that is a methodology that uses binary relations to compare alternatives via weak preference

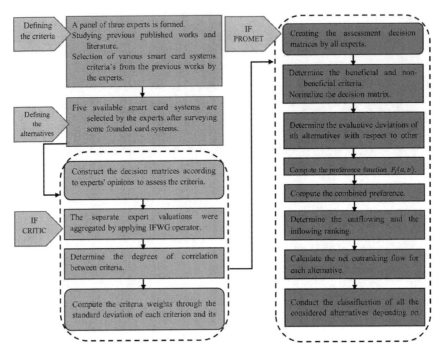

FIGURE 8.1
General illustration of the problem.

(Agrawal 2021). Examples of phrases that are used in PROMETHEE are "as least as" and "as excellent as." In order to successfully implement PROMETHEE, two different kinds of information are required. First are the weights, and then, there is the preference function of the decision-maker (Chai and Ngai 2020). The two variants of PROMETHEE that see the most application in the realm of research are PROMETHEE I and PROMETHEE II. On the contrary, PROMETHEE I only gives a partial ranking of the decision alternatives, whereas PROMETHEE II gives a full ranking of all of the options. In the course of this investigation, PROMETHEE II was designed to obtain credible outcomes by determining an exhaustive ranking of alternatives offered by providers. The PROMETHEE II approach is appropriate for addressing the MCDM issue (Goswami and Behera 2021).

8.2.2 Mathematical Model

In this part, the steps of the methodology used are presented, starting from the steps of data collection to the steps of determining the weights of the criteria and arranging the alternatives.

Step 1: The case is to be studied from all dimensions, and the points affecting understanding the problem are determined. After that, the criteria affecting the problem are identified to evaluate smart card systems for public transport and choose the best one. Also, it was agreed with some experts for the authors to participate in the compilation of data and advice on necessary matters. In this regard, some standards have been adopted for selecting experts, such as academic degrees and years of experience.

Step 2: Define the alternatives and associated criteria to establish the approach of the application. The set $SMS_i = \{SMS_1, SMS_2, ..., SMS_m\}$ having $i=1, 2 ... m$ alternatives is measured by n decision criteria of $C_j = \{C_1, C_2, ..., C_n\}$, with $j=1, 2, ..., n$. Let $w = (w_1, w_2, ..., w_n)$ be the vector set used for defining the criteria weights, $w_j > 0$ and $\sum_{j=1}^{n} w_j = 1$. Experts are presented with $E_1, E_2,..., E_K$, who are experts in their fields to make judgments.

Step 3: After studying the problem and identifying its most important dimensions, all the main and sub-aspects of the problem are organized, including the main objective, the criteria used, and the selected alternatives, in a hierarchical form to show the problem in an organized and audited form.

Step 4: Some linguistic terms are provided to help the experts participate in expressing their opinions for the evaluation of the criteria, as in Table 8.1. Also, some linguistic terms are provided to help evaluate and arrange the alternatives, as in Table 8.2.

Step 5: Build the decision matrices rendering to experts' estimations (E_k) to appraise the criteria by each expert by utilizing linguistic terms created in Table 8.1 and then by using IFNs as exhibited in Table 8.3.

Step 6: Combine the separate expert valuations on criteria weights by applying intuitionistic fuzzy weighted geometric (IFWG) presented in Eq. (8.1) (Xu and Yager 2006) as exhibited in Table 8.4. At this point, $(w_j)_{1 \times n}$ presents IFNs weight of jth criteria.

TABLE 8.1

Linguistic Terms and Their Equivalent IFNs for Assessing Factors

		IFNs	
Linguistic Terms	**Abbreviations**	u	ϑ
Absolutely low	ABL	0.10	0.85
Very low	VLO	0.20	0.75
Low	LOW	0.30	0.65
Medium low	MEL	0.40	0.55
Approximately	APP	0.50	0.45
Medium high	MEH	0.60	0.35
High	HIG	0.70	0.25
Very high	VEH	0.80	0.15
Absolutely high	ABH	0.90	0.05

TABLE 8.2

Linguistic Terms and Their Equivalent IFNs for Rating Alternatives

Linguistic Terms	Abbreviations	IFNs	
		u	ϑ
Absolutely low value	ABV	0.10	0.85
Very low value	VLV	0.20	0.75
Low value	LOV	0.30	0.65
Medium low value	MLV	0.40	0.55
Approximate value	APV	0.50	0.45
Medium high value	MHV	0.60	0.35
High value	HIV	0.70	0.25
Very high value	VEV	0.80	0.15
Absolutely high value	AHV	0.90	0.05

TABLE 8.3

Decision Matrix Based on IFNs According to Expert E_k

Criteria	Alternatives			
	SMS_1	SMS_2	...	SMS_m
C_1	$\left[u_{11_k}{}^C, \vartheta_{11_k}{}^C\right]$	$\left[u_{12_k}{}^C, \vartheta_{12_k}{}^C\right]$	...	$\left[u_{1m_k}{}^C, \vartheta_{1m_k}{}^C\right]$
C_2	$\left[u_{21_k}{}^C, \vartheta_{21_k}{}^C\right]$	$\left[u_{22_k}{}^C, \vartheta_{22_k}{}^C\right]$	...	$\left[u_{2m_k}{}^C, \vartheta_{2m_k}{}^C\right]$
$\vdots$	$\vdots$	$\vdots$	$\ddots$	$\vdots$
C_n	$\left[u_{n1_k}{}^C, \vartheta_{n1_k}{}^C\right]$	$\left[u_{32_k}{}^C, \vartheta_{32_k}{}^C\right]$	...	$\left[u_{nm_k}{}^C, \vartheta_{nm_k}{}^C\right]$

TABLE 8.4

Combined Decision Matrix Based on IFNs

Criteria	Alternatives			
	SMS_1	SMS_2	...	SMS_m
C_1	$\left[u_{11}{}^C, \vartheta_{11}{}^C\right]$	$\left[u_{12}{}^C, \vartheta_{12}{}^C\right]$	...	$\left[u_{1m}{}^C, \vartheta_{1m}{}^C\right]$
C_2	$\left[u_{21}{}^C, \vartheta_{21}{}^C\right]$	$\left[u_{22}{}^C, \vartheta_{22}{}^C\right]$	...	$\left[u_{2m}{}^C, \vartheta_{2m}{}^C\right]$
$\vdots$	$\vdots$	$\vdots$	$\ddots$	$\vdots$
C_n	$\left[u_{n1}{}^C, \vartheta_{n1}{}^C\right]$	$\left[u_{32}{}^C, \vartheta_{32}{}^C\right]$	...	$\left[u_{nm}{}^C, \vartheta_{nm}{}^C\right]$

$$IFWG\left(\widetilde{SMS}_1, \widetilde{SMS}_2, \ldots, \widetilde{SMS}_n\right) = \left(\prod_{i=1}^{n} u_{\overline{SMS}_i}{}^{w_i}, \left(1 - \prod_{i=1}^{n}\left(1 - \vartheta_{\overline{SMS}_i}\right)^{w_i}\right)\right) \quad (8.1)$$

Step 7: Describe the degrees of correlation between criteria. For this, the decision matrix is predominantly defuzzified by utilizing Eqs. (8.2) and

(8.3) by considering the criteria nature, which can be the advantage and non-advantage categories. Then, the standard deviation for each criterion is calculated by utilizing Eq. (8.4), and the correlation relationship of each criterion with other criteria is determined by applying Eq. (8.5).

$$
\phi_{ij} = \frac{1 - \dfrac{\mathcal{U}_{ij} \times \mathcal{U}_{-} + \vartheta_{ij} \times \vartheta_{-} + \pi_{ij} \times \pi_{-}}{\mathcal{U}_{ij}^{2} \vee \mathcal{U}_{-}^{2} + \vartheta_{ij}^{2} \vee \vartheta_{-}^{2} + \pi_{ij}^{2} \vee \pi_{-}^{2}}}{1 - \dfrac{\mathcal{U}_{-} \times \mathcal{U}_{+} + \vartheta_{-} \times \vartheta_{+} + \pi_{-} \times \pi_{+}}{\mathcal{U}_{-}^{2} \vee \mathcal{U}_{+}^{2} + \vartheta_{-}^{2} \vee \vartheta_{+}^{2} + \pi_{-}^{2} \vee \pi_{+}^{2}}},
\tag{8.2}
$$

$i = 1, 2, \dots, m; \; j = 1, 2, \dots, n$, for positive attributes

$$
\phi_{ij} = \frac{1 - \dfrac{\mathcal{U}_{ij} \times \mathcal{U}_{+} + \vartheta_{ij} \times \vartheta_{+} + \pi_{ij} \times \pi_{+}}{\mathcal{U}_{ij}^{2} \vee \mathcal{U}_{+}^{2} + \vartheta_{ij}^{2} \vee \vartheta_{+}^{2} + \pi_{ij}^{2} \vee \pi_{+}^{2}}}{1 - \dfrac{\mathcal{U}_{-} \times \mathcal{U}_{+} + \vartheta_{-} \times \vartheta_{+} + \pi_{-} \times \pi_{+}}{\mathcal{U}_{-}^{2} \vee \mathcal{U}_{+}^{2} + \vartheta_{-}^{2} \vee \vartheta_{+}^{2} + \pi_{-}^{2} \vee \pi_{+}^{2}}},
\tag{8.3}
$$

$i = 1, 2, \dots, m; \; j = 1, 2, \dots, n$, for negative attributes

$$
\sigma_{j} = \sqrt{\frac{\sum_{i=1}^{m}\left(\phi_{ij} - \bar{\phi}_{j}\right)^{2}}{m}}, \; j = 1, 2, \dots, n.
\tag{8.4}
$$

$$
r_{jk} = \frac{\sum_{i=1}^{m}\left(\phi_{ij} - \bar{\phi}_{j}\right)\left(\phi_{ik} - \bar{\phi}_{k}\right)}{\sqrt{\sum_{i=1}^{m}\left(\phi_{ij} - \bar{\phi}_{j}\right)^{2} \sum_{i=1}^{m}\left(\phi_{ik} - \bar{\phi}_{k}\right)^{2}}}, \; j = 1, 2 \dots n; \, k = 1, 2 \dots n.
\tag{8.5}
$$

where n_{-}, n_{+}, ϑ_{-}, and ϑ_{+} are the lowest and highest grades of membership and non-membership, respectively.

Step 8: Calculate the criterion weights through the standard deviation of each criterion and its correlation between other criteria by utilizing Eq. (8.6). Then, the objective weights of criteria were standardized, and the weight of each criterion is computed by applying Eq. (8.7).

$$
C_{j} = \sigma_{j} \sum_{k=1}^{n}\left(1 - r_{jk}\right), j = 1, 2 \dots n.
\tag{8.6}
$$

$$
w_{j} = \frac{C_{j}}{\sum_{j=1}^{n} C_{j}}
\tag{8.7}
$$

Step 9: Construct the appraisal judgment matrix by each expert specifically (E_k) between the identified criteria and the selected alternatives to analyze and evaluate the smart card systems by applying the linguistic terms presented in Table 8.2 and then applying the IFNs in Table 8.2 according to Table 8.5.

Step 10: Collect the appraisal judgment matrix by each expert specifically (E_k) between the identified criteria and the selected alternatives to analyze and evaluate the smart card systems into a single matrix by applying IFWG as presented in Eq. (8.1) as exhibited in Table 8.6.

Step 11: Defuzzification of the intuitionistic fuzzy combined appraisal judgment matrix into the crisp combined decision matrix by removing the IFNs by applying Eq. (8.8) according to Table 8.7. Also, Eq. (8.8) was mentioned in detail in the previous chapter. For better understanding, readers are advised to read Chapter 7, particularly the explanation corresponding to Eq. (7.5).

$$\Im\left(\widetilde{SMS}\right) = \mathcal{U}_{\widetilde{SMS}} + \left(\frac{\mathcal{U}_{\widetilde{SMS}}\vartheta_{\widetilde{SMS}}e^{\left(1-\mathcal{U}_{\widetilde{SMS}}-\vartheta_{\widetilde{SMS}}\right)}}{2}\right)^2, \text{ where } \Im\left(\widetilde{SMS}\right) \in [0,1] \quad (8.8)$$

TABLE 8.5

Decision Matrix for Substitutes in Terms of Criteria Based on IFNs

Criteria	SMS$_1$	SMS$_2$	...	SMS$_m$
		Alternatives		
C_1	$\left[\mathcal{U}_{11_k}{}^C, \vartheta_{11_k}{}^C\right]$	$\left[\mathcal{U}_{12_k}{}^C, \vartheta_{12_k}{}^C\right]$	...	$\left[\mathcal{U}_{1m_k}{}^C, \vartheta_{1m_k}{}^C\right]$
C_2	$\left[\mathcal{U}_{21_k}{}^C, \vartheta_{21_k}{}^C\right]$	$\left[\mathcal{U}_{22_k}{}^C, \vartheta_{22_k}{}^C\right]$	...	$\left[\mathcal{U}_{2m_k}{}^C, \vartheta_{2m_k}{}^C\right]$
⋮	⋮	⋮	⋱	⋮
C_n	$\left[\mathcal{U}_{n1_k}{}^C, \vartheta_{n1_k}{}^C\right]$	$\left[\mathcal{U}_{32_k}{}^C, \vartheta_{32_k}{}^C\right]$	...	$\left[\mathcal{U}_{nm_k}{}^C, \vartheta_{nm_k}{}^C\right]$

TABLE 8.6

Combined Decision Matrix for Substitutes in Terms of Criteria Based on IFNs

Criteria	SMS$_1$	SMS$_2$	...	SMS$_m$
		Alternatives		
C_1	$\left[\mathcal{U}_{11}{}^C, \vartheta_{11}{}^C\right]$	$\left[\mathcal{U}_{12}{}^C, \vartheta_{12}{}^C\right]$	...	$\left[\mathcal{U}_{1m}{}^C, \vartheta_{1m}{}^C\right]$
C_2	$\left[\mathcal{U}_{21}{}^C, \vartheta_{21}{}^C\right]$	$\left[\mathcal{U}_{22}{}^C, \vartheta_{22}{}^C\right]$	...	$\left[\mathcal{U}_{2m}{}^C, \vartheta_{2m}{}^C\right]$
⋮	⋮	⋮	⋱	⋮
C_n	$\left[\mathcal{U}_{n1}{}^C, \vartheta_{n1}{}^C\right]$	$\left[\mathcal{U}_{32}{}^C, \vartheta_{32}{}^C\right]$	...	$\left[\mathcal{U}_{nm}{}^C, \vartheta_{nm}{}^C\right]$

TABLE 8.7

Defuzzified Decision Matrix for Alternatives in Terms of Sub-Factors

Criteria	SMS$_1$	SMS$_2$	...	SMS$_m$
		Alternatives		
C_1	$x_{11} = [\mathcal{U}_{11}{}^C, \vartheta_{11}{}^C]$	$x_{12} = [\mathcal{U}_{12}{}^C, \vartheta_{12}{}^C]$	...	$x_{1m} = [\mathcal{U}_{1m}{}^C, \vartheta_{1m}{}^C]$
C_2	$x_{21} = [\mathcal{U}_{21}{}^C, \vartheta_{21}{}^C]$	$x_{22} = [\mathcal{U}_{22}{}^C, \vartheta_{22}{}^C]$	...	$x_{2m} = [\mathcal{U}_{2m}{}^C, \vartheta_{2m}{}^C]$
$\vdots$	$\vdots$	$\vdots$	$\ddots$	$\vdots$
C_n	$x_{n1} = [\mathcal{U}_{n1}{}^C, \vartheta_{n1}{}^C]$	$x_{32} = [\mathcal{U}_{32}{}^C, \vartheta_{32}{}^C]$	...	$x_{nm} = [\mathcal{U}_{nm}{}^C, \vartheta_{nm}{}^C]$

Step 12: Compute the normalized decision matrix according to Eq. (8.9) for advantageous criteria and Eq. (8.10) for non-advantageous criteria.

$$X_{ij} = \frac{[x_{ij} - \text{Min}(x_{ij})]}{[\text{max}(x_{ij}) - \text{Min}(x_{ij})]} \tag{8.9}$$

$$X_{ij} = \frac{[\text{max}(x_{ij}) - x_{ij}]}{[\text{max}(x_{ij}) - \text{Min}(x_{ij})]} \tag{8.10}$$

Step 13: Compute the evaluative dissimilarities of ith substitute for other substitutes.

Step 14: Calculate the preference function for the normalized decision matrix $P_j(a, b)$ according to Eqs. (8.11) and (8.12).

$$P_j(a, b) = 0 \text{ if } R_{aj} \leq R_{bj} \tag{8.11}$$

$$P_j(a, b) = (R_{aj} - R_{bj}) \text{ if } R_{aj} > R_{bj} \tag{8.12}$$

Step 15: Compute the weighted preference matrix according to Eq. (8.13) and the combined preference function according to Eq. (8.14).

$$w_j p_j(a, b) \tag{8.13}$$

$$\pi(a,b) = \frac{\sum_{j=1}^{n} w_j p_j(a, b)}{\sum_{j=1}^{n} w_j}, \text{ where } p_j(a,b) \text{ is the preference function} \tag{8.14}$$

Step 16: Calculate the outflowing ranking (leaving or optimistic) for ith alternative according to Eq. (8.15) and the inflowing ranking (entering or pessimistic) for ith alternative according to Eq. (8.16).

$$\varphi^+ = \frac{1}{M-1} \sum_{b=1}^{m} \pi(a,b), \quad a \neq b; \tag{8.15}$$

$$\varphi^- = \frac{1}{M-1} \sum_{b=1}^{m} \pi(b,a), \quad a \neq b; \tag{8.16}$$

where m refers to the number of substitutes.

Step 17: Calculate the net outranking flow for each substitute according to Eq. (8.17). Then, classify the substitutes in descending order of the values of $\varphi(SMS)$.

$$\varphi(SMS) = \varphi^+(SMS) - \varphi^-(SMS) \tag{8.17}$$

8.3 Model Implementation

The purpose of this chapter is to differentiate and verify some of the benefits of smart card systems that have been described in the literature. This will be accomplished by accurately comparing the old fare and smart card systems using opposing criteria. In light of this, the MCDM analysis takes into consideration not only the conventional system but also four other smart card systems, each of which has a distinct set of capabilities. In order to conduct an objective analysis, the technological parameters of the contactless smart cards have been standardized.

Step 1: The problem was studied, and the main objective was determined, which is the analysis and evaluation of smart card systems, in addition to determining the main criteria that affect the selection of the best smart card system. Also, four experts agreed to participate in data collection, and an effective weight for each expert was determined as 0.2, 0.3, 0.3, and 0.2.

Step 2: A set of five alternatives have been identified to be used in the evaluation process, including the traditional fare system and four smart card systems, namely, traditional fare system, smart card system 1, smart card system 2, smart card system 3, and smart card system 4 which are referred to by the following abbreviations SMS_1, SMS_2, SMS_1, SMS_2, and SMS_1, respectively. Also, a set of criteria were defined to evaluate the selected alternatives, as mentioned in Table 8.8.

TABLE 8.8

Description of Criteria

Criteria	Description
Transaction time, RRC_1	The amount of time, in seconds that an individual user spends interacting with a system.
Dwell time, DTC_2	The amount of time, measured in seconds, that a public transportation vehicle's door is left open at a certain stop.
On-time performance, OTC_3	A metric that is used to measure the capacity of different transport providers to arrive punctually at their respective destinations. It is a metric that may assess the presence of real-time information delivered to consumers and the correctness of that information.
Ridership, RSC_4	The total number of people using a certain mode of transportation at any given time. It gauges how easily the service may be used.
Service reliability, SRC_5	This system performance indicator calculates how likely it is that the system will fulfill a set of predetermined performance requirements.
Service coverage, SOC_6	The percentage of persons that may potentially benefit from the services that are being provided. This measure is connected to the number of different implementations of the system that are available.
Safety, STC_7	Examines how individuals feel about the many different payment methods, considering the importance of data and privacy protections for personal information and financial transactions.
Security, SEC_8	Assesses the degree of security mechanisms that have been put on infrastructure, as well as the efficiency with which these systems function.
Transfer time/ delay, TTC_9	The average amount of time, measured in minutes, is spent by riders of public transportation, which make their journey utilizing a combination of more than one method of transit and/or route.
Transit time reliability, TRC_{10}	The accuracy of the estimated travel time is calculated based on the frequency distribution of the departure and arrival timings.

Step 3: Based on the aspects of the problem, its goal, its criteria, and its alternatives, a hierarchical form of the problem was built as in Figure 8.2.

Step 4: Some linguistic terms were provided to help experts in evaluating the criteria as in Table 8.1. Also, some linguistic terms were provided to help experts in arranging the alternatives as in Table 8.2.

Step 5: The decision matrices rendering to experts' estimations (E_4) were created to appraise the criteria by each expert by utilizing linguistic terms created in Table 8.1 as exhibited in Table 8.9, and then by using IFNs according to Table 8.3 as presented in Table 8.10.

Step 6: The separate expert valuations on criteria were combined by applying IFWG operator in Eq. (8.1) according to Table 8.4 as presented in Table 8.11.

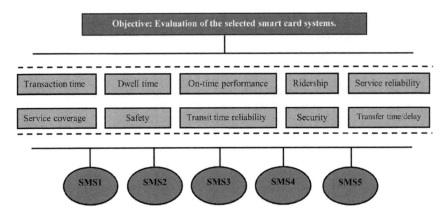

FIGURE 8.2

Hierarchical shape of the aspects of the problem.

TABLE 8.9

Decision Matrices Are Based on the Main Criteria for Each Expert Using Linguistic Terms

		RRC₁	DTC₂	OTC₃	RSC₄	SRC₅	SOC₆	STC₇	SEC₈	TTC₉	TRC₁₀
	SMS₁	ABL	VLO	APP	ABL	VEH	MEH	MEL	MEL	VLO	APP
	SMS₂	MEL	ABH	MEH	MEH	MEL	MEH	VEH	MEL	ABL	HIG
Expert₁	SMS₃	HIG	LOW	MEL	ABH	HIG	ABL	VLO	VEH	VEH	VLO
	SMS₄	MEL	HIG	ABL	ABL	ABH	LOW	APP	ABH	APP	VLO
	SMS₅	HIG	HIG	MEH	MEH	MEL	MEH	APP	MEL	LOW	VEH
		RRC₁	DTC₂	OTC₃	RSC₄	SRC₅	SOC₆	STC₇	SEC₈	TTC₉	TRC₁₀
	SMS₁	ABL	MEL	APP	ABL	VEH	MEH	MEL	MEL	VLO	APP
	SMS₂	APP	ABH	APP	MEH	MEL	MEH	VEH	LOW	ABL	HIG
Expert₂	SMS₃	HIG	LOW	MEL	ABH	VEH	ABL	VLO	VEH	VEH	VLO
	SMS₄	MEL	HIG	ABL	VLO	ABH	LOW	APP	ABH	APP	VLO
	SMS₅	HIG	HIG	MEH	MEH	MEL	APP	APP	MEL	LOW	VEH
		RRC₁	DTC₂	OTC₃	RSC₄	SRC₅	SOC₆	STC₇	SEC₈	TTC₉	TRC₁₀
	SMS₁	ABL	HIG	APP	ABL	VEH	MEH	APP	MEL	VLO	APP
	SMS₂	MEH	ABH	APP	MEH	MEL	MEH	VEH	LOW	ABL	HIG
Expert₃	SMS₃	HIG	LOW	MEL	ABH	ABH	ABL	VLO	VEH	VEH	VLO
	SMS₄	MEL	HIG	ABL	APP	ABH	LOW	APP	ABH	APP	VLO
	SMS₅	HIG	HIG	MEH	MEH	MEL	MEH	APP	MEL	LOW	VEH
		RRC₁	DTC₂	OTC₃	RSC₄	SRC₅	SOC₆	STC₇	SEC₈	TTC₉	TRC₁₀
	SMS₁	ABL	VLO	APP	ABL	VEH	MEH	MEL	MEL	VLO	APP
	SMS₂	LOW	ABH	HIG	MEH	MEL	MEH	VEH	MEL	ABL	HIG
Expert₄	SMS₃	HIG	LOW	MEL	ABH	VEH	ABL	VLO	VEH	VEH	VLO
	SMS₄	MEL	HIG	ABL	VLO	ABH	LOW	APP	ABH	APP	VLO
	SMS₅	HIG	HIG	MEH	MEH	MEL	HIG	APP	MEL	LOW	VEH

TABLE 8.10

Decision Matrices Based on Main Criteria for Each Expert Using IFNs

		RRC_1	DTC_2	OTC_3	RTC_4	SRC_5	SOC_6	STC_7	SEC_8	TTC_9	TRC_{10}
$Expert_1$	SMS_1	[0.10, 0.85]	[0.20, 0.75]	[0.50, 0.45]	[0.10, 0.85]	[0.80, 0.15]	[0.60, 0.35]	[0.40, 0.55]	[0.40, 0.55]	[0.20, 0.75]	[0.50, 0.45]
	SMS_2	[0.40, 0.55]	[0.90, 0.05]	[0.60, 0.35]	[0.60, 0.35]	[0.40, 0.55]	[0.60, 0.35]	[0.80, 0.15]	[0.40, 0.55]	[0.10, 0.85]	[0.70, 0.25]
	SMS_3	[0.70, 0.25]	[0.30, 0.65]	[0.40, 0.55]	[0.90, 0.05]	[0.70, 0.25]	[0.10, 0.85]	[0.20, 0.75]	[0.80, 0.15]	[0.80, 0.15]	[0.20, 0.75]
	SMS_4	[0.40, 0.55]	[0.70, 0.25]	[0.10, 0.85]	[0.10, 0.85]	[0.90, 0.05]	[0.30, 0.65]	[0.50, 0.45]	[0.90, 0.05]	[0.50, 0.45]	[0.20, 0.75]
	SMS_5	[0.70, 0.25]	[0.70, 0.25]	[0.60, 0.35]	[0.60, 0.35]	[0.40, 0.55]	[0.60, 0.35]	[0.50, 0.45]	[0.40, 0.55]	[0.30, 0.65]	[0.80, 0.15]
$Expert_2$	SMS_1	[0.10, 0.85]	[0.40, 0.55]	[0.50, 0.45]	[0.10, 0.85]	[0.80, 0.15]	[0.60, 0.35]	[0.40, 0.55]	[0.40, 0.55]	[0.20, 0.75]	[0.50, 0.45]
	SMS_2	[0.50, 0.45]	[0.90, 0.05]	[0.50, 0.45]	[0.60, 0.35]	[0.40, 0.55]	[0.60, 0.35]	[0.80, 0.15]	[0.30, 0.65]	[0.10, 0.85]	[0.70, 0.25]
	SMS_3	[0.70, 0.25]	[0.30, 0.65]	[0.40, 0.55]	[0.90, 0.05]	[0.80, 0.15]	[0.10, 0.85]	[0.20, 0.75]	[0.80, 0.15]	[0.80, 0.15]	[0.20, 0.75]
	SMS_4	[0.40, 0.55]	[0.70, 0.25]	[0.10, 0.85]	[0.20, 0.75]	[0.90, 0.05]	[0.30, 0.65]	[0.50, 0.45]	[0.90, 0.05]	[0.50, 0.45]	[0.20, 0.75]
	SMS_5	[0.70, 0.25]	[0.70, 0.25]	[0.60, 0.35]	[0.60, 0.35]	[0.40, 0.55]	[0.50, 0.45]	[0.50, 0.45]	[0.40, 0.55]	[0.30, 0.65]	[0.80, 0.15]
$Expert_4$	SMS_1	[0.10, 0.85]	[0.70, 0.25]	[0.50, 0.45]	[0.10, 0.85]	[0.80, 0.15]	[0.60, 0.35]	[0.50, 0.45]	[0.40, 0.55]	[0.20, 0.75]	[0.50, 0.45]
	SMS_2	[0.60, 0.35]	[0.90, 0.05]	[0.50, 0.45]	[0.60, 0.35]	[0.40, 0.55]	[0.60, 0.35]	[0.80, 0.15]	[0.30, 0.65]	[0.10, 0.85]	[0.70, 0.25]
	SMS_3	[0.70, 0.25]	[0.30, 0.65]	[0.40, 0.55]	[0.90, 0.05]	[0.90, 0.05]	[0.10, 0.85]	[0.20, 0.75]	[0.80, 0.15]	[0.80, 0.15]	[0.20, 0.75]
	SMS_4	[0.40, 0.55]	[0.70, 0.25]	[0.10, 0.85]	[0.50, 0.45]	[0.90, 0.05]	[0.30, 0.65]	[0.50, 0.45]	[0.90, 0.05]	[0.50, 0.45]	[0.20, 0.75]
	SMS_5	[0.70, 0.25]	[0.70, 0.25]	[0.60, 0.35]	[0.60, 0.35]	[0.40, 0.55]	[0.60, 0.35]	[0.50, 0.45]	[0.40, 0.55]	[0.30, 0.65]	[0.80, 0.15]
$Expert_4$	SMS_1	[0.10, 0.85]	[0.20, 0.75]	[0.50, 0.45]	[0.10, 0.85]	[0.80, 0.15]	[0.60, 0.35]	[0.40, 0.55]	[0.40, 0.55]	[0.20, 0.75]	[0.50, 0.45]
	SMS_2	[0.30, 0.65]	[0.90, 0.05]	[0.70, 0.25]	[0.60, 0.35]	[0.40, 0.55]	[0.60, 0.35]	[0.80, 0.15]	[0.40, 0.55]	[0.10, 0.85]	[0.70, 0.25]
	SMS_3	[0.70, 0.25]	[0.30, 0.65]	[0.40, 0.55]	[0.90, 0.05]	[0.80, 0.15]	[0.10, 0.85]	[0.20, 0.75]	[0.80, 0.15]	[0.80, 0.15]	[0.20, 0.75]
	SMS_4	[0.40, 0.55]	[0.70, 0.25]	[0.10, 0.85]	[0.20, 0.75]	[0.90, 0.05]	[0.30, 0.65]	[0.50, 0.45]	[0.90, 0.05]	[0.50, 0.45]	[0.20, 0.75]
	SMS_5	[0.70, 0.25]	[0.70, 0.25]	[0.60, 0.35]	[0.60, 0.35]	[0.40, 0.55]	[0.70, 0.25]	[0.50, 0.45]	[0.40, 0.55]	[0.30, 0.65]	[0.80, 0.15]

TABLE 8.11

Aggregated Decision Matrix Based on Main Criteria by All Experts

		RRC$_1$	DTC$_2$	OTC$_3$	RSC$_4$	SRC$_5$
Experts	SMS$_1$	[0.10, 0.85]	[0.36, 0.68]	[0.50, 0.45]	[0.10, 0.85]	[0.80, 0.15]
	SMS$_2$	[0.46, 0.49]	[0.90, 0.05]	[0.55, 0.37]	[0.60, 0.35]	[0.40, 0.55]
	SMS$_3$	[0.70, 0.25]	[0.30, 0.65]	[0.40, 0.55]	[0.90, 0.05]	[0.81, 0.18]
	SMS$_4$	[0.40, 0.55]	[0.70, 0.25]	[0.10, 0.85]	[0.23, 0.79]	[0.90, 0.05]
	SMS$_5$	[0.70, 0.25]	[0.70, 0.25]	[0.60, 0.35]	[0.60, 0.35]	[0.40, 0.55]
		SOC$_6$	STC$_7$	SEC$_8$	TTC$_9$	TRC$_{10}$
Experts	SMS$_1$	[0.60, 0.35]	[0.43, 0.55]	[0.40, 0.55]	[0.20, 0.75]	[0.50, 0.45]
	SMS$_2$	[0.60, 0.35]	[0.80, 0.15]	[0.34, 0.59]	[0.10, 0.85]	[0.70, 0.25]
	SMS$_3$	[0.10, 0.85]	[0.20, 0.75]	[0.80, 0.15]	[0.80, 0.15]	[0.20, 0.75]
	SMS$_4$	[0.30, 0.65]	[0.50, 0.45]	[0.90, 0.05]	[0.50, 0.45]	[0.20, 0.75]
	SMS$_5$	[0.59, 0.37]	[0.50, 0.45]	[0.40, 0.55]	[0.30, 0.65]	[0.80, 0.15]

TABLE 8.12

Normalized Decision Matrix Based on Main Criteria by All Experts

	RRC$_1$	DTC$_2$	OTC$_3$	RSC$_4$	SRC$_5$	SOC$_6$	STC$_7$	SEC$_8$	TTC$_9$	TRC$_{10}$
SMS$_1$	0.000	0.107	0.808	0.000	0.802	1.000	0.399	0.113	0.148	0.515
SMS$_2$	0.613	1.000	0.902	0.639	0.000	1.000	1.000	0.000	0.000	0.840
SMS$_3$	1.000	0.000	0.610	1.000	0.825	0.000	0.000	0.824	1.000	0.000
SMS$_4$	0.513	0.674	0.000	0.170	1.000	0.409	0.515	1.000	0.587	0.000
SMS$_5$	1.000	0.674	1.000	0.639	0.000	0.982	0.515	0.113	0.297	1.000
Standard deviation	0.414	0.423	0.398	0.402	0.486	0.456	0.357	0.465	0.396	0.464

Step 7: The standard deviation for the main criteria was calculated by utilizing Eq. (8.4) as presented in Table 8.12, and the correlation relationship of each criterion with other criteria was determined by applying Eq. (8.5) as exhibited in Table 8.12.

Step 8: The main criteria weights were calculated through the standard deviation of each criterion and its correlation among other criteria by applying Eq. (8.6). Then, the objective weights of the main criteria were normalized, and the weight of each criterion was calculated by applying Eq. (8.7) as presented in Table 8.13 and charted in Figure 8.3.

Step 9: The appraisal judgment matrix by each expert specifically (E_k) between the identified criteria and the selected alternatives was constructed to analyze and evaluate the smart card systems by applying

TABLE 8.13

Correlation Coefficient of the Relationship between the Main Criteria

	RRC_1	DTC_2	OTC_3	RSC_4	SRC_5	SOC_6	STC_7	SEC_8	TTC_9	TRC_{10}	Weights
RRC_1	1.00	0.14	0.13	0.88	−0.38	−0.42	−0.21	0.22	0.50	0.06	0.0828
DTC_2	0.14	1.00	0.05	−0.03	−0.65	0.49	0.90	−0.31	−0.58	0.53	0.0885
OTC_3	0.13	0.05	1.00	0.31	−0.77	0.61	0.22	−0.88	−0.51	0.83	0.0889
RSC_4	0.88	−0.03	0.31	1.00	−0.37	−0.44	−0.23	0.08	0.46	0.03	0.0827
SRC_5	−0.38	−0.65	−0.77	−0.37	1.00	−0.64	−0.64	0.77	0.60	−0.91	0.1443
SOC_6	−0.42	0.49	0.61	−0.44	−0.64	1.00	0.72	−0.89	−0.97	0.87	0.1093
STC_7	−0.21	0.90	0.22	−0.23	−0.64	0.72	1.00	−0.57	−0.84	0.63	0.0798
SEC_8	0.22	−0.31	−0.88	0.08	0.77	−0.89	−0.57	1.00	0.85	−0.92	0.1228
TTC_9	0.50	−0.58	−0.51	0.46	0.60	−0.97	−0.84	0.85	1.00	−0.79	0.1009
TRC_{10}	0.06	0.53	0.83	0.03	−0.91	0.87	0.63	−0.92	−0.79	1.00	0.1000

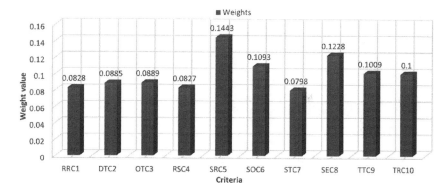

FIGURE 8.3
Final weights of criteria.

the linguistic terms in Table 8.2 according to Table 8.5 as presented in Table 8.14.

Step 10: The appraisal judgment matrix by each expert specifically (E_k) between the identified criteria and the selected alternatives was combined to analyze and evaluate the smart card systems into a single matrix by applying IFWG as in Eq. (8.1) according to Table 8.6 as exhibited in Table 8.15.

Step 11: The intuitionistic fuzzy combined appraisal judgment matrix was defuzzified by applying Eq. (8.8) for removing the IFNs according to Table 8.7, as presented in Table 8.16.

Step 12: The standardized decision matrix was calculated for advantageous criteria according to Eq. (8.9) and for non-advantageous criteria

TABLE 8.14

Decision Matrices of Five Smart Card Systems According to Criteria Using Linguistic Terms

		RRC$_1$	DTC$_2$	OTC$_3$	RSC$_4$	SRC$_5$	SOC$_6$	STC$_7$	SEC$_8$	TTC$_9$	TRC$_{10}$
	SMS$_1$	ABL	VLO	APP	ABL	VEH	MEH	MEL	MEL	VLO	APP
	SMS$_2$	MEL	ABH	MEH	MEH	MEL	MEH	VEH	MEL	ABL	HIG
Expert$_1$	SMS$_3$	HIG	LOW	MEL	ABH	HIG	ABL	VLO	VEH	VEH	VLO
	SMS$_4$	MEL	HIG	ABL	ABL	ABH	LOW	APP	ABH	APP	VLO
	SMS$_5$	HIG	HIG	MEH	MEH	MEL	MEH	APP	MEL	LOW	VEH
		RRC$_1$	DTC$_2$	OTC$_3$	RSC$_4$	SRC$_5$	SOC$_6$	STC$_7$	SEC$_8$	TTC$_9$	TRC$_{10}$
	SMS$_1$	ABL	MEL	APP	ABL	VEH	MEH	MEL	MEL	VLO	APP
	SMS$_2$	APP	ABH	APP	MEH	MEL	MEH	VEH	LOW	ABL	HIG
Expert$_2$	SMS$_3$	HIG	LOW	MEL	ABH	VEH	ABL	VLO	VEH	VEH	VLO
	SMS$_4$	MEL	HIG	ABL	VLO	ABH	LOW	APP	ABH	APP	VLO
	SMS$_5$	HIG	HIG	MEH	MEH	MEL	APP	APP	MEL	LOW	VEH
		RRC$_1$	DTC$_2$	OTC$_3$	RSC$_4$	SRC$_5$	SOC$_6$	STC$_7$	SEC$_8$	TTC$_9$	TRC$_{10}$
	SMS$_1$	ABL	HIG	APP	ABL	VEH	MEH	APP	MEL	VLO	APP
	SMS$_2$	MEH	ABH	APP	MEH	MEL	MEH	VEH	LOW	ABL	HIG
Expert$_3$	SMS$_3$	HIG	LOW	MEL	ABH	ABH	ABL	VLO	VEH	VEH	VLO
	SMS$_4$	MEL	HIG	ABL	APP	ABH	LOW	APP	ABH	APP	VLO
	SMS$_5$	HIG	HIG	MEH	MEH	MEL	MEH	APP	MEL	LOW	VEH
		RRC$_1$	DTC$_2$	OTC$_3$	RSC$_4$	SRC$_5$	SOC$_6$	STC$_7$	SEC$_8$	TTC$_9$	TRC$_{10}$
	SMS$_1$	ABL	VLO	APP	ABL	VEH	MEH	MEL	MEL	VLO	APP
	SMS$_2$	LOW	ABH	HIG	MEH	MEL	MEH	VEH	MEL	ABL	HIG
Expert$_4$	SMS$_3$	HIG	LOW	MEL	ABH	VEH	ABL	VLO	VEH	VEH	VLO
	SMS$_4$	MEL	HIG	ABL	VLO	ABH	LOW	APP	ABH	APP	VLO
	SMS$_5$	HIG	HIG	MEH	MEH	MEL	HIG	APP	MEL	LOW	VEH

according to Eq. (8.10) as presented in Table 8.17. After that, the evaluative dissimilarities of ith substitutes for other substitutes were computed as presented in Table 8.18.

Step 13: The preference function for the standardized decision matrix was computed according to Eqs. (8.11) and (8.12), as presented in Table 8.19.

Step 14: The weighted preference function matrix was calculated by applying Eq. (8.13), and the aggregated preference function was computed by applying Eq. (8.14) as presented in Table 8.20. Also, the grouped preference matrix was computed as presented in Table 8.21.

Step 15: The outflowing ranking for ith the alternative was computed according to Eq. (8.15), and the inflowing ranking for ith the alternative was calculated according to Eq. (8.16), as presented in Table 8.22.

TABLE 8.15

Aggregated Decision Matrix of Five Smart Card Systems According to Criteria

		RRC$_1$	DTC$_2$	OTC$_3$	RSC$_4$	SRC$_5$
Experts	SMS$_1$	[0.10, 0.85]	[0.36, 0.68]	[0.50, 0.45]	[0.10, 0.85]	[0.80, 0.15]
	SMS$_2$	[0.46, 0.49]	[0.90, 0.05]	[0.55, 0.37]	[0.60, 0.35]	[0.40, 0.55]
	SMS$_3$	[0.70, 0.25]	[0.30, 0.65]	[0.40, 0.55]	[0.90, 0.05]	[0.81, 0.18]
	SMS$_4$	[0.40, 0.55]	[0.70, 0.25]	[0.10, 0.85]	[0.23, 0.79]	[0.90, 0.05]
	SMS$_5$	[0.70, 0.25]	[0.70, 0.25]	[0.60, 0.35]	[0.60, 0.35]	[0.40, 0.55]
		SOC$_6$	STC$_7$	SEC$_8$	TTC$_9$	TRC$_{10}$
Experts	SMS$_1$	[0.60, 0.35]	[0.43, 0.55]	[0.40, 0.55]	[0.20, 0.75]	[0.50, 0.45]
	SMS$_2$	[0.60, 0.35]	[0.80, 0.15]	[0.34, 0.59]	[0.10, 0.85]	[0.70, 0.25]
	SMS$_3$	[0.10, 0.85]	[0.20, 0.75]	[0.80, 0.15]	[0.80, 0.15]	[0.20, 0.75]
	SMS$_4$	[0.30, 0.65]	[0.50, 0.45]	[0.90, 0.05]	[0.50, 0.45]	[0.20, 0.75]
	SMS$_5$	[0.59, 0.37]	[0.50, 0.45]	[0.40, 0.55]	[0.30, 0.65]	[0.80, 0.15]

TABLE 8.16

Defuzzified Aggregated Decision Matrix of Five Smart Card Systems According to Criteria

	RRC$_1$	DTC$_2$	OTC$_3$	RSC$_4$	SRC$_5$	SOC$_6$	STC$_7$	SEC$_8$	TTC$_9$	TRC$_{10}$
SMS$_1$	0.1020	0.3738	0.5140	0.1020	0.8040	0.6122	0.4446	0.4134	0.2062	0.5140
SMS$_2$	0.4740	0.9006	0.5621	0.6122	0.4134	0.6122	0.8040	0.3516	0.1020	0.7085
SMS$_3$	0.7085	0.3105	0.4134	0.9006	0.8154	0.1020	0.2062	0.8040	0.8040	0.2062
SMS$_4$	0.4134	0.7085	0.1020	0.2379	0.9006	0.3105	0.5140	0.9006	0.5140	0.2062
SMS$_5$	0.7085	0.7085	0.6122	0.6122	0.4134	0.6029	0.5140	0.4134	0.3105	0.8040

TABLE 8.17

Normalized Decision Matrix of Five Smart Card Systems According to Criteria

	RRC$_1$	DTC$_2$	OTC$_3$	RSC$_4$	SRC$_5$	SOC$_6$	STC$_7$	SEC$_8$	TTC$_9$	TRC$_{10}$
SMS$_1$	0.0000	0.1073	0.8075	0.0000	0.8018	1.0000	0.3987	0.1126	0.1485	0.5149
SMS$_2$	0.6135	1.0000	0.9019	0.6389	0.0000	1.0000	1.0000	0.0000	0.0000	0.8402
SMS$_3$	1.0000	0.0000	0.6103	1.0000	0.8252	0.0000	0.0000	0.8241	1.0000	0.0000
SMS$_4$	0.5134	0.6744	0.0000	0.1702	1.0000	0.4087	0.5149	1.0000	0.5869	0.0000
SMS$_5$	1.0000	0.6744	1.0000	0.6389	0.0000	0.9818	0.5149	0.1126	0.2970	1.0000

TABLE 8.18

Evaluative Differences between Alternatives (Smart Card Systems)

Differences	RRC_1	DTC_2	OTC_3	RSC_4	SRC_5	SOC_6	STC_7	SEC_8	TTC_9	TRC_{10}
$SMS_1 - SMS_2$	-0.613	-0.893	-0.094	-0.639	0.802	0.000	-0.601	0.113	0.148	-0.325
$SMS_1 - SMS_3$	-1.000	0.107	0.197	-1.000	-0.023	1.000	0.399	-0.712	-0.852	0.515
$SMS_1 - SMS_4$	-0.513	-0.567	0.808	-0.170	-0.198	0.591	-0.116	-0.887	-0.438	0.515
$SMS_1 - SMS_5$	-1.000	-0.567	-0.192	-0.639	0.802	0.018	-0.116	0.000	-0.149	-0.485
$SMS_2 - SMS_1$	0.613	0.893	0.094	0.639	-0.802	0.000	0.601	-0.113	-0.148	0.325
$SMS_2 - SMS_3$	-0.387	1.000	0.292	-0.361	-0.825	1.000	1.000	-0.824	-1.000	0.840
$SMS_2 - SMS_4$	0.100	0.326	0.902	0.469	-1.000	0.591	0.485	-1.000	-0.587	0.840
$SMS_2 - SMS_5$	-0.387	0.326	-0.098	0.000	0.000	0.018	0.485	-0.113	-0.297	-0.160
$SMS_3 - SMS_1$	1.000	-0.107	-0.197	1.000	0.023	-1.000	-0.399	0.712	0.852	-0.515
$SMS_3 - SMS_2$	0.387	-1.000	-0.292	0.361	0.825	-1.000	-1.000	0.824	1.000	-0.840
$SMS_3 - SMS_4$	0.487	-0.674	0.610	0.830	-0.175	-0.409	-0.515	-0.176	0.413	0.000
$SMS_3 - SMS_5$	0.000	-0.674	-0.390	0.361	0.825	-0.982	-0.515	0.712	0.703	-1.000
$SMS_4 - SMS_1$	0.513	0.567	-0.808	0.170	0.198	-0.591	0.116	0.887	0.438	-0.515
$SMS_4 - SMS_2$	-0.100	-0.326	-0.902	-0.469	1.000	-0.591	-0.485	1.000	0.587	-0.840
$SMS_4 - SMS_3$	-0.487	0.674	-0.610	-0.830	0.175	0.409	0.515	0.176	-0.413	0.000
$SMS_4 - SMS_5$	-0.487	0.000	-1.000	-0.469	1.000	-0.573	0.000	0.887	0.290	-1.000
$SMS_5 - SMS_1$	1.000	0.567	0.192	0.639	-0.802	-0.018	0.116	0.000	0.149	0.485
$SMS_5 - SMS_2$	0.387	-0.326	0.098	0.000	0.000	-0.018	-0.485	0.113	0.297	0.160
$SMS_5 - SMS_3$	0.000	0.674	0.390	-0.361	-0.825	0.982	0.515	-0.712	-0.703	1.000
$SMS_5 - SMS_4$	0.487	0.000	1.000	0.469	-1.000	0.573	0.000	-0.887	-0.290	1.000

TABLE 8.19

Preference Matrix for the Five Smart Card Systems

Differences	RRC₁	DTC₂	OTC₃	RSC₄	SRC₅	SOC₆	STC₇	SEC₈	TTC₉	TRC₁₀
SMS₁ – SMS₂	0.0000	0.0000	0.0000	0.0000	0.8018	0.0000	0.0000	0.1126	0.1485	0.0000
SMS₁ – SMS₃	0.0000	0.1073	0.1972	0.0000	0.0000	1.0000	0.3987	0.0000	0.0000	0.5149
SMS₁ – SMS₄	0.0000	0.0000	0.8075	0.0000	0.0000	0.5913	0.0000	0.0000	0.0000	0.5149
SMS₁ – SMS₅	0.0000	0.0000	0.0000	0.0000	0.8018	0.0182	0.6013	0.0000	0.0000	0.0000
SMS₂ – SMS₁	0.6135	0.8927	0.0944	0.6389	0.0000	0.0000	0.6013	0.0000	0.0000	0.3253
SMS₂ – SMS₃	0.0000	1.0000	0.2916	0.0000	0.0000	1.0000	1.0000	0.0000	0.0000	0.8402
SMS₂ – SMS₄	0.1000	0.3256	0.9019	0.4687	0.0000	0.5913	0.4851	0.0000	0.0000	0.8402
SMS₂ – SMS₅	0.0000	0.3256	0.0000	0.0000	0.0000	0.0182	0.4851	0.0000	0.0000	0.0000
SMS₃ – SMS₁	1.0000	0.0000	0.0000	1.0000	0.0235	0.0000	0.0000	0.7115	0.8515	0.0000
SMS₃ – SMS₂	0.3865	0.0000	0.0000	0.3611	0.8252	0.0000	0.0000	0.8241	1.0000	0.0000
SMS₃ – SMS₄	0.4866	0.0000	0.6103	0.8298	0.0000	0.0000	0.0000	0.0000	0.4131	0.0000
SMS₃ – SMS₅	0.0000	0.0000	0.0000	0.3611	0.8252	0.0000	0.0000	0.7115	0.7030	0.0000
SMS₄ – SMS₁	0.5134	0.5671	0.0000	0.1702	0.1982	0.0000	0.1162	0.8874	0.4384	0.0000
SMS₄ – SMS₂	0.0000	0.0000	0.0000	0.0000	1.0000	0.0000	0.0000	1.0000	0.5869	0.0000
SMS₄ – SMS₃	0.0000	0.6744	0.0000	0.0000	0.1748	0.4087	0.5149	0.1759	0.0000	0.0000
SMS₄ – SMS₅	0.0000	0.0000	0.0000	0.0000	1.0000	0.0000	0.0000	0.8874	0.2899	0.0000
SMS₅ – SMS₁	1.0000	0.5671	0.1925	0.6389	0.0000	0.0000	0.1162	0.0000	0.1486	0.4851
SMS₅ – SMS₂	0.3865	0.0000	0.0981	0.0000	0.0000	0.0000	0.0000	0.1126	0.2970	0.1598
SMS₅ – SMS₃	0.0000	0.6744	0.3897	0.0000	0.0000	0.9818	0.5149	0.0000	0.0000	1.0000
SMS₅ – SMS₄	0.4866	0.0000	1.0000	0.4687	0.0000	0.5731	0.0000	0.0000	0.0000	1.0000

TABLE 8.20

Weighted Preference Matrix for the Five Smart Card Systems

Differences	RRC_1	DTC_2	OTC_3	RSC_4	SRC_5	SOC_6	STC_7	SEC_8	TTC_9	TRC_{10}	Aggregated Preference
$W_j * P(SMS_1 - SMS_2)$	0.000	0.000	0.000	0.000	0.115	0.000	0.000	0.014	0.015	0.000	0.1443
$W_j * P(SMS_1 - SMS_3)$	0.000	0.010	0.018	0.000	0.000	0.109	0.032	0.000	0.000	0.051	0.2195
$W_j * P(SMS_1 - SMS_4)$	0.000	0.000	0.072	0.000	0.000	0.064	0.000	0.000	0.000	0.051	0.1878
$W_j * P(SMS_1 - SMS_5)$	0.000	0.000	0.000	0.000	0.115	0.002	0.000	0.000	0.000	0.000	0.1174
$W_j * P(SMS_2 - SMS_1)$	0.051	0.079	0.008	0.053	0.000	0.000	0.048	0.000	0.000	0.033	0.2724
$W_j * P(SMS_2 - SMS_3)$	0.000	0.089	0.026	0.000	0.000	0.109	0.080	0.000	0.000	0.084	0.3880
$W_j * P(SMS_2 - SMS_4)$	0.008	0.029	0.080	0.039	0.000	0.064	0.039	0.000	0.000	0.084	0.3437
$W_j * P(SMS_2 - SMS_5)$	0.000	0.029	0.000	0.000	0.000	0.002	0.039	0.000	0.000	0.000	0.0698
$W_j * P(SMS_3 - SMS_1)$	0.083	0.000	0.000	0.083	0.003	0.000	0.000	0.088	0.086	0.000	0.3429
$W_j * P(SMS_3 - SMS_2)$	0.032	0.000	0.000	0.030	0.119	0.000	0.000	0.101	0.101	0.000	0.3833
$W_j * P(SMS_3 - SMS_4)$	0.040	0.000	0.054	0.069	0.000	0.000	0.000	0.000	0.042	0.000	0.2053
$W_j * P(SMS_3 - SMS_5)$	0.000	0.000	0.000	0.030	0.119	0.000	0.000	0.088	0.071	0.000	0.3073
$W_j * P(SMS_4 - SMS_1)$	0.043	0.050	0.000	0.014	0.029	0.000	0.009	0.109	0.044	0.000	0.2985
$W_j * P(SMS_4 - SMS_2)$	0.000	0.000	0.000	0.000	0.144	0.000	0.000	0.123	0.059	0.000	0.3263
$W_j * P(SMS_4 - SMS_3)$	0.000	0.060	0.000	0.000	0.025	0.045	0.041	0.022	0.000	0.000	0.1926
$W_j * P(SMS_4 - SMS_5)$	0.000	0.000	0.000	0.000	0.144	0.000	0.000	0.109	0.029	0.000	0.2824
$W_j * P(SMS_5 - SMS_1)$	0.083	0.050	0.017	0.053	0.000	0.000	0.009	0.000	0.015	0.049	0.2764
$W_j * P(SMS_5 - SMS_2)$	0.032	0.000	0.009	0.000	0.000	0.000	0.000	0.014	0.030	0.016	0.1006
$W_j * P(SMS_5 - SMS_3)$	0.000	0.060	0.035	0.000	0.000	0.107	0.041	0.000	0.000	0.100	0.3429
$W_j * P(SMS_5 - SMS_4)$	0.040	0.000	0.089	0.039	0.000	0.062	0.000	0.000	0.000	0.100	0.3308

TABLE 8.21

Grouped Preference Matrix

	SMS_1	SMS_2	SMS_3	SMS_4	SMS_5
SMS_1	*	0.1443	0.2195	0.1878	0.1174
SMS_2	0.2724	*	0.3880	0.3437	0.0698
SMS_3	0.3429	0.3833	*	0.2053	0.3073
SMS_4	0.2985	0.3263	0.1926	*	0.2824
SMS_5	0.2764	0.1006	0.3429	0.3308	*

TABLE 8.22

Final Rating of the Alternatives

Alternatives	Leaving Flow $\varphi^+ (SMS)$	Entering Flow $\varphi^- (SMS)$	φ (SMS)	Ranking
SMS_1	0.1673	0.2976	−0.1303	5
SMS_2	0.2685	0.2386	0.0299	2
SMS_3	0.3097	0.2857	0.0240	3
SMS_4	0.2749	0.2669	0.0080	4
SMS_5	0.2627	0.1942	0.0684	1

Step 16: The net outranking flow for each substitute was computed by utilizing Eq. (8.17) as presented in Table 8.22 and shown in Figure 8.4. Eventually, the substitutes were classified in descending order of the values of $\varphi(SMS)$ as presented in Table 8.22 and shown in Figure 8.5.

8.4 Results and Discussion

This part discusses the results obtained from applying the methodology used to analyze and evaluate smart card systems for public transportation. The methodology used is divided into two parts. The first part refers to defining the priorities and weighting of the criteria. The second part refers to the arrangement of the alternatives according to the specified criteria.

Initially, according to the results obtained to determine the priorities of criteria as presented in Table 8.13 and shown in Figure 8.3, it is found that the service reliability SRC_5 criterion has the highest weight by weight

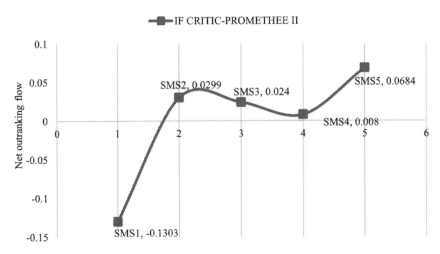

FIGURE 8.4
Final form of alternatives' value (net outranking flow).

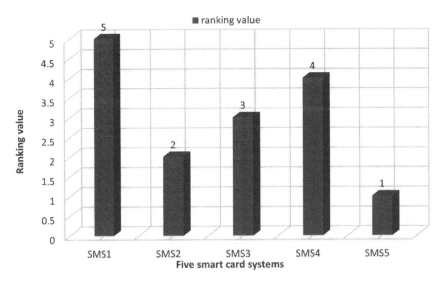

FIGURE 8.5
Final ranking of the selected smart card systems.

of 0.1443, followed by the security SEC_8 criterion with a weight of 0.1228, while the safety STC_7 criterion has the lowest weight by weight of 0.0798.

In the end, according to the results obtained for the ranking of smart card systems for public transport, as presented in Table 8.22 and shown in Figure 8.5, it is found that SMS_5 has the highest rank, followed by SMS_2, while SMS_1 occupies the last rank.

8.5 Summary

- This chapter comprehensively describes smart card systems and their relevant merits.
- This chapter reviews the importance and needs of assessing smart card systems for public transportation.
- This chapter presents the most important criteria for evaluating smart card systems for public transportation after a comprehensive analysis of several research articles.
- This chapter suggests the steps of a hybrid MCDM approach for evaluating smart card systems for public transportation.
- The hybrid MCDM approach consists of intuitionistic fuzzy CRiteria Importance through Intercriteria Correlation (IF-CRITIC) and the intuitionistic fuzzy Preference Ranking Organization Method for Enrichment Evaluation II (IF-PROMETHEE II) methods.
- This chapter presents a real case study while evaluating smart card systems.

8.6 Exercises

a. How do you define "smart card system"? Why is an evaluation of a smart card system necessary for public transportation?

b. What are the differences between the intuitionistic fuzzy CRiteria Importance through Intercriteria Correlation (IF-CRITIC) and the intuitionistic fuzzy Preference Ranking Organization Method for

Enrichment Evaluation II (IF-PROMETHEE II) methods? Discuss their relative advantages while making a decision.

c. What are the challenges in deciding on smart card systems?

d. Discuss the features of smart card systems in terms of the characteristics and formation of sustainable public transportation.

e. Why is the MCDM approach required to assess the smart card system for public transportation?

References

Agrawal, Nishant. 2021. "Multi-Criteria Decision-Making toward Supplier Selection: Exploration of PROMETHEE II Method." *Benchmarking: An International Journal.* https://doi.org/10.1108/BIJ-02-2021-0071.

Brans, Jean Pierre, and Ph. Vincke. 1985. "Note—A Preference Ranking Organisation Method." *Management Science* 31 (6): 647–56. https://doi.org/10.1287/mnsc.31.6.647.

Brans, Jean Pierre, Ph. Vincke, and Bertrand Mareschal. 1986. "How to Select and How to Rank Projects: The Promethee Method." *European Journal of Operational Research* 24 (2): 228–38. https://doi.org/https://doi.org/10.1016/0377-2217(86)90044-5.

Chai, Junyi, and Eric W T. Ngai. 2020. "Decision-Making Techniques in Supplier Selection: Recent Accomplishments and What Lies Ahead." *Expert Systems with Applications* 140: 112903. https://doi.org/https://doi.org/10.1016/j.eswa.2019.112903.

Goswami, Shankha Shubhra, and Dhiren Kumar Behera. 2021. "Evaluation of the Best Smartphone Model in the Market by Integrating Fuzzy-AHP and PROMETHEE Decision-Making Approach." *Decision* 48 (1): 71–96. https://doi.org/10.1007/s40622-020-00260-8.

Xu, Zeshui, and Ronald R. Yager. 2006. "Some Geometric Aggregation Operators Based on Intuitionistic Fuzzy Sets." *International Journal of General Systems* 35 (4): 417–33. https://doi.org/10.1080/03081070600574353.

Index

Note: **Bold** page numbers refer to tables and *italic* page numbers refer to figures.

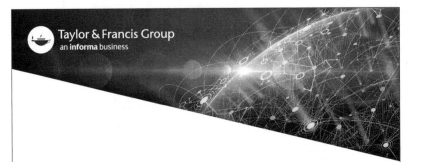